THE ANNUAL DIRECTORY OF

Southern Bed & Breakfasts

1999 Edition

D1528175

THE ANNUAL DIRECTORY OF

Southern Bed & Breakfasts

1999 Edition

Tracey Menges, *Compiler*

RUTLEDGE HILL PRESS®
NASHVILLE, TENNESSEE

Copyright © 1989, 1990, 1991, 1992, 1993, 1994, 1995, 1996, 1997, 1998 by Barbour & Company, Inc.

All rights reserved. Written permission must be secured from the publisher to use or reproduce any part of this book, except for brief quotations in critical reviews or articles.

Published in Nashville, Tennessee, by Rutledge Hill Press®, Inc., 211 Seventh Avenue North, Nashville, Tennessee 37219. Distributed in Canada by H. B. Fenn and Company, Ltd., 34 Nixon Road, Bolton, Ontario L7E 1W2. Distributed in Australia by The Five Mile Press Pty. Ltd., 22 Summit Road, Noble Park, Victoria, 3174. Distributed in New Zeland by Tandem Press, 2 Rugby Road, Birkenhead, Auckland 10. Distributed in the United Kingdom by Verulam Publishing, Ltd., 152a Park Street Lane, Park Street, St. Albans, Hertfordshire AL2 2AU.

Cover design and book design by Harriette Bateman
Page composition by Roger A. DeLiso, Nashville, Tennessee

Printed in the United States of America.

1 2 3 4 5 6—02 01 00 99 98

Contents

Introduction

Removed From Collec
of
Prince William Library

The 1999 edition of *The Annual Directory of Southern Bed & Breakfasts* is one of the most comprehensive directories available today. Whether planning your honeymoon, a family vacation or reunion, or a business trip (many bed and breakfasts provide conference facilities), you will find what you are looking for at a bed and breakfast. They are all here just waiting to be discovered.

Once you know your destination, look for it, or one close by, to see what accommodations are available. Each state has a general map with city locations to help you plan your trip efficiently. There are listings for all 50 states, Canada, Puerto Rico, and the Virgin Islands. Don't be surprised to find a listing in the remote spot you thought only you knew about. Even if your favorite hideaway isn't listed, you're sure to discover a new one.

How to Use This Guide

The sample listing below is typical of the entries in this directory. Each bed and breakfast is listed alphabetically by city and establishment name. The description provides an overview of the bed and breakfast and may include nearby activities and attractions. *Please note that the descriptions have been provided by the hosts. The publisher has not visited these bed and breakfasts and is not responsible for inaccuracies.*

Following the description are notes that have been designed for easy reference. Looking at the sample, a quick glance tells you that this bed and breakfast has four guest rooms, two with private baths (PB) and two that share a bath (SB). The rates are for two people sharing one room. Tax may or may not be included. The specifics of "Credit Cards" and "Notes" are listed at the bottom of each page.

GREAT TOWN

Favorite Bed and Breakfast

123 Main Street, 12345
(800) 555-1234

This quaint bed and breakfast is surrounded by five acres of award-winning landscaping and gardens. There are four guest rooms, each individually decorated with antiques. It is close to antique shops, restaurants, and outdoor activities. Breakfast includes homemade specialties and is served in the formal dining room at guests' leisure. Minimum stay of two nights.

Hosts: Sue and Jim Smith
Rooms: 4 (2 PB; 2 SB) $65-80
Full Breakfast
Credit Cards: A, B
Notes: 2, 5, 8, 10, 11, 12, 13

For example, the letter A means that MasterCard is accepted. The number 10 means that tennis is available on the premises or within 10 to 15 miles.

In many cases, a bed and breakfast is listed with a reservation service that represents several houses in one area. This service is responsible for bookings and can answer other questions you may have. They also inspect each listing and can help you choose the best place for your needs.

Before You Arrive

Now that you have chosen the bed and breakfast that interests you, there are some things you need to find out. You should always make reservations in advance, and while you are doing so you should ask about the local taxes. City taxes can be an unwelcome surprise. Make sure there are accommodations for your children. If you have dietary needs or prefer nonsmoking rooms, find out if these requirements can be met. Ask about check-in times and cancellation policies. Get specific directions. Most bed and breakfasts are readily accessible, but many are a little out of the way.

When You Arrive

In many instances you are visiting someone's home. Be respectful of their property, their schedules, and their requests. Don't smoke if they ask you not to, and don't show up with pets without prior arrangement. Be tidy in shared bathrooms, and be prompt. Most places have small staffs or may be run single-handedly and cannot easily adjust to surprises.

With a little effort and a sense of adventure you will learn firsthand the advantages of bed and breakfast travel. You will rediscover hospitality in a time when kindness seems to have been pushed aside. With the help of this directory, you will find accommodations that are just as exciting as your traveling plans.

We would like to hear from you about any experiences you have had or any inns you wish to recommend. Please write us at the following address:

The Annual Directory of
Southern Bed & Breakfasts
211 Seventh Avenue North
Nashville, Tennessee 37219

THE ANNUAL DIRECTORY OF

Southern Bed & Breakfasts

1999 Edition

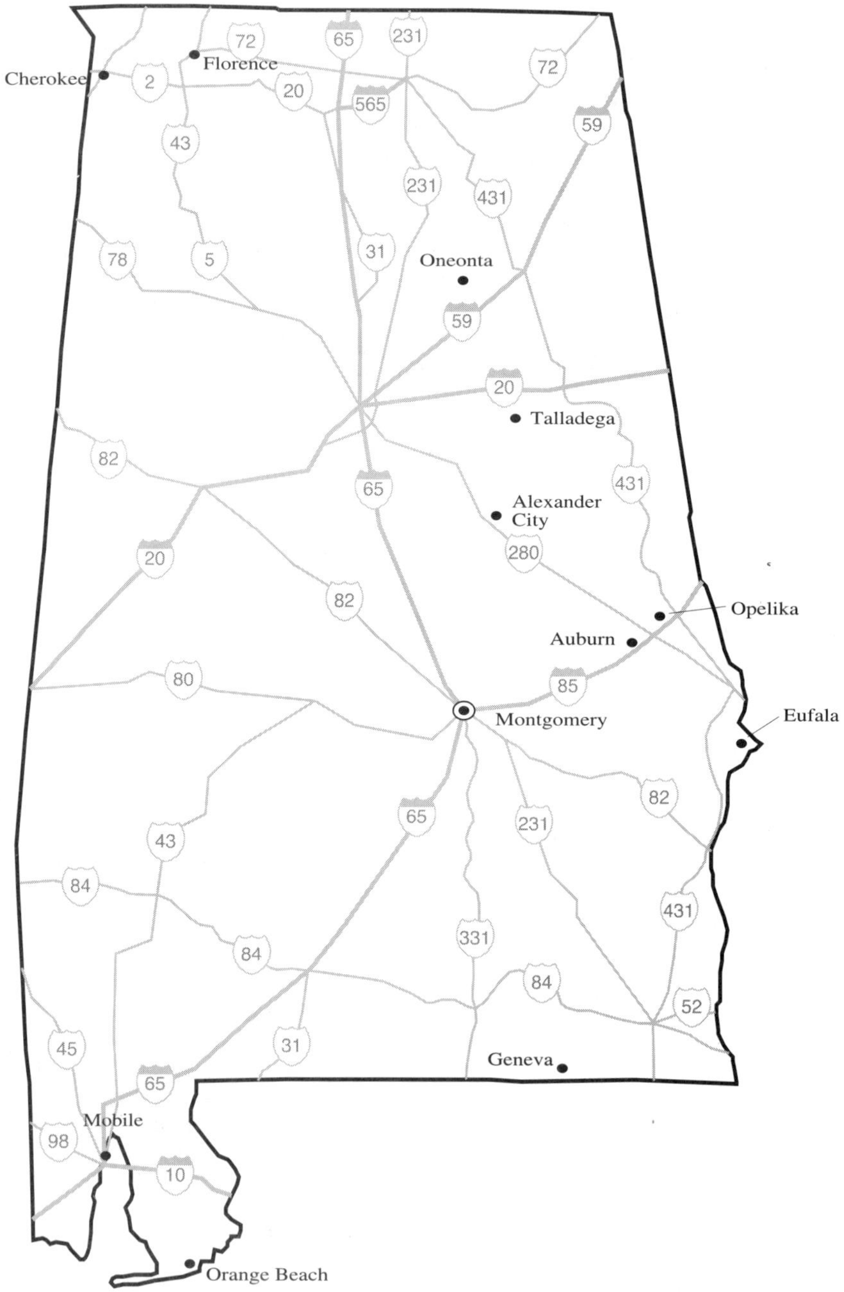
Cherokee
Florence
Oneonta
Talladega
Alexander City
Opelika
Auburn
Montgomery
Eufala
Geneva
Mobile
Orange Beach

Alabama

Alabama

Mistletoe Bough

ALEXANDER CITY

Mistletoe Bough Bed and Breakfast

497 Hillabee Street, 35010
(256) 329-3717

Mistletoe Bough offers guests a retreat into years gone by with all the comforts and conveniences of modern days. The moment guests enter, they will sense the elegance and charm of this lovely Victorian home. A distinctive decorating style creates a relaxing environment that is perfect for lingering and unwinding. Enjoy the elegant parlors and bedrooms decorated in an eclectic collection of traditional, Victorian, and European antiques. Stroll through the beautiful gardens, or relax on one of the porches.

Hosts: Jean and Carlice Payne
Rooms: 5 (PB) $85-110
Full Breakfast
Credit Cards: None
Notes: 2, 5, 7, 10, 11, 12

AUBURN

The Crenshaw Guest House

371 North College Street, 36830
(334) 821-1131; (800) 950-1131
FAX (334) 826-8123
e-mail: crenshaw-gh@mindspring.com
www.crenshawguesthouse.com

A gracious bed and breakfast in Auburn's historic district, rich in history and late-Victorian detail. Spacious rooms include private baths, touch-tone telephones, cable TV, VCR, and clock/radio cassette players. Gleaming porcelain, brass, and ornately carved mantels provide the perfect setting for a collection of comfortable antiques. Suite or kitchenette units available. Room service breakfast. Just a short drive to world-class golf, three blocks to campus, downtown, and restaurants. AAA-rated

The Crenshaw Guest House

NOTES: Credit cards accepted: A MasterCard; B Visa; C American Express; D Discover; E Diner's Club; F Other; 2 Personal checks accepted; 3 Lunch available; 4 Dinner available; 5 Open all year; 6 Pets welcome; 7 No smoking; 8 Children welcome; 9 Social drinking allowed; 10 Tennis nearby; 11 Swimming nearby; 12 Golf nearby; 13 Skiing nearby; 14 May be booked through a travel agent; 15 Handicapped accessible.

three diamonds and Mobil Travel Guide. Take exit 51 from I-85, four miles north on College Street.

Hosts: Fran and Peppi Verma
Rooms: 6 (PB) $58-75
Continental Breakfast
Credit Cards: A, B, C
Notes: 2, 5, 7, 8, 9, 10, 11, 12, 14

CHEROKEE

Natchez Trace Bed and Breakfast Reservation Service

P.O. Box 193, Hampshire, TN 38461
(931) 285-2777; (800) 377-2770
e-mail: natcheztrace@worldnet.att.net

Easterwood House. Just three miles from the trace and four miles from the Tennessee River and Pickwick Lake, this home was burned during the Civil War, rebuilt at the turn of the century, and recently refurbished. Guests love the charm of this old home with its antique furnishings. Relax on the porch or stroll around the 12 acres of giant old cedar trees. $75.

EUFALA

Kendall Manor Inn

534 West Broad Street, 36021
(334) 687-8847; FAX (334) 616-0678
e-mail: kmanorinn@aol.com
www.bbonline.com/al/kendall

Come, capture a memory in an elegant antebellum home with a warm and friendly atmosphere. The six spacious guest rooms are well appointed, and the wraparound veranda, upstairs sitting porch, and deck in the rear offer opportunities to relax and unwind. A welcome beverage served on arrival. Wonderful breakfasts and tour of the historic home with a trip to the belvedere (cupola) and opportunity to add your name to the walls where generations have signed. Fishing, antique shops, and historic district nearby.

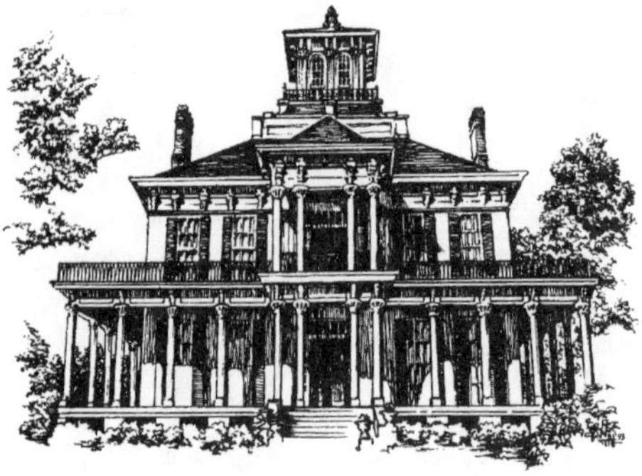

Kendall Manor Inn

Hosts: Barbara and Tim Lubsen
Rooms: 6 (PB) $89-125
Full Breakfast
Credit Cards: A, B, C, D
Notes: 2, 4, 5, 7, 9, 10, 11, 12, 14

FLORENCE

Natchez Trace Bed and Breakfast Reservation Service

P.O. Box 193, Hampshire, TN 38461
(931) 285-2777; (800) 377-2770
e-mail: natcheztrace@worldnet.att.net

Limestone Manor. This 1915 Georgian Revival home is 12 miles from the trace. Built from blocks of local limestone and one of Florence's most treasured landmarks. Previous guests in the home include Henry Ford, Thomas Edison, and Humphrey Bogart! Two guest rooms, one with private sitting room, large sun porch, library with games. $80.

Wood Avenue Inn. Milepost 332. This magnificent Queen Anne Victorian mansion, circa 1889, is in the historic district of Florence, just 12 miles from the trace. Its octagonal and square towers, wraparound porch, 10 fireplaces, 14-foot ceilings, and antique furnishings provide elegance at its best. Full English breakfast. Rooms available with twin, king- or queen-size beds. A suite available for $62-95.

NOTES: Credit cards accepted: A MasterCard; B Visa; C American Express; D Discover; E Diner's Club; F Other; 2 Personal checks accepted; 3 Lunch available; 4 Dinner available; 5 Open all year; 6 Pets welcome;

Wood Avenue Inn

658 North Wood Avenue, 35630
(205) 766-8441

In the picturesque Tennessee Valley, just 13 miles off the Natchez Trace in historical Florence, this Victorian mansion, built in 1889, offers five beautiful private rooms and four public areas for relaxation or a small conference. Walk to nearby restaurants, horse-drawn carriage ride, museum, shopping, and live theaters. An unforgettable, elegant experience in this romantic setting.

Hosts: Gene and Alvern Greeley
Rooms: 5 (PB) $65.50-115
Full Breakfast
Credit Cards: A, B
Notes: 2, 4, 5, 7, 8, 10, 11, 12

Wood Avenue Inn

GENEVA

Live Oaks of Geneva

307 South Academy Street, 36340
(334) 684-2489

Beautifully restored 1918 home one block from downtown in southeast Alabama, this bed and breakfast offers comfortable bedrooms, private baths, and TVs. Enjoy the large porch, sunroom, and living room as a family member. A guest entrance allows visitors to come and go as they wish.

Live Oaks of Geneva

Smoking is restricted to the porch. No pets in bedrooms.

Hosts: Horace and Pamela Newman
Rooms: 3 (PB) $40
Continental Breakfast
Credit Cards: None
Notes: 2, 5, 8, 12

MOBILE

Malaga Inn

359 Church Street, 36602
(334) 438-4701; (800) 235-1586

The Malaga Inn, in the historic district of downtown, is the only hotel of its kind in the state. Originally the two townhouses were built in 1862 by two brothers-in-law when the Civil War was going well for the South. The two homes have been lovingly restored around a quiet patio garden. All rooms are furnished with a great deal of individuality, reminiscent of the finest southern tradition. The friendly and courteous attention afforded to each guest, the convenient location next to the civic center, and all the historic sites of Mobile have attracted those who relish the inn's Old Town atmosphere for many years. Mayme's, a full-service restaurant, a lounge, and a pool on the premises. Breakfast is not included in the rates.

Host: Julie Beem
Rooms: 40 (PB) $69-79
Credit Cards: A, B, C, D
Notes: 2, 3, 4, 5, 7, 8, 9, 11, 12, 14

7 No smoking; 8 Children welcome; 9 Social drinking allowed; 10 Tennis nearby; 11 Swimming nearby; 12 Golf nearby; 13 Skiing nearby; 14 May be booked through a travel agent; 15 Handicapped accessible.

Towle House

1104 Montauk Avenue, 36604
(334) 432-6440; (800) 938-6953
FAX (334) 433-4381; e-mail: jfvereen@aol.com

Lovely home, circa 1874, in the heart of Mobile's historic Old Dauphin Way District. Only minutes away from the convention center, Mobile Auditorium, historic homes, antique shopping, and the revitalized downtown area. The location also offers convenient access to the City of Mobile Museum, Fort Condé, the battleship USS *Alabama*. Within easy walking distance of the parade routes for Mardi Gras visitors. Gourmet breakfast served daily.

Hosts: Felix and Carolyn Vereen
Rooms: 3 (1 PB: 2 SB) $70-85
Full Breakfast
Credit Cards: A, B
Notes: 2, 5, 7, 9, 10, 12, 14

MONTGOMERY

Red Bluff Cottage

551 Clay Street, P.O. Box 1026, 36101
(334) 264-0056; FAX (334) 263-3054
e-mail: redblufbnb@aol.com
www.bbonline.com/al/redbluff

The Waldos built Red Bluff Cottage in 1987 high above the Alabama River in the historic Cottage Hill district. A raised cottage, it has all guest rooms on the ground floor, with easy access to off-street parking, gazebo, and fenced playyard. Upstairs, guests will enjoy pleasantly light and airy public rooms, including dining, living, music (piano and harpsichord), and sitting (TV) rooms. A deep porch overlooks downtown, the state capitol, and the river plain.

Red Bluff Cottage

Hosts: Anne and Mark Waldo
Rooms: 4 (PB) $75
Full Breakfast
Credit Cards: A, B, C, D
Notes: 2, 5, 7, 8, 9, 14

ONEONTA

Capps Cove Bed and Breakfast and Antiques

4126 County Highway 27, 35121
(800) 583-4750; e-mail: cappscov@nacell.net

Capps Cove is a unique country experience—combining bed and breakfast hospitality with antique and gift shopping. Rooms with private baths are available in a two-story Colonial home—or stay in one of the comfortable cabins. Guests will find antiques and other gift ideas in the General Store or just sit and rest a spell on the porch overlooking the creek. The Country Chapel is a perfect setting for a wedding, business meeting, reception, or afternoon tea.

Hosts: Cason and Sybil Capps
Rooms: 4 (PB) $80-150
Full Breakfast
Credit Cards: A, B
Notes: 2, 5, 7, 12

OPELIKA

The Heritage House Inn

714 Second Avenue, 36801
(334) 705-0485

Spacious accommodations in a comfortably elegant home in one of Opelika's historic neighborhoods and just blocks from the downtown area. Championship golf, Auburn University, fine restaurants, and other area attractions are minutes away. Facilities are also available for meetings and special events. Touch-tone telephone, TV, clock/radio in every room. Room rates include a full gourmet breakfast. Gift shop in Old Carriage House on premises. Take exit 62 from I-85.

Hosts: Richard Patton and Barbara Patton
Rooms: 5 (PB) $65-85
Full Breakfast
Credit Cards: A, B, C
Notes: 2, 5, 7, 9, 10, 11, 12, 14

ORANGE BEACH

The Original Romar House

23500 Perdido Beach Boulevard, 36561
(334) 974-1625; (800) 487-6627
FAX (334) 974-1163
e-mail: original@gulftel.com
www.bbonline.com/al/romarhouse/

The Original Romar House is Alabama's first seaside bed and breakfast inn. This 1920s beach house has a romantic feeling with its Art Deco furniture, stained glass, and charmingly historic atmosphere. Enjoy complimentary wine and cheese at sundown in the Purple Parrot bar. Enjoy the private beach for an early morning walk or fast tan, the hot tub for a midnight dip, or a brief drive to the Gulf Coast's finest seafood restaurants, nightclub entertainment, or seven golf courses.

Host: Darrell Finley
Owner: Jerry M. Gilbreath
Rooms: 6 (PB) $79-129
Cottage: 1 (PB) $89-185
Full Breakfast
Credit Cards: A, B, C
Notes: 2, 5, 9, 10, 11, 12

TALLADEGA

The Governor's House

Lincoln (location)
500 Meadowlake Lane, 35160 (mailing)
(205) 763-2186; FAX (205) 362-2391

The Governor's House was built in Talladega in 1850 by former Alabama governor, Lewis Parsons. In 1990 it was moved to the hosts' polled Hereford farm overlooking Logan Martin Lake in Lincoln where it was renovated, furnished with family antiques, and established as a bed and breakfast for those who enjoy quiet country life. A tennis court, bass pond, and picnic area are on the premises. Relax on the wraparound front porch and watch the sunset while enjoing a cold drink. Take exit 165 off I-20 and go two miles south on county road 207. Guest house also available on the premises.

Hosts: Mary Sue and Ralph Gaines
Rooms: 3 (1 PB; 2 SB) $75-85
Full Breakfast
Credit Cards: None
Notes: 2, 3, 4, 5, 9, 10, 11, 12

Bella Vista
62
Eureka Springs
65
62
Hardy
62
62
Johnson
Fayetteville
62
Kingston
71
65
167
67
63
55
40
64
71
Conway
40
67
40
40
Jessieville
270
Hot Springs
49
Helena
71
70
Pine Bluff
65
71
30
167
165
Magnolia
82
71
82

Arkansas

Arkansas

BELLA VISTA

The Inn at Bella Vista

1 Chelsea Road, 72714
(501) 876-5645; (888) 876-5645
e-mail: iabv@arkansas.net

Built of native fieldstone, cedar, and glass, the inn is in the beautiful Ozark Mountains in northwest Arkansas. The 900-square-foot inn sits on 14 acres and offers incredible views. Access to seven golf courses, eight lakes, and lots to do.

Hosts: Bill and Beverly Williams
Rooms: 5 (PB) $95-140
Full Breakfast
Credit Cards: A, B, C, D
Notes: 2, 5, 7, 9, 10, 11, 12, 14

CONWAY

The Cottage

1221 Watkins Street, 72032
(501) 329-7703; e-mail: sshadrach@stumo.org
www.rimstarintl.com/cgh00001.htm

This quaint 1,000-square-foot home is in the middle of Old Conway and is safe, private, and convenient to the downtown and colleges as well as the business, shopping, and restaurant districts. At the Cottage guests are not just renting a room, but an entire home that is exclusively theirs during their stay in Conway. It is completely furnished and has two bedrooms, bathroom, living room, kitchen (including stove, refrigerator, microwave, etc.), and dining area. Beautifully landscaped and decorated with many antiques and quilts, the Cottage has many amenities including cable TV/VCR, telephone, and a daily Continental breakfast. Weekly and monthly rates available.

Hosts: Carol and Marietta Shadrach
Entire House: $60 per night
Continental Breakfast
Credit Cards: F
Notes: 2, 5, 7, 8, 10, 11, 12

EUREKA SPRINGS

Angel at Rose Hall

56 Hillside, 72632
(501) 253-5405; (800) 828-4255
www.the-angel.com

Step back into time and enjoy the romantic ambiance of breathtaking Victorian furnishings, grand fireplaces, and Jacuzzis for two. Twenty-eight century-old stained-glass windows invite glorious streams of light into the Angel where rich fabrics, designer linens, and fresh flowers splash vibrant colors into rooms. Specializing in weddings, honeymoons, anniversaries, and special getaways. Adults only. No smoking.

Angel at Rose Hall

NOTES: Credit cards accepted: A MasterCard; B Visa; C American Express; D Discover; E Diner's Club; F Other; 2 Personal checks accepted; 3 Lunch available; 4 Dinner available; 5 Open all year; 6 Pets welcome; 7 No smoking; 8 Children welcome; 9 Social drinking allowed; 10 Tennis nearby; 11 Swimming nearby; 12 Golf nearby; 13 Skiing nearby; 14 May be booked through a travel agent; 15 Handicapped accessible.

Host: Sandy Latimer
Rooms: 5 (PB) $125-150
Full Breakfast
Credit Cards: A, B, C, D
Notes: 2, 5, 7, 9, 12, 14

Antiques and Lace at Evening Shade Inn

Highway 62 East, 72632
(501) 253-6264; (800) 992-1224
e-mail: eveshade@ipa.net
www.eveningshade.com

Antiques and Lace is the newest honeymoon cottage at Evening Shade Inn. Two exceptional honeymoon suites filled with antiques make this cottage very special and romantic. Fireplace, Jacuzzi for two, king-size bed, and private deck are just some of the luxuries guests will enjoy. All cottages and rooms have private baths, TV with HBO, VCR with free movies, in-room telephones, breakfast at guests' leisure, champagne and snacks each evening. In the heart of Eureka Springs, on the trolley route, yet quiet and serene, in the woods. The best of both worlds! Small weddings. AAA-rated three diamonds.

Hosts: Ed and Shirley Nussbaum
Rooms: 7 (PB) $115-150
Continental Breakfast
Credit Cards: A, B, C, D, E
Notes: 2, 5, 7, 9, 12, 14

Arbour Glen Bed and Breakfast Victorian Inn and Guest House

7 Lema, 72632
(501) 253-9010; (800) 515-GLEN

The Arbour Glen (circa 1896) offers cottage-style lodging with Victorian romantic charm complete with Jacuzzis for two, fireplaces, antique furnishings. This inn on Eureka Springs's historic district loop and trolley route, is only a five-minute walk from downtown shops and cafés. Completely renovated with guests' comfort in mind. On the veranda guests may relax and enjoy the picturesque setting of the tree-covered hollow for an unforgettable experience.

Rooms: 5 (PB) $75-125
Full Breakfast
Credit Cards: A, B, C, D
Notes: 2, 4, 5, 7, 9, 10, 11, 12, 14

Arsenic and Old Lace

Arsenic and Old Lace Bed and Breakfast Inn

60 Hillside, 72632
(800) 243-5223; FAX (501) 253-2246
www.eureka~usa.com/arsenic

Victorian mansion in the historic district within easy walking distance of shopping, dining, and attractions. In-room Jacuzzis, fireplaces, balconies, cable TV and VCRs, antiques, fresh flowers, full gourmet breakfasts, 24-hour snack and beverage bar. Surrounded by trees, flower gardens, and wicker-filled verandas. Mobil and AAA three-diamond-rated. Featured in Gail Greco's *Romance of Country Inns* and featured in March 1997 *Houston Chronicle* travel section.

Hosts: Gary and Phyllis Jones
Rooms: 5 (PB) $110-160
Full Breakfast
Credit Cards: A, B, C, D
Notes: 2, 5, 7, 9, 10, 11, 12, 14, 15

Beaver Lake Bed and Breakfast

1234 County Road 120, 72631
(501) 253-9210; (888) 253-9210
www.bbonline.com/ar/beaverlake/

In the beautiful Ozark Mountains at the end of a country road find the perfect escape. Secluded nine acres of pristine Beaver Lake

NOTES: Credit cards accepted: A MasterCard; B Visa; C American Express; D Discover; E Diner's Club; F Other; 2 Personal checks accepted; 3 Lunch available; 4 Dinner available; 5 Open all year; 6 Pets welcome;

with a private covered dock for fishing and swimming. Fifteen minutes from the many attractions in historic Eureka Springs. Four guest rooms all with incredible lake views and private bathrooms. Full breakfast every morning. Sorry, no smoking, children, or pets permitted.

Hosts: David and Elaine Reppel
Rooms: 4 (PB) $75-95
Full Breakfast
Credit Cards: A, B, D
Notes: 2, 7, 9, 11, 12, 14

Bonnybrooke Farm Atop Misty Mountain

Route 2, Box 335A, 72631
(501) 253-6903
www.rosemart.com/bonnybrooke

If guests' hearts are in the country—or long to be—the hosts invite them to come share in the sweet quiet and serenity that await them in their home away from home. Five cottages are distinctly different in their tempting pleasures: fireplace and Jacuzzi for two, full glass fronts, mountaintop views, shower under the stars in the glass shower, wicker porch swing in front of the fireplace, and a waterfall Jacuzzi. Guests are going to love it! In order to preserve privacy, the location is not made public and is given to registered guests only. Featured in *Country Heart* magazine as the Most Romantic Accommodation in Arkansas.

Hosts: Bonny and Josh
Cottages: 5 (PB) $95 and up

Credit Cards: None
Notes: 2, 5, 7, 9, 11, 14

Bridgeford House Bed and Breakfast

263 Spring Street, 72632
(888) 567-2422
e-mail: bridgefordbb@earthlink.net
www.bridgefordhouse.com

Nestled in the heart of Eureka Springs's historic residential district, Bridgeford House is an 1884 Victorian delight. Hailed by many guests as "the best bed and breakfast in Eureka Springs." Outside are shady porches that invite guests to pull up a chair and watch the world go by on Spring Street. Each room has a private entrance, antique furnishings, and private bath. Fresh coffee in the suite, a selection of fine teas, color TV, air conditioning, and a gourmet southern-style breakfast. Jacuzzis and private decks!

Hosts: Linda and Henry Thornton
Rooms: 4 (PB) $85-105
Full Breakfast
Credit Cards: A, B, C, D
Notes: 2, 5, 7, 8, 9, 10, 11, 12, 14

Brownstone Inn

75 Hillside Avenue, 72632
(800) 973-7505
www.eureka-usa.com/brownstone

Built in 1895, for 70 years it served as the site for the Ozarka Water Company. The two-story limestone structure retains the original façade while the interior has been converted into the uniquely finished Victorian decor with modern amenities, along with ample off-street parking. Beverage basket delivered to guests' doorstep before full breakfast in the morning. Featured in "Best Places to Stay in the South." A member of PAII and the state Bed and Breakfast Association.

Hosts: Marvin and Donna Shepard
Rooms: 4 (PB) $85-105
Full Breakfast
Credit Cards: A, B, D
Notes: 2, 7, 9, 10, 12, 14

Enchanted Cottages

18 Nut Street, 72632
(501) 253-6790; (800) 862-2788

Secluded parklike setting in Eureka Springs historic district. Romantic private cottages just three blocks to shops and restaurants. Storybook cottages surrounded by woods with neighborhood family of deer. Each cottage has either an indoor Jacuzzi for two or a private hot tub under the stars, wood or gas fireplace, king- or queen-size bed, antique furnishings, cable TV, kitchens, and patios with grills. Special honeymoon and anniversary packages. Weekday discounts. "We will beat any similar accommodations rates!"

Hosts: Barbara Kellogg and David Pettit
Cottages: 3 (PB) $79-149
Continental Breakfast
Credit Cards: A, B
Notes: 2, 5, 7, 8, 9

The Gardener's Cottage

11 Singleton Street, 72632
(501) 253-9111; (800) 833-3394

Tucked away in a private, wooded, historic district location, this delightful cottage is decorated in charming country decor with romantic touches and a Jacuzzi for two. This cozy retreat features a beamed cathedral ceiling, skylights, full kitchen, TV, VCR, and gas log fireplace. Relax and listen to the local wildlife from the porch with its swing and hammock or walk to the shops and cafés. Open April through November. Breakfast not included, but can be prearranged for $12 at Singleton House.

The Gardener's Cottage

Host: Barbara Gavron
Cottage: 1 (PB) $95-125
Credit Cards: A, B, C, D
Notes: 2, 7, 9, 11, 12, 14

Harvest House

Harvest House

104 Wall Street, 72632
(501) 253-9363; (800) 293-5665

Vintage Victorian house filled with lovely antiques, collectibles, and family favorites. The guest rooms have private entrances and private baths. A full breakfast is served in the dining room or, weather permitting, in the screened-in gazebo overlooking pine and oak trees. Bill is a native Arkansan and knows all the hidden treasures of the area. Patt is the shopper with a particular interest in antiques and the local attractions.

Hosts: Bill and Patt Carmichael
Rooms: 4 (PB) $89-129
Full Breakfast
Credit Cards: A, B, D
Notes: 2, 5, 6, 7, 9, 14

The Heartstone Inn and Cottages

35 Kings Highway, 72632
(501) 253-8916
www.eureka-springs-usa.com/lodging/heartstone.html

The nationally acclaimed historic district Victorian inn combines nostalgic charm

NOTES: Credit cards accepted: A MasterCard; B Visa; C American Express; D Discover; E Diner's Club; F Other; 2 Personal checks accepted; 3 Lunch available; 4 Dinner available; 5 Open all year; 6 Pets welcome;

Heartstone Inn

with all modern conveniences. Inviting rooms filled with antiques, all with king- or queen-size beds plus private entrances and bathrooms. Experience the luxury of on-site therapeutic massage; savor gourmet breakfasts; laze awhile on tree-shaded verandas; enjoy the golf privileges; or indulge in bountiful shopping, entertainment, and restaurants nearby. AAA-, Mobil-, Fodor's-approved. Recommended by all.

Hosts: Iris and Bill Simantel
Rooms: 10 (PB) $68-125
Cottages: 2 (PB)
Full Breakfast
Credit Cards: A, B, C, D
Notes: 2, 7, 8, 9, 11, 12, 14

Ridgeway House Bed and Breakfast

28 Ridgeway, 72632
(501) 253-6618; (800) 477-6618

Gracious southern hospitality makes this lovely, immaculately restored bed and breakfast in the historic district the perfect place to have that much-needed getaway, or to celebrate that special occasion. Built in 1908 by W. O. Perkins, the inn has large porches and decks, robes in each room, high ceilings, guest kitchens, and other amenities. Excellent location, quiet street within walking distance of downtown. Jacuzzi suites available. Smoking allowed on porches and decks. Children welcome in the suites.

Hosts: Becky and "Sony" Taylor
Rooms: 5 (PB) $79-149
Full Breakfast
Credit Cards: A, B, D
Notes: 2, 5, 9, 11, 14

Singleton House Bed and Breakfast

11 Singleton Street, 72632
(501) 253-9111; (800) 833-3394

This country Victorian home in the historic district is an old-fashioned place with a touch of magic. Each guest room is whimsically decorated with a delightful collection of antiques and folk art. Breakfast is served on the balcony overlooking the fantasy wildflower garden below, with its goldfish pond and curious birdhouse collection. Guests park and walk a scenic wooded pathway to Eureka's shops and cafés. Innkeeper apprenticeship program available.

Host: Barbara Gavron
Rooms: 5 (PB) $65-105
Full Breakfast
Credit Cards: A, B, C, D
Notes: 2, 5, 7, 8, 9, 11, 12, 14

Singleton House

FAYETTEVILLE

Eton House

1485 Eton, 72703
(501) 443-7517

This buff brick, ranch-style home has a cathedral ceiling and is furnished in delicate pastels, Victorian wicker, and more staid European pieces. Guests are welcome to relax in the living room by a cozy fireplace during winter months, but the screened-in patio overlooking a parklike setting is a spring and summer delight. A gazebo can be used for weddings. Fayetteville boasts the University of Arkansas and Walton Arts Center, plus arts and crafts.

Host: Patricia Parks
Rooms: 3 (PB) $49
Continental Breakfast
Credit Cards: None
Notes: 5, 9, 10, 11, 12

Hill Avenue Bed and Breakfast

131 South Hill Avenue, 72701
(501) 444-0865

In a residential neighborhood, this home is near the University of Arkansas, Walton Arts Center, the town square, and Bud Walton Arena. Guests will find immaculate and comfortable accommodations with king-size beds and private baths.

Hosts: Dale and Cecelia Thompson
Room: 3 (PB) $60
Full Breakfast
Credit Cards: None
Notes: 5, 7

HARDY

Hideaway Inn

Rural Route 1, Box 199, 72542
(870) 966-4770; (888) 966-4770

Modern bed and breakfast on 376 acres, three guest rooms, queen-size beds, central heat and air. Gourmet full breakfast and evening dessert snack. Log cabin with a Continental breakfast for those seeking solitude. Playground, gardens, and swimming pool for guests' enjoyment. Available packages include honeymoon, fly-fishing, anniversary, birthday, romance in the Ozarks, canoeing, and golfing. Hosts can also create special packages. Ten miles from antiques, fishing, parks, shopping, theater, and water sports. "If you are looking for a unique bed and breakfast experience, at a comfortable home, you've found it."

Host: Julia Baldridge
Rooms: 5 (3 PB; 2 SB) $55-95
Full or Continental Breakfast
Credit Cards: A, B, C, D
Notes: 2, 5, 7, 8, 9, 11, 12, 14

Olde Stonehouse Bed and Breakfast Inn

511 Main Street, 72542
(870) 856-2983; (800) 514-2983 (reservations only)
FAX (870) 856-4036

Native Arkansas stone house in the National Register of Historic Places has large porches lined with jumbo rocking chairs, is comfortably furnished with antiques, and features zoned heat and air, ceiling fans, queen-size beds, and private baths. One block from Spring River and the shops of Old Hardy Town. Country music theaters, golf courses, horseback riding, canoeing, and fishing nearby. Local attractions include Mammoth Spring State Park, Grand Gulf, Evening Shade, Arkansas Traveller Theater, and country music and comedy theaters. Two-room "special occasion" suites are in a separate 1905 cottage. Smoking permitted on porches. Mystery, trout fishing, golf, and other packages available. Approved by AAA and BBAA.

Host: Peggy Volland
Rooms: 9 (PB) $69-99
Full Breakfast
Credit Cards: A, B, C, D
Notes: 2, 3, 5, 7, 9, 10, 11, 12, 14

HELENA

Foxglove

229 Beech, 72342
(870) 338-9391; (800) 863-1926

On a ridge overlooking historic Helena and the Mississippi River. Stunning antiques abound in this nationally registered inn. Parquet floors, quarter-sawn oak woodwork, stained glass, and six original fireplaces are complemented by private marble baths, whirlpool tubs, telephones, cable TV, fax, air conditioning, and other modern conveniences. Points of interest include Delta Cultural Center, Confederate Military Cemetery, antiques shops, and a casino, all within five minutes' travel. Complimentary evening beverage/snack. Inquire about accommodations for children over 12.

Host: John Butkiewicz
Rooms: 8 (PB) $69-109
Full Breakfast
Credit Cards: A, B, C
Notes: 2, 5, 7, 9, 12, 14

HOT SPRINGS NATIONAL PARK

The Gables Inn Bed and Breakfast

318 Quapaw Avenue, 71901
(501) 623-7576; (800) 625-7576

Featured in the *Dallas Morning News* travel section. Walk only four blocks to downtown historic district, shops, restaurants, and Bathhouse Row. Come enjoy the charm and history of this beautiful home and relax in the ambiance of a bygone era. This 1905 Victorian home with four romantic guest rooms each featuring antiques, cable TV, VCR, and private baths. Price includes a full breakfast served each morning in the elegant dining room. Scrumptious dessert always available with choice of coffee, tea, or soft drinks. Elegant wedding, honeymoon, anniversary, and special occasion packages available. No facilities available for children. No smoking or pets.

Hosts: Judy and David Peters
Rooms: 4 (PB) $69-89
Full Breakfast
Credit Cards: A, B, C, E
Notes: 2, 5, 7, 9, 10, 11, 12, 14

The Gables Inn

Williams House Inn

Williams House Inn

420 Quapaw Avenue, 71901
(501) 624-4275; (800) 756-4635 (reservations)
e-mail: willmbnb@ipa.net
www.bbonline.com/ar/williamshouse

The Williams House Inn is a nationally registered 1890 brownstone and brick Victorian mansion with carriage house. It has five antique-filled rooms with a romantic setting offering attention to comfort and detail. Two rooms have private sitting rooms. Breakfast offered 7:30-9:00 A.M. Only four blocks to the national park visitor center, Bathhouse Row, hiking trails, art galleries, restaurants, and shopping. Spring water, wine, baby grand piano, upper and lower wraparound porches, common rooms, and patios for guests' enjoyment. Reservations preferred. Inquire about bungalow accommodations for families. Children 12 and older welcome.

Hosts: David and Karen Wiseman
Rooms: 5 (PB) $75-112
Full Breakfast
Credit Cards: A, B, C, D
Notes: 2, 5, 7, 9, 10, 11, 12, 14

KINGSTON

Fools Cove Ranch Bed and Breakfast

P.O. Box 10, 72742
(501) 665-2986; fax (501) 665-2372
e-mail: foolscoveranchbandb@angelfire.com

A family farm in the Ozark Mountains, Fools Cove Ranch has a rustic setting with beautiful views of mountains and wildlife. Trails and back roads to explore, fishing for catfish or bass in private ponds. Porches and decks for lounging and relaxing, comfortable parlor with large-screen TV on satellite system. Full country breakfast. Accommodations for children with prior approval. Minutes to area attractions, Buffalo National River, Eureka Springs, the War Eagle Mill, and Fayetteville. Astronomical observatory on premises.

Host: Mary Jo Sullivan
Rooms: 4 (1 PB: 3 SB) $55-75
Full Breakfast
Credit Cards: A, B, C, D, E
Notes: 2, 3, 4, 6, 7, 11, 14, 15

Fools Cove Ranch

JESSIEVILLE

Mountain Thyme Bed and Breakfast Inn

10860 Scenic Byway 7 North, 71949
(501) 984-5428; e-mail: bedthyme@cswnet.com

The inn was built from the ground up by innkeepers who are bed and breakfast travelers who know what makes a comfortable and luxurious inn. Good beds, expensive linens, ample light, individual temperature control, fireplaces, whirlpool tubs, and delicious breakfasts served in a dining room looking out on the Ouachita Mountains make this an excellent spot for a romantic weekend or an extended stay in the Hot Springs area. Smoking permitted on porch only. Children over 10 welcome.

Hosts: Rhonda and Michael Hicks; Polly Felker
Rooms: 8 (PB) $70-120
Full Breakfast
Credit Cards: A, B, D
Notes: 2, 9, 12 15

JOHNSON

Inn at the Mill

3906 Greathouse Springs Road, 72741-0409
(501) 443-1800; (501) 521-8091
(800) CLARION

Timeless elegance awaits guests at the Inn at the Mill. Nestled in the Ozark Mountains between the communities of Fayetteville and Springdale, guests will feel worlds apart from the hassles of the city while being only minutes away. The Inn at the Mill embraces a historic landmark, listed in the National Register of Historic Places, formerly known as the Johnson Mill. The water wheel is powered by four million gallons of fresh spring water daily, rushing down the falls. The elegantly appointed guest rooms marry with the serenity of the Ozarks to afford guests the ultimate lodging experience.

Hosts: James and Joyce Lambeth
Rooms: 48 (PB) $89-225
Continental Breakfast

NOTES: Credit cards accepted: A MasterCard; B Visa; C American Express; D Discover; E Diner's Club; F Other; 2 Personal checks accepted; 3 Lunch available; 4 Dinner available; 5 Open all year; 6 Pets welcome;

Credit Cards: A, B, C, D, E
Notes: 3, 4, 5, 7, 8, 9, 12, 14

MAGNOLIA

Magnolia Place

510 East Main, 71753
(501) 234-6122; (800) 237-6122
FAX (501) 234-1254
e-mail: magplace@magnolia-net.com
www.bbonline.com/ar/magnolia

This stately 1910 Craftsman home has been beautifully restored to its former elegance. Soft music, complimentary snacks and beverages greet guests. Relax on the wraparound porch or in the library or walk to the nearby historic courthouse square to shop and view the colorful downtown murals. Antiques throughout, with queen-size beds, TVs, private baths, and telephones. Full breakfasts. Come and enjoy the charm and hospitality of the Old South. Featured in September 1996 *Southern Living* magazine.

Hosts: Carolyne Hawley and Ray Sullivent
Rooms: 5 (PB) $89-149
Full Breakfast
Credit Cards: A, B, C, D
Notes: 5, 7, 11, 12, 14

Magnolia Place

PINE BLUFF

Margland

Margland Bed and Breakfast

703 West Second Street, 71601
(870) 536-6000; (800) 545-5383

Southern hospitality as it was meant to be—four historic southern homes—each suite is carefully furnished for the perfect combination of atmosphere and comfort. Guests may savor breakfast on the terrace or in the formal dining room and have access to cable TV, private baths, VCRs, fax machine, and whirlpools. Full or queen-size beds; swimming pool; exercise room. Margland II is handicapped accessible. All buildings are equipped with sprinkler fire protection system. Lunch and dinner reservations are required for groups of eight or more.

Host: Wanda Bateman
Rooms: 22 (PB) $85-105
Continental Breakfast
Credit Cards: A, B, C, D, E
Notes: 2, 5, 7, 8, 9, 10, 12, 14, 15

Havana
Tallahassee
Destin
Apalachicola
Amelia Island
Jacksonville
Wellborn
St. Augustine
Steinhatchee
Micanopy
San Mateo
Daytona Beach
Cedar Key
Cedar Key
Ocala
Mount Dora
Orlando
Cape Canaveral
Brooksville
Tarpon Springs
Dunedin
Clearwater
Tampa
Palm Bay
Lake Wales
St. Petersburg Beach
Ruskin
St. Petersburg
Vero Beach
Anna Maria Island
Fort Pierce
Sarasota
Arcadia
Stuart
Jupiter
West Palm Beach
Palm Beach
Lake Worth
Sanibel Island
Fort Lauderdale
Everglades City
Miami
Marathon
Big Pine Key
Key West

Florida

Florida

The Bailey House

AMELIA ISLAND

The Bailey House

28 South 7th Street, Fernandina Beach, 32034
(904) 261-5390

Completed in 1895, this fine old home is an outstanding example of the Queen Anne style. Filled with a vast collection of carefully chosen period antiques collected across the nation. The guest rooms are furnished with authentic antique furniture and decorator pieces, yet offer the modern conveniences of a private bath. Central heat and air for year-round comfort. Near Fort Clinch State Park, horseback riding, and beautiful beaches. Come enjoy the charm and history of this beautiful turn-of-the-century home and relax in the ambiance of a bygone era. In consideration of all guests, the hosts must say no to pets and children under eight years of age.

Hosts: Tom and Jenny Bishop
Rooms: 9 (PB) $95-150
Full Breakfast
Credit Cards: A, B, C
Notes: 2, 5, 7, 10, 11, 12

Elizabeth Pointe Lodge

98 South Fletcher Avenue, 32034
(904) 277-4851

This seaside lodge, an 1890s Nantucket Shingle-style structure, has large porches that overlook the ocean. Enjoy the great room with fireplace and library. Each guest room has an oversize tub, remote color cable TV, fresh flowers, and newspaper delivered to room. Wine at 6:00 P.M. Homemade snack and desserts always available. Rock on the porch with a glass of lemonade. Baby-sitting, laundry room service, and concierge assistance. Historic seaport of Fernandina nearby. Bikes available for touring the island.

Hosts: David and Susan Caples
Rooms: 25 (PB) $125-230
Full Breakfast
Credit Cards: A, B, C, D
Notes: 2, 3, 4, 5, 7, 8, 9, 10, 11, 12, 14, 15

Elizabeth Pointe Lodge

NOTES: Credit cards accepted: A MasterCard; B Visa; C American Express; D Discover; E Diner's Club; F Other; 2 Personal checks accepted; 3 Lunch available; 4 Dinner available; 5 Open all year; 6 Pets welcome; 7 No smoking; 8 Children welcome; 9 Social drinking allowed; 10 Tennis nearby; 11 Swimming nearby; 12 Golf nearby; 13 Skiing nearby; 14 May be booked through a travel agent; 15 Handicapped accessible.

The Fairbanks House

The Fairbanks House

227 South Seventh Street, 32034
(904) 277-0500; (800) 261-4838

The Fairbanks House is an Italianate villa, built in 1885 and listed in the National Register of Historic Places. It has 12 rooms, suites, or cottages, telephones, and TVs. Four-poster king, queen, or twin beds are available with claw-foot tubs, showers, or Jacuzzis. The Fairbanks House has been completely restored. Furnished in antiques, period pieces, and oriental rugs. Enjoy the swimming pool and gardens. Gourmet breakfast and complimentary afternoon refreshments included in rates.

Hosts: Bill and Theresa Hamilton
Rooms: 12 (PB) $125-225
Full Breakfast
Credit Cards: A, B, C, D
Notes: 2, 5, 7, 9, 10, 11, 12, 14, 15

The 1735 House

584 South Fletcher Avenue, Fernandina Beach, 32034
(800) 872-8531; FAX (904) 261-9200

Come and enjoy personal service at this 1920s inn on Amelia Island near the Georgia border, 35 miles north of Jacksonville. The white wooden building has a New England look to it, and it's filled with nautical items such as sea chests and marine charts. All suites are on the ocean, and guests may enjoy the private beach. There are five suites, each sleeping four, as well as a four-story lighthouse which sleeps four. Gourmet breakfast is brought to the guests' door along with the morning paper. Area attractions include fishing, sailboat or powerboat charters, horseback riding, tennis, and golf. Shopping in historic Fernandina Beach, gourmet dining, historic Fort Clinch, and much more.

Host: William L. Auld
Suites: 5 (PB) $101-161
Continental Breakfast
Credit Cards: A, B, C, D, E
Notes: 2, 5, 7, 8, 9, 10, 11, 12, 13, 14

ANNA MARIA ISLAND

Harrington House Beachfront Bed and Breakfast

5626 Gulf Drive, Holmes Beach, 34217
(941) 778-5444; FAX (941) 778-0527
www.harhousebb.com

The charm of Old Florida architecture and the casual elegance of beachfront living are beautifully combined at the Harrington House. Built in 1925, this home has been lovingly restored. Most rooms have French doors leading to balconies over-

Harrington House

NOTES: Credit cards accepted: A MasterCard; B Visa; C American Express; D Discover; E Diner's Club; F Other; 2 Personal checks accepted; 3 Lunch available; 4 Dinner available; 5 Open all year; 6 Pets welcome;

looking the pool, the beach, and the blue-green Gulf of Mexico. Relax by the pool, take a moonlit stroll on the beach, or listen to the surf. AAA-rated; Mobil Guide-rated; ABBA-rated. Children over 12 welcome.

Hosts: Frank and Jo Adele Davis
Rooms: 13 (PB) $119-225
Full Breakfast
Credit Cards: A, B
Notes: 2, 5, 9, 10, 11, 12

APALACHICOLA

Magnolia Hall

177 Fifth Street, 32320
(904) 653-2431

Southern plantation home erected in 1838, overlooking the Apalachicola River. Totally remodeled, the home is, once more, grandly inviting and comfortable. Lush gardens, shaded walkways, and swimming pool. A wonderful getaway on a grand scale. Two beautifully appointed guest rooms are on the second floor. Sitting areas, gas log fireplaces, designer bed and bath linens, and special amenities to pamper guests are common to both individually decorated rooms.

Innkeepers: Anna and Doug Gaidry
Rooms: 2 (PB) $100-150
Full Breakfast
Credit Cards: A, B
Notes: 2, 5, 7, 9, 11

ARCADIA

Historic Parker House

427 West Hickory Street, 34266-3703
(941) 494-2499; (800) 969-2499

The Historic Parker House, circa 1895, immediately transports guests back to a simpler, yet grander time. This 6,000-square-foot home is chock full of Victorian antiques, a wonderful clock collection, and bits of Florida's past. Within walking distance is downtown Arcadia's antique district, the Peace River for canoeing and fishing, and all of south-central Florida's attractions are nearby. Relax out back under the oak trees with the hosts as the garden railroad entertains guests before retiring to their elegantly furnished rooms.

Hosts: Bob and Shelly Baumann
Rooms: 4 (2 PB; 2 SB) $60-75
Continental Breakfast
Credit Cards: A, B, C
Notes: 2, 5, 7, 9, 14

BIG PINE KEY

Deer Run—Bed and Breakfast on the Atlantic

Long Beach Road, Box 431, 33043
(305) 872-2015; (305) 872-2800

Deer Run is a Florida cracker-style house nestled among lush native trees on the ocean. Breakfast is served on the large veranda overlooking the ocean. Dive at Looe Key National Marine Sanctuary, fish the Gulf Stream, or lie on the beach. A nature lover's paradise and a bird watcher's heaven. All rooms have ocean views and king-size beds. Bikes and a canoe are available to guests. Two-night minimum stay required. Adults only.

Host: Sue Abbott
Rooms: 2 (PB) $95-150
Full Breakfast
Credit Cards: None
Notes: 5, 7, 9, 10, 11, 12, 14, 15

BROOKSVILLE

Verona House

201 South Main Street, 34601
(352) 796-4001; (800) 355-6717
FAX (352) 799-0612
www.bbhost.com/veronabb/

The Verona House is a unique 1925 Sears, Roebuck and Company catalog house in downtown Brooksville, among the rolling hills and the large oak tree-canopied streets

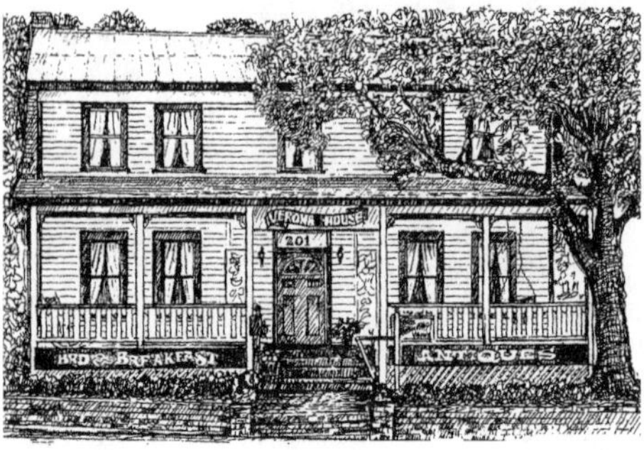

Verona House

of a historical town established in 1856. A truly cozy and quiet getaway with Jan's special baked casserole, fruit, and southern hospitality for breakfast. All four rooms, with queen-size beds and private baths are furnished in a warm atmosphere of antiques and collectible pieces. The welcome mat is always out.

Hosts: Bob and Jan Boyd
Rooms: 4 (PB) $65-80
Full Breakfast
Credit Cards: A, B, C, D
Notes: 2, 5, 7, 8, 9, 10, 12, 14, 15

CAPE CANAVERAL

Beachside Bed and Breakfast

629 Adams Avenue, 32920
(407) 799-4320

See a space launch from the beach. The ocean is only a few yards from the guest suite with private entrance, bedroom with twin beds, one and one-half private baths, living room, and kitchen stocked for breakfast, which guests can enjoy at their leisure. Port Canaveral and Kennedy Space Center are minutes away. Walt Disney World and Orlando are just an hour's drive. Orlando International Airport (45 minutes) shuttle service available.

Hosts: Tony and Dorothy Dean Saccaro
Suite: 1 (PB) $65
Continental Breakfast
Credit Cards: None
Notes: 2, 5, 7, 9, 10, 11, 12

CEDAR KEY

The Island Hotel

P.O. Box 460, 32625
(352) 543-5111; (800) 432-4640
e-mail: ishotel@gnv.fdt.net
www.gnv.fdt.net/~ishotel/

This pre-Civil War building with Jamaican-style architecture is rustic and authentic, with much of the original structure. In the National Register of Historic Places. Gourmet seafood dining room, serving local Cedar Key specialties. Like stepping back in time, with muraled walls, paddle fans, French doors, and a wide wraparound porch which catches gulf breezes. A cozy lounge bar completes a perfect place to get away from it all. No smoking in bedrooms. Inquire about children being welcome.

Hosts: Dawn and Tony Cousins
Rooms: 13 (11 PB; 2 S1B) $85-95
Full Breakfast
Credit Cards: A, B, D
Notes: 4, 5, 10, 11, 12

The Island Hotel

CLEARWATER

Lanning's Green Gables

1040 Sunset Point Road, 34615
(813) 443-3675 (phone/FAX)

Built in 1910, this Old Florida house has plenty of charm and space to relax. Decorated and furnished for comfort, the rooms are spacious, each bedroom with private bath. Two beautiful porches with swing and rockers. Guests will love the private dock at sunset or bird watching. The Continental plus breakfast is loaded with fresh fruits, breads, and cereals, and served in the cheery dining room. Licensed by city and state. Member Inn Route, Clearwater and Dunedin Chambers of Commerce, and Superior Small Lodgings.

Hosts: Sue and Tom Lanning
Rooms: 3 (PB) $69-89
Continental Breakfast
Credit Cards: A, B, C
Notes: 2, 5, 7, 9, 10, 11, 12, 14, 15

DAYTONA BEACH

Live Oak Inn

444-448 South Beach, 32114
(904) 252-4667; (800) 881-4667

Relax and romance at one of Florida's top 10 historic inns. Live Oak Inn offers the best of Daytona. The restful atmosphere of the Intracoastal Waterway and the excitement of "the World's Most Famous Beach" only a mile away. In the historic district, guests are able to escape into the leisurely pace of days gone by. Twelve guest rooms with their own private baths, TVs, VCRs, and telephones. Some include balconies and in-room Jacuzzis. Enjoy lunch and dinner in the casual fine-dining restaurant.

Hosts: Del and Jessie Glock
Rooms: 12 (PB) $80-150
Continental Breakfast
Credit Cards: A, B
Notes: 2, 3, 4, 5, 7, 9, 10, 11, 12, 14

Live Oak Inn

The Villa

The Villa Bed and Breakfast

801 North Peninsula Drive, 32118
(904) 248-2020

Enjoy elegant accommodations in a historic Spanish mansion in the heart of Daytona Beach. Decorated with fine antiques, this lovely inn has richly detailed public areas, a formal living room, dining and breakfast rooms, and a library/entertainment room. Enjoy the private walled flower gardens, the pool, and the sunning area. Guests are within walking distance of Daytona's famous beach, restaurants, shopping, nightlife, and the boardwalk and arcade area.

Host: Jim Camp
Rooms: 4 (PB) $90-170
Continental Breakfast
Credit Cards: A, B, C
Notes: 5, 10, 11, 12, 14

DESTIN

Henderson Park Inn—A Beachside Bed and Breakfast

2700 Highway 98E-Beach Route, 32541
(800) 336-4853; www.abbott-resorts.com

Destin's first and only beachside bed and breakfast combines the charm of a Queen Anne-style inn with the amenities of a modern resort. The perfect place for couples and romantics; rooms are decorated with cozy impressionistic themes, antique hand-crafted reproductions, high ceilings; some rooms have fireplaces and four-poster beds, private

Henderson Park Inn

balconies and baths, some of which have Jacuzzis. Southern beachside breakfast, beach service, maid service, turndown service, room service, evening happy hour, heated pool, veranda, palm grove, and restaurant.

Host: Susie Nunnelley
Rooms: 20 (PB) $94-279
Full Breakfast
Credit Cards: A, B, C, D
Notes: 2, 3, 4, 5, 9, 10, 11, 12, 14, 15

DUNEDIN

J. O. Douglas House

209 Scotland Street, 34698
(813) 735-9006; FAX (813) 736-0626
e-mail: hudson19@ix.netcom.com
www.jodouglashouse.com

Built in 1878, the J. O. Douglas House is the oldest home in historic Dunedin. This fully restored Victorian home is furnished with antiques and is listed in the National Register of Historic Places. A large swimming pool, hot tub, and screened porch are available for relaxation. Smoke-free establishment. Walk to the marina, shops, galleries, restaurants. Biking, boating, and

J. O. Douglas House

blading on the 42-mile Pinellas Trail. Continental plus breakfast served.

Hosts: Jeffrey and Sherril Melio
Rooms: 5 (1 PB; 4 SB) $85-110
Continental Breakfast
Credit Cards: A, B
Notes: 2, 5, 7, 9, 10, 11, 12, 15

EVERGLADES CITY

The Ivey House Bed and Breakfast

107 Camellia Street, P.O. Box 5038, 34139
(941) 695-3299; FAX (941) 695-4155
e-mail: sandee@iveyhouse.com
www.iveyhouse.com

This quaint bed and breakfast is for those who want to explore the Everglades National Park without leaving the comforts of home. There are 10 air-conditioned rooms with shared bathrooms and a large living room that includes an Everglades-area library. Cottage with private bath also available. Smoking and drinking are allowed only on the outside porches. Guided adventures, including canoeing, kayaking, boating, and sea shelling, are provided daily. Also available are canoe, kayak, and skiff rentals (bikes are complimentary for guests).

Hosts: The Harraden Family
Rooms: 11 (1 PB; 10 SB) $50-85
Full Breakfast
Credit Cards: A, B
Notes: 2, 3, 4, 7, 8, 10, 11, 14

On the Banks of the Everglades ...a bed and breakfast inn

201 West Broadway, P.O. Box 570, 34139
(941) 695-3151; (888) 431-1977
FAX (941) 695-3335
e-mail: patty@banksoftheeverglades.com
www.banksoftheeverglades.com

On the Banks of the Everglades is a bed and breakfast inn that derives its name from the fact that it is tranquilly nestled in the historic Bank of Everglades building. Chartered in 1923, therefore taking its place in history. Built by the Baron Collier family of

Collier County, the Bank building served as the first bank in Collier County during those roaring 20s. Enjoy breakfast served in the first bank vault of Collier Country!

Host: Patty Flick Richards
Rooms: 11 (5 PB; 6 SB) $55-105
Full Breakfast
Credit Cards: A, B, C, D
Notes: 2, 7, 8, 9, 10, 14, 15

FORT LAUDERDALE

Phoenix South Guest House

3609 NE 27th Street, 33308
(954) 733-7701 (Monday through Saturday)
(954) 563-6665 (Sundays and evenings)
FAX (954) 739-0282
e-mail: info@beachguesthouse.com
www.beachguesthouse.com

At Phoenix House each guest suite includes a queen-size bed, private bath, living room, kitchenette, and patio terrace with beach access just footsteps to the sand and water. Guests can take an early evening water-taxi tour of the Intracoastal Waterway or relax comfortably on their own terrace enjoying the moonlit nights and tropical breezes. Whatever one decides to do, the friendly proprietor at Phoenix House will make sure the stay will be memorable and one will leave guests wanting to come back for more. Continental breakfast optional.

Hosts: Sandra and Tony
Rooms: 5 (PB) $125-175
Continental Breakfast
Credit Cards: None
Notes: 2, 5, 7, 11, 12, 13, 14

FORT PIERCE

The Mellon Patch Inn

3601 North A1A, 34949
(561) 461-5231; (800) 656-7824
www.sunet.net/mlnptch

Escape to a beach setting. "Let us pamper you." Wake up to freshly ground coffee and a full gourmet breakfast. The ocean is just across the street. Explore the parks and nature preserve. Play tennis, golf, and bicycle. Canoe and fish from the dock. Poke through little-known galleries and shop for antiques. Relax in the spa. Read while relaxing in the hammock or the swing. Two hours from Orlando and Pompano Beach.

Hosts: Andrea and Arthur Mellon
Rooms: 4 (PB) $90-120
Full Breakfast
Credit Cards: A, B, C, D
Notes: 2, 3, 5, 7, 9, 10, 11, 12, 14, 15

HAVANA

Historic Havana House

301 East Sixth Avenue, 32333
(904) 539-5611

This bed and breakfast, found on a quiet residential street two blocks from the center of town, is a likely stop for collectors. At last count, Havana had 60 antique shops plus many related businesses. Tallahassee, the state capital and home of Florida State University, is only 15 minutes away by car. Gaver's restored 1907 frame house has a large screened porch. Guests are welcome to watch cable TV in the common area. For breakfast, the hosts will design a menu to suit guests' preferences. Children over eight welcome. Special rates, accommodation restrictions, and reservation policy apply to Florida State University graduation weekends, F.S.U. home football games, and selected special events.

Hosts: Shirley and Bruce Gaver
Rooms: 2 (PB) $70-90
Full Breakfast
Credit Cards: A, B, D
Notes: 2, 5, 7, 9, 14

JACKSONVILLE

Club Continental Suites

2143 Astor Street, P.O. Box 7059, Orange Park, 32073
(904) 264-6070; (800) 877-6070

The Club Continental Suites is a Mediterranean-style inn overlooking the

Club Continental Suites

broad St. Johns River, featuring romantic Continental dining with "Old Florida charm." The Club, built in 1923 as the Palmolive family estate, now hosts 22 river-view suites with expansive grounds, giant live oaks, lush gardens, and the pre-Civil War Riverhouse Pub with live entertainment. Sunday brunch available. Lunch and dinner available Tuesday through Friday. Inquire about accommodations for pets. Nonsmoking rooms available.

Hosts: Caleb Massee and Karrie Stevens
Rooms: 22 (PB) $65-160
Continental Breakfast
Credit Cards: A, B, C, D, E
Notes: 2, 5, 8, 9, 10, 11, 12, 14, 15

House on Cherry Street

1844 Cherry Street, 32205
(904) 384-1999; FAX (904) 384-5013
e-mail: houseoncherry@compuserve.com

Historic restored home on the St. Johns River near downtown Jacksonville features antiques, wine, snacks, and canoe, kayak, and bicycles for guest use. Children over nine welcome.

Host: Carol Anderson
Rooms: 4 (PB) $84.50-118.30
Continental Breakfast
Credit Cards: A, B, C
Notes: 2, 5, 9, 10, 12, 14

The San Marco Point House

1709 River Road, 32207
(904) 396-1448; FAX (904) 396-7760
e-mail: sanmarcopt@aol.com

Charming Craftsman-style five-bedroom bungalow in the heart of historic San Marco. Within walking distance to shops, restaurants, and theaters. Enjoy a leisurely walk along the river and view the skyline of downtown Jacksonville, which is only five minutes away.

Hosts: Todd and Kemp and Linda Olsavsky
Rooms: 5 (PB) $75-150
Full Breakfast
Credit Cards: A, B, C
Notes: 2, 5, 7, 9, 10, 12, 14

JUPITER

Innisfail

17576 Bridle Court, 33478
(561) 744-5902; FAX (561) 744-3387
e-mail: kathie@vannoorden.com

Innisfail, in the farms of Jupiter, is a gracious new home, framed with royal palms and palmettos. Start the day with a dip in the heated pool and enjoy a leisurely Continental breakfast on the lanai. Browse through the VanNoorden gallery or stroll out to the studio to observe the sculpture studio in action. It helps to be a pet lover as Innisfail is home to three royal standard poodles and three cats. Children over 10 welcome. One night surcharge of $10.

Host: Katherine VanNoorden
Rooms: 2 (PB) $75-85
Continental Breakfast
Credit Cards: None
Notes: 2, 5, 7, 9, 10, 11, 12

Innisfail

KEY WEST

Andrew's Inn

Zero Walton Lane, 33040
(305) 294-7730; FAX (305) 294-0021
e-mail: andrewsinn@aol.com

Central Old Town Key West and down a shaded lane off Duval Street. Each queen-size or king-size deluxe room is distinctive and beautiful. Each guest room has private entrance, full bath, remote control TV, air conditioning, and telephone. Guests will be served a full breakfast each morning and will enjoy complimentary happy hour in the evening. Overlooking the Hemingway estate.

Hosts: Scott and Tammy Saunders
Rooms: 9 (PB) $115-405
Full Breakfast
Credit Cards: A, B, C, D
Notes: 2, 5, 8, 9, 14

Center Court Historic Inn and Cottages

916 Center Street, 33040
(305) 296-9292; (800) 797-8787
FAX (305) 294-4104
www.centercourtkw.com

One-half block off famous Duval Street in the very center of historic Old Town. Nestled in lush tropical gardens, the beautifully renovated 1874 shipbuilder's home and cigar maker's cottage are uniquely furnished with original art, sculpture, and photos, air conditioning, ceiling fan, cable TV, in-room safe, telephone, and hair dryer. The guest house and cottages surround the heated pool, Jacuzzi, exercise pavilion, fish and lily pond, and gardens, which extend along Center Street.

Host: Naomi Van Steelandt
Rooms and Cottages: 16 (PB) $88-298
Continental Breakfast
Credit Cards: A, B, C, D
Notes: 2, 5, 6, 7, 8, 9, 10, 11, 12, 14, 15

The Cypress House

601 Caroline Street, 33040
(305) 294-6969; (800) 525-2488
FAX (305) 296-1174; e-mail: cypress@conch.net
www.cypresshousekw.com

Affordable luxury just one block from Duval Street. Grand Bahamian mansion, listed in the National Register of Historic Places. Spacious rooms feature air conditioning, color cable TV, telephone, and Bahama ceiling fans. A Continental plus breakfast is served daily. Lush tropical garden features a 40-foot lap pool and second-floor sun deck. Afternoon happy hour. Free parking nearby for registered guests. Two blocks to historic seaport.

Host: Dave Taylor
Rooms: 16 (10 PB; 6 SB) $79-250
Continental Breakfast
Credit Cards: A, B, C, D
Notes: 5, 9, 14

Duval House

815 Duval Street, 33040
(305) 294-1666; (800) 22 DUVAL
FAX (305) 292-1701

This beautifully restored century-old Victorian house has a special charm and deluxe amenities. Enjoy the large swimming pool and quiet tropical gardens. Walk to any one of the many nearby

Duval House

7 No smoking; 8 Children welcome; 9 Social drinking allowed; 10 Tennis nearby; 11 Swimming nearby; 12 Golf nearby; 13 Skiing nearby; 14 May be booked through a travel agent; 15 Handicapped accessible.

restaurants and attractions. AAA- and Mobil Travel Guide-approved.

Host: Richard Kamradt
Rooms: 28 (PB) $90-300
Continental Breakfast
Credit Cards: A, B, C, D, E, F
Notes: 5, 9, 10, 11, 12, 14

Heron House

512 Simonton Street, 33040
(305) 294-9227; (800) 294-1644
FAX (305) 294-5692

Key West's Heron House offers a refreshing new alternative. It has all of the intimacy of a quaint Key West guest house while possessing all of the style of a small luxury hotel. Local artists have painstakingly hand-crafted each room to enrich one's experience. Oak, redwood, and cedar adorn the walls of the guest rooms. Enjoy the coolness of Italian tile and marble under one's feet. Rest on huge oak beds as the morning sunlight filters through hand-crafted stained-glass transoms. And the exceptional full guest hospitality—turn-down service, full concierge, morning newspaper, orchid gardens and tours, robes, and much more—expresses a genuine caring. Everyone is treated as a friend.

Hosts: Fred Geibelt and Robert Framarin
Rooms: 23 (PB) $110.39-299.94
Continental Breakfast
Credit Cards: A, B, C, E
Notes: 5, 7, 9, 10, 11, 12, 14

Heron House

The Island City House Hotel

411 William Street, 33040
(305) 294-5702; (800) 634-8230
www.islandcityhouse.com

The Island City House Hotel is three historic Victorian guest houses offering 24 one- and two-bedroom suites with tropical gardens and red brick walkways winding throughout. Enjoy a complimentary breakfast buffet of fruits, breads, and coffee on a secluded patio, or relax on the deck in the crystalline pool and Jacuzzi in this lush tropical paradise. Children welcome.

Hosts: Stanley and Janet Corneal
Rooms: 24 (PB) $95-225
Continental Breakfast
Credit Cards: A, B, C, D, E, F
Notes: 5, 8, 9, 10, 11, 12, 14

Key West Bed and Breakfast—The Popular House

415 William Street, 33040
(305) 296-7274; (800) 438-6155
FAX (305) 293-0306

The Key West Bed and Breakfast (circa 1898) is one of the oldest and more established guest houses in Old Town. On a quiet tree-lined street this historically registered Victorian is only three blocks from all Duval Street has to offer. With over a 20-year history in Key West, it houses an extensive collection of local art, and guests can learn about the folklore and the hidden Key West, the outrageous, the creative, and the truly laid back. Complimentary Continental plus breakfast at guests' leisure. Smoking permitted in designated areas only.

Host: Jody Carlson
Rooms: 8 (5 PB; 3 SB) $59-250
Continental Breakfast
Credit Cards: A, B, C
Notes: 5, 9, 10, 11, 12, 13

L'Habitation Bed and Breakfast

408 Eaton Street, 33040
(305) 293-9203; FAX (305) 296-1313

This bed and breakfast, in the heart of the historic preservation district, was built in

1874. L'Habitation reflects all the architectural charm of a true Key West Conch house with Victorian and Bahamian accents. One-half block from Duval Street, five minutes' walking distance from Mallory Square, museum, and restaurants. All rooms have private bath, telephone, cable color TV, air conditioning, refrigerator, and some have a kitchen. From the tropical terrace, guests enjoy a well-prepared Continental breakfast.

Hosts: Helene Gironet and Stuart Butler
Rooms: 8 (PB) $59-129
Continental Breakfast
Credit Cards: A, B, C, D
Notes: 5, 6, 8, 9, 11, 12, 14

Merlinn Inn

811 Simonton Street, 33040
(305) 296-3336; (800) 642-4753

Lush tropical gardens, decks, and pool in the heart of Old Town. Freshly baked breakfast served among exotic birds in the secluded garden. Twenty rooms and apartments with private baths, TV, and air conditioning. Also wheelchair accessible unit with private garden. The staff can arrange a day on the water—snorkeling, fishing, sailing, or playing. Guests never want to leave!

Host: Julia Fondriest
Rooms: 20 (PB) $79-199
Continental Breakfast

Merlinn Inn

Credit Cards: A, B, C, D
Notes: 5, 7, 8, 9, 11, 12, 14, 15

Nassau House

1016 Fleming Street, 33040
(305) 296-8513; (800) 296-8513

In Old Town Key West, Nassau House is a century-old bed and breakfast offering rooms and suites on three floors, as well as some very special island cottages. All accommodations feature hospitality refrigerators, air conditioning, color cable TV, telephones, and clock radios. The Treetop Suites feature living rooms and full kitchens. Relax on the large airy front porch or the lush tropical garden with lagoon-style pool/spa nestled into the foliage. Complimentary beverages available in the evenings. Bicycle rental and full concierge service available on-site. Minimum stay during holidays.

Hosts: Damon Leard and Bob Tracy
Rooms: 8 (PB) $79-200
Continental Breakfast
Credit Cards: A, B, C, D
Notes: 5, 6, 7, 9, 10, 11, 12, 14, 15

The Paradise Inn

819 Simonton Street, 33040
(305) 293-8007; (800) 888-9648
FAX (305) 293-0807

In historic Old Town, just one block from Duval Street. Eighteen island-inspired luxury suites and one- and two-bedroom cottages with private marble baths, air conditioning, telephones, TVs, safes, bathrobes, and concierge services. Outdoor heated pool and Jacuzzi in a secluded, lushly landscaped tropical courtyard. Congenial multilingual staff. Convenient secured on-premise parking. Beaches, shopping, dining, and entertainment all within walking distance. Children over five welcome.

Host: Shel Segel
Rooms: 18 (PB) $160-300
Continental Breakfast
Credit Cards: A, B, C, D, E
Notes: 5, 9, 10, 11, 12, 14, 15

Treetop Inn Historic Bed and Breakfast

806 Truman Avenue, 33040
(305) 293-0712; (800) 926-0712
FAX (305) 294-3668

Built at the turn of the century, Treetop Inn has been restored to provide modern comforts in a 1900s setting. It received the 1994 Key West Chamber of Commerce's Business for Beauty award. In central Old Town, Treetop Inn is within walking distance of beaches, restaurants, and shops. The hosts are knowledgeable about all Key West activities. The spacious rooms are graciously furnished and include private baths, cable TV, air conditioning, refrigerators, and telephones. Poolside breakfast are served.

Hosts: Sue and Fred Leake
Rooms: 3 (PB) $98-178
Full Breakfast
Credit Cards: A, B
Notes: 5, 7, 9, 10, 11, 12

Tropical Inn

812 Duval Street, 33040
(305) 294-9977; FAX (305) 292-1656
e-mail: tropicainn@aol.com

The Tropical Inn is in the heart of the historical district and is listed in the National Register of Historic Places. Within walking distance of beaches, historic sites, shops, art galleries, and the most popular restaurants and night spots. All rooms have private baths, air conditioning, ceiling fans, cable TV, telephones—some with private balconies and decks amid lush tropical gardens. Two suites with kitchens and garden Jacuzzi can accommodate up to four people. Complimentary Continental breakfast offered in season in the lovely gardens. Staffed by friendly and helpful people.

Host: Dennis
Rooms: 10 (PB) $85-140
Continental Breakfast
Credit Cards: A, B, D
Notes: 5, 7, 9, 10, 11, 12, 14

Whispers Bed and Breakfast Inn

409 William Street, 33040
(305) 294-5969; (800) 856-SHHH
FAX (305) 294-3899

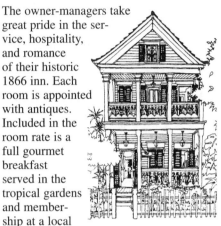

The owner-managers take great pride in the service, hospitality, and romance of their historic 1866 inn. Each room is appointed with antiques. Included in the room rate is a full gourmet breakfast served in the tropical gardens and membership at a local beach club and health spa. Hot tub and sun deck on premises. Inquire about children.

Host: John Marburg
Rooms: 7 (PB) $80-175
Full Breakfast
Credit Cards: A, B, C, D
Notes: 2, 5, 7, 9, 10, 11, 12, 14

The Wicker Guest House: An Island Bed and Breakfast

913 Duval Street, 33040
(305) 296-4275; (800) 880-4275
FAX (305) 294-7240

This spacious complex of six houses, 21 rooms, on colorful Duval Street, has been family owned and operated since 1984. The main house dates to 1890 and the guest house is within easy walking distance to all downtown attractions. A large variety of affordable accommodations is offered. Most rooms include kitchenettes and cable TV, off-street parking, and full concierge service on the property. A delicious Continental breakfast is served poolside in the lovely, tranquil tropical garden. Boasting the friendliest and most helpful staff. Families are always welcome.

Hosts: Mark and Libby Curtis
Rooms: 21 (18 PB: 3 SB) $63-205
Continental Breakfast
Credit Cards: A, B, C, D, E
Notes: 5, 8, 9, 10, 11, 12, 14, 15

LAKE WALES

Chalet Suzanne Country Inn and Restaurant

3800 Chalet Suzanne Drive, 33853-7060
(941) 676-6011; (800) 433-6011
FAX (941) 676-1814
e-mail: info@chaletsuzanne.com
www.chaletsuzanne.com

Discover Europe in the heart of Florida. Bordered by fragrant orange groves, this historic 30-room family-run inn has become an oasis for travelers, weary executives, and discriminating diners. The award-winning dining room is now open daily, including Mondays. Be sure to ask about the Sunset Serenade summer packages.

Hosts: Vita Hinshaw and Family
Rooms: 30 (PB) $159-219
Full Breakfast
Credit Cards: A, B, C, D, E, F
Notes: 2, 3, 4, 5, 8, 9, 10, 11, 12, 14, 15

Chalet Suzanne

LAKE WORTH

Mango Inn Bed and Breakfast

128 North Lakeside Drive, 33460
(561) 533-6900 (phone/FAX)
www.mangoinn.com

The inn is a short 10-minute walk to the white sandy beaches of the Atlantic Ocean. Amenities include a heated pool, bicycles, guest rooms with central air conditioning, cable TV, refrigerators, private baths, queen-size beds, designer monogrammed bed linens, and plump down pillows. Deep-sea fishing, golfing, snorkeling, scuba-diving are within minutes of the inn. Two blocks from historic downtown Lake Worth, burgeoning with antique shops, art galleries, and sidewalk cafes. Ten minutes from Palm Beach International Airport and Palm Beach.

Hosts: Erin and Bo Allen
Rooms: 8 (PB) $60-120
Full and Continental Breakfast
Credit Cards: A, B, D, E
Notes: 2, 5, 9, 10, 11, 12, 14

MARATHON

Latigo Bed and Breakfast Cruise

1021 11th Street, Ocean, 33050
(305) 289-1066 (phone/FAX)

On this 56-foot luxury yacht with three private staterooms, guests begin their experience on a sunset cruise sipping champagne with a variety of hors d'oeuvres, followed by a first-class gourmet dinner. Champagne, wine, and beer are complimentary. The yacht is anchored overnight behind a cluster of islands offering complete privacy. The following morning after breakfast, guests may snorkel over the beautiful coral reef or swim before

Latigo Cruise

7 No smoking; 8 Children welcome; 9 Social drinking allowed; 10 Tennis nearby; 11 Swimming nearby; 12 Golf nearby; 13 Skiing nearby; 14 May be booked through a travel agent; 15 Handicapped accessible.

returning dockside. Extended cruises are also available to Key West, Dry Tortugas, Bahamas. Fishing, diving, water-skiing are available. Rate includes two meals, lodging, sunset and snorkel cruises.

Hosts: Ken and Valerie Waine
Rooms: 3 (1 PB; 2 SB) $179 (per person)
Full or Continental Breakfast
Credit Cards: A, B
Notes: 2, 3, 4, 5, 8, 9, 10, 11, 13, 14

MIAMI

Redland's Bed and Breakfast

19521 SW 128 C, 33177
(305)238-5285

The romantic tropical guest house is 750 square feet with a fully furnished kitchen, living room, bedroom, and private bath. It sleeps four (two private) and has private entrance, TV, air conditioning, pool, and Jacuzzi. Self-catered breakfast can be enjoyed poolside or at the garden gazebo. Bicycles also available for the nearby bike trails. Near Miami's farming community, 25 minutes from Florida Keys and Miami International Airport.

Hosts: Marianne and Tim Hamilton
Rooms: 1 (PB) $50
Continental Breakfast
Credit Cards: None
Notes: 2, 5, 7, 8, 9, 10, 11, 12

MICANOPY

Herlong Mansion

402 Northeast Cholokka Boulevard, P.O. Box 667, 32667
(352) 466-3322; (800) HERLONG

"Micanopy is the prettiest town in Florida. The Herlong Mansion is its crown jewel"—*Florida Trend*, November 1989. The brick Greek Revival structure has four Corinthian columns, 10 fireplaces, six different types of wood, and is decorated in period antiques. Built in 1845 and 1910, the three-story house has 12 bedrooms, all with private baths, on two acres with moss-draped oaks, pecans, dogwoods, and magnolias.

Herlong Mansion

Host: H. C. "Sony" Howard Jr.
Rooms: 12 (PB) $55-160
Full Breakfast
Credit Cards: A, B
Notes: 2, 7, 8, 9, 12, 14, 15

MOUNT DORA

The Emerald Hill Inn

27751 Lake Jem Road, 32757
(352) 383-2777; (800) 366-9387
FAX (352) 383-6701; e-mail: Emerldhill@aol.com

On a country road in a natural, Old Florida setting, is this serene, sprawling 1941 lakefront estate amidst orange groves, on more than two acres with tall oaks, Spanish moss, broad sweeping lawn down to lake. Resembling a lodge, the stunning living room has a majestic coquina rock

Emerald Hill Inn

fireplace, wood cathedral ceiling, polished oak floors. Lake-view rooms have patio, TV/VCR. Ten minutes to Mount Dora antique shops, restaurants, festivals. Forty-five minutes to Orlando/Disney attractions. Many area lakes for water sports, boat cruises. AAA three-diamond rating. Children over 10 welcome.

Hosts: Michael and Diane Wiseman
Rooms: 4 (PB) $99-149
Full Breakfast
Credit Cards: A, B, D
Notes: 5, 7, 9, 12, 14

Farnsworth House Bed and Breakfast

1029 East 5th Avenue, 32757
(352) 735-1894

On one and one-half acres in the historic town of Mount Dora with its many boutiques and antique shops, this home was built in 1886. Three suites and two efficiencies, each decorated in a unique theme with private bath and kitchen. Guests can enjoy the large screened porch, living and dining room, and hot tub enclosed within a screened gazebo. Twenty-five miles northwest of Orlando.

Hosts: Dick and Sandy Shelton
Rooms: 5 (PB) $85-115
Credit Cards: A, B, D
Notes: 2, 5, 7, 8, 9, 10, 11, 12, 14

OCALA

Seven Sisters Inn

820 SE Fort King Street, 34471
(352) 867-1170; FAX (352) 867-5266

"Florida's Enchantress" named Inn of the Month by *Country Inns* magazine. Featured in *Southern Living*, this 1888 Queen Anne Victorian mansion is in the historic district of Ocala. Eight rooms feature king- and queen-size suites, fireplaces, canopied beds, private baths, soaking tubs, Jacuzzis. Award-winning gourmet breakfast and afternoon tea are included. Murder mysteries and candlelight dinners are available. Canoeing, golf, horseback riding, hiking, antiquing, and famous Silver Springs attractions nearby.

Hosts: Bonnie and Ken Oden
Rooms: 8 (PB) $105-165
Full Breakfast
Credit Cards: A, B, C, D
Notes: 2, 4, 5, 7, 9, 10, 11, 12, 14, 15

ORLANDO

Perri House Bed and Breakfast Inn

10417 Centurion Court, 32836
(407) 876-4830; (800) 780-4830
FAX (407) 876-0241
www.perrihouse.com

Perri House is a quiet, private, country estate inn secluded on three acres of land adjacent to the Walt Disney World Resort. Bird sanctuary project, bird feeders, bird house museum. Outstanding location! Five minutes to Disney World. Upscale Continental breakfast buffet, pool, hot tub. Eight guest "nests" with private bath, entrance, TV, telephone. Four bird house cottages by late 1998, featuring king-size canopied beds, whirlpool tubs for two. Three-, five-, seven-day vacation packages will be offered.

Hosts: Nick and Angi Perretti
Rooms: 8 (PB) $89-129
Continental Breakfast
Credit Cards: A, B, C, D, E
Notes: 5, 7, 8, 9, 10, 12, 14

ORLANDO (WINTER GARDEN)

Meadow Marsh Bed and Breakfast

940 Tildenville School Road, Winter Garden, 34787
(407) 656-2064; (888) 656-2064

For a wonderful treat, visit this romantic getaway where the hectic pace of today fades into the sweet peace of yesteryears.

Just west of Orlando this Victorian farmhouse sits on 12 acres of Old Florida. Huge oaks and stately palms filter sunlight to the spacious lawn below. A leisurely stroll across the meadow takes guests to a "rails-to-trails" path for biking, skating, or an early morning walk. Close to all central Florida attractions yet far enough away to provide a haven from the fast lane. Guests can enjoy two-person whirlpools in the suites and cottage or old-fashioned tubs and showers in the smaller bedrooms. Cozy fireplaces and heart-pine floors add to the warmth and beauty of this country estate. A lovely one-room cottage sits just behind the main house for those seeking privacy in their own "little house." Southern hospitality is offered by the native Floridian, Cavelle, and her "transplanted" husband, John.

Hosts: Cavelle and John Pawlack
Rooms: 2 (PB) $95-215
Suites: 2 (PB)
Garden Cottage: $215
Full Breakfast
Credit Cards: A, B, D
Notes: 5, 7, 12, 14

PALM BAY

Casa Del Sol

Country Estates, 232 Rheine Road Northwest, 32907
(407) 728-4676

This award-winning home is on Florida's central east coast. Breakfast is served on the lanai, with breathtaking foliage. From here see a spaceship launched. Enjoy the luxury of a Roman tub. Minutes away from the space pad, all Disney attractions, and the Marlins' winter quarters. Closed April 16 through November 7.

Casa Del Sol

Host: Stanley Finkelstein
Rooms: 3 (1 PB; 2 SB) $55-135
Full Breakfast
Credit Cards: None
Notes: 2, 8, 9, 10, 11, 12, 13, 14

PALM BEACH

Plaza Inn

215 Brazilian Avenue, 33480
(561) 832-8666; (800) 233-2632
FAX (561) 835-8776; e-mail: plazainn@aol.com
www.plazainnpalmbeach.com

Circa 1940. Just one block from the beach on the island of Palm Beach. This elegant but unpretentious European-style boutique hotel exudes Old World charm. The lobby is decorated with antiques, hand-crafted gilded ceilings with Austrian chandeliers, Persian rugs, Louis XIV front desk, and a baby grand piano. Pick the ambiance of one's choice: French, Italian, or traditional four-poster beds. All deluxe rooms are decorated differently. Some rooms feature hand-blown Murano chandeliers and French draperies. The inn features the Stray Fox Pub, twice a week entertainment and a Charleston-style courtyard. Other amenities include heated pool, Jacuzzi, full American breakfast, and parking.

Room: 50 (PB) $95-225
Full Breakfast
Credit Cards: A, B, C
Notes: 2, 5, 6, 7, 8, 9, 10, 12, 14

RUSKIN

Ruskin House Bed and Breakfast

120 Dickman Drive SW, 33570
(813) 645-3842

In rural Hillsborough County within easy driving distance of Tampa, St. Petersburg, and Saratoga, this landmarked Victorian house features columned verandas and a tower, a massive dogleg staircase, a fireplace, hardwood floors, high ceilings, and original wall coloring. Every room is furnished with period antiques and oriental rugs; rocking chairs and a hammock grace the upper veranda. The house looks over the Ruskin Inlet, which winds around three acres of lawn, tropical glades, and flower gardens.

Hosts: Melanie Hubbard and Mac Miller
Rooms: 3 (PB) $75-110
Continental Breakfast
Credit Cards: A, B, C
Notes: 2, 5, 7, 8, 9, 11, 12, 14, 15

ST. AUGUSTINE

Carriage Way

Carriage Way Bed and Breakfast

70 Cuna Street, 32084
(904) 829-2467; (800) 908-9832
FAX (904) 826-1461

A beautifully restored 1883 Victorian home in the heart of the historic district is within walking distance of the waterfront, shops, restaurants, and historic sites. Rooms are decorated with antiques and reproductions. Private baths have showers or antique clawfoot tubs with showers. The atmosphere is leisurely and casual. Complimentary beverages, newspaper, cookies, and full gourmet breakfast. Roses, fruit and cheese tray, gourmet picnic lunch, carriage rides, and breakfast in bed are available as "special touches." Selected one of the 125 facilities in *Best Places to Stay in Florida.*

Hosts: Bill and Diane Johnson
Rooms: 9 (PB) $69-150
Full Breakfast
Credit Cards: A, B, C, D
Notes: 2, 5, 7, 9, 10, 11, 12, 14

Casa de la Paz

22 Avenida Menendez, 32084
(904) 829-2915; (800) 929-2915
www.oldcity.com/delapaz

Enjoy views of Matanzas Bay from the elegant guest rooms or the second-story veranda at this Mediterranean-style inn decorated with antique furnishings. From the veranda, an open stairway leads to a beautiful walled garden courtyard. The inn is central to all historic sites, fine restaurants, and miles of ocean beaches. Complimentary wines and a full buffet breakfast. AAA-rated three diamonds. Listed in the National Register of Historic Places.

Hosts: Bob and Donna Marriott
Rooms: 6 (PB) $89-189
Full Breakfast
Credit Cards: A, B, C, D
Notes: 2, 5, 7, 9, 10, 11, 12

Casa de Solana Bed and Breakfast Inn

21 Aviles Street, 32084-4441
(904) 824-3555; e-mail: solana@aug.com
www.oldcity.com/solana

A lovingly renovated Colonial home, circa 1763, is in the heart of St. Augustine's historical area within walking distance of

Casa de Solana

7 No smoking; 8 Children welcome; 9 Social drinking allowed; 10 Tennis nearby; 11 Swimming nearby; 12 Golf nearby; 13 Skiing nearby; 14 May be booked through a travel agent; 15 Handicapped accessible.

restaurants, museums, and quaint shops. There are four antique-filled guest accommodations. All are suites; some have fireplaces, others have balconies that overlook the beautiful garden, and others have a breathtaking view of Matanzas Bay. All have private baths. Tariff includes a full breakfast served in the formal guest dining room, cable TV, chocolates, decanter of sherry.

Host: Fayé Lang-McMurry
Rooms: 4 (PB) $125-145
Full Breakfast
Credit Cards: A, B, C, D
Notes: 2, 5, 7, 9, 10, 11, 12, 13, 14

The Cedar House Inn

Castle Garden

15 Shenandoah Street, 32084
(904) 829-3839; FAX (904) 829-9049
e-mail: castleg@aug.com

"Stay at a Castle and be treated like royalty!" Relax and enjoy the peace and quiet of royal treatment at this newly restored 100-year-old castle of Moorish Revival design. Awaken to the aroma of freshly baked goodies as hosts prepare a full mouth-watering country breakfast just like Mom used to make! This former Castle Warden carriage house boasts three beautiful bridal rooms with sunken beds, soothing in-room Jacuzzis, and cathedral ceilings. Amenities include complimentary wine or champagne, chocolates, and bicycles. Packages and specialty gift baskets available. Children five and older are welcome.

Hosts: Bruce Kloeckner and Kimmy Van Kooten Kloeckner
Rooms: 7 (PB) $75-150
Full Breakfast
Credit Cards: A, B, C, D
Notes: 2, 5, 7, 10, 11, 12, 14

The Cedar House Inn

79 Cedar Street, 32084
(904) 829-0079; (800) CEDAR-INN
FAX (904) 825-0916; e-mail: russ@aug.com
www.cedarhouseinn.com

Capture romantic moments at this 1893 Victorian home in the heart of the ancient city. Escape into a Jacuzzi suite or an antique-filled bedroom with claw-foot tub or enjoy the parlor with its fireplace, player piano, and antique Victrola. Elegant full breakfast, complimentary beverages, evening snack, convenient on-premises parking. Garden Jacuzzi tub and bicycles. Walk to all historic sites. Easy drive to I-95, Atlantic Ocean beaches, tennis, and golf. Midweek specials. AAA three-diamond-rated. Picnic lunches available.

Hosts: Nina and Russ Thomas
Rooms: 6 (PB) $64-155
Full Breakfast
Credit Cards: A, B, C, D
Notes: 2, 4, 5, 7, 9, 10, 11, 12, 14

The Kenwood Inn

38 Marine Street, 32084
(904) 824-2116; FAX (904) 824-1689

Local maps and early records show the inn was built between 1865 and 1885 and was functioning as a private boarding

The Kenwood Inn

NOTES: Credit cards accepted: A MasterCard; B Visa; C American Express; D Discover; E Diner's Club; F Other; 2 Personal checks accepted; 3 Lunch available; 4 Dinner available; 5 Open all year; 6 Pets welcome;

house as early as 1886. In the historic district, the inn is within walking distance of many fine restaurants and all historic sights. One block from the Intracoastal Waterway, with its passing fishing trawlers, yachts at anchor, and the classic Bridge of Lions. Beautiful ocean beaches are just across the bridge. Children over eight welcome.

Hosts: Mark Kerrianne and Caitlin Constant
Rooms: 14 (PB) $85-115
Suite: $150
Continental Breakfast
Credit Cards: A, B, D
Notes: 2, 5, 7, 9, 10, 11, 12

Old Powder House Inn

38 Cordova Street, 32084
(904) 824-4149; (800) 447-4149
e-mail: ahowes@aug.com
www.oldcity.com/powderhouse

High ceilings and wraparound verandas distinguish this Victorian home built in 1899 on the site of an 18th-century Spanish powder magazine. It's in the heart of the historic area with horse and buggies going right past the house. Restaurants, antique stores, and quaint shops are within walking distance. Full gourmet breakfast, sparkling juice, wine, and hors d'oeuvres each day. Single and tandem bicycles available. Inground Jacuzzi and on-site parking. Weddings and special packages.

Hosts: Al and Eunice Howes
Rooms: 8 (PB) $79-165
Full Breakfast
Credit Cards: A, B, D
Notes: 2, 5, 7, 9, 10, 11, 12, 14

St. Francis Inn

279 St. George Street, 32084
(904) 824-6068; (800) 824-6062
FAX (904) 810-5525; www.stfrancisinn.com

The St. Francis Inn, in the historic district, was built as a private home for a Spanish soldier in 1791. It is a Spanish Colonial structure with a private courtyard, fireplaces, balconies, and the

St. Francis Inn

modern additions of a swimming pool, telephones, and some whirlpool tubs. The warmth and peacefulness of the inn itself, its location, and the kind of guests it attracts are all strong assets. Buffet breakfast served. Inquire about accommodations for children.

Host: Joe Finnegan
Rooms: 14 (PB) $80-180
Full Breakfast
Credit Cards: A, B, C, D, E
Notes: 2, 5, 7, 9, 10 ,11, 12, 14, 15

Segui Inn Bed and Breakfast

47 San Marco Avenue, 32084-3276
(904) 825-2811; (800) 858-5719
FAX (904) 824-3967; e-mail: seguiinn@aug.com
www.jax-ads.com/segui.inn

"Your home away from home." Between downtown and uptown St. Augustine. Join the hosts at their 1914 home filled with family antiques, spacious bedrooms, private baths, air conditioning, ceiling fans, on-premises parking, and cable TV in the parlor. Enjoy a full breakfast, freshly baked goodies, complimentary beverages, and a warm welcome. Pick-up available at the St. Augustine airport.

Hosts: George and Nikki Lent
Rooms: 3 (PB) $75-150
Full Breakfast
Credit Cards: A, B, D
Notes: 2, 5, 7, 8, 9, 10, 11, 12

Southern Wind Inn Bed and Breakfast

18 Cordova Street, 32084
(904) 825-3623; (800) 781-3338
FAX (904) 810-5212; e-mail: swind@aug.com

Surrender to the gracious southern hospitality at the inn renowned for its turn-of-the-century elegance. From this central location, guests can explore beautiful St. Augustine. Spend some relaxing moments on one of the shaded verandas, enjoy some home-baked cookies, and sip a glass of lemonade or wine while enjoying the passing horse-drawn carriages. The hosts offer all the contemporary comforts of king- and queen-size beds, central air, cable TV, private in-room baths (some even have Jacuzzi tubs). The full gourmet buffet breakfast features organically grown fruits and vegetables. Children over 10 welcome.

Hosts: Bob and Alana Indelicato
Rooms: 10 (PB) $85-165
Full Breakfast
Credit Cards: A, B, C, D
Notes: 5, 7, 9, 10, 11, 12, 14

Victorian House Bed and Breakfast

11 Cadiz Street, 32084
(904) 824-5214

In the heart of the historic district, the Victorian House was built in 1897 and has been restored and furnished in period antiques. Enjoy canopied beds, handwoven coverlets, quilts, stenciled walls, and hand-hooked rugs on heart-pine floors. Featured in *Country Home*, *Better Homes and Gardens*, *Southern Homes*, *Country Almanac*, and *Innsider* magazines. Guests are within walking distance of fine restaurants, the waterfront, shops, museums, and the plaza. Weekly and monthly rates are available upon request.

Host: Daisy Morden
Room: 8 (PB) $85-115
Continental Breakfast
Credit Cards: A, B, C
Notes: 2, 5, 7, 9, 10, 11, 12, 14

Westcott House

Westcott House

146 Avenida Menendez, 32084
(904) 824-4301

One of St. Augustine's most elegant guest houses overlooking Matanzas Bay. Circa 1890, restored in 1983, in the historic area and within walking distance to historic sites. All rooms have private baths, king-size beds, cable TV, private telephones, and are furnished in antiques. Year-round climate control. Complimentary afternoon wine. One-half block from the city's yacht pier.

Hosts: Sherry and David Dennison
Rooms: 9 (PB) $95-175
Continental Breakfast
Credit Cards: A, B, C, D
Notes: 2, 5, 7, 9, 10, 11, 12

ST. PETE BEACH

Beach Haven Villas

4980 Gulf Boulevard, 33706
(813) 367-8642

Directly on the sparkling Gulf of Mexico, Beach Haven harkens back to the days when much of Florida offered vacationers colorful Art Deco-style motels. Still in pink, Beach Haven retains its charming personality, while providing updated interiors and furnishings. Close to shopping, dining, and entertainment. Add the peaceful set-

Beach Haven Villas

ting, a gulf-front pool, and a sandy beachfront setting and guests will know why Beach Haven is so popular. Non-smoking units available.

Hosts: Jone and Millard Gamble
Rooms: 18 (PB) $50-125
Continental Breakfast
Credit Cards: A, B
Notes: 2, 5, 8, 9, 11, 12

Island's End Resort

1 Pass-A-Grille Way, 33706
(813) 360-5023; FAX (813) 367-7890

At the southernmost tip of St. Pete Beach, Island's End has a combination of sand, sea, and sky creating a unique atmosphere of rustic charm among gray weathered cottages. Experience the brilliant sunrises while sipping freshly squeezed orange juice. Later, enjoy the spectacular sunsets so famous along the Florida Suncoast. All cottages have modern kitchens and bathrooms. Furnishings are contemporary and extremely comfortable. Quality accommodations that enhance the beauty of the waterfront are at guests' disposal.

Island's End Resort

Hosts: Jone and Millard Gamble
Rooms: 6 (PB) $61-175
Continental Breakfast
Credit Cards: A, B
Notes: 2, 5, 8, 9, 11, 12

ST. PETERSBURG

Bayboro House Bed and Breakfast

1719 Beach Drive Southeast, 33701
(813) 823-4955; e-mail: bayborohouse@juno.com

Turn-of-the-century Queen Anne home furnished in antiques. Old-fashioned porch swing to enjoy sea gulls and sailboats on Old Tampa Bay. Minutes from the Dali Museum, pier, Suncoast Dome, Bayfront Center, and Al Lang Stadium. Many fine restaurants in the area. Personal suite available on request. Historic designated. AAA-rated three diamonds. Smoking on the veranda only. Pool and spa now available.

Hosts: Gordon and Antonia Powers
Rooms: 4 (PB) $95-145
Continental Breakfast
Credit Cards: A, B
Notes: 2, 5, 9, 10, 11, 12, 14

Bay Gables Bed and Breakfast

136 Fourth Avenue NorthEast, 33701
(813) 822-8855; (800) 822-8803
FAX (813) 824-7223

Nestled behind the tranquil garden and gazebo lies Bay Gables Bed and Breakfast, a three-story Key West-style building with nine spacious rooms that will suit guests' every need. Cheerfully decorated with antiques and an attention to detail, all rooms have private baths and separate entrances from spacious, covered, wide porches. A delicious Continental breakfast is offered in the breakfast room, garden, verandas or porches, or may be enjoyed in the privacy of the guest's room. Just one-half block from the bay, shopping, parks, and major museum.

Rooms: 9 (PB) $85-165
Continental Breakfast
Credit Cards: A, B
Notes: 2, 5, 7, 8, 10, 11, 12, 14, 15

Mansion House

Mansion House

105 Fifth Avenue NE, 33701
(813) 821-9391 (phone/FAX); (800) 274-7520
e-mail: mansion1@ix.netcom.com
www.mansionbandb.com

Historic award-winner Mansion House is owner-occupied; AAA three diamonds, AB&BA three-crowns 1997 excellence award, and rated St. Pete/Clearwater Superior Small Lodging. Ideal location in the art and entertainment district. Guests can walk to restaurants, sports, waterfront, museums, galleries, theaters, and shops. Rates include complimentary full breakfast, wine, snacks, and soft drinks. Customized packages for stays Sunday through Thursday. Six common areas including a Jacuzzi spa, library, and screened-in porch. Boat cruises available. InnPoints airline/lodging incentive awards given. Portuguese and French spoken.

Hosts: Robert and Rose Marie Ray
Rooms: 5 (PB) $95-150
Carriage House: $95-150
Full Breakfast
Credit Cards: A, B, C
Notes: 2, 5, 7, 8, 9, 10, 11, 12, 14

SANIBEL ISLAND

Sanibel's Seaside Inn

541 East Gulf Drive, 33957
(941) 472-1400; (800) 831-7384 (reservations)

Sanibel's Seaside Inn, a cozy beachfront inn that exudes Old Florida charm, offers newly renovated studios, one-bedroom cottages and apartments, and a three-bedroom suite. Guests will enjoy such complimentary amenities as a heated pool, shuffleboard, bicycles, library of videos and books, a daily Continental breakfast, and outdoor barbecue grills.

Host: Jack Reed
Rooms: 32 (PB) $150-350
Continental Breakfast
Credit Cards: A, B, C, D, E
Notes: 2, 5, 8, 10, 11, 12, 14, 15

Sanibel's Song of the Sea

863 East Gulf Drive, 33957
(941) 472-2220; (800) 231-1045 (reservations)

Song of the Sea, Sanibel Island's romantic European-style seaside inn, features luxurious studios and one-bedroom suites, each with a fully equipped kitchen, microwave, color cable TV, and screened patios. Guests enjoy complimentary wine and fresh flowers upon

NOTES: Credit cards accepted: A MasterCard; B Visa; C American Express; D Discover; E Diner's Club; F Other; 2 Personal checks accepted; 3 Lunch available; 4 Dinner available; 5 Open all year; 6 Pets welcome;

Sanibel's Song of the Sea

arrival, a heated gulfside pool and whirlpool, pristine white beach, library of books and videos, bicycles, daily newspapers, and Continental plus breakfasts alfresco, served on the terrace.

Host: Linda Logan
Rooms: 30 (PB) $160-350
Continental Breakfast
Credit Cards: A, B, C, D, E
Notes: 2, 5, 10, 11, 12, 14, 15

SAN MATEO

Ferncourt Bed and Breakfast

150 Central Avenue, P.O. Box 758, 32187
(904) 329-9755

This 1889 "painted lady" is known for her comfortable rooms and wonderful food. Voted to have the best breakfast by a leading bed and breakfast directory. Country Victorian atmosphere with real crowing roosters. The happy hens lay luscious eggs for guests' enjoyment. House specialities include rice pudding, and bourbon-sauced bread pudding. Short 25-minute drive to historic St. Augustine.

Hosts: Jack and Dee Morgan
Rooms: 6 (5 PB; 1 SB) $55-75
Full Breakfast
Credit Cards: A, B, C, D
Notes: 2, 5, 7, 9, 12, 14, 15

STEINHATCHEE

Steinhatchee Landing Resort

Highway 51 North, 32359
(800) 584-1709; e-mail: sli@dixie.4ez.com
www.steinhatcheelanding.com

A mystic setting surrounds the cottages as stately moss-laden oaks stand along meandering roadways. Nestled along the Steinhatchee River and tucked into Florida's Nature Coast, Steinhatchee Landing Resort offers guests an architectural delight punctuated with wildlife and luxury. Horseback riding, fishing, canoeing, cycling, tennis, basketball, shuffleboard, a children's playground, pool, and health club all on property (and most are free). Florida's capital, state parks, and national forests are within an easy drive. Week-long inclusive packages available.

Host: R. Dean Fowler
Rooms: 20 (PB) $120-280
Continental Breakfast
Credit Cards: A, B
Notes: 2, 4, 5, 6, 7, 8, 9, 10, 11, 14, 15

STUART

The Homeplace Bed and Breakfast

501 Akron Avenue, 34994
(561) 220-9148; FAX (561) 221-3265
e-mail: suzanne@homeplacebb.com
www.homeplacebb.com

The Homeplace, Stuart's premier bed and breakfast inn, was built in 1913 and lovingly restored in 1989. Totally dedicated to guests, it is best known for its romantic ambiance, quality, and unequaled graciousness. Four rooms with private baths, each distinctly

7 No smoking; 8 Children welcome; 9 Social drinking allowed; 10 Tennis nearby; 11 Swimming nearby; 12 Golf nearby; 13 Skiing nearby; 14 May be booked through a travel agent; 15 Handicapped accessible.

The Homeplace

different, are air conditioned and comfortably appointed with antiques. Also available is a garden suite. The wickered sun porch and turn-of-the-century parlor create a Victorian setting in which to recall pleasurable reminiscences of times gone by. The lush patio garden, pool, and heated spa beckon. Wine and cheese served at 5:30 P.M.

Hosts: Suzanne and Michael Pescitelli
Rooms: 4 (PB) $85-110
Suite: $160
Full Breakfast
Credit Cards: A, B
Notes: 2, 5, 7, 9, 10, 11, 12, 14

TALLAHASSEE

Calhoun Street Inn Bed and Breakfast

525 North Calhoun Street, 32301
(850) 425-5095; e-mail: gailrei@juno.com

Turn-of-the-century house less than a mile from the capitol, government offices, and Florida State University. Historic residential neighborhood with nearby parks for jogging and walking (inn's golden retriever available). From Tallahassee it's a short drive to gulf beaches and national forest recreation areas. Large, sunny, uncluttered rooms have good lights for reading. Breakfast served at small tables in the dining room or a Continental breakfast can be brought to guest room.

Host: Gail Reinertsen
Rooms: 5 (3 PB; 2 SB) $50-95
Full Breakfast
Credit Cards: A, B
Notes: 2, 7, 8, 9

Governors Inn

209 South Adams Street, 32301
(904) 681-6855

The Governors Inn combines original woodwork, exposed beams, and brilliant skylights to create a French country environment. The 41 guest rooms and suites are furnished with antique armoires and English pub tables. No two rooms are alike. Some have French four-poster beds and framed prints. Others have loft bedrooms and fireplaces, spiral staircases, and clerestory windows. The Spessard Holland Suite has a wet bar and vaulted ceilings. Conferences for up to 75 people can be arranged. One-half block from the state capitol.

Rooms: 40 (PB) $119-229
Continental Breakfast
Credit Cards: A, B, C, D, E
Notes: 5, 8, 14, 15

Governors Inn

TAMPA

Gram's Place Bed and Breakfast Guest House

3109 North Ola, 33603
(813) 221-0596; e-mail: GramsPl@aol.com
www.members.aol.com/GramsPL/index.html

Named in honor of legendary singer/songwriter Gram Parsons, Gram's Place is a

Gram's Place

relaxing, eclectic Key West-style bed and breakfast, reminiscent of the music of jazz, blues, folk, country, and rock and roll. Two cottage houses were built in 1945. Three rooms have shared bath (European style with sinks in rooms), and three rooms have private baths with canopied beds and hardwood floors. Each house has full kitchen and dining area. A working class neighborhood two miles northwest of downtown Tampa and historic Ybor City is well lighted on an off street for secure parking. Amenities include oversized Jacuzzi, waterfall, sun deck, courtyard with BYOB bar, outside shower/toilet facilities, cable TV, and HBO. In-room telephones. Personal secretary on telephone and a separate line for e-mail.

Host: Mark Holland
Rooms: 7 (4 PB; 3 SB) $45-85
Continental Breakfast
Credit Cards: A, B, C
Notes: 5, 8, 9, 14

TARPON SPRINGS

East Lake Bed and Breakfast

421 Old East Lake Road, 34689
(727) 937-5487
e-mail: littleflower@prodigy.com

Private home on two and one-half acres, on a quiet road along Lake Tarpon. Bedroom and adjoining private bath are at the front of the house, away from the family quarters. Twenty-four-hour access. Room has color TV and telephone. The hosts are retired business people who enjoy new friends and are well informed about the area. A full home-cooked breakfast is served. Limited smoking allowed.

Hosts: Marie and Dick Fiorito
Room: 1 (PB) $35-40
Full Breakfast
Credit Cards: None
Notes: 2, 5, 9, 10, 11, 12

Spring Bayou Inn Bed and Breakfast

32 West Tarpon Avenue, 34689
(813) 938-9333

A large, elegant home built in 1905 is in the center of the historical district. Enjoy the beautiful Spring Bayou, downtown antique shops, and area attractions of a small Greek village. Excellent restaurants are nearby, and guests have a short drive to the beach. Well-appointed rooms have antique furnishings and modern conveniences, and guests enjoy spacious wraparound front porch.

Host: Sharon Birk
Rooms: 5 (3 PB; 2 SB) $60-110

Spring Bayou

Full Breakfast
Credit Cards: None
Notes: 2, 5, 7, 9, 10, 11, 12

VERO BEACH

Redstone Manor Bed and Breakfast

806 43rd Avenue, 32960
(561) 562-8082

Enjoy this Florida ranch-style home on two and one-half acres with palm trees, swimming pool, and spa all surrounded on two sides by an orange grove. There are four beautifully decorated rooms with private baths and patios. A full breakfast and afternoon refreshments are served in gracious style. Large common areas to relax in. Minutes from beaches, shopping malls, restaurants, river, major league baseball spring training site, and minor class A team.

Hosts: Butch and Joyce Redstone
Rooms: 4 (PB) $80-110
Full Breakfast
Credit Cards: A, B, F
Notes: 2, 5, 7, 10, 11, 12, 13, 15

WELLBORN

1909 McLeran House

12408 County Road 137, 32094
(904) 963-4603

A beautifully restored two-story Victorian home on five landscaped acres features a lovely garden area with gazebo, garden swing, deck area, goldfish pond, and an abundance of trees and shrubs. Guests enjoy a large, comfortable room with mini-refrigerator and cable TV. The private bath downstairs features a claw-foot tub with shower. Enjoy the many antiques throughout the house, relax in the garden, stroll the grounds, or visit the "collectibles" shop in the old barn. Additional charge for extra people.

Hosts: Bob and Mary Ryals
Rooms: 2 (PB) $70-80
Full Breakfast
Credit Cards: None
Notes: 2, 5, 7, 9, 10, 11, 12

1909 McLeran House

WEST PALM BEACH

Southern Palm Ranch Bed and Breakfast

1120 Royal Palm Beach Boulevard #280, 33411
(561) 790-1413; FAX (561) 790-3035

Built in 1997. Five spacious guest rooms, with hardwood floors, all with private baths, on an estate nestled on 20 wooded acres. A beautiful pond which includes ducks, black swans, and Japanese koi invites guests to swim or stroll along the edge to the island and sit under the chee-kee hut to enjoy the tranquility. Magnificent exotic birds (endangered species breeding facility) and camels add to the ambiance of this tropical paradise. Guests are just minutes from the polo grounds, Coral Sky Amphitheater, Palm Beach nightlife, and the beaches.

Rooms: 5 (PB) $125
Continental Breakfast
Credit Cards: A, B, C, D
Notes: 2, 5, 7, 10, 11, 12, 15

Tropical Gardens Bed and Breakfast

419 Thirty-second Street, 33407-4809
(561) 848-4064; (800) 736-4064
FAX (561) 848-2422; e-mail: wpbbed@aol.com

A cozy Key West-style cottage built in the 1930s has all of today's conveniences: private baths, air conditioning, paddle fans, and cable TV. The hosts have retained the charm of Old Florida with white wicker furniture in a colorful Caribbean decor; sun by the lush tropical pool, ride complimentary bicycles, or just relax! In the Old Northwood Historic District, just one block from the waterway, and minutes to the tropical waters of the Atlantic or to Palm Beach. A Continental plus breakfast is served.

Hosts: Robert Rosario and Emil Scipioni
Room: 4 (PB) $55-125
Continental Breakfast
Credit Cards: A, B, C, D
Notes: 2, 5, 7, 9, 10, 11, 12, 14

Hiawassee
Eton
Dalton
Blue Ridge
Chickamauga
Helen
Clarksville
Dahlonega
Sautee
Gainesville
Commerce
Flowery Branch
Athens
Marietta
Chamblee
Stone Mountain
Oxford
Atlanta
Decatur
Madison
Thomson
Augusta
Palmetto
Eatonton
Greenville
Thomaston
Hamilton
Columbus
Hawkinsville
Americus
Savannah
Fitzgerald
Darien
St. Simons Island
St. Simons
Jekyll Island
Thomasville
St. Marys
59
75
19
441
85
27
20
129
1
301
185
16
341
82
84
95
319

Georgia

Georgia

1906 Pathway Inn

AMERICUS

1906 Pathway Inn Bed and Breakfast

501 South Lee Street, 31709
(912) 928-2078; (800) 889-1466

Parlors, porches, whirlpools, down comforters, fireplaces, friends, muffins, and more await guests at an English Colonial Revival inn. Stained glass, sumptuous candlelight breakfast. Near Civil War Andersonville and Plains, where President Carter teaches Sunday school. Thirty minutes west of I-75 and two hours south of Atlanta. Romantic getaway. "Pampering's our specialty." Pets welcome with prior approval.

Hosts: Sheila and David Judah
Rooms: 5 (PB) $77-137
Full Breakfast
Credit Cards: A, B, D
Notes: 2, 5, 8, 9, 10, 12, 14

ATHENS

The Nicholson House

6295 Jefferson Road, 30607
(706) 353-2200; FAX (706) 353-7799

The casual elegance of the Nicholson House makes this property unique. Built in 1820 on the Old Federal Road, this historic inn is set on six acres of rolling land, with streams and wooded areas surrounding. Three miles from downtown Athens, home of the University of Georgia, the Nicholson House offers nine spacious rooms, each with private bath, TV, and telephone. The warmth of antiques, jewel-tone walls, and a rocking-chair porch brings guests back in time. A full healthy breakfast is served.

Host: Stuart J. Kelley, proprietor
Rooms: 9 (PB) $75-85
Full Breakfast
Credit Cards: A, B, C, D, F
Notes: 5, 7, 9, 10, 12, 14

Nicholson House

NOTES: Credit cards accepted: A MasterCard; B Visa; C American Express; D Discover; E Diner's Club; F Other; 2 Personal checks accepted; 3 Lunch available; 4 Dinner available; 5 Open all year; 6 Pets welcome; 7 No smoking; 8 Children welcome; 9 Social drinking allowed; 10 Tennis nearby; 11 Swimming nearby; 12 Golf nearby; 13 Skiing nearby; 14 May be booked through a travel agent; 15 Handicapped accessible.

ATLANTA

Ansley Inn

253 Fifteenth Street NorthEast, 30309
(800) 446-5416; FAX (404) 892-2318
e-mail: ansleyinn@aol.com

A stay at Ansley Inn enables guests to experience Old World charm with all of the modern conveniences that guests expect. Every room is equipped with cable TV, direct dial telephone, in-room coffee maker, individual climate control, and private Jacuzzi bath. The full breakfast buffet is included in the room rate. Inquire about accommodations for pets.

Rooms: 22 (PB) $125-145
Full Breakfast
Credit Cards: A, B, C
Notes: 2, 5, 8, 9, 10, 12, 14

Ansley Inn

Bed & Breakfast Atlanta

1608 Briarcliff Road, Suite 5, 30306
(404) 875-0525; (800) 967-3224
FAX (404) 875-8198
e-mail: bnbinfo@mindspring.com
www.bedandbreakfastatlanta.com

A-1. This early 1900s neighborhood of winding streets and beautiful parks is on the historic register. Guest accommodation is a private cottage behind a Dutch Colonial home in the midtown/Ansley Park area. Bright, spacious unit has bedroom alcove, living/dining space with double sleeper-sofa and breakfast table, full bath, and minor kitchen. Provisions set in by host for a self-catered breakfast. Cable TV, desk, attractive private outdoor area, and off-street parking are among the amenities offered at this nonsmoking bed and breakfast. Good access to major transportation arteries and MARTA. $88-100.

A-2. Bed and breakfast is two to three miles to downtown and has excellent public transportation with many points of interest nearby. The private entry guest suite offers a bedroom with twin beds, adjacent sitting room with cable TV (an additional single bed as well), private shower only bath, and special amenities for minor cooking such as a small refrigerator, coffee maker, toaster, and a microwave. Breakfast provisions are stocked for self-catering. A second room with king-size bed, small refrigerator, coffee maker, and full bath is available upstairs; with Continental breakfast provided. Nonsmokers welcome. Resident cat and dog. $68-80.

A-13. Hardscrabble Cottage is a painted Craftsman-style brick bungalow built in the 1920s and is within walking distance to the Botanical Garden, High Museum, Woodruff Arts Center, and the Arts Center MARTA station. Guest accommodation is a private-entry suite with an antique extra-long spool bed, full bath, and a small sitting room with cable TV. Gracious Continental breakfast is served. Nonsmokers, please. $72-80.

A-16. This 1903 English Tudor mansion built by Atlanta department store magnate George Muse in the beautiful neighborhood of Ansley Park. Walk to Piedmont Park, High Museum, Arts Center Marta station, and midtown business district. Twenty-two rooms available. All rooms feature newly restored private baths with Jacuzzi tubs, cable TV, private line telephone, and indi-

NOTES: Credit cards accepted: A MasterCard; B Visa; C American Express; D Discover; E Diner's Club; F Other; 2 Personal checks accepted; 3 Lunch available; 4 Dinner available; 5 Open all year; 6 Pets welcome;

vidual climate control. Lounge in front of the huge original fireplace in the parlor, and enjoy a large Continental breakfast in the dining room under a beautiful arched ceiling. Evening iced tea and hors d'oeuvres served in the living room. Plenty of off-street parking. Rates from $125.

A-17. Walk to Georgia Tech, Piedmont Park, and midtown business district; easy walking distance to MARTA. Enjoy a great neighborhood ambiance while visiting this spectacular 1896 mansion. Relax in the large parlors under Palladiam windows and stained glass. Many original fixtures, beautiful tiled fireplaces. Two guest bedrooms are offered. Italian and French are spoken. One cat in residence. Nonsmokers only. $85-95.

B-2. Renovated two-story brick traditional home is minutes from Peachtree Road; close-in Buckhead location serves business or pleasure travelers well. Two guest rooms are offered, one with small refrigerator and small desk, and one with TV, radio, and built-in closet; they share one full bath on the second floor. Only one room is used unless party is traveling together; there is an additional full bath available for guest use downstairs. Continental breakfast is offered. One cat in residence. Nonsmokers only. $72-90.

B-10. Spacious Buckhead guest cottage with large fully furnished screened porch viewing rear wooded area is the setting for this wonderful bed and breakfast unit. Fortunate bed and breakfast guests will enjoy the expansive living room with luxurious leather sofa and chairs, TV, stereo with CD player, and fireplace; well-equipped kitchen with full-size refrigerator and oven. Guest bedroom is comfortable, with queen-size bed, inviting chair, and ample storage space, and an adjoining bath with large stall shower. Host stocks provisions for a self-catered breakfast. Personal security system, and washer/dryer are among the amenities in this guest cottage. $135-200.

B-15. Quiet condominium complex four miles from downtown, with MARTA nearby. Guest accommodation, on the main floor, has ample storage, remote control TV and VCR, and adjacent private bath. Guests enjoy a plentiful Continental breakfast. Amenities available to guests include beautiful patio and swimming pool. Nonsmokers. $68-80.

E-1. Charming traditional two-story house with spectacular swimming pool is on 10 beautifully wooded acres one mile from Emory University. Two guest rooms share one bath. Both rooms have traditional furniture, handmade quilts, and tastefully chosen family collectibles. Gracious Continental breakfast each morning. $68-76.

E-2. "The 1223 at Emory," an authentically restored Colonial Revival home built in 1925, within the Druid Hills national register historic district, offers exceptional comfort and hospitality. Walking distance of Emory University, Emory and Egelston Hospitals, the Carlos Museum, and CDC, four to five miles from downtown Atlanta, with good access to expressway system and MARTA. Four well-proportioned second-floor bedrooms with private baths are presided over by very genial and competent hosts. $80-100.

I-3. In Atlanta's only Victorian neighborhood, Inman Park, only two miles east of downtown. Excellent public transit. Upstairs, the Santa Fe Suite is a private living unit with huge bedroom, sitting room, kitchen and breakfast area, office, bath with shower stall and dressing room. Two first-floor guest rooms are also available. Both rooms share one bath. Host

Bed and Breakfast Atlanta (continued)

speaks French and German. Secured parking is available. Cat in residence. Nonsmokers, please. $68-100.

I-5. This 1892 Queen Anne Victorian in Atlanta's first planned suburb, two miles east of downtown, great for meetings downtown, easy access to MARTA and highway. Three guest accommodations are available in main house offering complete privacy—none of the rooms even has adjoining walls. Just behind the main house is a guest cottage with living room, fireplace, kitchen, loft bedroom, full bath with whirlpool tub, and brick patio. Continental breakfast served in the dining room. No smoking. $75-120.

I-8. This Victorian-style house built in 1904 is just minutes to downtown and MARTA rail. Many restaurants, theaters, art galleries, and coffee shops nearby. Accommodation is a private-entry apartment with bedroom, sitting room/library (with day bed), kitchen equipped with full refrigerator, stove, coffee maker, and dishwasher, and full bath. A gourmet Continental breakfast is served each morning from 7:00 to 9:00 A.M. Amenities at this nonsmoking bed and breakfast include spacious wicker-filled front porch and cable TV. $95.

K-1. Kosher bed and breakfast in northeast Atlanta, near Toco Hills-Emory area. Downtown convention center reached via public transportation or in 15 minutes by car. Recently renovated 1960s brick ranch-style home offers two sunny guest rooms, each with private bath. Free parking available at curbside or in driveway. Central air conditioning. Nutritious Continental or full breakfast. Nonsmokers, please. $68-88.

M-1. Brick Colonial, built in 1921, in Morningside, one of Atlanta's charming intown neighborhoods. Excellent public transportation, walk to shops, restaurants, and points of interest. Three bed and breakfast accommodations. One third-floor suite has private bath. One second-floor guest room has private bath, and a second guest room can be utilized as an additional room if the party is traveling together. Full breakfast served daily. Off-street parking. Dog in residence. Smoking permitted on outside screen porch only. $80-98.

M-2. Large private-entry apartment in a 1920s neighborhood with good access to major transportation arteries and public transportation. This immaculately kept second-floor guest suite offers a bedroom, spacious living/dining room, well-equipped kitchen, and private full bath. A second guest room with an antique sleigh bed is across the hall from the suite, used only for overflow guests in the apartment. This room shares the suite's bath and kitchen. Host sets in ample provisions for self-catered breakfast. Cable TV, separate heat and air conditioning, and private-line telephone. Nonsmokers, please. $68-100.

M-3. Walk to shops and restaurants in nearby Virginia-Highland, attend meetings with ease. Private guest cottage is an efficiency unit with double bed, kitchen equipped for minor cooking (microwave, full refrigerator, toaster oven, coffee maker, and dishwasher). Breakfast provisions are set in daily for self-catering. Amenities include washer and dryer, off-street parking, and TV with remote control. Nonsmokers, please. $80.

M-7. English country home built in the early '80s as charming as older Morningside neighbors. Walk to shops and restaurants in Virginia-Highland and attend meetings with ease using public transit.

Guest accommodation is an upstairs bedroom with full bath. Continental plus breakfast. Special amenity is a cable TV and VCR with an extensive tape library. Dog and cat in residence. Nonsmokers. $72.

M-11. This 1917 Tudor home is within walking distance to midtown business district, Piedmont Park, Civic Center, and Margaret Mitchell's beloved "the Dump," birthplace of *Gone With the Wind*. Easy access to MARTA and major transportation arteries. Three guest rooms are available, each with a private bath. Continental breakfast is served daily. Guests are invited to enjoy County Waterford, one of the common areas, a lovely sitting room with an outdoor deck. Two dogs in residence. Nonsmokers only. $72-98.

O-1. Enjoy small-town charm of Conyers with easy access to Atlanta, the Conyers Monastery, Stone Mountain, and other communities outside the eastern I-285 perimeter. Fernewood is a large traditional two-story Colonial home, custom built for its current owners. Two second-floor bedrooms are offered, each with a private bath. Guests are welcome to enjoy the downstairs living areas as well as the lovely outdoor garden. Southern hospitality and a Continental or full breakfast are offered. This bed and breakfast is pet free. Smoking is permitted only on the lovely outdoor grounds. $52-60.

O-12. Quiet, residential neighborhood in southwest Atlanta, convenient to downtown, airport, and MARTA. Guest accommodations include three guest rooms, each with a distinct international motif. One room has a private bath and the other two share a bath. Guests' favorite breakfast will be prepared (with adequate notice to host) daily. All guests are invited to enjoy use of the sunroom, recreation room (with cable TV and stereo), exercise room (with exercise bike, treadmill, weights), and outdoor basketball half-court. No smoking. $72-88.

V-1. Modest garden cottage behind a large home in Virginia-Highland, a neighborhood with unique shops, diverse entertainment, and wonderful restaurants. Bed and breakfast offers a living room, TV, bedroom with double bed, bath, and well-equipped kitchen. Provisions are set in for a self-served Continental breakfast. Guests also enjoy a rear patio and private-line telephone. Nonsmokers. $68-80.

V-2. Atkins Park, a small neighborhood listed in the National Register of Historic Places, is part of Virginia-Highland. MARTA bus is available and expressways are easily accessible. The private cottage has a bedroom, adjoining bath with shower, full kitchen, and color TV. Breakfast provisions are stocked for self-catering. $64-72.

V-3. Built in 1913 and completely renovated in 1990, this Craftsman-style home is in close proximity to some of the city's most popular restaurants. Good access to expressways and public transportation. Inn offers six guest rooms with private baths. Some with whirlpool tubs, fireplaces, or laundry facilities. Continental breakfast served in the dining room. $95-195.

V-4. Caruso Manor is a Georgian-style brick home built in 1910 in the popular intown Virginia-Highland neighborhood. Easy access to MARTA bus. Two large guest rooms share a bath with shower. Each room has cable TV, clock, and radio. Continental breakfast is served. Please, no smoking. $60-80.

V-5. Virginia-Highland private-entry room with kitchen privileges only three to five miles from Emory/Egleston Complex. Blue dormer bedroom with a full bath across the hall. Parquet hardwood floors, good light, ceiling fans, separate upstairs heating and air-conditioning unit, and a well-equipped kitchen make this an exceptional accommodation for short and long-term stays. Weekly and monthly discount rates available upon request. $120.

Beverly Hills Inn

Beverly Hills Inn

65 Sheridan Drive, 30305
(404) 233-8520; www.beverlyhillsinn.com

A charming city retreat one-half block from public transportation, one and one-half miles from Lenox Square, and five minutes from the Atlanta Historical Society. Full kitchens, library, free parking, color TV, and Continental breakfast.

Host: Mit Amin
Rooms: 18 (PB) $90-160
Continental Breakfast
Credit Cards: A, B, C, E, F
Notes: 2, 5, 6, 8, 14

Buckhead Bed and Breakfast Inn

70 Lenox Pointe, Northeast, 30324
(404) 261-8284; (888) 224-8797
e-mail: bandb@mindspring.com
www.mindspring.com/~bandb

Enjoy the cascading waterfall at the Buckhead Bed and Breakfast Inn where guests will find 18 rooms, each unique in design and decor. The rooms are appointed with four-poster beds, rake beds, or wrought iron beds, formal writing desks, private baths, cable TV, and modem telephone lines. Built in 1995 as an engaging alternative to corporate hotels, it is nestled among Atlanta's affluent restaurants and shopping districts with immediate access to downtown.

Host: Mr. Jerry H. Cates
Rooms: 18 (PB) $85-105
Continental Breakfast
Credit Cards: A, B, C
Notes: 2, 7, 9, 10, 11, 12, 14, 15

Gaslight Inn Bed and Breakfast

1001 St. Charles Avenue, 30306
(404) 875-1001; FAX (404) 876-1001
www.gaslightinn.com

Urbane sophistication in one of Atlanta's most popular and historic in-town neighborhoods. Historic inn featured in national and local publications and on international travel TV. Fireplaces, whirlpools, steam showers, multiple verandas, courtyard gardens. Within walking distance are antique shops, galleries, restaurants, museums, theaters. Five minutes to downtown Atlanta. A-rated and triple crowns by ABBA.

Host: Jim Moss
Rooms: 6 (PB) $95-195
Continental Breakfast
Credit Cards: A, B, C, D
Notes: 2, 5, 7, 8, 9, 10, 11, 12, 14, 15

Gaslight Inn

NOTES: Credit cards accepted: A MasterCard; B Visa; C American Express; D Discover; E Diner's Club; F Other; 2 Personal checks accepted; 3 Lunch available; 4 Dinner available; 5 Open all year; 6 Pets welcome;

Inman Park Bed and Breakfast

100 Waverly Way Northeast, 30307
(404) 688-9498; FAX (404) 524-9939

The honeymoon cottage of Robert Woodruff, Atlanta's famous soft-drink magnate, is a totally restored Victorian in historic Inman Park. One block from the subway station, close to dining. Its 12-foot ceilings, heart-pine woodwork, fireplaces, antiques, screened porch, and private garden are to enjoy. Secured parking available on-site. Personal checks accepted for deposit only.

Host: Eleanor Matthews
Rooms: 3 (PB) $85-95
Continental Breakfast
Credit Cards: A, B, C
Notes: 5, 7, 9, 10, 12, 14

King-Keith House

889 Edgewood Avenue Northeast, 30307
(404) 688-7330; (800) 728-3879
www. travelbase.com/destinations/atlanta/king-keith/

One of Atlanta's most photographed houses. The 1890 Victorian "painted lady" close to Atlanta's most popular in-town shopping, restaurant, and theater districts. Two miles to downtown Atlanta. Two and a half blocks to MARTA (subway) with direct connections to the airport. Unusually spacious guest rooms, filled with antiques and collectibles. This bed and breakfast has all the bells and whistles one is looking for.

Hosts: Jan and Windell Keith
Rooms: 4 (PB) $75-115
Full Breakfast
Credit Cards: A, B, C
Notes: 2, 5, 7, 8, 9, 12, 14

The Woodruff Bed and Breakfast

223 Ponce de Leon Avenue, 30308
(404) 875-9449; (800) 473-9449 (reservations only)
FAX (404) 875-2882
e-mail: RSVP@mindspring.com

Southern hospitality and charm await guests at this historic, beautifully restored bed and breakfast inn. In midtown Atlanta and convenient to everything. Filled with antiques, oriental rugs, stained glass, and hardwood floors. A full southern breakfast cooked by the on-site owners is a real treat.

Hosts: Douglas and Joan Jones
Rooms: 12 (10 PB; 4 SB) $89-149
Full Breakfast
Credit Cards: A, B, C, D
Notes: 5, 7, 8, 9, 11, 14

ATLANTA (SENOIA)

The Veranda

252 Seavy Street, P.O. Box 177,
Senoia, 30276-0177
(770) 599-3905; FAX (770) 599-0806

Guests stay in beautifully restored spacious Victorian rooms in a 1907 hotel on the National Register of Historic Places. Just 30 miles south of Atlanta airport. Freshly prepared southern gourmet meals by reservation. Unusual gift shop featuring kaleidoscopes. Memorabilia and 1930 Wurlitzer player piano pipe organ. One room has a whirlpool bath; all have private baths and air conditioning.

Hosts: Jan and Bobby Boal
Rooms: 9 (PB) $99-150
Full Breakfast
Credit Cards: A, B, C, D
Notes: 2, 4, 5, 7, 8, 10, 12, 14, 15

AUGUSTA

The Perrin Guest House Inn

208 LaFayette Drive, 30909
(706) 731-0920; (800) 668-8930
FAX (706) 731-9009

The Perrin Place is an old cotton plantation established in 1863. The plantation has long since become the site for the Augusta National, home of the Masters, while the three acres of the homeplace remain a little spot of magnolia heaven surrounded by shopping, golfing, and fine dining. The guest house has bedrooms that feature

7 No smoking; 8 Children welcome; 9 Social drinking allowed; 10 Tennis nearby; 11 Swimming nearby; 12 Golf nearby; 13 Skiing nearby; 14 May be booked through a travel agent; 15 Handicapped accessible.

fireplaces and Jacuzzis. Share the pleasure of a front porch rocker, the comfort of a cozy parlor, or the cool of a scuppernong arbor with other guests. Weddings, receptions, and other social functions, treasured events when held at the Perrin Inn. Available by reservation only.

Hosts: Ed and Audrey Peel
Rooms: 10 (PB) $75-125
Continental Breakfast
Credit Cards: A, B, C
Notes: 2, 5, 7, 8, 9, 10, 11, 12, 13, 14

BLUE RIDGE

Appalachian Trails End

11375 Doublehead Gap Road, 30513
(706) 838-2000

Appalachian Trails End Lodge, a new bed and breakfast, is in the scenic north Georgia mountains a few miles from the terminus of the Appalachian Trail. Surrounded by national forests and wilderness areas, this bed and breakfast is the ideal starting place for trout fishing, white-water sports, hiking, and antiquing. Relax in the lodge room by the fireplace, enjoy refreshments on the spacious front porch overlooking splendid mountain scenery, and indulge in private hot tub.

Hosts: Jerry and Susan Frith
Suites: 2 (PB) $100-140
Full Breakfast
Credit Cards: None
Notes: 2, 3, 4, 5, 6, 7, 8, 9, 10, 11, 12

CHAMBLEE

Bed & Breakfast Atlanta

1608 Briarcliff Road, Suite 5, Atlanta, 30306
(404) 875-0525; (800) 967-3224
FAX (404) 875-8198
e-mail: bnbinfo@mindspring.com
www.bedandbreakfastatlanta.com

C-1. Ideal apartment for relocating business persons. Contemporary multilevel home. Good expressway access, just outside of the perimeter, is the location of this private-entry bed and breakfast unit. The apartment has full kitchen, dining area, living room with sleeper-sofa, private-line telephone, TV, VCR, stereo, full bath, work space with desk, and washer and dryer. Provisions for a self-catered breakfast are set in by the hostess. A large patio with porch swing and chairs overlooking a deep wooded lot and creek is bound to be a favorite spot for guests. Smoking acceptable. Discounted monthly. $88.

CLARKESVILLE

Glen-Ella Springs Inn

1789 Bear Gap Road, 30523
(706) 754-7295; FAX (706) 754-1560
www.glenella.com

Deep in the woods in a peaceful valley lies an inn in the National Register of Historic Places. Relax in heart-pine rooms furnished in antiques and folk art, some with fireplaces. Share gardens and meadows with deer, butterflies, and hummingbirds. Enjoy fine dining and swim in the pool. Find serenity and exceptional service for personal or executive retreats on the edge of the Blue Ridge Mountains. Waterfalls, trails, antiques, folk art, and charming villages nearby.

Hosts: Barrie and Bobby Aycock
Rooms: 16 (PB) $100-180
Full Breakfast
Credit Cards: A, B, C
Notes: 2, 4, 5, 7, 9, 11, 12, 14, 15

Glen-Ella Springs Inn

NOTES: Credit cards accepted: A MasterCard; B Visa; C American Express; D Discover; E Diner's Club; F Other; 2 Personal checks accepted; 3 Lunch available; 4 Dinner available; 5 Open all year; 6 Pets welcome;

CHICKAMAUGA

Gordon-Lee Mansion Bed and Breakfast Inn

217 Cove Road, 30707
(706) 375-4728; (800) 487-4728

Circa 1847. Step back in time and enjoy this beautifully restored antebellum plantation house, set on seven acres with formal gardens and furnished with museum-quality period antiques in the atmosphere of early southern aristocracy. Used as a Union headquarters and hospital. Near the Chickamauga Battlefield and 15 miles from Chattanooga, Tennessee. Breakfast served in the elegant dining room. Civil War artifacts museum. Private baths. Cable TV. National Register of Historic Places. Civil War Trust Discovery Trail.

Host: Richard Barclift
Rooms: 5 (PB) $70-125
Full Breakfast
Credit Cards: A, B
Notes: 2, 5, 7, 9, 10, 12, 14

COLUMBUS

The Woodruff House and the Mansion

1414 Second Avenue, 31901
(888) 320-9309; FAX (706) 320-9304
e-mail: lbussey@mindspring.com

In the high uptown historic district, the Woodruff House is the birthplace of Robert W. Woodruff. Through his vision and leadership, Coca-Cola became the world's refreshment. Built in 1885, the Woodruff House remains a picture of charm and beauty. With nearby corporate offices, dining establishments, and entertainment, guests' convenience is assured. The Woodruff House is guests' home away from home offering 12 luxury guest suites, each with private bath, fireplace, cable TV, and telephone. A Continental plus breakfast is included.

The Woodruff House

Host: Larry W. Bussey
Rooms: 13 (PB) $95-160
Continental Breakfast
Credit Cards: A, B, C, D
Notes: 5, 7, 8, 9, 10, 12, 14, 15

COMMERCE

The Pittman House

81 Homer Road, 30529
(706) 335-3823

This house is a grand 1890 Colonial completely furnished with period antiques. Wraparound porch just waiting to be rocked on. In the northeastern Georgia foothills near many interesting places. One hour northeast

The Pittman House

7 No smoking; 8 Children welcome; 9 Social drinking allowed; 10 Tennis nearby; 11 Swimming nearby; 12 Golf nearby; 13 Skiing nearby; 14 May be booked through a travel agent; 15 Handicapped accessible.

of Atlanta just off I-85. Tennis, golf, discount shopping mall, fishing, antiquing, and water sports all nearby. Seventy-two-hour cancellation notice required.

Hosts: Tom and Dot Tomberlin
Rooms: 4 (2 PB; 2 SB) $55-75
Full Breakfast
Credit Cards: A, B
Notes: 2, 5, 7, 10, 11, 12, 13, 14

DAHLONEGA

Mountain Top Lodge at Dahlonega

447 Mountain Top Lodge Road, 30533
(706) 864-5257

Share the magic of a secluded bed and breakfast inn surrounded by towering trees and spectacular views. Enjoy antique-filled rooms, cathedral ceiling, great room, spacious decks, and heated outdoor spa; some rooms have fireplaces, whirlpool tubs, and porches. Deluxe room accommodations also available. Generous country breakfast with homemade biscuits. Two-night minimum stay required for holidays and weekends during the fall season. Children over 12 are welcome.

Host: Karen Lewan
Rooms: 13 (PB) $67.20-140
Full Breakfast
Credit Cards: A, B, C, F
Notes: 2, 5, 7, 9, 12

The Smith House

84 South Chestatee Street, 30533
(706) 867-7000; (800) 852-9577
FAX (706) 864-7564
e-mail: info@smithhouse.com
www.smithhouse.com

Just one block from Dahlonega's historic town square is one of Georgia's most famous inns. The Smith House has been serving its famous family-style menu for over 50 years. After enjoying a home-cooked feast, retreat to one of the 16 guest rooms offered for overnight visitors to Dahlonega. Each room offers private bath, cable TV, coffee maker, and Continental breakfast in the morning.

Hosts: The Welch Family
Rooms: 16 (PB) $55-145
Continental Breakfast
Credit Cards: A, B, C, D
Notes: 3, 4, 5, 7, 8, 11, 15

Worley Homestead Inn

168 Main Street West, 30533
(706) 864-7002
www.bbonline.com/ga/worley

Step back into the past when staying at this restored 1845 ancestral home. Only two blocks from Dahlonega's famous courthouse square, the inn is across from the gold-topped steeple of North Georgia College, site of the U.S. Mint when Dahlonega was the gold center of the United States. Member of the National Trust for Historic Preservation. Please note that rates are subject to change during holidays and special events.

Hosts: Bill and Frances
Rooms: 8 (PB) $85-95
Full Breakfast
Credit Cards: A, B
Notes: 2, 5, 7, 9, 12

DALTON

The Holly Tree House

217 West Cuyler Street, 30720
(706) 278-6620; FAX (706) 278-1851

Lovely restored home, circa 1924, in historical district of noteworthy Civil War and Cherokee Indian area. Convenient to many points of interest, the home is furnished in antiques and collectibles from around the world. Each spacious room has a private bath, TV, and VCR. A video library is available for guests' use. A three-course breakfast is served of carefully prepared specialities. Before retiring, cordials are available. The home is 100 miles north of Atlanta and 30 miles south of Chattanooga.

Host: Doris FioRito
Rooms: 4 (PB) $75-85
Full Breakfast
Credit Cards: A, B, C, D
Notes: 2, 5, 7, 12

DARIEN

Open Gates Bed and Breakfast

Vernon Square National Historic District, 31305
(912) 437-6985

Explore untrammeled barrier islands and the Altamaha River delta via a scenic byway one and one-half miles east of I-95. This 1876 timber baron's home has been featured on the cover of *Southern Homes*, in *Georgia Off the Beaten Path*, *Fodor's: Bed and Breakfasts*, and *Country Inns*. Locally harvested seafood and caviar and a hostess knowledgeable about Georgia's second oldest town enhance guests' stay. Ecological and historical tours by boat to barrier islands and the Altamaha River delta. Bicycling, canoeing, bird watching groups advised on routes to interest spots. Fishing nearby.

Host: Carolyn Hodges
Rooms: 4 (2 PB; 2 SB) $63.80-69.30
Full Breakfast
Credit Cards: None
Notes: 2, 5, 7, 9

Open Gates

DECATUR

Bed & Breakfast Atlanta

1608 Briarcliff Road, Suite 5, Atlanta, 30306
(404) 875-0525; (800) 967-3224
FAX (404) 875-8198
e-mail: bnbinfo@mindspring.com
www.bedandbreakfastatlanta.com

D-2. This 1924 Tudor-style home retains many of its original features. Two guest rooms are offered, each with private bath and cable TV. The queen room has a working fireplace, bath with shower only. Twin room has a private entry, bath with tub only and hand-held shower. Bountiful, Continental breakfast, afternoon tea if desired, and comfortable inviting common rooms add to guest comfort. Walk to the square in Decatur for restaurants, shops, and entertainment. Delightful Irish wolfhound shares this home with host and her two small sons. Nonsmokers, please. $52-80.

D-3. This cream-colored Victorian brick house is in an ideal residential setting for downtown meetings (three blocks to MARTA rail), walking to the square in Decatur, and Agnes Scott College. Private-entry suite has large front porch with rocking chairs, library/sitting room with wood burning fireplace, bedroom with antique bed, and adjoining shower-stall bath. Another guest room with private bath is offered upstairs. Full or Continental breakfast served. Resident dogs and cats. Smoking outdoors only, please. $80-120.

EATONTON

The Crockett House

671 Madison Road, 31024
(706) 485-2248
www.bbonline.com/ga/crocketthouse/

The Crockett House, circa 1895, is nestled amongst 100-year-old red pecan, oak, pine,

The Crockett House

and magnolia trees, and is gracefully adorned by its beautiful weeping willows. Experience a new adventure as one steps back in time to luxurious accommodations, fine dining, and a slower pace at this historic Victorian home. "The Crockett House is the perfect place for a romantic rendezvous"—*Atlanta Journal*. Features include: 11 fireplaces, large wraparound porch, antique-filled guest rooms, claw-foot tubs beside working fireplaces, refreshments upon arrival, and Christa's memorable gourmet breakfast served in elegant style. The Crockett House is on Georgia's historic antebellum trail.

Hosts: Christa and Peter Crockett
Rooms: 6 (PB) $85-95
Full Breakfast
Credit Cards: A, B
Notes: 2, 4, 5, 9, 10, 11, 12, 14, 15

ETON

Ivy Inn

245 Fifth Avenue, E., P.O. Box 406, 30742
(706) 517-0526
www.bbonline.com/ga/ivyinn/

This inn reminds its guests of those restful, secure nights at Grandmother's or a favorite aunt's country home. Rooms are furnished in pieces from the '30s and '40s. A casual air with rocking chair porches is waiting for weary travelers. The Ivy Inn has bicycles for guests' use. Horseback riding and stables are next door; white-water rafting is only 25 minutes away. Smoking is limited to front porch and grounds. Twelve miles from carpet capital of the world; three miles from crafts and antique shops.

Hosts: Gene and Juanita Twiggs
Rooms: 3 (PB) $87
Full Breakfast
Credit Cards: A, B, C
Notes: 2, 5, 8, 10, 11, 12, 13

Ivy Inn

FITZGERALD

Dorminy-Massee House

516 West Central Avenue, 31750
(912) 423-3123

Just 20 miles east of I-75, this beautiful family-owned 1915 Colonial home, designed by architect T. F. Lockwood, contains eight charmingly furnished, air-conditioned bedrooms, with TV, telephone, computer modem, and private bath. Guests enjoy the dining, living, and parlor areas. Spacious, beautifully landscaped grounds include fish pool, gazebo, smokehouse, carriage house, and private parking. Walk three blocks to the Blue-Gray museum and learn Fitzgerald's history—the only town colonized by Union and Confederate veterans.

Hosts: Mark and Sherry Massee;
Marion and Joyce Massee
Rooms: 8 (PB) $75-85
Continental Breakfast

Dorminy-Massee House

Credit Cards: A, B, C
Notes: 5, 7, 8, 10, 12, 15

FLOWERY BRANCH

Whitworth Inn

6593 McEver Road, 30542
(770) 967-2386; FAX (770) 967-2649
e-mail: visit@whitworthinn.com
www.whitworthinn.com

Contemporary country inn on five wooded acres offers relaxing atmosphere, 11 uniquely decorated guest rooms, and two guest living rooms. Full country breakfast served in large sunlit dining room. Meeting and party space available. Thirty minutes northeast of Atlanta at Lake Lanier. Nearby attractions and activities include boating, golf, beaches, and water parks. Close to Road Atlanta and Chateau Elan Winery and Golf Course. Easily accessible from major interstates. Three-diamond AAA rating.

Hosts: Ken and Chris Jonick
Rooms: 10 (PB) $59-89
Full Breakfast
Credit Cards: A, B, C
Notes: 2, 5, 7, 8, 10, 11, 12, 14, 15

Whitworth Inn

GAINESVILLE

Bed & Breakfast Atlanta

1608 Briarcliff Road, Suite 5, Atlanta, 30306
(404) 875-0525; (800) 967-3224
FAX (404) 875-8198
e-mail: bnbinfo@mindspring.com
www.bedandbreakfastatlanta.com

G-1. Heron Cove guest house 60 miles northeast of downtown Atlanta on Lake Lanier. Wonderful suite in a semirural neighborhood sits on a nearly three-acre National Wildlife Federation-certified Backyard Wildlife Habitat. This lake-level, private-entry suite offers a den with color TV, bedroom, and a full bath with shower/sauna. A full or Continental breakfast served daily. Amenities include fireplace in the living room, baby grand piano in the library, and spotting scope and binoculars available for viewing wildlife through the full-length atrium windows. $88-110.

The Dunlap House

635 Green Street, 30501
(770) 536-0200; (800) 276-2935
FAX (770) 503-7857
e-mail: dunlaphouse@applied.net

Built in 1910, this 10-room bed and breakfast inn is on Gainesville's historic Green Street, a convenient location for the business or leisure traveler. Period furnishings decorate each room. Private baths, TV, telephone. Enjoy morning breakfast in guests' room, common area, or on the wicker-furnished veranda. Fax and computer services are available. Be surrounded with the ambiance of the Old South in a modern setting. Experience the difference at the Dunlap House.

Hosts: Dave and Karen Peters
Rooms: 10 (PB) $105-155
Full Breakfast
Credit Cards: A, B, C
Notes: 5, 7, 10, 11, 12, 14

GREENVILLE

Georgian Inn

566 South Talbotton Street, Hwy. 18 & 27 A, P.O. Box 1000, 30222
(706) 672-1600; FAX (706) 672-1666
e-mail: georgianinn@hotmail.com
www.bbonline.com/ga/georgian/

Enjoy true southern elegance and hospitality in this historic home. Refreshments and delicious breakfast served. Great getaway conveniently off I-85, just 45 minutes south of Atlanta's Hartsfield airport, minutes from Warm Springs, Roosevelt's beloved Little White House, and beautiful Callaway Gardens. Imagine refreshing the spirit, awakening the senses, and soothing the soul. A stay at Georgian Inn is a worthy memory for anyone who savors life in the South and wishes to indulge in memories of bygone days.

Host: Angela Hand
Rooms: 5 (3 PB; 2 SB) $95-125
Full Breakfast
Credit Cards: A, B, C
Notes: 2, 3, 4, 5, 7, 8, 9, 10, 11, 12, 13, 14

Samples Plantation Inn 1832

15380 Roosevelt Highway 27 South, P.O. Box 649, 30222
(706) 672-4765

Circa 1832 and historically registered. Catering to romance. Great getaway. Authentic plantation breakfast; 50 miles to Atlanta airport; near FDR's Little White House, Callaway Gardens, Warm Springs, shopping, and Pine Mountain. Come taste the South.

Hosts: Carl and Marjorie Samples
Rooms: 7 (PB) $149-289
Full Breakfast
Credit Cards: A, B, C, D, E
Notes: 2, 5, 7, 10, 11, 12, 13

HAMILTON

Magnolia Hall Bed and Breakfast

127 Barnes Mill Road, P.O. Box 326, 31811
(706) 628-4566

Magnolia Hall is a beautifully restored 1890 Victorian home furnished with antiques. All five guest quarters have queen-size beds and private baths. Lovely Callaway Gardens is five miles away, and FDR's Little White House at historic Warm Springs is only a short drive.

Hosts: Dale and Kendrick Smith
Rooms: 5 (PB) $90-105
Full Breakfast
Credit Cards: None
Notes: 2, 5, 7, 9, 10, 11, 12, 14, 15

Magnolia Hall

HAWKINSVILLE

New Hope Guest House Ministry

115 Thunder Road, 31036
(912) 987-8096

Come treat oneself to a relaxing stay at this renovated country guest house. New Hope Guest House is in the middle of Georgia just 10 minutes from I-75 and the National Fairgrounds. This home is a labor of love specially designed for people with disabili-

NOTES: Credit cards accepted: A MasterCard; B Visa; C American Express; D Discover; E Diner's Club; F Other; 2 Personal checks accepted; 3 Lunch available; 4 Dinner available; 5 Open all year; 6 Pets welcome;

ties. Amenities include a full kitchen, living area, two bedrooms beautifully decorated with magnolias and ivy, and a large bathroom featuring a whirlpool tub and a wheelchair-accessible shower. Rate is a suggested donation.

Hosts: Samuel and Christine Vines
Rooms: 2 (1 PB) $40
Continental Breakfast
Credit Cards: None
Notes: 2, 5, 6, 7, 8, 11, 12, 15

HELEN

Chattahoochee Ridge Lodge and Cottages

P.O. Box 175, 30545
(706) 878-3144; (800) 476-8331
e-mail: rooms@stc.net

Perched on a wooded ridge a mile from Alpine Helen, each new unit has cable TV, air conditioning, refrigerator, coffee maker, free telephone, and large Jacuzzi. Some have a full kitchen, extra bedroom, and fireplace. There is also a gas grill on the back deck. Hosts are "earth friendly" with double insulation and back-up solar heating. Everything guests need is furnished and on the premises, including hosts who can fill guests in on attractions. Cottages in the woods are also available; please inquire.

Hosts: Bob and Mary Swift
Rooms: 5 (PB) $45-80
Credit Cards: A, B, C, D
Notes: 2, 5, 8, 9, 10, 11, 12

Dutch Cottage Bed and Breakfast

P.O. Box 757, 30545
(706) 878-3135

Come, relax by a waterfall or on the porch at this bed and breakfast in the mountains of northeast Georgia on an old gold mining site. Spacious rooms include cable TV and VCR. Shopping in Alpine Helen, fishing, or tubing down the Chattahoochee River, all within walking distance. Other local attractions include mountain biking, hiking, waterfalls, and Unicoi Lake. At the day's end relax in the hot tub or quietly rock in the hammock among the trees.

Rooms: 4 (PB) $55-95
Full Breakfast
Credit Cards: A, B
Notes: 2, 5, 7, 9, 11, 12

HIAWASSEE

Henson Cove Place Bed and Breakfast

3840 Car Miles Road, 30546
(706) 896-6195; (800) 714-5542
FAX (706) 896-5252
www.yhc.edu/users/nle

Henson Cove Place Bed and Breakfast prides itself on putting guests at ease and helping them feel at home. The furniture, quilts, and memorabilia are from the hosts' families. Guests are encouraged to enjoy the large library, watch TV in the sitting room, or relax on the porch and unwind. Breakfast features the hosts' homemade breads baked in a 1929 Tappan gas range. A three-bedroom, one and one-half bath separate cabin in the wood is also available. No smoking inside.

Hosts: Bill and Nancy Leffingwell
Rooms: 2 (PB) $70
Full Breakfast
Credit Cards: A, B
Notes: 2, 5, 7, 9, 10, 11, 12, 13

MADISON

The Brady Inn

250 North Second Street, 30650
(706) 342-4400

Two Victorian cottages linked together by an extended porch filled with rockers welcome guests to this bed and breakfast. All rooms have private baths, heart-pine floors, and antiques. Come enjoy southern hospitality and see "the town Sherman refused to burn."

Hosts: C. G. and L. J. Rasch
Rooms: 7 (PB) $55-75
Full Breakfast
Credit Cards: A, B, C, D, F
Notes: 2, 3, 4, 5, 8, 9, 10, 11, 12

MARIETTA

Sixty Polk Street, A Bed and Breakfast

60 Polk Street, 30064
(770) 419-1688; (800) 845-7266
e-mail: jmertes@aol.com

Fully restored to its original glory, this French Regency Victorian home built in 1872 features four warm and inviting bedrooms. Delight in the exquisite period antiques as one peruses the library, relax in the parlor, or savor afternoon sweets in the dining room. Wake up to early coffee, then a sumptuous southern breakfast before walking to the many antique shops, restaurants, museums, or theater on the Marietta Square.

Hosts: Joe and Glenda Mertes
Rooms: 4 (PB) $95-175
Full Breakfast
Credit Cards: A, B, C
Notes: 2, 5, 7, 10, 12, 14

Sixty Polk Street

The Whitlock Inn

57 Whitlock Avenue, 30064
(770) 428-1495; FAX (770) 919-9620
www.mindspring.com/~whitlock inn/

Grand southern mansion in national historic district with other outstanding Victorian homes. Beautifully furnished, cozy and elegant. Rocking-chair porches beckon guests to "sit a spell." One block to town square, wonderful restaurants, antique shops, carriage rides, live concerts in the summertime. The Whitlock Inn is like living in great-grandmother's day. Hop on the freeway to Atlanta—20 miles and a century away. Best to stay Sunday through Thursday as the inn is the area's most popular place for weekend weddings and receptions. Children over 12 are welcome.

Host: Alexis Edwards
Rooms: 5 (PB) $100-125
Continental Breakfast
Credit Cards: A, B, C, D
Notes: 2, 5, 7, 10, 11, 12, 14

OXFORD

Hopkins House Bed and Breakfast

1111 Wesley Street, 30054
(770) 784-1010; FAX (770) 784-0706
www.bbonline.com/ga/hopkins/

This 1847 Greek Revival cottage only 35 miles east of Atlanta in Oxford's historic district. Decorated in comfortable blend of antique and contemporary furniture. Each guest room features handmade quilt, queen-size bed, private telephone, and cable TV. Relax in a rocker on the spacious screen porch or enjoy the pool. Complimentary refreshments. Bottomless cookie jar featuring the best chocolate chip cookies in Georgia. Continental breakfast served weekdays; full breakfast served Saturday and Sunday.

Hosts: Nancy and Ralph Brian
Rooms: 5 (PB) $85-100
Full and Continental Breakfast
Credit Cards: A, B, C, D
Notes: 2, 5, 7, 8, 9, 12, 14, 15

NOTES: Credit cards accepted: A MasterCard; B Visa; C American Express; D Discover; E Diner's Club; F Other; 2 Personal checks accepted; 3 Lunch available; 4 Dinner available; 5 Open all year; 6 Pets welcome;

PALMETTO

Serenbe

10950 Hutcheson Ferry Road, 30268
(770) 463-2610; FAX (770) 463-4472
e-mail: serenbe.com

A turn-of-the-century farm in the rolling hills 32 miles southwest of Atlanta. Rooms are furnished with antiques accented with traditional, modern, and folk art. Flower and vegetable gardens, a large pool and hot tub, three streams, two waterfalls, a well-stocked lake with canoes, many trails, and over 100 farm animals are some of the attractions to explore. Afternoon tea, evening sweets, and a full country breakfast included. See web site for pictures.

Hosts: Marie and Steve Nygren
Rooms: 7 (PB) $95-150
Full Breakfast
Credit Cards: None
Notes: 2, 5, 7, 8, 9, 11, 12, 14

ST. MARYS

Spencer House Inn Bed and Breakfast

200 Osborne Street, 31558
(912) 882-1872; FAX (912) 882-9427
www.spencerhouseinn.com

Built in 1872, this charming three-story home with elevator is furnished with fine antiques, beautiful reproductions, selected fabrics, and comfortable furnishings. Original moldings, high ceilings, and heart-pine floors add warmth and beauty to the sunny, many-windowed inn. The village of St. Marys is nestled in the southeast corner of Georgia's historic colonial coast. Local attractions include Cumberland Island National Seashore and ferry, Kings Bay Naval Submarine Base, and Okefenokee National Wildlife Refuge. Ferry and restaurants within walking distance.

Spencer House Inn

Hosts: Mary and Mike Neff
Rooms: 14 (PB) $65-95
Suite: $125
Full Breakfast
Credit Cards: A, B, C, D
Notes: 2, 5, 7, 8, 9, 10, 12, 15

ST. SIMONS

The Lodge on Little St. Simons Island

P.O. Box 21078ABB, 31522
(912) 638-7472; (888) 733-5774
FAX (912) 634-1811
e-mail:issi@mindspring.com

Privately owned, 10,000-acre barrier island retreat has seven miles of pristine beaches. Comfortable accommodations, bountiful family-style meals with hors d'oeuvres and wine. Endless recreational activities include horseback riding, fishing, boating, canoeing, bird watching, and naturalist expeditions. Fly-fishing instruction and excursions available. Limited boat docking also available. A unique experience in an unspoiled, natural environment. Day trips and full island rentals available. Smoking permitted in designated areas only. Inquire about accommodations for children. Full American Plan.

Host: Debbie McIntyre
Rooms: 13 (PB) $300-540 FAP
Full Breakfast
Credit Cards: A, B
Notes: 2, 3, 4, 5, 9, 11, 14, 15

7 No smoking; 8 Children welcome; 9 Social drinking allowed; 10 Tennis nearby; 11 Swimming nearby; 12 Golf nearby; 13 Skiing nearby; 14 May be booked through a travel agent; 15 Handicapped accessible.

SAUTEE

The Stovall House

1526 Highway 255 North, 30571
(706) 878-3355

This 1837 Victorian farmhouse, restored in 1983, is listed in the National Register of Historic Places. The inn has views of the mountains from all directions on the 26 acres in the historic Sautee Valley. The recipient of several awards for its attentive restoration, the inn is furnished with family antiques and decorated with hand stenciling. The restaurant, open to the public, features regional cuisine prepared with a fresh difference served in an intimate yet informal setting. It's a country experience.

Host: Ham Schwartz
Rooms: 5 (PB) $68-80
Continental Breakfast
Credit Cards: A, B
Notes: 2, 4, 5, 7, 8, 10, 11, 12

SAVANNAH

Bed and Breakfast Inn

117 West Gordon Street at Chatham Square, 31401
(912) 238-0518; FAX (912) 233-2537
e-mail: bnbinn@email.msn.com

Elegant 19th-century home nestled among magnificent moss-draped live oaks in the heart of Savannah's historic district. Relax among antiques, original artwork, and oriental carpets. Most guest rooms have queen-size beds and private baths. Enjoy the full hearty breakfast and freshly baked breads seated on the deck overlooking the garden courtyard with its colorful fragrant flowers. Then stroll Savannah's streets and squares to the many shops and restaurants all within an easy walk from the inn.

Rooms: 15 (PB) $80-110
Full Breakfast
Credit Cards: A, B, C, D
Notes: 2, 5, 7, 8, 9, 10, 12, 14

East Bay Inn

225 East Bay Street, 31401
(912) 238-1225; (800) 500-1225
FAX (912) 232-2709

The East Bay Inn has 28 charming guest rooms that invite guests to relax and enjoy Savannah. Walk to historic house museums and through the beautiful city squares. Return for evening wine and cheese reception. All rooms are furnished in a 19th-century style; with private baths and coffee makers in each room. Enjoy Continental plus breakfast each morning, a wine and cheese social each evening, and turndown service with chocolates at night. Higher rates apply for special events. Nonsmoking rooms available.

Innkeeper: Glenn Anderson
Rooms: 28 (PB) $119-169
Continental Breakfast
Credit Cards: A, B, C, D, E
Notes: 3, 4, 8, 9, 10, 11, 12, 14

Eliza Thompson House

5 West Jones Street, 31401
(912) 236-3620; (800) 348-9378

An 1847 three-story mansion on Savannah's finest street in the historic district. Twenty-three rooms, all with private baths, antiques, color TVs, and telephones. A lovely carriage house connected by a brick courtyard with three fountains. Complimentary wine and cheese served each evening and cheesecake and coffee served after dinner hour every night. Continental plus

Eliza Thompson House

NOTES: Credit cards accepted: A MasterCard; B Visa; C American Express; D Discover; E Diner's Club; F Other; 2 Personal checks accepted; 3 Lunch available; 4 Dinner available; 5 Open all year; 6 Pets welcome;

breakfast. All rooms renovated in 1996 by new owners.

Hosts: Carol and Steve Day
Rooms: 23 (PB) $89-189
Full Breakfast
Credit Cards: A, B
Notes: 2, 5, 7, 9, 14

Foley House Inn

14 West Hull Street, 31401
(912) 232-6622; (800) 647-3708
FAX (912) 231-1218

On beautiful Chippewa Square, in the heart of the historic landmark district, this wonderful 1896 inn awaits its guests. The individually decorated rooms offer four-poster rice beds, oriental rugs, and English antique furnishings. Most of the rooms have fireplaces, some have Jacuzzi baths, and all have cable TV. After a full day exploring the historic city of Savannah, return to the inn for tea, cordials, and snacks. An extensive film library is available if guests want to curl up and relax. If guests want more activity, the innkeepers can make arrangements for tennis and golf.

Hosts: Inge Svensson Moore and Mark Moore
Rooms: 19 (PB) $120-225
Continental Breakfast
Credit Cards: A, B, C, D, E
Notes: 2, 5, 8, 9, 10, 12, 14

The Forsyth Park Inn

102 West Hall Street, 31401
(912) 233-6800

Circa 1893 Queen Anne Victorian mansion with 16-foot ceilings and 14-foot doors. Ornate woodwork, floors, stairways, some fireplaces, antiques, some whirlpool baths, and courtyard cottage. Faces a 25-acre park in large historic district. Complimentary wine. Fine dining, tours, museum homes, river cruises, and beaches nearby. Personal checks accepted in advance.

Hosts: Virginia and Hal Sullivan
Rooms: 10 (PB) $135-200

Forsyth Park Inn

Continental Breakfast
Credit Cards: A, B, C, D
Notes: 5, 8, 9, 10, 11, 12

The Gastonian

220 East Gaston Street, 31401
(912) 232-2869

Rated one of the 12 most romantic inns, this pair of 1868 mansions are furnished with English antiques. Each of the 17 rooms has its own fireplace. All rooms have private baths; many have Jacuzzi baths. Enjoy complimentary wines and cheese with afternoon tea. A full gourmet breakfast is served daily. *Great Country Inns* calls the Gastonian the "Grande Dame of Savannah Inns."

Host: Anne Landers
Rooms: 17 (PB) $195-350
Full Breakfast
Credit Cards: A, B, C, D
Notes: 2, 5, 7, 9, 12, 14

Joan's on Jones Bed and Breakfast

17 West Jones Street, 31401
(912) 234-3863; (800) 407-3863

In the heart of the historic district, two charming bed and breakfast suites distinguish the garden level of this three-story Victorian private home. Each suite has private entry, off-street parking, sitting room,

kitchen, private telephone, cable TV. Note the original heart-pine floors, period furnishings, and Savannah gray brick walls. The innkeepers live upstairs and invite guests on a tour of their home if they are staying two nights or more. Inquire about accommodations for pets.

Hosts: Joan and Gary Levy
Suites: 2 (PB) $125-140
Continental Breakfast
Credit Cards: None
Notes: 2, 5, 7, 8, 9, 10, 11, 12, 14

Lion's Head Inn

120 East Gaston Street, 31401
(912) 232-4580; (800) 355-LION

A stately 19th-century home is in a quiet neighborhood just north of picturesque Forsyth Park. This lovely 9,200-square-foot mansion is filled with fine Empire antiques. Each guest room is exquisitely appointed with four-poster beds, private baths, period furnishings, fireplaces, TVs, VCRs, and telephones. Each morning enjoy a Continental plus breakfast, and in the evening enjoy wine and cheese served on the sweeping veranda overlooking the marbled courtyard.

Lion's Head Inn

Host: Christy Dell'Orco
Rooms: 7 (PB) $100-210
Continental Breakfast
Credit Cards: A, B, C, D
Notes: 2, 5, 7, 8, 9, 10, 11, 12, 14, 15

Magnolia Place Inn

Magnolia Place Inn

503 Whitaker Street, 31401
(912) 236-7674; (800) 238-7674
FAX (912) 236-1145
e-mail: b.b.magnolia@mci2000.com
www.magnoliaplaceinn.com

This 1878 steamboat Gothic overlooks Forsyth Park. Birthplace of Pulitzer Prize-winning poet Conrad Aiken. In the main house, 13 bedrooms with private baths. Eleven of the rooms have fireplaces and six have double Jacuzzi tubs, plus two suites in the adjoining historic property, both with fireplaces and one with a jumbo Jacuzzi tub. Limited handicapped accessibility.

Hosts: Kathy Medlock; Jane and Rob Sales
Rooms: 15 (PB) $145-250
Continental Breakfast

Credit Cards: A, B, C, D
Notes: 2, 5, 7, 9, 10, 11, 12, 14

Oglethorpe Lodge

117 East Bay Street, 31401
(912) 234-8888; FAX (912) 231-0440

The Oglethorpe Lodge is an elegant and enchanting retreat within historic Savannah. Experience the comfort and serenity of three exquisite suites that offer spacious living areas, beautifully decorated bedrooms, private baths, and fully equipped kitchens with ice makers. Enjoy complimentary Continental breakfast delivered to suites daily, free daily newspaper, and complimentary parking. The one- and two-bedroom suites feature cable TV, VCR, stereo system, hair dryers, coffee makers, iron and ironing boards, and work desk with data ports.

Suites: 3 (PB) $199-325
Continental Breakfast
Credit Cards: A, B, C, D, E
Notes: 5, 7, 8, 9, 10, 11, 12

Olde Harbour Inn

508 East Factor's Walk, 31401
(912) 234-4100; (800) 553-6533
FAX (912) 233-5979

Overlooking the Savannah River, the Olde Harbour Inn offers 24 guest suites. All suites have a full kitchen. Rooms are decorated in 19th-century style, and range from studio suites to two bedrooms with loft. Within walking distance to Savannah's beautiful city squares and historic homes. Return to the Grand Salon for wine and cheese reception in the evening, and retire to find the guest room "turned down" and a special treat. Higher rates apply for special events. Evening cordials included in rates.

Innkeeper: Glenn Anderson
Rooms: 24 (PB) $130-195
Continental Breakfast
Credit Cards: A, B, C, D, E
Notes: 5, 8, 9, 10, 11, 12, 14

Remshart-Brooks House

106 West Jones Street, 31401
(912) 234-6928

Enjoy casual southern hospitality at this historic Savannah home built in 1853. The guest suite is furnished with comfortable country antiques. Share the garden for a Continental breakfast. Private off-street covered parking is free. Rates slightly higher for three to four persons staying in the suite.

Host: Anne E. Barnett
Suite: 1 (PB) $85 plus tax
Continental Breakfast
Credit Cards: None
Notes: 2, 5, 7, 9, 10, 11, 12

The President's Quarters (A Premier Historic Inn on Oglethorpe Square)

225 East President Street, 31401
(912) 233-1600; (800) 233-1776
FAX (912) 238-0849

Four-diamond award-winning inn in the heart of historic district. Spacious rooms and suites with antiques, four-poster and canopied beds, Jacuzzis, working fireplaces, some with balconies overlooking beautiful courtyard. Complimentary amenities include fruit and wine on arrival, afternoon hors d'oeuvres, nightly turn-down with sweet and cordial, and Continental plus breakfast. Private parking and elevator accessible with 24-hour concierge and bellman.

7 No smoking; 8 Children welcome; 9 Social drinking allowed; 10 Tennis nearby; 11 Swimming nearby; 12 Golf nearby; 13 Skiing nearby; 14 May be booked through a travel agent; 15 Handicapped accessible.

Hosts: Stacy Stephens and Hank Smalling
Rooms: 16 (PB) $137-225
Continental Breakfast
Credit Cards: A, B, D
Notes: 2, 3, 5, 7, 8, 9, 10, 11, 12, 14, 15

STONE MOUNTAIN

Bed & Breakfast Atlanta

1608 Briarcliff Road, Suite 5, Atlanta, 30306
(404) 875-0525; (800) 967-3224
FAX (404) 875-8198
e-mail: bnbinfo@mindspring.com
www.bedandbreakfastatlanta.com

S-3. This inn is a reproduction of a southern plantation one mile outside of Stone Mountain National Park, in the village of Stone Mountain. Five guest rooms with private baths and three rooms with Jacuzzi baths. Also available is a guest cottage with two bedrooms, living room with fireplace, and kitchen. The inn is family owned and operated. Southern hospitality abounds. Full breakfast. Nonsmoking. Wheelchair accessible. $98-108.

THOMASTON

Woodall House

324 West Main Street, 30286
(706) 647-7044

The interior gingerbread is original in this restored Victorian home built by the county physician at the turn of the century. Private baths with individual air conditioning and cable TV. One-half block from beautiful old courthouse square, 10 miles from Flint River, 40 miles from Roosevelt's Little White House and Andersonville Confederate Cemetery, and 60 miles from Plains, Georgia, home of former President Jimmy Carter. Only 50 miles from Atlanta, Columbus, and Macon. "Home away from home" is the management philosophy.

Hosts: Bill and Charlene Woodall
Rooms: 3 (PB) $65
Full Breakfast
Credit Cards: None
Notes: 2, 5, 7, 8, 9, 10, 11, 12

THOMASVILLE

Evans House Bed and Breakfast

725 South Hansell Street, 31792
(912) 226-1343; (800) 344-4717
FAX (912) 226-0653

In the Parkfront Historical District, this restored Victorian home is directly across from the 27-acre Paradise Park near fine downtown antique shops and dining. Featuring four guest rooms with private baths. Full breakfast served in the country kitchen or dining room. Bikes and many other amenities. AAA three-diamond rating.

Hosts: Lee and John Puskar
Rooms: 4 (PB) $70-135
Full Breakfast
Credit Cards: None
Notes: 2, 5, 7, 8, 9, 12, 14

Evans House

NOTES: Credit cards accepted: A MasterCard; B Visa; C American Express; D Discover; E Diner's Club; F Other; 2 Personal checks accepted; 3 Lunch available; 4 Dinner available; 5 Open all year; 6 Pets welcome;

THOMSON

Four Chimneys

2316 Wire Road Southeast, 30824
(706) 597-0220

Early 1800s plantation-plain country house has original hand-planed pine-board floors, walls, and ceilings. Furnished with antiques and reproductions; all guest rooms have fireplaces and four-posters. Beautiful grounds with colonial-style herb and flower garden. Continental plus breakfast served. Afternoon tea available. Equestrian events, golf, and antique shops are nearby. Easy access to I-20 and Augusta. Two miles to town and restaurants. Higher rates for special events. Inquire about picnics or suppers. No smoking in guest rooms.

Hosts: Maggie and Ralph Zieger
Rooms: 4 (2 PB; 2 SB) $35-60
Continental Breakfast
Credit Cards: A, B
Notes: 2, 5, 9, 12

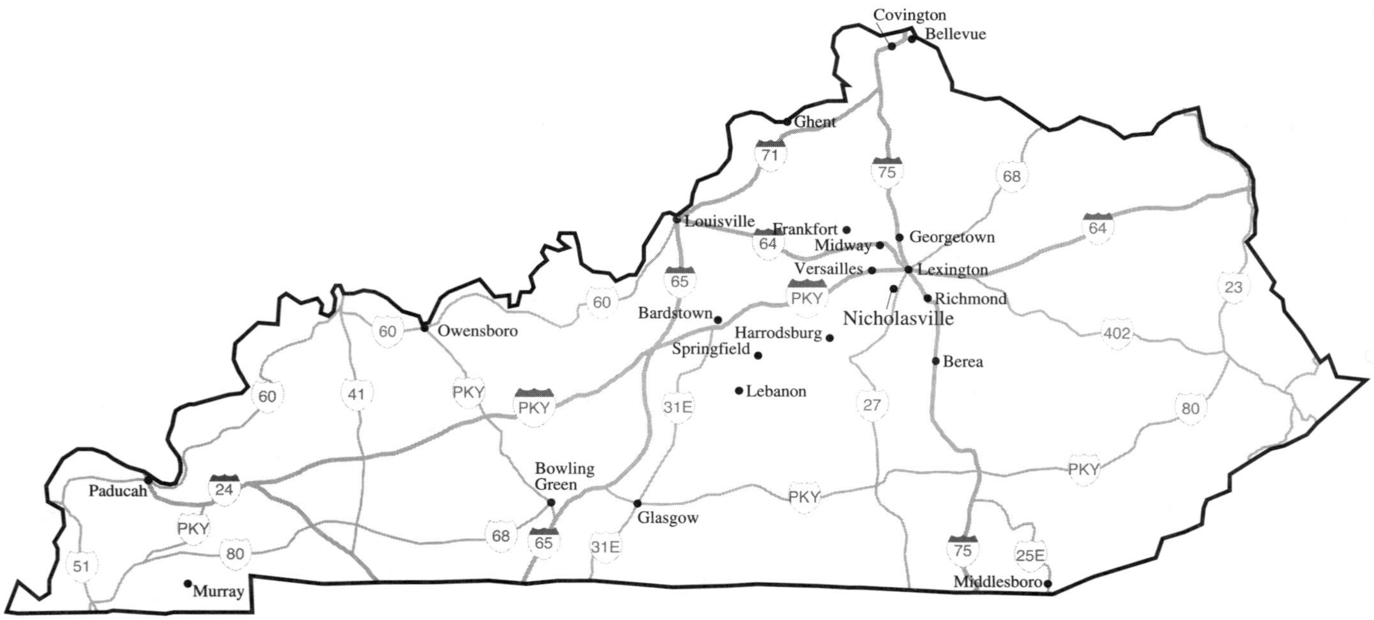
Covington
Bellevue
Ghent
71
75
68
64
Louisville
Frankfort
Georgetown
Midway
Versailles
Lexington
65
PKY
Richmond
Nicholasville
23
60
Bardstown
Harrodsburg
Springfield
402
Owensboro
Berea
Lebanon
60
41
PKY
PKY
31E
27
80
Bowling
Green
PKY
Paducah
24
PKY
Glasgow
PKY
68
65
31E
75
25E
80
51
Murray
Middlesboro

Kentucky

Kentucky

BARDSTOWN

Arbor Rose

209 East Stephen Foster, 40004
(502) 349-0014; (888) 828-3330

This 1820 Victorian home is in the historic district of Bardstown, the town associated with Stephen Foster. It has king-size beds and a garden terrace with pond. Minutes from shopping for antiques, tours of mansions, four distilleries, golfing, Civil War history, and much more.

Hosts: Derrick and Judy Melzer
Rooms: 5 (PB) $79-99
Full Breakfast
Credit Cards: A, B, C, D
Notes: 2, 5, 7, 8, 9, 10, 11, 12, 14

Beautiful Dreamer Bed and Breakfast

440 East Stephen Foster Avenue, 40004
(502) 348-4004; (800) 811-8312

Antiques and cherry furniture complement this newly built Federal-design home that overlooks historic My Old Kentucky Home. The Beautiful Dreamer Room has a double Jacuzzi. The Captain's Room has a single Jacuzzi and fireplace. The Stephen Foster Room is conveniently on the first floor. All rooms are air conditioned and have queen-size beds. Hearty breakfast included. Within walking distance of *The Stephen Foster Story*.

Host: Lynell Ginter
Rooms: 3 (PB) $89-109
Full Breakfast
Credit Cards: A, B, C, D
Notes: 2, 5, 7, 10, 11, 12, 15

Bruntwood Inn

714 North Third Street, 40004
(502) 348-8218

This gracious antebellum mansion built in 1830, complete with spiraling staircase, grand entry foyer, elegant chandeliers, antique furnishings, and decorative original fireplaces in every room, may have been the type of setting that moved Stephen Foster to write about his "Old Kentucky Home." The poplar and ash floors with oriental rugs and the 12- and 13-foot-high ceilings add to the charm and spaciousness of the house. A full plantation breakfast is served daily at 9 A.M. Bruntwood Inn is within five minutes of many historic sites for touring.

Host: Susan Danielak
Rooms: 7 (5 PB; 2 SB) $80-100
Full Breakfast
Credit Cards: A, B
Notes: 2, 5, 7, 8, 9, 10, 11, 14

Jailer's Inn

111 West Stephen Foster Avenue, 40004
(502) 348-5551

Iron bars on windows, 30-inch thick stone walls, and a heavy steel door slamming behind one may not sound like the typical tourist accommodation and Jailer's Inn is anything but typical. The historic Jailer's Inn, circa 1819, offers a unique and luxurious way to "do time." Jailer's Inn is a place of wonderful, thought-provoking contrasts. Each of the six guest rooms is beautifully

NOTES: Credit cards accepted: A MasterCard; B Visa; C American Express; D Discover; E Diner's Club; F Other; 2 Personal checks accepted; 3 Lunch available; 4 Dinner available; 5 Open all year; 6 Pets welcome; 7 No smoking; 8 Children welcome; 9 Social drinking allowed; 10 Tennis nearby; 11 Swimming nearby; 12 Golf nearby; 13 Skiing nearby; 14 May be booked through a travel agent; 15 Handicapped accessible.

Jailer's Inn

decorated with antiques and heirlooms, all in the renovated front jail. The back jail, built in 1874, is basically unchanged; guests will get a chilling and sobering look at what conditions were like in the old Nelson County jail that was in full operation as recently as 1987. Call for rates.

Host: Paul McCoy
Rooms: 6 (PB)
Full Breakfast
Credit Cards: A, B, C, D
Notes: 2, 7, 8, 9, 10, 11, 12, 14

Kenmore Farms Bed and Breakfast

1050 Bloomfield Road, 40004
(800) 831-6159
www.bbonline.com/ky/kenmorefarms/

Drop the hurried ways and enjoy the charm and warmth of days gone by. This beautifully restored 1860s Victorian home features antiques, Oriental rugs, gleaming poplar floors, and a cherry stairway. Air-conditioned guest rooms are furnished with queen-size four-poster or Lincoln beds, and lovely linens, including period pieces. Large, private baths; spacious vanities. A hearty country breakfast is served—all home-cooked. The decor and the hosts' brand of hospitality create a relaxing and enjoyable atmosphere. AAA-approved. Children over 12 welcome.

Hosts: Dorothy and Bernie Keene
Rooms: 4 (PB) $80-90
Full Breakfast
Credit Cards: None
Notes: 2, 5, 7, 9, 10, 11, 12

The Mansion Bed and Breakfast

1003 North 3rd Street, 40004
(502) 348-2586; (800) 399-2586

This beautiful Greek Revival mansion, built in 1851, is in the National Register of Historic Places. On more than three acres of land with magnificent trees and plantings, it reminds one of more genteel times. The Mansion is on the site where the Confederate flag the Stars and Bars was raised in Kentucky for the first time. The rooms feature period antiques, hand-crocheted bedspreads, dust ruffles, shams, king-size beds, and private baths. Continental plus breakfast. Smoking restricted. Children over 10 welcome.

Host: Joseph D. Downs
Rooms: 8 (PB) $75-125
Continental Breakfast
Credit Cards: A, B, C, D
Notes: 2, 5, 9, 10, 11, 12, 14

BELLEVUE

Weller Haus Bed and Breakfast

319 Poplar Street, 41073
(606) 431-6829; (800) 431-4287
FAX (606) 431-4332
www.bbonline.com/ky/weller/

Savor the casual elegance of an era past in these historic preservation-awarded 1880s Victorian Gothic homes. The inn is 1.7 miles from downtown Cincinnati, Ohio, antique-appointed, and offers an exquisite candlelit breakfast. Other amenities include two Jacuzzi suites for two, private English garden, ivy-covered gathering kitchen.

Riverboat Row with its attractions and dining spots is within walking distance. Smoking in restricted areas only. Corporate amenities include in-room telephones, and a fax is available.

Hosts: Mary and Vernon Weller
Rooms: 5 (PB) $75-145
Full Breakfast
Credit Cards: A, B, C, D, E
Notes: 2, 5, 8, 9, 10, 11, 12, 13, 14, 15

BEREA

The Doctor's Inn of Berea

617 Chestnut Street, 40403-1550
(606) 986-3042 (phone/FAX)
e-mail: docsinn@mis.net

The Doctor's Inn is Berea's premier bed and breakfast, nestled in the foothills of the Appalachians just off I-75 in the heart of Kentucky's designated capital of folk arts and crafts. The hosts offer a warm welcome along with the "hound of the inn," Coco. For leisure time there is satellite TV, a baby grand piano, library of books, or lively conversation during evening social hour before leaving for dinner. Shopping for crafts, jewelry, pottery, fine furniture, hand-woven items, antiques, tours of Berea College are all within walking distance.

The Doctor's Inn of Berea

Hosts: Dr. Bill and Bisi Baker
Rooms: 3 (PB) $125
Full Breakfast
Credit Cards: None
Notes: 2, 5, 9, 10, 11, 12

BOWLING GREEN

Alpine Lodge

5310 Morgantown Road, 42101-8201
(502) 843-4846

Alpine Lodge is a spacious Swiss chalet-style home that has more than 6,000 square feet and is built on a little more than 11 acres. The furnishings are mostly antiques. A typical breakfast, southern style, of eggs, sausage, biscuits, gravy, fried apples, grits, coffee, and orange juice starts the guests' day. Swimming pool, gazebo, outdoor spa, and lots of trails to stroll through. All rooms have telephones and cable TVs. Inquire about accommodations for pets.

Hosts: Dr. and Mrs. David Livingston
Rooms: 5 (3 PB; 2 SB) $45-85
Full Breakfast
Credit Cards: None
Notes: 2, 3, 4, 5, 7, 8, 9, 10, 11, 12, 14

Walnut Lawn Bed and Breakfast

1800 Morgantown Road, 42101
(502) 781-7255

This is a restored Victorian house, part of which was built in 1805. It is furnished with family antiques of the period. On a farm three miles from the center of Bowling Green and just off Natcher Parkway and I-65. The place has been in the family for more than 125 years. Walnut Lawn requires reservations and serves a Continental breakfast.

Host: George Anna McKenzie
Rooms: 4 (3 PB; 1 SB) $65
Continental Breakfast
Credit Cards: None
Notes: 2, 5, 7, 9

COVINGTON

Licking Riverside Historic Bed and Breakfast

516 Garrard Street, 41011
(606) 291-0191; (800) 483-7822
FAX (606) 291-0939
www.bbonline.com/ky/riverside/

Relax in the Jacuzzi with a view. All rooms have private baths, Jacuzzis, TVs, VCRs, refrigerators. Suite has Jacuzzi for two, fireplace, view of river. Historic home in the historic area on the Licking River. European decor, Victorian flavor. Contemporary style for the comfort one expects. Expect southern hospitality at this bed and breakfast. Continental plus breakfast. Call for current events and reservations.

Host: Lynda L. Freeman
Rooms: 4 (PB) $99-149
Continental Breakfast
Credit Cards: A, B, D
Notes: 2, 5, 7, 8, 10, 11, 12, 13, 14

Sandford House

1026 Russell Street, 41011-3065
(606) 291-9133; (888) 291-9133

Enjoy a delicious full breakfast in the gazebo in the award-winning garden. The original Federal design, now French Empire, 1820s mansion is 10 minutes from Cincinnati, Ohio, and 20 minutes from the airport. This bed and breakfast is in the city with the feel of the country. Casual yet elegant. Public rooms have 12-foot ceilings with ornate cornices. Accommodations available for extended stay include penthouse and two-bedroom/two-bath carriage house.

Hosts: Dan and Linda Carter
Rooms: 4 (PB) $55-95
Full Breakfast
Credit Cards: A, B, C
Notes: 2, 5, 6, 7, 8, 9, 12, 14

FRANKFORT

Bluegrass Bed and Breakfast Reservation Service

2964 McCracken Pike, Versailles, 40383
(606) 873-3208; e-mail: BPRATT9905@aol.com

High Meadow. Get away from it all at this small country cottage perched on a rural hilltop. Sit around the big fireplace on a cold winter night or stroll the hillside in warmer weather. There is one large living/dining/kitchen area and one first-floor bedroom with double bed and bath (tub only). Air conditioning. No TV. Second-floor room with two double beds and a bath with shower. $75.

GHENT

Ghent House Bed and Breakfast

411 Main Street (US 42), P.O. Box 478, 41045
(502) 347-5807
www.bbonline.com/ky/ghent/

Ghent House is a gracious reminder of the antebellum days of the Old South. Federal style with a beautiful fantail window, two slave walls, rose and English gardens, gazebo, crystal chandeliers, fireplaces, outdoor hot tub, and whirlpool. Ghent House has a spectacular view of the Ohio River halfway between Cincinnati and Louisville, and one can almost visualize the steamboats. Go back in time and stay at the Ghent House. Come as a guest—leave as a friend.

Hosts: Wayne and Diane Young
Rooms: 3 (PB) $60-120
Full Breakfast
Credit Cards: A, B, C, D
Notes: 2, 5, 7, 8, 9, 11, 12, 14

NOTES: Credit cards accepted: A MasterCard; B Visa; C American Express; D Discover; E Diner's Club; F Other; 2 Personal checks accepted; 3 Lunch available; 4 Dinner available; 5 Open all year; 6 Pets welcome;

GEORGETOWN

Blackridge Hall

4055 Paris Pike, 40324
(502) 863-2069; (800) 768-9308

Blackridge Hall is an upscale, luxurious southern Georgian-style mansion on five acres in Bluegrass horse country. There are six guest suites/rooms containing antique and reproduction furnishings. Two master suites have marble Jacuzzi tubs, while all baths are private. A full gourmet candlelight breakfast is served in the dining room or on the veranda. A cozy guest kitchenette is available with snacks and soft drinks. Minutes to Lexington, Kentucky Horse Park, Keeneland and Red Mile racetracks, University of Kentucky, Toyota Motor Corporation tours, and historic Georgetown antique shops. Near I-64 and I-75.

Host: Jim D. Black, proprietor
Rooms: 6 (PB) $89-179
Full Breakfast
Credit Cards: A, B, C, D
Notes: 2, 5, 7, 9, 10, 11, 12, 14

Blackridge Hall

GLASGOW

Four Seasons Country Inn

4107 Scottsville Road, 42141
(502) 678-1000

Charming Victorian-style inn built in 1989. Most rooms have queen-size, four-

Four Seasons Country Inn

poster beds, private baths, remote-equipped TVs with cable. Continental breakfast served in inviting lobby with wood-burning fireplace. Some rooms open out to spacious deck or large front porch. Swimming pool. Honeymoon suite. Near the caves, lakes, and Corvettes.

Host: Charles Smith
Rooms: 21 (PB) $60-99
Continental Breakfast
Credit Cards: A, B, C, D, E
Notes: 5, 9, 10, 11, 12, 14, 15

HARRODSBURG

Bauer Haus Bed and Breakfast

362 North College Street, 40330
(606) 734-6289

Savor the craftsmanship of the past in this 1880s Victorian home listed in the National Register of Historic Places and designated a Kentucky landmark. Nestle in the sitting room, sip tea or coffee in the dining room, repose in the parlor, or ascend the staircase to a private room for a relaxing visit. In Kentucky's oldest settlement, Bauer Haus is within walking distance of Old Fort Harrod State Park and historic Harrodsburg.

Hosts: Dick and Marian Bauer
Rooms: 4 (2 PB; 2 SB) $60-75
Full Breakfast
Credit Cards: A, B, C, D
Notes: 2, 5, 7, 9, 10, 12

Inn at Shaker Village of Pleasant Hill

3501 Lexington Road, 40330
(606) 734-5411

The Shaker Village of Pleasant Hill offers a one-of-a-kind guest experience. Its 80 guest rooms in buildings where Shakers once lived and worked are simply and beautifully furnished with Shaker-crafted furniture. This national historic landmark sits on 2,700 acres of rolling bluegrass farmland. The village offers tours, daily exhibitions of Shaker crafts, and hearty country dining. Riverboat excursions from April through October.

Host: James Thomas
Rooms: 80 (PB) $55-100
Full and Continental Breakfast
Credit Cards: A, B
Notes: 2, 3, 4, 5, 8, 9, 11, 12, 14

LEBANON

Myrtledene

370 North Spalding Avenue, 40033
(502) 692-2223; (800) 391-1721

Four rooms in the heart of Kentucky, Myrtledene is a place to go back in time, to slow down, to unwind. Make this gracious Georgian home, built in 1833 and furnished in period antiques, the headquarters for traveling to area attractions. Come, stay a while and experience the rich heritage of an area noted for its Southern hospitality.

Host: James Spragens
Rooms: 4 (2 PB; 2 SB) $65
Full Breakfast
Credit Cards: A, B
Notes: 2, 5, 8, 9, 10, 11, 12, 14

LEXINGTON

Bluegrass Bed and Breakfast Reservation Service

2964 McCracken Pike, Versailles, 40383
(606) 873-3208; e-mail: BPRATT9905@aol.com

Lexington III. A lovely in-town house so surrounded by woods that guests scarcely realize there are neighbors. Contemporary in style with spacious feeling deriving from its two-storied living room and generous use of glass. Guests may select a king-size bed with adjacent private bath or twin mahogany four-posters and attached private bath. Air conditioned. $75.

Brand House at Rose Hill

461 North Limestone Street, 40508
(606) 226-9464; (800) 366-4942
FAX (606) 252-7940
e-mail: loganleet@uky.campus.mci.net

This 1812 nationally registered home in the center of the Bluegrass is on 1.3 acres adjacent to Lexington's downtown historic district and minutes from the legendary horse farms of central Kentucky. Casually elegant, all rooms feature whirlpool tubs, cable TV, and telephones. Most with fireplaces. The home has been featured in *Country Inns*, *National Geographic*, and *Southern Living* magazines.

Hosts: Pam and Logan Leet
Rooms: 5 (PB) $89-199
Full Breakfast
Credit Cards: A, B, C, D
Notes: 2, 5, 7, 9, 10, 11, 12, 13, 14

LOUISVILLE

Aleksander House Bed and Breakfast

1213 South First Street, 40203
(502) 637-4985; FAX (502) 635-1398

The Aleksander House is a gracious 1882 Victorian Italianate home in historical Old Louisville. Tastefully decorated in antiques, the home features original fireplaces, wood floors, light fixtures, stained glass, and staircases. The four guest rooms and one suite are spacious with TVs, VCRs, fireplaces, telephones, air conditioning, and heat control. Aleksander House is near downtown, the airport, the

NOTES: Credit cards accepted: A MasterCard; B Visa; C American Express; D Discover; E Diner's Club; F Other; 2 Personal checks accepted; 3 Lunch available; 4 Dinner available; 5 Open all year; 6 Pets welcome;

university, I-65, and Kentucky Expo Center. A full gourmet breakfast is served each morning. Discount rates are available. Children are welcome.

Host: Nancy Hinchliff
Rooms: 4 (2 PB; 2 SB) $75-119
Full Breakfast
Credit Cards: A, B, C
Notes: 2, 5, 7, 8, 9, 10, 11, 12, 14

Ashton's Victorian Secret Bed and Breakfast

1132 South First Street, 40203
(502) 581-1914; (800) 449-4691 (#0604)

In historic Old Louisville, guests will find a three-story brick mansion appropriately named the Victorian Secret Bed and Breakfast. Its 14 rooms offer spacious accommodations, high ceilings, 11 fireplaces, and original woodwork. Recently restored to its former elegance, the 110-year-old structure provides a peaceful setting for enjoying period furnishings and antiques.

Hosts: Nan and Steve Roosa
Rooms: 3 (1 PB; 2 SB) $53-89
Continental Breakfast
Credit Cards: B
Notes: 5, 8, 9, 10, 11, 12, 13, 14

Bluegrass Bed and Breakfast Reservation Service

2964 McCracken Pike, Versailles, 40383
(606) 873-3208; e-mail: BPRATT9905@aol.com

Land O'Goshen. Eighteen rooms and breakfast eggs fresh from the henhouse are available at this country bed and breakfast on a Thoroughbred farm. Stone walls, a pond, flower and vegetable gardens, iron gates, and a boxwood *allée* contribute to an unforgettable experience. Two rooms are available. Both rooms have fireplaces, private baths, and are furnished with antiques. Air conditioned. Resident dogs and cat. $85-90.

Inn at the Park

1332 South Fourth Street, 40208
(502) 637-6930; FAX (502) 637-2796
e-mail: innatpark@aol.com
www.bbonline.com/ky/innatpark/

This Victorian mansion was built in 1886 as a premier example of Richardsonian Romanesque architecture. The inn is elegantly furnished in Victorian antiques and antique reproductions. Very spacious with 14-foot ceilings, eight fireplaces, picturesque porches overlooking Central Park, and rich hardwood floors. The grand, sweeping staircase is magnificent! Appropriate for special occasions and the very particular guest. Enjoy an evening stroll in the park, personal attention from the innkeepers, and an excellent full breakfast.

Hosts: John and Sandra Mullins
Rooms: 7 (PB) $79-149
Full Breakfast
Credit Cards: A, B, C, D
Notes: 2, 5, 7, 9, 10, 11, 12, 14

Old Louisville Inn

1359 South Third Street, 40208
(502) 635-1574; FAX (502) 637-5892
e-mail oldlouin@aol.com
www.oldlouinn.com

Wake up to the aroma of freshly baked popovers and muffins when staying in one of the 10 guest rooms or suites. Conveniently between downtown and the airport. Stay for a romantic getaway or relax on a business trip and consider this inn home away from home.

Old Louisville Inn

Host: Marianne Lesher
Rooms: 10 (PB) $75-195
Full Breakfast
Credit Cards: A, B, C, D
Notes: 2, 5, 8, 9, 10, 12, 14

The Red Room Bed and Breakfast

1028 Cherokee Road #1, 40204
(502) 458-7197

Spacious condo just five minutes from midcity. Tree-lined street in an older established neighborhood. One block from Bardstown Road and its wall-to-wall antique shops and restaurants. Queen-size and twin bedrooms with private baths. Smokers welcome. Inquire about rates during Kentucky Derby weekend. Cookbook author hostess may surprise her guests with strawberry shortcake at breakfast.

Rooms: 2 (PB) $60
Full Breakfast
Credit Cards: None
Notes: 2, 5, 9

Rocking Horse Manor Bed and Breakfast

1002 South Third Street, 40203
(502) 583-0408; (888) HORSE BB
FAX (502) 583-6077 ext#129
www.bbonline.com/ky/rockinghorse/

Stay in an 1888 Victorian mansion. Five guest rooms each with en suite private bath, cable TV, telephone, and heat /air-condition control. Conveniently in Old Louisville. A gourmet breakfast and complimentary evening snacks provided. Relax in the Victorian parlor or library with wet bar, or choose the third-floor sitting area that has a mini-office for those who can't leave work behind. Jacuzzi suite. Corporate rates. AAA-rated. Gift certificates available.

Hosts: Diana Jachimiak and Brad Vossberg
Rooms: 5 (PB) $60-120
Full Breakfast
Credit Cards: A, B, C
Notes: 2, 5, 9, 10, 14

Welcome House Bed and Breakfast

1613 Forest Hill Drive, 40205
(502) 452-6629

Gracious Colonial home in a lovely suburban neighborhood offers two queen-size, two double, and two single bedrooms with three baths. Off the beaten path, but convenient to antique shops, shopping malls, and the expressways. Great for reunions and conventions. Close to fairgrounds.

Host: Jo DuBose Boone
Rooms: 5 (3 PB; 2 SB) $50-65
Full Breakfast
Credit Cards: None
Notes: 2, 5, 8, 9, 10, 11, 12, 14

Woodhaven Bed and Breakfast

401 South Hubbards Lane, 40207
(502) 895-1011; (888) 895-1011
www.bbonline.com/ky/woodhaven/

Beautiful Gothic Revival mansion, built in 1853, features elaborately carved woodwork, winding staircases, and spacious rooms tastefully decorated with antiques. The seven bedrooms and one cottage suite offer private baths (some with whirlpools), TVs, telephones, clock radios, and complimentary coffee and tea stations. Guests enjoy a welcoming snack and a full gourmet breakfast in the formal dining room.

Woodhaven

Common areas have 14-foot ceilings and floor-to-ceiling windows. Three porches and perennial gardens circle the property.

Host: Marsha Burton
Rooms: 7 (PB) $70-150
Full Breakfast
Credit Cards: A, B, C
Notes: 2, 4, 5, 7, 8, 9, 10, 11, 12, 14, 15

MIDDLESBORO

The RidgeRunner Bed and Breakfast

208 Arthur Heights, 40965
(606) 248-4299
www.bbonline.com/ky/ridgerunner/

This 1891 Victorian home is furnished with authentic antiques and is nestled in the Cumberland Mountains. A picturesque view is enjoyed from the 60-foot front porch, welcoming guests with rocking chairs, swings, and hammocks. Guests are treated like special people, in a relaxed, peaceful atmosphere. Five minutes from Cumberland Gap National Park, the newly opened Twin Tunnels through historical Cumberland Gap, 12 minutes from Pine Mountain State Park, 50 miles from Knoxville, Tennessee, 2 miles from the P-38 Restoration Project Museum.

Hosts: Sue Richards and Irma Gall
Rooms: 4 (2PB; 2SB) $55-65
Full Breakfast
Credit Cards: None
Notes: 2, 5, 7, 9, 10, 12

The RidgeRunner

MIDWAY

Bluegrass Bed and Breakfast Reservation Service

2964 McCracken Pike, Versailles, 40383
(606) 873-3208; e-mail: BPRATT9905@aol.com

Scottwood. This 1795 brick house is an Early American jewel restored and furnished to perfection. Step back in time in a room of choice: a ground-floor room with fireplace flanked by tea table and wing chair, antique bed, and modern private bath; upstairs beneath the eaves, two bedrooms. Both open onto a sitting room with fireplace and games table. Charming guest cottage has a deck overlooking a lazy bend of the Elkhorn, four-poster bed, fireplace, and sleeping loft with an extra three-fourths bed. No smoking, please. Air conditioned. Two-night minimum stay. Three-night minimum Derby weekend. Thirty-five dollars for third person in cottage. $125.

MURRAY

Diuguid House Bed and Breakfast

603 Main Street, 42071
(502) 753-5470; (888) 261-3028

This beautiful home, listed in the National Register of Historic Places, features a sweeping oak staircase, comfortable and spacious rooms, and a generous guest lounge area. This bed and breakfast is in town near the university, lake area, and many antique shops. Full breakfast is included in the reasonable rates, and the area has the reputation for being a top-rated retirement area.

Hosts: Karen and George Chapman
Rooms: 3 (SB) $40
Full Breakfast
Credit Cards: A, B, D, E
Notes: 2, 5, 7, 8, 10, 12, 14

NICHOLASVILLE

Bluegrass Bed and Breakfast Reservation Service

2964 McCracken Pike, Versailles, 40383
(606) 873-3208; e-mail: BPRATT9905@aol.com

This comfortable home overlooking a creek and farmland is in a rural subdivision with the old-time gracious living of two-acre lots. Great neighborhood for a stroll or jogging. Twenty-minute drive to Keeneland. Thirty minutes to Shakertown. Two guest bedrooms share a hall bath (tub only, though a shower may be available). Swimming pool. Air conditioned. No smoking. $80.

Sandusky House and O'Neal Log Cabin

1626 Delaney Ferry Road, 40356
(606) 223-4730; e-mail: humphlin@aol.com

A tree-lined drive to the Sandusky House is just a prelude to the handsome Greek Revival residence built about 1850 with bricks fired on the premises. Today the bed and breakfast sits on a 10-acre estate amid horse farms, yet close to downtown Lexington, Keeneland Race Track, Kentucky Horse Park, and many other attractions. The 180-year-old authentic log cabin has been reconstructed and has two bedrooms, kitchen, living room with a fireplace, whirlpool tub, and air conditioning. Full breakfast for house guests and Continental plus breakfast for cabin guests. Children over 12 welcome in house. Children of all ages welcome in cabin.

Sandusky House

Hosts: Jim and Linda Humphrey
House: 3 (PB) $79
Cabin: $99
Full or Continental Breakfast
Credit Cards: A, B
Notes: 2, 5, 7, 9

OWENSBORO

Trail's End

5931 Highway 56, 42301
(502) 771-5590; FAX (502) 771-4723
e-mail: jramey@mindspring.com
www.mindspring.com/~jramey

A condo cottage, in Indiana, furnished with antiques and gas-log fireplace, has three bedrooms, fully equipped kitchen with stocked refrigerator of breakfast fixings, laundry facilities, patio, and stables for lessons or trail riding on the property. A second condo cottage, in Kentucky, has three bedrooms. Guests may enjoy indoor/outdoor tennis, Nautilus fitness, and a sauna. Country-style breakfast served at the tennis club on property. Pool and a fireplace. Cottages are air conditioned. Also available is a two-bedroom trailer with two baths. Weekly rates available. Ten dollars for additional persons over two.

Host: Joan G. Ramey
Condo: 2 (PB) $50-75
Trailer: 2 (PB) $35
Full Breakfast
Credit Cards: A, B, D
Notes: 2, 5, 6, 7, 8, 9, 10, 11, 12, 14, 15

PADUCAH

The 1857's Bed and Breakfast

127 Market House Square; P.O. Box 7771, 42002-7771
(502) 444-3960; (800) 264-5607
FAX (502) 444-6751

This three-story brick building, listed in the National Register of Historic Places, has a warm, friendly Victorian atmosphere. The first floor houses Cynthia's Ristorante; the second floor houses two guest rooms and a hot tub on the deck; and the third floor houses the family room and game room with a billiards table. This home is in the downtown historic district, with antique stores, carriage rides, quilt museum, restaurants, and the Market House Cultural Center within walking distance. The entire second floor with private bath may be booked for $95; two-night minimum stay.

Hosts: Deborah and Steve Bohnert
Rooms: 3 (SB) $65-95
Continental Breakfast
Credit Cards: A, B
Notes: 2, 5, 10, 11, 12, 13, 14

Farley Place Bed and Breakfast

166 Farley Place, 42003
(502) 442-2488

Farley Place Bed and Breakfast is the mid-Victorian home of Emily Grant Garrett (1820-1889) who defied Gen. Ulysses S. Grant. On a quiet side street convenient to downtown Paducah. Lovely yard, porches, goldfish pond, and fountains. Spacious antique-filled rooms. Coffee and local paper outside guests' bedroom door at 6:00 A.M., if requested.

Host: Bernice Jones
Rooms: 3 (1 PB; 2 SB) $55-85
Full Breakfast
Credit Cards: A, B, C, D
Notes: 2, 5, 6, 8, 10, 11, 12

Trinity Hills Farm Bed and Breakfast Home and Stained Glass Studio

10455 Old Lovelaceville Road, 42001
(502) 488-3999; (800) 488-3998
e-mail: trinity8@apex.net
www.bbonline.com/ky/trinityhills

Share the serenity of this 17-acre country retreat, ideal for romantic getaways or family gatherings. Enjoy nature at its best—bird watching, hiking, boating, fishing, farm animals, peacocks, or simply relaxing in the spa near water gardens. New three-story home features romantic third-floor suites with private whirlpool or spa and first-floor guest rooms with private entrances; unique stained glass, fireplaces, vaulted ceilings, TV/game/exercise room. Amenities include bathrobes, candles, clock radio, stereo, and evening refreshments. Some pets welcome with prior notice. Social drinking permitted in rooms.

Hosts: Mike and Ann Driver
Jim and Nancy Driver (Mike's parents)
Rooms: 5 (PB) $70-105
Full Breakfast
Credit Cards: A, B, D
Notes: 2, 5, 7, 8, 10, 11, 12, 15

RICHMOND

Bluegrass Bed and Breakfast Reservation Service

2964 McCracken Pike, Versailles, 40383
(606) 873-3208; e-mail: BPRATT9905@aol.com

Bennett House. In downtown Richmond with two bedrooms, queen-size beds, with private baths. A Victorian house with stunning cherry staircase. Continental breakfast. Air conditioned. Ten miles to Berea, a crafts center; 25 miles to Lexington; eight miles to Bybee Pottery. $75.

SPRINGFIELD

Glenmar Plantation Bed and Breakfast

2444 Valley Hill Road, 40069
(606) 284-7791; (800) 828-3330

Relax and be invigorated at this very romantic 250-acre horse farm. In the national historic register. A recipient of the Kentucky Commemorative Historic Farm award. Guests may stroll the trails, go horseback riding, ride bicycles built for two, fish, or even have a marshmallow roast. This pre-Civil War farm has historic buildings, slave quarters, and the main house is the oldest brick home in Kentucky. Enjoy the horses, llamas, cattle, peacocks, and sheep. Full breakfast and evening desserts served.

Host: Kenny Mandell
Rooms: 8 (6 PB; 2 SB) $75-150
Full Breakfast
Credit Cards: A, B, C
Notes: 2, 3, 4, 5, 7, 8, 9, 10, 11, 12, 14

VERSAILLES

Bluegrass Bed and Breakfast Reservation Service

2964 McCracken Pike, Versailles, 40383
(606) 873-3208; e-mail: BPRATT9905@aol.com

Daisy Hill. This stately brick home on extensive tree-shaded grounds has been in the owner's family since 1812. It's a glorious combination of antique furnishings and modern luxuries. A large downstairs bedroom with elegantly canopied double bed and private bath en suite opens onto a brick courtyard and lawn. A large upstairs bedroom with king-size bed and private bath overlooks the grounds, including farm and Thoroughbreds. Another room available for family group. Air conditioned. $110.

Peacham. Nine fireplaces typify the charm of this house built in 1829 from brick fired on the farm. Set amid ancient trees on a knoll a half-mile from the highway, this home is a quiet oasis bordered by horse farms. One second-floor room with twin beds and private bath. Very private first-floor suite—living room, bedroom with queen-size canopied bed, air conditioning, and private bath. No smoking, please. Two-night minimum during Keeneland race meets in April and October. $65-100.

Polly Place. An artist's dream studio: beautiful, comfortable, yet with touches of whimsy. First level is one great room oriented around a huge fireplace. Above are open-balconied bedrooms and bath with Jacuzzi. Studio rests on a shaded knoll on a 200-acre farm. Sleeps four friendlies beautifully, six in a pinch. Guests have the entire house. Two-night minimum. Air conditioned. $115.

Shadewell. Deep in the country, this home begins with the original 1810 room and rambles on through additions and restorations. The newest is a kitchen cum garden room designed by the gourmet cook and artist owner, overlooking extensive boxwood gardens. Steep, twisting stairs lead up to two bedrooms sharing a bath with shower. Separate stairs lead up to another private suite, with sitting area and bath with shower. Air conditioning. Fourth bedroom is available on lower level with bath on floor above. No smoking. $125.

Springdale. Nestled on a grassy slope above a stone springhouse, this fine old home is the perfect setting for those who want to experience quiet country living. The original dwelling, built about 1800, forms the nucleus of the airy brick home shaded by old trees. One air-conditioned bedroom has double bed and private bath. Another bedroom is available for additional family or friends. Crib available. No smoking, please. Two-night minimum during Keeneland race meets in April and October. $85.

Welcome Hall. Built in 1792, when Kentucky was still the westernmost segment of Virginia, this handsome stone house and its grounds are a prime example of that period's self-sufficient country estate. Now devoted to blooded horses, as well as general farming, it provides a unique experience to its guests. Restored air-conditioned two-room cabin with double four-poster bed. Two-night minimum. $100.

NOTES: Credit cards accepted: A MasterCard; B Visa; C American Express; D Discover; E Diner's Club; F Other; 2 Personal checks accepted; 3 Lunch available; 4 Dinner available; 5 Open all year; 6 Pets welcome;

Shepherd Place

US 60 and Heritage Road, 40383
(606) 873-7843; (800) 278-0864

Shepherd Place

Marlin and Sylvia invite guests to share their pre-Civil War home, built between 1820 and 1850. The house has windows that go all the way to the floor, crown moldings, hardwood floors, and large rooms with private baths, as well as a parlor and front porch swing for relaxation. Stroll up to the barn and meet the resident ewes, or ride through the Bluegrass horse farms. Horseback riding nearby.

Hosts: Marlin and Sylvia Yawn
Rooms: 3 (PB) $75
Full Breakfast
Credit Cards: A, B
Notes: 2, 5, 7, 8, 12

71
167
165
20
Shreveport
20
171
65
165
49
Natchitoches
167
28
171
165
49
St. Francisville
Jackson
55
Husser
New Roads
61
190
190
Prairieville
190
171
165
12
10
Vacherie
10
Slidell
10
Lafayette
St. Martinville
Napoleonville
Kenner
New Orleans
90
23

Louisiana

Louisiana

HUSSER

Grand Estate Mansion Bed and Breakfast

55314 Highway 445, 70442
(504) 748-2915; (888) 792-2915

An elegant three-story southern mansion that is the perfect setting for a romantic getaway. Private majestic bedrooms and baths. Queen-size beds, fireplaces, period antiques, library, sunroom, formal parlor, great room with big screen TV/VCR. Honeymoon suite with double oversized pink marble Jacuzzi tub with columns. Three porches with rocking chairs. Large wraparound balcony overlooking built-in swimming pool and fishing pond. Ballroom suitable for weddings, receptions, business meetings, and special events. One-hour drive from New Orleans, Baton Rouge, or MSY airport.

Host: Mary Ann Brauninger
Rooms: 5 (3 PB; 2 SB) $85-175
Full Breakfast
Credit Cards: A, B
Notes: 2, 5, 7, 8, 9, 10, 11, 12, 14

JACKSON

Milbank

3045 Bank Street, 70748
(504) 634-5901

Built in 1836, Milbank is a romantic antebellum mansion with irresistible charm. Sleep in a queen-size canopied Mallard bed. Historic walking tour includes homes, churches, cemeteries, commemorative area, museum, winery, and antique shops.

Milbank

Hostess: Marjorie Collamer
Rooms: 3 (PB) $75
Suite: 1 (SB) $125
Full Breakfast
Credit Cards: A, B, D
Notes: 2, 5, 7, 8, 9, 12

KENNER (NEW ORLEANS)

Seven Oaks Plantation

2600 Gay Lynn Drive, 70065
(504) 888-8649

This 10,000-square-foot West Indies-style home overlooking the lake is convenient to the airport and is 20 minutes from the New Orleans French Quarter. Guest rooms open into a large living room and onto 12-foot galleries. A full plantation breakfast is served and the entire home can be toured. Antiques and Mardi Gras memorabilia are found throughout. Seven Oaks offers southern hospitality and makes guests' visits full of warm, pleasant memories.

NOTES: Credit cards accepted: A MasterCard; B Visa; C American Express; D Discover; E Diner's Club; F Other; 2 Personal checks accepted; 3 Lunch available; 4 Dinner available; 5 Open all year; 6 Pets welcome; 7 No smoking; 8 Children welcome; 9 Social drinking allowed; 10 Tennis nearby; 11 Swimming nearby; 12 Golf nearby; 13 Skiing nearby; 14 May be booked through a travel agent; 15 Handicapped accessible.

Hosts: Kay and Henry Andressen
Rooms: 2 (PB) $95-115
Full and Continental Breakfast
Credit Cards: A, B, C
Notes: 2, 5, 7, 8, 9, 12, 14

LAFAYETTE

Alida's: A Bed and Breakfast

2631 SE Evangeline Throughway,70508-2168
(318) 264-1191; (800) 9 CAJUN 7 (922-5867)
e-mail:info@alidas.com
www.alidas.com

In the heart of Cajun Country, Alida's is characterized by the gracious hospitality that its innkeepers provide. They give generously of themselves, making every guest feel comfortable, at ease, and at home. At the end of the day, guests can slip into one of the huge antique claw-foot tubs, sip a glass of wine in the parlor, or just relax on one of the swings on the front porch or rear patio. Smoking outside only.

Hosts: Tanya and Douglas Greenwald
Rooms: 4 (PB) $75-150
Full Breakfast
Credit Cards: A, B, C, D
Notes: 2, 3, 4, 7, 9, 10, 12, 14

Maison Mouton

402 Garfield Street, 70501
(318) 234-4661; FAX (318) 235-6755

Twelve beautiful guest rooms furnished with wonderful, heavenly carved bedroom sets made of mahogany and oak, with superb canopied beds. All jewels of Louisiana and symbols of the mid-19th century gifted craftsmen. Downtown one-half block from the children's museum. Near the Natural History Museum and world-famous restaurants. Full breakfast is served by friendly and attentive hosts with the typical French touch.

Host: Karen deLaunay
Rooms: 14 (8 PB; 7 SB) $50-85
Full Breakfast
Credit Cards: A, B
Notes: 5, 8, 9, 12

NAPOLEONVILLE

Madewood Plantation House

4250 Highway 308, 70390
(504) 369-7151

A national historic landmark, Madewood is a stately Greek Revival mansion on Bayou Lafourche about 75 miles from New Orleans's French Quarter. Set on 20 acres in front of a working sugar cane plantation, Madewood is furnished with antiques. Bedrooms have canopied beds. Guests eat southern specialties by candlelight, family-style, after a wine and cheese party in the library. Featured in *Country Home*, *Country Inns* (cover story, one of the 12 best of the year), and *National Geographic Traveler* (one of the South's five featured inns). All accommodations include a full breakfast and dinner for two. Closed Thanksgiving, Christmas, and New Year's.

Hosts: Keith and Millie Marshall
Rooms: 8 (PB) $215
Full Breakfast
Credit Cards: A, B, C, D
Notes: 2, 4, 7, 8, 9, 14

NATCHITOCHES

Breazeale House Bed and Breakfast

926 Washington Street, 71457
(318) 352-5630; (800) 352-5631

Built for Congressman Phanor Breazeale in the late 1800s, Breazeale House is within walking distance of the historic downtown district. This Victorian home features 11 fireplaces, 12-foot ceilings, 9 stained-glass windows, a set of servants' stairs, 3 balconies, 8 bedrooms, and 3 floors with over 6,000 square feet of living space. President Taft slept here, and this house can be seen in *Steel Magnolias*.

Hosts: Willa and Jack Freeman
Rooms: 4 (PB) $70-85
Full Breakfast
Credit Cards: A, B, C
Notes: 2, 5, 7, 8, 9, 10, 11, 12, 14

NOTES: Credit cards accepted: A MasterCard; B Visa; C American Express; D Discover; E Diner's Club; F Other; 2 Personal checks accepted; 3 Lunch available; 4 Dinner available; 5 Open all year; 6 Pets welcome;

Fleur de Lis

Fleur de Lis Bed and Breakfast Inn

336 Second Street, 71457
(318) 352-6621; (800) 489-6621

This grand old Victorian house is in the oldest settlement in the Louisiana Purchase and is listed in the National Register of Historic Places. Guests at the inn may expect a warm welcome, a room tastefully decorated with king- or queen-size bed, private bath, make-up vanity, sitting area, as well as the many amenities one expects in a friend's home. Delicious full breakfast with rich Louisiana coffee and orange juice.

Hosts: Tom and Harriette Palmer
Rooms: 5 (PB) $75
Full Breakfast
Credit Cards: A, B, C, D, E, F
Notes: 2, 5, 7, 8, 9, 10, 11, 12, 14

The Levy-East House Bed and Breakfast Inn

358 Jefferson Street, 71457
(800) 840-0662

A most luxurious bed and breakfast in the heart of the historic district. The beautiful Greek Revival house, circa 1838, has been recently restored and tastefully renovated to capture the spirit of an earlier time. Furnished with fine antiques that have been in the house for over 100 years. The Levy-East House offers a gourmet breakfast, queen-size bed, private whirlpool bath, telephone, and TV and VCR in each room. Private parking. Enjoy elegant rooms and luxurious leisure.

Hosts: Judy and Avery East
Rooms: 4 (PB) $105-200
Full Breakfast
Credit Cards: A, B
Notes: 2, 5, 7, 9, 10, 11, 12

NEW ORLEANS

Beau Séjour Bed and Breakfast

1930 Napoleon Avenue, 70115
(504) 897-3746; (888) 897-9398
FAX (504) 891-3340; e-mail: bosejour@aol.com

This turn-of-the-century mansion is uptown on the Mardi Gras parade route and near the historic streetcar that carries guests to the French Quarter, convention center, Superdome, aquarium, and universities. Beau Séjour boasts a casual, tropical atmosphere with spacious rooms, queen-size beds, and antiques, embodying the charm and ambiance of old New Orleans.

Hosts: Gilles and Kim Gagnon
Rooms: 5 (PB) $99-150
Continental Breakfast
Credit Cards: B, C
Notes: 2, 8, 9, 10, 11, 12, 14

Bed and Breakfast & Beyond Reservation Service

3225 Napoleon Avenue, 70125
(504) 822-8525; (800) 886-3709
FAX (504) 822-8547; e-mail: Mshimon@ibm.net
www.nolabandb.com

Corporate Suites. Suites in a relaxed, friendly atmosphere in the French Quarter. Pool, private voice mail, business services. Continental breakfast. $90-129.

1880s Italianate. In picturesque midcity, this renovated home is an art lover's delight.

Pickled floors, 14-foot ceilings, and a short stroll to the fairgrounds, home to the Jazz and Heritage Festival. Personal checks accepted. Open year-round. No smoking. Children welcome. Social drinking allowed. Tennis, swimming, and golf nearby. Rates may differ during special events. Continental breakfast. $95-125.

Esplanade Ridge. This beautiful Eastlake Victorian romantically set along oak-lined avenue close to the French Quarter offers a suite decorated with European antiques. Kitchen. Southern hospitality at its best. Continental breakfast. $130

French Quarter 1. Luxury suite on one of the most exciting streets in the world. This two-bedroom suite boasts its own balcony and special glimpse into the French Quarter. Personal checks accepted. Open year-round. No smoking. Children welcome. Social drinking allowed. Tennis, swimming, and golf nearby. Rates may differ during special events. Continental breakfast. $175-325.

French Quarter 2. This 1880 Greek Revival has been renovated to its original grandeur. The guest suite offers stunning views of the French Quarter. Cottage opening onto beautiful courtyard also available. Continental breakfast. $125-140.

Garden District Carriage House 1. Nestled in a secluded courtyard, this 1870s carriage house beckons guests. A spiral staircase leads guests from the living area, complete with pullman kitchen, to a separate area containing the bedroom and bath. Personal checks accepted. Open year-round. No smoking. Children welcome. Social drinking allowed. Tennis, swimming, and golf nearby. Rates may differ during special events. Continental breakfast. $125.

Garden District Carriage House 2. This two-story bed and breakfast has a balcony, outdoor whirlpool and gazebo. Enjoy the walking tours along the beautiful, colorful streets in the Garden District. Continental breakfast. $125-140.

Grandeur and Comfort. On one of the most beautiful avenues in uptown New Orleans rests this renovated southern mansion. From the stunning stairwell leading to the second floor, to the high ceilings and polished wood floor, this is a bed and breakfast classic in style without sacrificing its welcoming comfort. Personal checks accepted. Open year-round. No smoking. Children welcome. Social drinking allowed. Tennis, swimming, and golf nearby. Rates may differ during special events. Continental plus breakfast. $105-150.

Uptown Mansion. Resting on the most picturesque avenue off St. Charles Avenue. Quiet elegance and friendly charm. Guests love this homey atmosphere and grand architecture. Private baths. Close to streetcar. $100-150.

Uptown Victorian. Renovated to show elegance and comfort among the 14-foot ceilings and balconies. Suites with Jacuzzi. Guests can expect fresh flowers and "roll out the red carpet" services. Continental breakfast. $100-150.

Uptown Victorian Steamboat Mansion. Experience southern hospitality at its best. From the grand beveled glass entrance hall and period billiard room to the formal dining room and enticing swimming pool, guests will marvel at the gracious and welcoming appeal. Three suites with individual appeal. Personal checks accepted. Open year-round. No smoking. Children welcome. Social drinking allowed. Tennis, swimming, and golf nearby. Rates may differ during special events. Continental plus breakfast. $130-150.

Bed and Breakfast Inc.

1021 Moss Street, Box 52257, 70152-2257
(504) 488-4640; (800) 729-4640
FAX (504) 488-4639
e-mail: bedbreak@gnofn.org

Bayou St. John Home. This home is of the "box step cottage" design typical of this area. Its street is named after scenic Bayou St. John which passes nearby. Several small French cafés, coffee shop, and New Orleans Museum of Art are just a stroll away. Friendly hosts enjoy collecting everything from Mardi Gras memorabilia to antique match books. Bus to the French Quarter and downtown where convention centers are nearby in under 15 minutes (5 minutes by car). Continental breakfast. $50-80.

The Chimes. A special place filled with romance and decorated with antiques and architectural details, the cottages look onto a patio and antique swing. The streetcar is downtown at the French Quarter in just 15 minutes. Guests enjoy antiques, famous bistros, and music nearby. Two cottages with private baths; three guest rooms with private baths. Continental breakfast. $60-125.

Desoto Suite. Built in the 1880s, this raised Victorian home displays the architectural charm so typical of New Orleans cottages. Set in an area of ongoing restorations. Several small French restaurants, a specialty coffee shop, and a gourmet grocery-deli are nearby. Along the banks of Bayou St. John is City Park, one of America's largest metropolitan parks and home of the New Orleans Museum of Art. A New Orleans native, the host gladly shares his extensive knowledge of the city. Guest suite is spacious with separate entrance and kitchenette. Continental breakfast. $75-95.

The Dive Inn. Once a scuba diving school, once a gymnasium for the family of the Mexican ambassador to the United States in the early 1900s, this interesting building is now an eclectic bed and breakfast. Guests enter a large atrium which is dominated by an indoor heated swimming pool and large bar where guests sit for Continental breakfast or after a morning swim. The hosts' unique taste is evident everywhere. $70-125.

French Quarter Lanaux House. Featured in 1997 *Country Inns Bed & Breakfast* magazine's 10th anniversary issue, this magnificent Renaissance Revival mansion is a favorite background for movies filmed in New Orleans. The host first fell in love with her home at age 17, but not until years later did she purchase her dream. Her restoration includes the return of original pieces and warrants high national regard. A private entrance leads to each guest suite. Continental breakfast. $96-276.

Guest Suite in Greek Revival Cottage. Greek Revival cottage offers a well-appointed guest apartment with its own private entrance overlooking the swimming pool. Hosts have tastefully decorated their home. The streetcar ride to downtown is just 10 minutes. A short walk takes guests to other attractions. One bedroom with private bath. Continental breakfast. $50-90.

La Maison Marigny. In the French Quarter area, this petite bed and breakfast inn dates from the 19th century. Each bedroom has Old World charm, designer fabrics, and private bath. Enjoy Continental breakfast downstairs or outside in the traditional New Orleans patio. Guests may relax in their own French Quarter retreat or stroll to see Jackson Square's street performers and artists. Famous restaurants, jazz clubs, antique shoppes, galleries, and much more are nearby. $85-105.

Parkview Marigny. Just at the edge of the French Quarter, this side-hall Creole home affords a serene location steps from the action. The house was built in the middle 1800s and exhibits a lot of historic, original architectural detail. Guest bedrooms have beautiful antique or antique reproduction beds and private bathrooms. The charming hosts enjoy helping guests plan their stay. They are experts on local history and love to share knowledge of the area. $80-110.

St. Charles Avenue Home. Hosts love sharing their enthusiasm for New Orleans in a historic, homespun setting. Walking distance to the interesting Riverbend area with its specialty shops, coffee houses, and popular restaurants. The host was born in this house that boasts some of the original antiques. Two bedrooms with hall bath; Continental breakfast. $60-70.

Southern Comfort. This 100-year-old raised cottage is just two blocks to the St. Charles Avenue streetcar. Guests stroll or streetcar to galleries, specialty shops, restaurants, and more. Recently renovated, the home reflects lovely architectural details in its inlaid hardwood floors and large windows—New Orleans ambiance. After living around the world, the host returned to enjoy her city and spend time with her family. Her knowledge and enthusiasm are a boon to guests! Continental breakfast. $90-115.

Bougainvillea House

841 Bourbon Street, 70116
(504) 522-3983

Antique ambiance with all of the modern conveniences in the heart of the French Quarter. Off-street parking, cable TV, balconies, patios, elegant decor, central air and heat, private telephones, walk to riverboats, bars, restaurants, aquarium, and the convention center.

Host: Flo Cairo
Rooms: 3 (PB) $90-200
Continental Breakfast
Credit Cards: B, C
Notes: 5, 7, 9, 12

The Cornstalk Hotel

915 Royal Street, 70116
(504) 523-1515; FAX (504) 522-5558

A small but elegant national register hotel in the heart of the French Quarter. The early 1800s home of Judge François Xavier-Martin, first Chief Justice of the Louisiana Supreme Court and author of the first history of Louisiana. Location is central to the sights, sounds, gourmet foods, and night life of old New Orleans. Guests may enjoy their complimentary Continental breakfast and morning newspaper in their room, on the front gallery, balcony, or patio.

The Cornstalk Hotel

Hosts: Debi and David Spencer
Rooms: 14 (PB) $75-165
Continental Breakfast
Credit Cards: A, B, C
Notes: 5, 8, 9, 10, 12

The Cotton Brokers Houses of Esplanade Avenue "Benachi House" and "Esplanade Villa"

2216 Esplanade Avenue, 70119
(504) 525-7040; (800) 308-7040
FAX (504) 525-9760; e-mail: cotton@nolabb.com
www.nolabb.com

Choose from the distinctive bed and breakfasts of Esplanade Avenue. Sensitive restorations of classic New Orleans homes. Rooms and suites. Private baths. Gardens, patios, and porches. Delightful gourmet breakfast. Secure, free parking. Convenient

NOTES: Credit cards accepted: A MasterCard; B Visa; C American Express; D Discover; E Diner's Club; F Other; 2 Personal checks accepted; 3 Lunch available; 4 Dinner available; 5 Open all year; 6 Pets welcome;

The Cotton Brokers

to French Quarter and central business district. Triples and small groups welcome.

Hosts: James G. Derbes and Cecilia J. Rau
Rooms: 9 (7 PB; 2 SB) $105-175
Full Breakfast
Credit Cards: A, B, C, D
Notes: 2, 5, 7, 8, 9, 10, 12, 14

The Dusty Mansion

2231 General Pershing, 70115
(504) 895-4576; FAX (504) 891-0049

Rooms in this turn-of-the-century home have hardwood floors and are uniquely decorated with a New Orleans flavor. Amenities include ceiling fans and air conditioning. Sun deck on third floor. Pool table. Enclosed hot tub. Close to historic St. Charles streetcar, which provides easy access to French Quarter, aquarium, Garden District, zoo, and more. Excellent restaurants nearby.

Host: Cynthia Riggs
Rooms: 4 (2 PB; 2 SB) $50-75
Continental Breakfast
Credit Cards: A, B, C, D
Notes: 2, 5, 8, 9, 10, 12, 14

The Glimmer Inn

1631 Seventh Street, 70115
(504) 897-1895

This restored 1891 Victorian home features 12-foot cove ceilings, cypress woodwork, side and front galleries, wraparound porch, and enclosed brick patio. Across the street from the Garden District, just a half-block to St. Charles streetcar, and easy access to French Quarter and Audubon Park and Zoo. A private carriage house is also available. All rooms are air conditioned. Continental plus breakfast served.

Hosts: Sharon Agiewich and Cathy Andros
Rooms: 6 (1 PB; 5 SB) $70-85
Continental Breakfast
Credit Cards: None
Notes: 2, 5, 6, 8, 9, 10, 12, 14

The Glimmer Inn

Hotel St. Pierre

911 Burgundy Street, 70116
(504) 524-4401; (800) 535-7785

Hotel St. Pierre embodies the architecture and ambiance of the 18th-century French Quarter. The 75 guest rooms and suites are set among courtyards and swimming pools. Each morning, complimentary coffee and doughnuts await guests in the Louis Armstrong Breakfast Room. Two blocks off Bourbon Street and all that jazz!

Host: James Lentz
Rooms: 75 (PB) $109-159
Continental Breakfast
Credit Cards: A, B, C, D, E
Notes: 5, 8, 9, 10, 11, 12, 14

Hotel Villa Convento— In the French Quarter

616 Ursulines Street, 70116
(504) 522-1793; FAX (504) 524-1902
e-mail: convento@aol.com
www.neworleansonline.convento.html

Family-owned and -operated like European pensions, this Creole townhouse was built in 1848. All rooms have full baths, TVs, and telephones. Complimentary croissant, coffee, and tea. Some rooms have balconies. Spanish also spoken. On-street parking. Nightly rate based on occupancy in season.

Hosts: Lela, Larry, and Warren Campo
Rooms: 25 (PB) $79-155
Continental Breakfast
Credit Cards: A, B, C, D, E
Notes: 2, 5, 9, 14

Lafitte Guest House

1003 Bourbon Street, 70116
(504) 581-2678; (800) 331-7971
www.lafitteguesthouse.com

This elegant French manor house, in the heart of the French Quarter, is meticulously restored to its original splendor and furnished in fine antiques and reproductions. Every modern convenience, including air conditioning, is provided for guests' comfort. Complimentary Continental breakfast; wine and hors d'oeuvres at cocktail hour. On-site parking at $9.00 per night.

Host: Dr. Robert Guyton
Rooms: 14 (PB) $89-179
Continental Breakfast
Credit Cards: A, B, C, D, E, F
Notes: 5, 7, 8, 9, 11, 12, 14

Lafitte Guest Hotel

La Maison

La Maison

608-10 Kerlerec Street, 70116
(504) 271-0228 (phone/FAX); (800) 307-7179

Built in 1805 by Bernard De Marigny in the historical area called Faubourg Marigny, an area of architectural significance with the Creole cottage as the predominant form of early development. All suites include private baths, parlor with color cable TV and telephone, and bedroom. Special events rates are given upon request. Cancellation policy is seven days' advance notice.

Host: Alma F. Hulin
Suites: 8 (PB) $85-165
Continental Breakfast
Credit Cards: A, B, C, D
Notes: 2, 5, 7, 9, 14

NOTES: Credit cards accepted: A MasterCard; B Visa; C American Express; D Discover; E Diner's Club; F Other; 2 Personal checks accepted; 3 Lunch available; 4 Dinner available; 5 Open all year; 6 Pets welcome;

Macarty Park Guest House/Historic Homes

3820 Burgundy Street, 70117-5708
(504) 943-4994; (800) 521-2790
e-mail: macpar@aol.com
www.macartypark.com

Feel right at home in a century-old classic Victorian guest house and cottages just five minutes from the French Quarter. Step out of your room into lush tropical gardens and jump into the sparkling heated swimming pool. Rooms are tastefully decorated in antique, reproduction, or contemporary furnishings, each with private bath, color cable TV, telephone, and air conditioning. Free parking. Full gym.

Host: John Maher
Rooms: 8 (PB) $45-160
Continental Breakfast
Credit Cards: A, B, C, D
Notes: 5, 9, 11, 14

Melrose Mansion

937 Esplanade Avenue, 70116
(504) 944-2255

The Melrose is an 1884 Victorian mansion that has been completely restored to perfection. This opulent, galleried mansion features nine antique-filled guest rooms with luxurious private baths, spacious heated pool and tropical patio, whirlpools, and wet bars with refrigerators in the rooms. Cocktail hour and a Creole breakfast. New Orleans grandeur at its very finest. Limited smoking.

Melrose Mansion

Hosts: Melvin and Rosemary Jones
Rooms: 8 (PB) $225-425
Full Breakfast
Credit Cards: A, B, C, D
Notes: 2, 5, 9, 11, 14

New Orleans Bed and Breakfast and Accommodations: A Reservation Service

P.O. Box 8163, New Orleans, 70182
(504) 838-0071; FAX (504) 838-0140
e-mail: smb@neworleansbandb.com
www.neworleansbandb.com

Grand Home. Magnificent home in historic district one block to streetcar line. Executives, VIPs, families, couples or friends traveling together can experience the best the hosts have to offer in this beautiful home with room for six people. Fifteen-foot ceilings, lush gardens, antiques, and modern amenities. Available for weekly and monthly rentals.

A2. A stately Spanish home just steps off St. Charles Avenue and streetcar line. Three bedrooms and three baths. Hostess shares beautiful living area with guests. Continental breakfast and pool. $100.

A3. On the third floor in a newly renovated Victorian home, the hosts have created an airy haven for their guests' pleasure. A double bed and private bath accommodate two. A Continental breakfast is served downstairs or on a tray in the room. $85.

A4. A short distance from French Quarter and downtown, one block from St. Charles Avenue, the streetcar line, and the Garden

District. A late-1800s house, newly renovated, has two bedrooms with shared bath. The guests are welcome into the comfortable living/dining area. A Continental breakfast is provided for guest enjoyment. $75.

CP1. In the historic district of the city and to the rear of an 1890 Creole cottage is a spacious efficiency apartment with double bed, double sofa bed, private bath, kitchenette, and private entrance. Walking distance to the Museum of Art, St. Louis Cemetery, plantation homes, and the beautiful 150-year-old oaks in City Park. Continental breakfast. $65-75.

CP2. A comfortable one-bedroom apartment, completely private with twin beds and a fully furnished kitchen. A double sofa bed is in the living room. Walk to activities in City Park or catch a bus to the French Quarter. No smoking. Continental breakfast. $90-100.

FM1. Five blocks to French Quarter. Apartment with private entrance off beautiful garden with pool. Living/dining/kitchen area, bedroom with twin beds and private bath. Additional half-bath. Continental breakfast. $85-150.

GE1. On this tree-shaded boulevard, one large brick house has three bedrooms. The master bedroom is done in rose and black, has five tall windows, king-size bed, and private bath. Two other rooms share a bath. Continental breakfast. $65-75.

GE2. A pretty cottage has a king-size bed or two twin beds, a kitchen, bath, and loads of off-street parking. Continental breakfast. $65-75.

LV2. In a delightful lake-view subdivision, a cozy bungalow offers one bedroom with twin beds and private bath, private entrance, and off-street parking. The guests will find a restful den and lovely back yard garden. Continental breakfast. $60-75.

UP4. One moderately priced, luxurious home is near first-class restaurants. Two bedrooms with private baths. Hostess loves to travel. Continental breakfast. $75.

UP6. In a lovely uptown home with serene atmosphere is a large two-bedroom and bath suite, one with king-size bed and the other with a queen-size bed. Antiques, private entrance. Just steps away from St. Charles Avenue and streetcar line. Continental breakfast. $75.

UP10. This renovated historic uptown residence was once a plantation home. It consists of five bedrooms, each with a private bath. Built in 1840, the house is furnished with antiques or reproductions of antiques. Three bedrooms have queen-size beds. A fourth bedroom has a king-size bed and one twin bed. The fifth bedroom has a double Edwardian bed. One block from St. Charles Avenue and the streetcar line. Near many fine restaurants. Continental breakfast. $95-135.

UP11. Guests in this historic 1840 home enjoy a suite that has a sitting room overlooking the pool, a spacious bedroom with a king-size bed, two marble bathrooms, and a wet bar. The sitting area is furnished with a day bed that accommodates two singles or another couple. $95.

UP11A. Adjoining this property is another newly restored home. One bedroom has private bath, and two bedrooms have shared bath. A common sitting room. Suitable for three congenial couples or a family. Continental breakfast is served in the dining room of the main house or on the veranda. $65-75.

UP12. Near the historic streetcar line, a cozy guest house is often available for the enjoyment of guests. There is a living room, kitchen/dining area, and bath. Breakfast is in the refrigerator for guests' convenience. $95.

UP13. In a historic uptown neighborhood is a beautifully restored home with two rooms on the second floor. Both have private baths. One has a queen-size bed and one has a twin bed. Continental plus breakfast. Near streetcar line. $95.

UP15. An apartment on the lower level of owner's home with a private entrance. Two bedrooms, a living and dining area, kitchen, and one independent bath. French doors open to patio. Two blocks to St. Charles Avenue and streetcar. $150.

New Orleans First Bed and Breakfast (Essem's House)

3660 Gentilly Boulevard, 70122
(504) 947-3401; (888) 240-0070
FAX (504) 838-0140
e-mail: smb@neworleansbandb.com

New Orleans First Bed and Breakfast (Essem's House) is a 10-room Mediterranean style on a boulevard lined with majestic live oak trees. It is furnished in Art Deco and traditional styles. Guests are welcome to relax, watch TV, or visit with each other in the spacious living room. Especially cozy in winter with the fire flickering. Books on many topics are available for guests' perusal (if they have time in New Orleans). Safe. Off-street parking. Children over 10 welcome.

Host: Sarah Margaret Brown
Rooms: 4 (2 PB; 2 SB) $55-65
Suite: $120
Continental Breakfast
Credit Cards: A, B, C, D, F
Notes: 5, 7, 10, 11, 12, 14, 15

New Orleans Guest House

1118 Ursulines Street, 70116
(504) 566-1177; (800) 562-1177

An 1848 Creole cottage with lush courtyard where a complimentary Continental breakfast is served each morning. Private baths, free parking, tastefully decorated with antiques or contemporary furnishings, air conditioning, telephones, and TV. Three blocks to famous Bourbon Street.

Hosts: Ray and Alvin
Rooms: 14 (PB) $79-99
Continental Breakfast
Credit Cards: A, B, C
Notes: 5

Nine-O-Five Royal Hotel

905 Royal Street, 70116
(504) 523-0219

This quaint European-style hotel is in the heart of the French Quarter. One of the first smaller hotels in the French Quarter. Built in the 1890s, the Nine-O-Five has a courtyard and balconies overlooking the southern charm and hospitality of Royal Street. Period furnishings, high ceilings, and kitchenettes in all rooms.

Rooms and Suites: 10 (PB) $75-125 and up
Credit Cards: A, B
Notes: 5, 8

The Prytania Inn

1415 Prytania Street, 70130
(504) 566-1515

Restored to its pre-Civil War glory, this inn in the historic district received the 1984 Commission Award. Tender care; full gourmet breakfast. Patio, slave quarters, 18 rooms with private baths, and most with kitchen facilities or microwave and refrigerator. Five minutes to the French Quarter and one-block walk to St. Charles Avenue and the streetcar. Free parking. Hosts speak German. Nonsmoking rooms available.

Hosts: Sally and Peter Schreiber
Rooms: 18 (PB) $35-55
Full Breakfast
Credit Cards: A, B, C, D, E, F
Notes: 2, 3, 5, 6, 8, 9, 10, 11, 15

Terrell House

1441 Magazine Street, 70130
(504) 524-9859 (phone/FAX); (800) 878-9859
www.lacajun.com/terrellhouse.htm/

Terrell House was built in the Classical Revival style in 1858 by Richard Terrell as his family residence. The main mansion rooms are the original bedrooms of the house. Original carriage house has been converted to four guest rooms. The house contains oriental rugs, marble mantels, gold-leaf mirrors. Gaslight-era chandeliers and lamps grace every room, along with Mardi Gras memorabilia to recreate the ambiance of Old New Orleans.

Hosts: Bobby and Cindy Hogan
Rooms: 10 (PB) $85-200
Full Breakfast
Credit Cards: A, B, C
Notes: 2, 5, 7, 9, 10, 12, 14

NEW ROADS

Pointe Coupee Bed and Breakfast—Samson House

405 Richey Street, 70760-3451
(504) 638-6254; FAX (504) 638-6060

National register home featured in *Country Victorian* magazine, circa 1835. In historic district near lake with dining and shopping. Lovely Creole plantation house with private courtyard and fireplace on patio. Owners have collection of antiques and collectibles to browse. Jim is a veteran of U.S. Air Force missile program, and Sam is an interior designer. A full southern breakfast is served in high style in formal dining room or on gallery.

Hosts: Jim McVea and Lynda "Sam" McVea
Rooms: 2 (PB) $100
Full Breakfast
Credit Cards: A, B
Notes: 5, 7, 9, 10, 11, 12, 14

PRAIRIEVILLE

Tree House in the Park

16520 Airport Drive, 70769
(800) LE CABIN (532-2246)

A Cajun cabin in the swamp, high among the cypress trees and Spanish moss. Three guest rooms each have a private deck with a hot tub, queen-size waterbed, private bath, and a small refrigerator. A Cajun supper is served the evening of arrival, as well as a full breakfast each morning. The Tree House sits among four large ponds on five wooded acres. The bed and breakfast is perfect for a honeymoon hideaway, birthday surprise, or for rest and relaxation.

Hosts: Vic and Vikki Hotopp
Rooms: 3 (PB) $125-150
Full Breakfast
Credit Cards: A, B, C, D
Notes: 2, 3, 5, 7, 9, 11, 14

ST. FRANCISVILLE

Barrow House Inn

9779 Royal Street, Box 700, 70775-0700
(504) 635-4791

Sip wine and relax in a wicker rocker on the front porch while enjoying the ambiance of a quiet neighborhood of antebellum homes. Guest rooms are all furnished in beautiful antiques from 1840 to

Barrow House

NOTES: Credit cards accepted: A MasterCard; B Visa; C American Express; D Discover; E Diner's Club; F Other; 2 Personal checks accepted; 3 Lunch available; 4 Dinner available; 5 Open all year; 6 Pets welcome;

1870. Delicious gourmet candlelight dinners are available upon request, and a cassette walking tour of the historic district is included for guests.

Hosts: Shirley Dittloff and Chris Dennis
Rooms: 5 (PB) $85-105
Suites: 3 (PB) $130-150
Full or Continental Breakfast
Credit Cards: A, B, D
Notes: 2, 4, 5, 7, 8, 9, 12, 14

Butler Greenwood Plantation

8345 U.S. Highway 61, 70775
(504) 635-6312; FAX (504) 635-6370
e-mail: ButlerGree@aol.com
www.butlergreenwood.com

The 1790s plantation in English Louisiana is still owned and occupied by original family. Full of priceless antiques. Listed in National Register of Historic Places. Overnight accommodations in six private cottages on peaceful grounds. Pool, pond, plenty of live oaks, and gardens. Cottages all have baths, kitchens, porches or decks, cable TV, ceiling fans. Some have Jacuzzis and fireplaces. Rates include breakfast and tour of main antebellum home.

Host: Anne Butler
Rooms: 6 (PB) $100-110
Continental Breakfast
Credit Cards: A, B, C
Notes: 2, 5, 6, 8, 9, 11, 12, 14

Lake Rosemound Inn

10473 Lindsey Lane, 70775
(504) 635-3176; FAX (504) 635-2224

Amid towering trees and rolling hills Lake Rosemound Inn, on picturesque Lake Rosemound, is midway between Baton Rouge and Natchez, Mississippi, in the heart of plantation country. All four beautifully decorated rooms have lake views. For guests' enjoyment amenities include: king- and queen-size beds, fireplace, Jacuzzis for two, air conditioning, TV, canoe, paddleboat, fishing gear, hammocks, porch swings, and famous "help yourself" ice cream parlor with Brunswick pool table.

Lake Rosemound Inn

Full country breakfast. Smoking permitted outside only.

Host: Jeane Peters
Rooms: 4 (PB) $75-105
Full Breakfast
Credit Cards: A, B, C, D
Notes: 2, 5, 6, 7, 8, 9, 11, 12, 15

ST. MARTINVILLE

Old Castillo Bed and Breakfast

220 Evangeline Boulevard, 70582
(318) 394-4010; (800) 621-3017
FAX (318) 394-7983; e-mail: phylin@worldnet.net

Beneath the moss-draped branches of the legendary Evangeline Oak, the Greek Revival structure of the Old Castillo Bed and Breakfast, circa 1825, rises from the banks of the historic Bayou Teche. Now both tourists and area residents can step back in time to share the warmth of Acadian culture and cuisine. Cherish time spent leisurely beside the slow-moving waters of

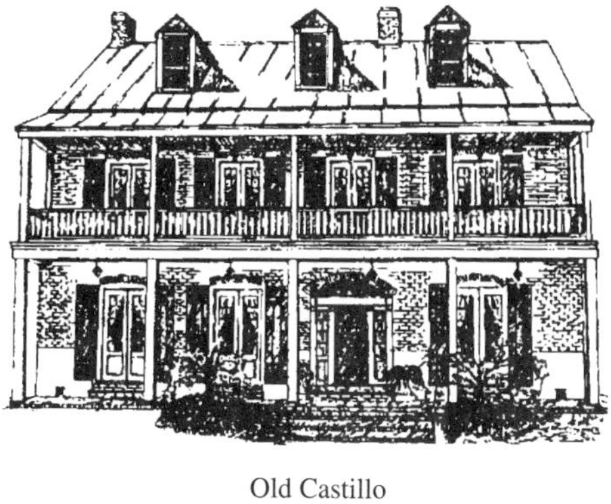

Old Castillo

7 No smoking; 8 Children welcome; 9 Social drinking allowed; 10 Tennis nearby; 11 Swimming nearby; 12 Golf nearby; 13 Skiing nearby; 14 May be booked through a travel agent; 15 Handicapped accessible.

Bayou Teche. Listed in the National Register of Historic Places since 1978.

Host: Peggy Hulin
Rooms: 5 (PB) $50-80
Full Breakfast
Credit Cards: A, B, C
Notes: 3, 4, 5, 8, 9, 10, 11, 12, 13, 14, 15

SHREVEPORT

The Columns on Jordan

615 Jordan, 71101-4748
(800) 801-4950; FAX (318) 459-1155
www.BBonline.com/la/columns

"We cordially invite you to be our guest at the Columns." Enjoy the time-honored traditions and gracious elegance of southern living amid the atmosphere of another era. "We look forward to welcoming you." Inquire about accommodations for children.

Rooms: 5 (3 PB; 2 SB) $85-125
Full Breakfast
Credit Cards: A, B, C, D
Notes: 2, 5, 7, 11, 12, 14

SLIDELL

Salmen-Fritchie House Bed and Breakfast

127 Cleveland Avenue, 70458
(504) 643-1405; (800) 235-4168

Built before the turn of the century by one of the founders of the city, this Victorian mansion is listed in the National Register of Historic Places. Just 30 minutes from New Orleans's famous French Quarter. Beautiful grounds have 300-year-old trees. Several bedrooms have fireplaces. All have private baths, telephones, and TVs. Beautiful period antique furnishings with huge poster beds. A cottage that sleeps two to four people has living room/kitchen combination, bedroom with marble Jacuzzi for two, a courtyard and screened porch, and laundry facilities. Smoking permitted on porches only. Children over 10 welcome.

Salmen-Fritchie House

Hosts: Sharon and Homer Fritchie
Rooms: 5 (PB) $85-95
Suites: $115-125
Cottage: $150
Full Breakfast
Credit Cards: A, B, C, D
Notes: 2, 5, 9, 10, 12

VACHERIE

Oak Alley Plantation, Restaurant, and Inn

3645 Highway 18 (Great River Road), 70090
(800) 44 ALLEY
e-mail: oakalleyplantation@worldnet.att.net
www.oakalleyplantation.com

Nowhere in the Mississippi Valley is there a more spectacular setting! Turn-of-the-century Creole cottages, decorated in a quaint country style, are on the grounds of Oak Alley Plantation, a national historic landmark. A full country breakfast is served in the restaurant from 8:30 to 10:30 A.M. Just one hour from New Orleans and Baton Rouge. Tours of the mansion are not included in rate.

Owner: Zeb Mayhew Jr.
Rooms: 5 (PB) $95-125
Full Breakfast
Credit Cards: A, B, C, D
Notes: 3, 5, 7, 8, 9, 14

Mississippi

BAY ST. LOUIS

Lincoln, Ltd.; Bed and Breakfast Mississippi

P.O. Box 3479, Meridian, 39303
(601) 482-5483 (information)
(800) 633-MISS (reservations)
FAX (601) 693-7447
e-mail: blincolnh@aol.com

79. Overlooking the Mississippi Sound Bay, this turn-of-the-century home welcomes guests to the ambiance and quaintness of Bay St. Louis. Enjoy the view from bay windows in the room or rock on the front porch and watch for dolphins playing in the water. All rooms decorated in the taste of their former owners. Seven rooms. Continental breakfast. Children accepted by arrangement. $75-85.

BELMONT

Natchez Trace Bed and Breakfast Reservation Service

P.O. Box 193, Hampshire, TN 38461
(931) 285-2777; (800) 377-2770
e-mail: natcheztrace@worldnet.att.net

Belmont Hotel. This Georgian-style hotel in downtown Belmont was built in 1924 and is six miles from the trace. It is newly restored, with all the comforts of a modern hotel, but with the charm and decor of an earlier, more gracious time. Truly a gem, with wide hallways, high ceilings, and a relaxing atmosphere. A Continental breakfast is served in the elegant dining room. Children welcome. $55-60.

BILOXI

The Old Santini House Bed and Breakfast

964 Beach Boulevard, 39530
(228) 436-4078; (800) 686-1146
www.waidsoft.com/santinibnb

The Old Santini House, listed in the National Register of Historic Places, was built in 1837. The hosts offer the perfect romantic getaway for newlyweds or just a special occasion. The exquisite furnishings feature a brass wet bar, lush leather furniture, king-size bed, and Jacuzzi tub. Wake up to the smell of freshly brewed coffee and sit down to a full breakfast on fine china. Guests will take home fond memories of their moonlight stroll on the beach with their loved one. Children over 12 welcome.

Hosts: James and Patricia Dunay
Rooms: 4 (PB) $100-150
Full Breakfast
Credit Cards: A, B, C
Notes: 2, 5, 7, 9, 11, 12

The Old Santini House

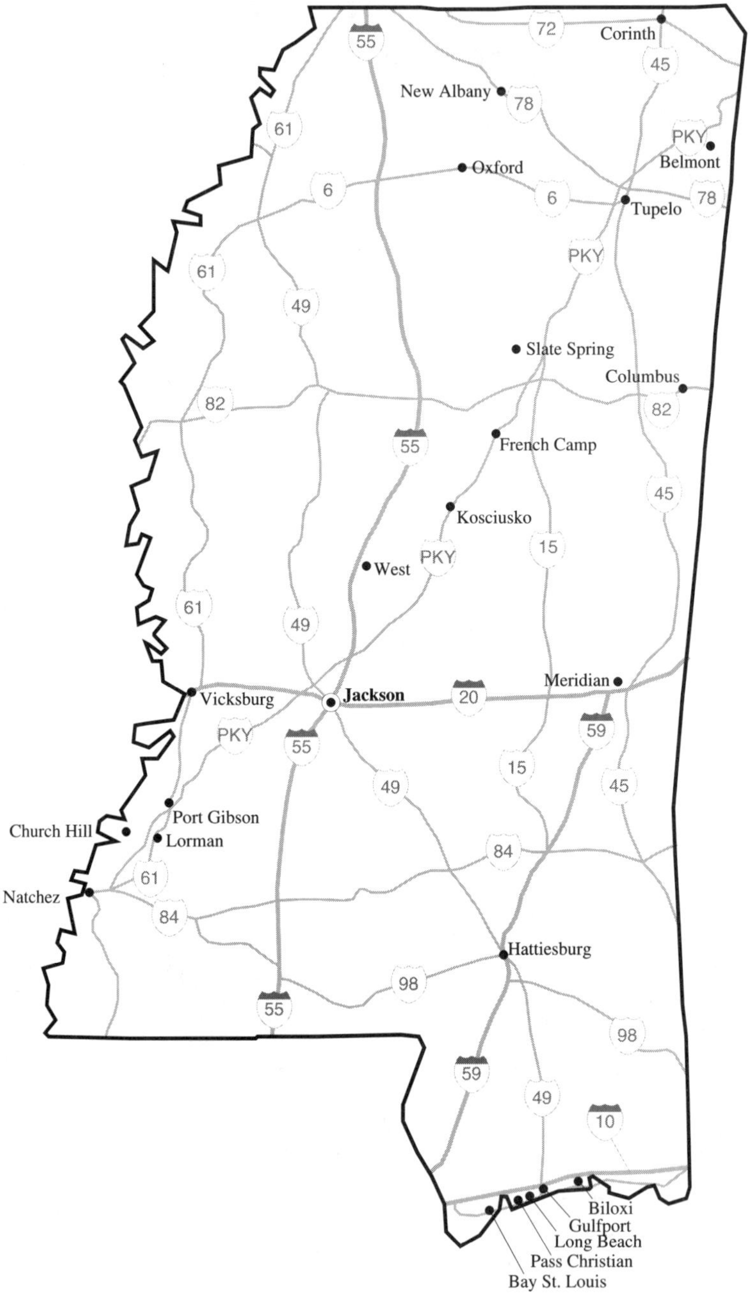

Mississippi

BILOXI (LONG BEACH)

Red Creek Inn, Vineyard and Racing Stable

7416 Red Creek Road, Long Beach, 39560
(228) 452-3080 (information)
(800) 729-9670 (reservations)

This three-story raised French cottage is on 11 acres of live oaks and magnolias. The 64-foot porch and six fireplaces add to the relaxing atmosphere of this circa 1899 brick-and-cypress home. English, French, and Victorian antiques, wooden radios, and a Victrola are for guests' use. Casinos are nearby. Vineyard and racing stable are under development. The inn is one and one-half miles south of I-10 off exit 28. Or from Beach Highway 90, via Espy Avenue in Long Beach or Menge Avenue in Pass Christian, then north on Red Creek Road. Biloxi is 20 minutes away and New Orleans an hour. Come bed and breakfast awhile! Continental plus breakfast served.

Hosts: Karl and "Toni" Mertz
Rooms: 7 (5 PB; 2 SB) $49-99
Continental Breakfast
Credit Cards: None
Notes: 2, 5, 7, 8, 9, 10, 11, 12, 14

CHURCH HILL

Natchez Trace Bed and Breakfast Reservation Service

P.O. Box 193, Hampshire, TN 38461
(931) 285-2777; (800) 377-2770
e-mail: natcheztrace@worldnet.att.net

The Cedars. Just north of Mount Locust, only six miles from the trace, overlooking 176 acres of wooded landscape, accented with beautiful moss-draped trees and ponds, this magnificent plantation home was previously owned by actor George Hamilton. There's a classic Greek Revival front section with a double gallery and white columns. A gracious southern plantation breakfast is served. Large bedrooms, one with a fireplace, and a third-floor suite with fireplace and Jacuzzi are available. $150-200.

COLUMBUS

Lincoln, Ltd.; Bed and Breakfast Mississippi

P.O. Box 3479, Meridian, 39303
(601) 482-5483 (information)
(800) 633-MISS (reservations)
FAX (601) 693-7447
e-mail: blincolnh@aol.com

5. This is a Federal-style house and the oldest brick house in Columbus. It was built in 1828, the same year Andrew Jackson was elected president. The house has been completely restored and is furnished with antiques of the period. Three bedrooms, each with private bath. Full breakfast is included. $100.

71. Enjoy this Italian villa-style home built in 1848 and owned by the family of the original builders. Furnished in period antiques and in the National Register of Historic Places. A full southern breakfast is served. Four guest rooms with private baths. $100.

CORINTH

Lincoln, Ltd.; Bed and Breakfast Mississippi

P.O. Box 3479, Meridian, 39303
(601) 482-5483 (information)
(800) 633-MISS (reservations)
FAX (601) 693-7447
e-mail: blincolnh@aol.com

37. A beautiful Victorian home, completely furnished with antiques. Convenient to

Memphis, Tennessee, and Shiloh National Military Park, a Civil War battlefield. A full southern breakfast is served to guests. Lunch and dinner are also available. Four guest rooms. $75-90.

75. Circa 1869, this southern-style Colonial house is on two acres of oak and dogwood in the city of Corinth. The host is a native of Oxford, England, and he and his wife are very knowledgeable about the area. Enjoy the original pine floors and walls of two-inch-thick planks. A full breakfast is served on the back veranda as guests relax in antique wicker furniture. Three guest rooms available. $85-90.

103. The aroma of freshly baked bread and cozy fireside chairs serve as a warm welcome at one of Corinth's finest homes. Built in 1892, this restored home is furnished with exquisite Victorian antiques. Outdoors, guests can enjoy the formal gardens, lawn games, and four verandas with fans, rockers, and swings. $75.

Natchez Trace Bed and Breakfast Reservation Service

P.O. Box 193, Hampshire, TN 38461
(931) 285-2777; (800) 377-2770
e-mail: natcheztrace@worldnet.att.net

Carriage House. This cottage, originally the carriage house for a wealthy cotton merchant, is now a charming and rustic retreat, offering two comfortable bedrooms with one bath, living/dining room, and full kitchen. (It is rented to only one traveling party at a time.) Screened-in porch overlooks old-fashioned gardens. Complimentary tour of the main house and its minimuseum, Continental breakfast, and afternoon refreshments. $65.

The General's Quarters. Milepost 320. Built circa 1870s. In the historic district of the old Civil War village of Corinth, near Battery Robinett and the site of Fort Williams. Only 22 miles from Shiloh National Military Park; host will be happy to tell guests all about the history of the area. Five rooms with private baths. Full southern breakfast is served. $75-90.

Robbins' Nest Bed and Breakfast. Milepost 270, 320, or 320-A. This southern Colonial-style home, circa 1870, is on two acres of oak trees, dogwoods, boxwoods, and azaleas in historic Corinth. Guests can enjoy a delicious breakfast on the back porch, relaxing in antique wicker furniture with veranda ceiling fans. Complimentary afternoon tea and refreshments are served on arrival. Convenient to Shiloh and Pickwick Lake and state park. $85.

Samuel D. Bramlitt House. Built in 1892 and just opened as a bed and breakfast, this home sits atop a hill, deserving of its reputation as a small town mansion. Wrapped in upper and lower verandas, perfect places for sipping homemade lemonade or iced tea. Guests will enjoy the rose gardens, fountain, and an old magnolia tree with a bench for resting in its shade. Five fireplaces, original walnut staircase, beautifully decorated. If guests call ahead, hosts may be able to serve guests dinner. $75.

Ravenswood Bed and Breakfast

1002 Douglas Street (at Linden), 38834-4227
(601) 665-0044

A 1929 Arts and Crafts-style home with spacious public areas featuring a fireplace, library, TV/VCR, and two porches with swings. Sited on one and one-half acres, the grounds contain Civil War earthworks and abundant wildlife. Antebellum and Victorian homes, Civil War walking tours, an information and visitor center, and museum are all within walking distance in historic downtown. Continental breakfast buffet in

Ravenswood

the breakfast room. Private guest rooms on second floor. Twenty-three miles to Shiloh National Military Park. Seasonal watersports and fishing at Pickwick Landing State Park, about 20 miles. Near the Natchez Trace. Inquire about accommodations for pets.

Hosts: Ron Wayne Smith and Timothy Hodges
Rooms: 3 (1 PB; 2 SB) $70-80
Continental Breakfast
Credit Cards: A, B
Notes: 2, 8, 9, 10, 11, 12

The Samuel D. Bramlitt House

1125 Cruise Street, 38834
(601) 286-5370; e-mail: thom112@avisa.com

Starry skies. Soft breezes. Sweet fragrance of magnolia and roses. The aroma of freshly baked bread. A good book. All offered at

The Samuel D. Bramlitt House

the Samuel D. Bramlitt House, circa 1892. Filled with antiques, this gracious and warm Victorian mansion promises visitors a return to days when life was not so hectic. Walk to Mississippi's oldest drug store and soda fountain. Explore streets lined with historic homes, steeped in Civil War history. Taste the world-famous "slug burgers." Water skiing nearby.

Hosts: Cindy and Kevin Thomas
Rooms: 5 (PB) $75
Full Breakfast
Credit Cards: A, B, C, D, F
Notes: 2, 4, 5, 7, 8, 10, 11, 12, 13

FRENCH CAMP

Natchez Trace Bed and Breakfast Reservation Service

P.O. Box 193, Hampshire, TN 38461
(931) 285-2777; (800) 377-2770
e-mail: natcheztrace@worldnet.att.net

French Camp Bed and Breakfast. Milepost 181. Two blocks from the trace, a rustic inn constructed from two century-old log cabins. Known as French Camp, this area is steeped in early trace history. Enjoy a breakfast of sorghum-soaked biscuits, creamy grits, fresh eggs, crispy bacon, and homemade jams and jellies. Hosts will share the tale of the origin of this historic two-story log cabin and their collection of quilts, antique books, and linens. $60.

GULFPORT

Magnolia Plantation

16391 Robinson Road, 39503-4817
(800) 700-7858; FAX (601) 832-3010

Thirty-two luxurious king- and queen-size rooms and suites that are on ground level and self-contained. Guests enjoy a tranquil backdrop of lakes and waterfalls and are only minutes from white-sand beaches, golf courses, casinos, and many

7 No smoking; 8 Children welcome; 9 Social drinking allowed; 10 Tennis nearby; 11 Swimming nearby; 12 Golf nearby; 13 Skiing nearby; 14 May be booked through a travel agent; 15 Handicapped accessible.

other exciting attractions. Complimentary in-room coffee, breakfast buffet, afternoon tea, and evening social hour. Corporate meetings, retreats, and receptions. Lunch and dinner available for groups. Heated pool and Jacuzzi. Complimentary local airport transportation. Arrange in advance.

Host: Ralph Burton
Rooms: 32 (PB) $85-150
Suites: $250
Full Breakfast
Credit Cards: A, B, C
Notes: 5, 7, 8, 9, 10, 11, 12, 14, 15

HATTIESBURG

Lincoln, Ltd.; Bed and Breakfast Mississippi

P.O. Box 3479, Meridian, 39303
(601) 482-5483 (information)
(800) 633-MISS (reservations)
FAX (601) 693-7447
e-mail: blincolnh@aol.com

80. In the historic neighborhood of Hattiesburg and in the National Register of Historic Places. Guests will enjoy this turn-of-the-century-style home with its 11 fireplaces and two-story wraparound porch. Guests are greeted with a complimentary drink and may enjoy the homemade jellies and preserves with their breakfast. Three rooms. $75 and up.

Tally House

402 Rebecca Avenue, 39401
(601) 582-3467

Tally House, a 1907 mansion with 13,000 square feet of floor space in a large national register district, has been restored to its original grandeur. The Tally House sits on large grounds with formal gardens, fountains, and statuary. Tally House is furnished throughout with antiques. Hosts are avid collectors; therefore, Tally House has something to interest everyone. Antiques, shopping malls, the zoo, three golf courses, the university, and nice restaurants within five minutes. Children over 12 welcome.

Rooms: 4 (PB) $60-75
Full Breakfast
Credit Cards: A, B
Notes: 2, 5, 7, 9, 10, 12, 14

JACKSON

Fairview Inn

734 Fairview Street, 39202
(601) 948-3429; (888) 948-1908
FAX (601) 948-1203
e-mail: fairview@fairviewinn.com
www.fairviewinn.com

A grand Colonial Revival mansion on national historic register offers luxury accommodations and fine dining for groups along with dataports and voice mail. Fairview Inn was named a Top Inn of 1994 by *Country Inns* magazine. AAA four-diamond-rated. "The Fairview Inn is southern hospitality at its best."—*Travel & Leisure.* Dinner available for groups.

Hosts: Carol and William Simmons
Rooms: 8 (PB) $115-165
Full Breakfast
Credit Cards: A, B, C, D
Notes: 2, 5, 7, 8, 9, 10, 12, 14, 15

Lincoln, Ltd.; Bed and Breakfast Mississippi

P.O. Box 3479, Meridian, 39303
(601) 482-5483 (information)
(800) 633-MISS (reservations)
FAX (601) 693-7447
e-mail: blincolnh@aol.com

50. Circa 1888. Step through the door and step back across 100 years into a graceful world of sparkling chandeliers and finely crafted furnishings in this 19th-century home. Mere moments away from the city's central business and government districts. Convenient to many of Jackson's finest shopping, dining, and entertainment opportunities. The bedrooms are individually decorated, each accompanied by a fully modern private bath. Eleven guest rooms. Single rates available. $85-180.

KOSCIUSKO

Lincoln, Ltd.; Bed and Breakfast Mississippi

P.O. Box 3479, Meridian, 39303
(601) 482-5483 (information)
(800) 633-MISS (reservations)
FAX (601) 693-7447
e-mail: blincolnh@aol.com

63. One of the finest examples of Queen Anne architecture, this historic inn stands as a visual example of the lifestyle and culture of 1884. Four lovely bedrooms, furnished with antiques. Lunch and dinner are available by reservation. Breakfast included. $75-125.

Natchez Trace Bed and Breakfast Reservation Service

P.O. Box 193, Hampshire, TN 38461
(931) 285-2777; (800) 377-2770
e-mail: natcheztrace@worldnet.att.net

Redbud Inn. Milepost 160. Stately two-story structure built in 1884, one of Kosciusko's finest examples of Queen Anne architecture, with a distinctive Victorian multicolor scheme, a three-story octagonal corner tower, and fishscale shingles. Houses a tea room as well, which serves lunch Monday through Friday, dinner by prior arrangement for guests. Only two miles from the trace. $75-100.

LONG BEACH

Lincoln, Ltd.; Bed and Breakfast Mississippi

P.O. Box 3479, Meridian, 39303
(601) 482-5483 (information)
(800) 633-MISS (reservations)
FAX (601) 693-7447
e-mail: blincolnh@aol.com

The Wilson House, circa 1922, rustic log construction, pine floors, large wraparound porch for enjoying warm, friendly breezes and the fresh southern air. Six guest rooms, two of which contain fireplaces with gas logs. Enjoy a hearty southern breakfast, welcoming beverage, and a cozy atmosphere. Children over 12 welcome. $55-110.

LORMAN

Lincoln, Ltd.; Bed and Breakfast Mississippi

P.O. Box 3479, Meridian, 39303
(601) 482-5483 (information)
(800) 633-MISS (reservations)
FAX (601) 693-7447
e-mail: blincolnh@aol.com

84. Circa 1855, this Italianate Revival home is on a working plantation. It is a wildlife preserve with guided jeep tours of the area, nature trails, and a heated swimming pool. Enjoy a wood-burning fireplace or stove and see wild deer or turkey on a tour or walking the nature trails. A full, seated breakfast and dinner are included in the price. $165-195.

Natchez Trace Bed and Breakfast Reservation Service

P.O. Box 193, Hampshire, TN 38461
(931) 285-2777; (800) 377-2770
e-mail: natcheztrace@worldnet.att.net

Rosswood. Milepost 30. Completed in 1857 by an architect of Windsor, whose awesome ruins stand nearby. Classic Greek Revival with 14 rooms, 14-foot ceilings, columned galleries, winding stairway, and original slave quarters. Visitors may read in the diary of an early owner of the house about plantation life before and during the Civil War. Even a resident ghost! Rooms are upstairs; canopied beds, private baths, TV, movies, and telephones. Refreshments on arrival, full breakfast, heated pool, and spa. AAA-approved. $99-125.

Rosswood Plantation

Rosswood Plantation

Route 552, 39096
(601) 437-4215; (800) 533-5889
FAX (601) 437-6888; e-mail: whylander@aol.com
www.rosswood.net

Authentic antebellum mansion, close to Natchez and Vicksburg, offering luxury, comfort, charm, and hospitality on a serene country estate. Once a cotton plantation, Rosswood now grows Christmas trees. Ideal for honeymoons. A Mississippi landmark; national register; AAA-rated three diamonds. Closed during the months of January and February.

Hosts: Jean and Walt Hylander
Rooms: 4 (PB) $115-135
Full Breakfast
Credit Cards: A, B, C, D
Notes: 2, 7, 8, 9, 11, 14

MERIDIAN

Lincoln, Ltd.; Bed and Breakfast Mississippi

P.O. Box 3479, Meridian, 39303
(601) 482-5483 (information)
(800) 633-MISS (reservations)
FAX (601) 693-7447
e-mail: blincolnh@aol.com

16. A charming guest suite in a home in one of Meridian's historic neighborhoods. Bedroom, bath, and a living area decorated in antiques. Kitchen privileges. Private entrance. Continental breakfast. Weekly and monthly rates available. $75-85.

18. In one of Meridian's loveliest neighborhoods, this home is set among flowering shrubs and dogwood trees. The host and hostess have always been active in civic and cultural activities, both locally and throughout the state. Attractively furnished, two bedrooms with shared bath (for family or four people traveling together, only) or a double room with private bath. Full Mississippi breakfast. $65-100.

58. A contemporary inn convenient to I-59 and I-20 with 100 beautiful, spacious guest rooms. Meeting space for up to 60 people. Swimming pool and whirlpool on premises. Weekly and monthly rates available. Continental breakfast. $45-55.

NATCHEZ

Bed and Breakfast Mansions of Natchez

P.O. Box 347, Canal Street Depot, 39121
(601) 446-6631; (800) 647-6742
FAX (601) 446-8687

Aunt Clara's Cottage. Circa 1878. This quaint country cottage was moved from back of the Burn to next door to the Burn. Seven blocks from historic downtown Natchez. Enjoy a full southern breakfast. Two bedrooms with private baths, TV, and telephone usage. Welcomes children of all ages. $75.

Aunt Pitty Pat's. Enjoy the hospitality for which Natchez is famous at Aunt Pitty Pat's. This quaint Victorian cottage is nestled on a quiet street in the Garden District within easy walking distance to downtown shopping and tour sites. Relax on the porch swing. Enjoy a full southern breakfast in the sunroom overlooking the secluded courtyard. After a day of touring, enjoy refreshments in the kitchen or relax in the parlor with a magazine or TV. Three bedrooms. Children welcome. No smoking. No pets. $75-125.

The Bailey House. Enjoy relaxed atmosphere and southern hospitality, served with an artist's touch. The Bailey House, built circa 1890-1900, features broad verandas and a private courtyard on a prominent corner of the quiet residential Garden District of Natchez. Five bedrooms, full southern breakfast, handicapped-sensitive room. $125-145.

Bartley Guest House. Efficiency apartment-type accommodations with facilities for preparation of light meals if guest chooses. In-room satellite color TV and private telephone. Small deck off kitchen area to enjoy the outdoors. Complimentary wine and fruit basket provided upon arrival. Daily Continental breakfast furnished in room. Covered off-street parking. Two blocks from historic downtown Natchez and the Garden District. $90.

The Briars. Elegant southern plantation architecture, circa 1814, on 19 acres of lush and beautiful gardens overlooking the Mississippi River. Amenities include 13 antique-filled bedrooms with telephones and TVs and 24-hour use of living areas of house, gardens, and pool. Delicious four-course seated breakfast served in Riverview Pavilion. AAA-rated four diamonds. Smoking in designated areas. $125-230.

The Burn. Historic elegance, circa 1834, combines the traditions of the antebellum South with present-day comfort. Exquisite antiques and canopied beds in seven warm, inviting rooms. Nightly turndown with sweets and wine. Guests feast on a full, seated, hot southern breakfast. Pool. TV in room. Smoking in designated areas only. $100-160.

Cedar Grove Plantation. Circa 1830. An active retreat in the country: swimming pool, kennels for dogs, bicycles available, walking trails, fishing ponds, full southern breakfast. Five guest rooms in the main house, two guest rooms in the original carriage house. Entire house open for guests to enjoy. Welcomes children 12 and older. $110-145.

Cedars Plantation. Circa 1830. The inn is in Church Hill on a rise overlooking a park-like setting encompassing 176 acres of wooded landscape and manicured grounds, accented with ponds and beautiful moss-draped trees and shrubs typical of southern gardens. Experience the peacefulness of plantation life along with modern-day amenities. Three large bedrooms with private baths and a third-floor suite of rooms with fireplace and Jacuzzi are available. Accommodations are all in the main house. Full southern plantation breakfast is served. Children 12 or older are welcome. Sorry, no pets. $150-200.

Coyle House. Circa 1793-94. Listed in the National Register of Historic Places. Private entrances with convenient off-street parking. Central air and heat. Suite one has a private parlor with TV, private bath with shower, and accommodates four with day bed. Suite two has a TV in the bedroom, large private bath with whirlpool, veranda overlooking beautifully landscaped grounds, and accommodates three with day bed. Full southern breakfast served. Children eight and older welcome. $110.

Dixie. Circa 1795-1853. Dixie stands on land granted by the Spanish crown to Maurice Stackpoole. One suite in the main

Bed and Breakfast Mansions of Natchez (continued)

house and one suite in the 1795 wing of Dixie. Self-serve Continental breakfast in rooms. TV and telephone in rooms. Private entrances. Welcomes children 12 and older. $100-125.

Dorsey House. Circa 1835. Listed in the National Register of Historic Places. This antebellum townhouse is in historic downtown Natchez. Full southern breakfast is served in the formal dining room. Three large guest rooms have modern, private baths and fireplaces. Member of Pilgrimage Tour Association. Children welcome. $130-160.

Dunleith. Picturesque Greek Revival mansion, circa 1856, on a 40-acre landscaped park near downtown Natchez, is a national historic landmark. Eleven rooms, three in the main house and eight in the courtyard wing. All rooms have working fireplaces and TVs. Full southern breakfast. Children 18 and older welcome. $95-140.

Elgin. Guests enjoy a plantation experience in the 1853 guest house. Bedrooms with antique furnishings open onto a private gallery. Downstairs are sitting room, kitchen, and dining room where seated breakfast is served. Ten minutes from city center. Featured in *Gourmet*, April 1993. Smoking in designated areas only. $90-150.

Glenburnie. Circa 1833. Escape to the charm of history and ambiance of country gardens in a quaint three-room cottage on grounds of Glenburnie. Standing near the heart of downtown Natchez, the cottage features beautifully appointed rooms and caters to the demands of today's traveler with kitchen, washer, and dryer. No smoking. Continental breakfast. $100.

Glenfield. Charming English Gothic house, circa 1812 and 1845, in a country setting, yet only a short distance from downtown Natchez. House is furnished with period antiques. Five generations of the owner's family have lived at Glenfield. Enjoy the hospitality of descendants of early Natchez families. Smoking in designated areas only. $100.

The Governor Holmes House. Circa 1794. One of the oldest and most historic houses in the Old Spanish Quarter. It was the home of the last governor of the Mississippi Territory and the first governor of Mississippi when it became a state in 1817. The house is decorated with period furnishings and paintings. AAA-rated three diamonds. TV in room. Smoking in designated areas only. $95.

Harper House. An outstanding example of the many quaint and colorful Victorian homes in Natchez. Within easy walking distance of Natchez-Under-the-Hill and many of the antebellum homes. An overnight stay is enhanced by wicker-filled porches providing for a relaxing afternoon, custom, hand-stenciled rooms, antique oak and wicker furniture, TV in room, private baths, and off-street parking. Two guest rooms available for nonsmoking guests only. Full southern breakfast served outdoors in the gazebo, weather permitting. $100-130.

Hope Farm. This home, circa 1775-89, served the Spanish governor in 1789. Four bedrooms furnished in authentic antiques include distinctive four-poster beds with draped testers. Breakfast served in formal dining room. Surrounded by 20 acres of old-fashioned gardens, a short distance from the Natchez city park. Smoking in designated areas only. $90-100.

NOTES: Credit cards accepted: A MasterCard; B Visa; C American Express; D Discover; E Diner's Club; F Other; 2 Personal checks accepted; 3 Lunch available; 4 Dinner available; 5 Open all year; 6 Pets welcome;

Linden. An imposing Federal plantation home, circa 1800, in a parklike setting. Its front doorway was copied for *Gone With the Wind.* Seven bedrooms furnished with exquisite heirlooms and canopied beds from six generations. Delectable southern breakfast served in the formal banquet room. AAA three-diamond-rated. Smoking in designated areas only. $90-120.

Lisle House. Circa 1880. A charming Victorian cottage one block from the Mississippi River and within walking distance of shops and dining areas. It offers two bedrooms with queen-size tester beds, a full bath, kitchen, dining area, sitting room, TV, and telephone. Self-serve Continental breakfast. Welcomes children 12 and older. $110.

Main Street Balcony. Circa 1865-1872. The Flood Building currently is home to an impeccably appointed, furnished apartment in historic downtown Natchez. Includes a master bedroom, a second bedroom, private baths, living room, dining area, fully furnished kitchen, front and back balcony, TV, telephone. Continental breakfast or a voucher for the breakfast buffet at the Natchez Eola Hotel. Welcomes children 12 and older. $140.

Miss Lucy's Cottage. Circa 1850. Miss Lucy's Cottage is an old kitchen building separated from a Greek Revival townhouse by a patio and attractive gardens. The two-storied dependency features a bedroom, dressing room, bath, and balcony. The downstairs has a sitting room with telephone and kitchen. Both levels have cable TV and period antiques. It offers a variety of Continental breakfast items. $125.

Mistletoe. Circa 1811. Mistletoe, a quaint and charming home, is adorned with porches and galleries. Decorated in the Federal style; period antiques and reproductions are found throughout the house. Three spacious bedrooms in the main house, telephones, and private baths, with two rooms featuring Jacuzzi baths. The entire living area is open for everyone to enjoy. Only minutes from the heart of Natchez. Southern breakfast. Welcomes children 10 and older. $100-135.

Monmouth. On 27 landscaped acres, Monmouth, circa 1818, is a national historic landmark. Twenty-five rooms and suites. Four-diamond-rated; member Small Luxury Hotels of the World. Candlelight dinner served Tuesday through Saturday. Pond, fishing, croquet course, and nature walks. Groups and corporate retreats welcome. TV in room. $125-255.

Oakwood. Circa 1836. Oakwood is a Mississippi planter's cottage owned by the family for whom it was constructed, containing many of its original furnishings. The entire house is reserved for only one party at a time. Two bedrooms, three baths, living room, dining room, kitchen. Ten miles south of Natchez in the historic Kingston area. Full southern breakfast. Welcomes children 12 and older. $150.

The Orchard Bed and Breakfast. Circa 1858. A brick townhouse in the historic district. Each of the three units is a complete floor suite with kitchen, dining room, parlor, TV, telephone, private entrance. The private off-street parking with security fencing is bordered by an orchard. Offers a Continental-style, self-serve breakfast or a voucher for a breakfast buffet at the Natchez Eola Hotel. Welcomes children of all ages. $175.

Pleasant Hill. Circa 1840. A wooden cottage with high quality Greek Revival trim in the historic district within walking distance of the Mississippi River, shopping,

7 No smoking; 8 Children welcome; 9 Social drinking allowed; 10 Tennis nearby; 11 Swimming nearby; 12 Golf nearby; 13 Skiing nearby; 14 May be booked through a travel agent; 15 Handicapped accessible.

and dining areas. Four bedrooms with private baths. Full southern breakfast served in the Garden Room. Off-street parking, TV, and telephone usage. Welcomes children six and older. $90.

Ravenna. Elegant family home, circa 1835, secluded in three acres of an old-fashioned garden a few blocks from downtown Natchez. Known for its three-story elliptical stairway. Three large antique-filled bedrooms in main house; one-bedroom guest house by swimming pool. Seated breakfast served in formal dining room. $95-110.

Ravennaside. Circa 1880-1900. Designed for entertainment, the house lived up to its original purpose. Ravennaside offers nine bedrooms in the main house plus two cottages, all with private bath, and TV. Telephone usage. A complimentary horse-drawn carriage tour of historic downtown Natchez. Full southern breakfast. Welcomes children of all ages. $85-115.

Rosswood Plantation. Circa 1857. A classic Greek Revival structure completely restored and furnished with beautiful antiques. Once a thriving cotton plantation of 1,250 acres, it now has 100 acres of rolling fields and stately trees. Four bedrooms are upstairs in the mansion with private baths, TV, and telephone. Full southern breakfast. In Lorman, 40 miles north of Natchez. Welcomes children of all ages. $115-135.

Shields Town House. Circa 1860. Exclusive bed and breakfast suites in beautiful private setting feature modern amenities, antique charm, and individual landscaped courtyards. Garage parking adjacent to each suite. Main house courtyard features a large three-tier fountain and splendid gardens. Telephone and TV in room. Continental breakfast. $100-110.

Terrace Suite. Circa 1890. An award-winning 1997 restoration and warehouse conversion in the heart of downtown Natchez on Antiques Row, which boasts 19th-century charm with 20th-century luxury and convenience. Featuring two queen-size beds, one and one-half baths, a Jacuzzi, CATV, telephone, indoor garage, and a rooftop terrace with a panoramic view of the historic district. All amenities, very spacious and private. Welcomes children 12 and older. $150.

Texada. First brick house, circa 1792, in the Mississippi Territory. Elegant townhouse in Spanish Quarter. English and American period antiques with four-poster beds. Four large bedrooms and central sitting room with private entrance. Guest house with sitting room accommodates four. Enclosed landscaped courtyard. Smoking in designated areas only. $100.

Wensel House. Circa 1888. Three guest rooms furnished in antiques, each with a private modern bath, cable TV, telephone. Off-street parking, full use of the parlor and dining room, full southern breakfast. Just a few steps to restaurants, visitor center, shops, trolley stop, and carriage rides. Smoking permitted on the porch. Welcomes children of all ages. $75.

Dunleith

84 Homochitto, 39120
(601) 446-8500; (800) 433-2445

A national historic landmark, circa 1856, this picturesque Greek Revival mansion is on a 40-acre landscaped park near downtown Natchez. There are 11 guest rooms: three in the main house, eight in the courtyard wing. All rooms have working fireplaces. Full southern breakfast is served in the Poultry House.

Host: Nancy Gibbs
Rooms: 11 (PB) $95-140

NOTES: Credit cards accepted: A MasterCard; B Visa; C American Express; D Discover; E Diner's Club; F Other; 2 Personal checks accepted; 3 Lunch available; 4 Dinner available; 5 Open all year; 6 Pets welcome;

Dunleith

Full Breakfast
Credit Cards: A, B, D
Notes: 7

The Governor Holmes House

207 South Wall Street, 39120
(601) 442-2366; (888) 442-0166
FAX (601) 442-0166

The Governor Holmes House was built in 1794, one of the oldest and most historic homes in the Old Spanish Quarter. It was the home of the last governor of the Mississippi Territory and the first governor of the state of Mississippi when it became a state in 1817. The home was also in the painting of Natchez that Audubon painted in 1823 and is in the National Register of Historic Places. Rates are subject to change without notice. No smoking permitted in rooms.

Host: Robert Pully, owner/manager
Rooms: 4 (PB) $95-125
Full Breakfast
Credit Cards: A, B, C, D
Notes: 2, 5, 9, 10, 11, 12, 14

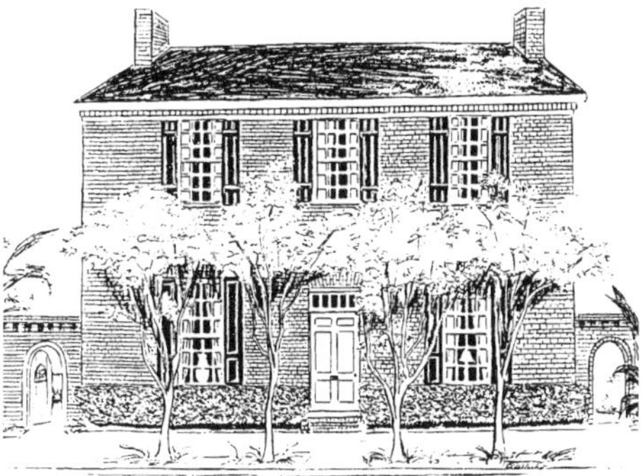

The Governor Holmes House

Lincoln, Ltd.; Bed and Breakfast Mississippi

P.O. Box 3479, Meridian, 39303
(601) 482-5483 (information)
(800) 633-MISS (reservations)
FAX (601) 693-7447
e-mail: blincolnh@aol.com

19. Circa 1832. This three-story mansion's outstanding architectural feature is the semi-elliptical stairway. Horses once trod where a collection of priceless furnishings and fine paintings now reside. Listed in the National Register of Historic Places. Swimming pool on premises. Ten guest rooms. Full breakfast served. $90-135.

20. Dating from 1774 to 1789 and surrounded by old-fashioned gardens, this home was once the home of a Spanish governor. In keeping with the period of the house, it is charmingly furnished with family heirlooms and other rare antiques. Formerly the home of Mr. and Mrs. J. Balfour Miller. The late Mrs. Miller was the originator of the Natchez Pilgrimage. Listed in the National Register of Historic Places. Four guest rooms. Full breakfast served. $90.

21. Circa 1790. Once the home of Thomas B. Reed, first elected U.S. senator from Mississippi, this architectural gem of the Federal period has been occupied since 1849 by the Conner family. Listed in the National Register of Historic Places. Seven guest rooms. Full breakfast served. $95 and up.

22. Circa 1818. The former home of Gen. John A. Quitman, an early Mississippi governor of Mexican War fame. This antebellum home contains many original Quitman pieces. Listed in the national register. Fourteen guest rooms; suite available. $110-210.

30. An outstanding historical home with a panoramic view of the Mississippi River.

Furnished with an impressive collection of antiques, including the works of John Belter and P. Mallard. Welcoming beverage, tour of the home, and a large plantation-style breakfast are included. Five guest rooms. $85-95.

69. Once owned by the last territorial governor and the first U.S. governor of Mississippi, this home was built in 1794 in the heart of Natchez. Many of the rooms have original 18th-century paneling and are furnished in period antiques. Enjoy the formal drawing room and eat a full plantation breakfast in the elegant dining room or cozy breakfast room. Five guest rooms and one suite available. $85-120.

98. Circa 1883-1889. This beautifully ornate home was once the gathering place of famous writers, publishers, politicians, and the elite of Natchez. In it guests will find treasures such as the parquet floor in the Gold Room, a bas relief design around the ceiling in the dining room, and a beautiful sweeping staircase in the grand entrance hall. With the price of a guest room, guests will enjoy a tour of the home, carriage ride around Natchez, and cocktails. $100-115.

102. Circa 1894. On the bluff, guests will get a panoramic view of the Mississippi River from this home. Mornings, guests will enjoy a full southern breakfast brought right to their room. An excellent home for families. Only blocks away from shops, historic homes, and restaurants. $110.

Linden

1 Linden Place, 39120
(601) 445-5472; (800) 2-LINDEN

Linden sits on seven landscaped acres and has been in the present owner's family for six generations. All seven bedrooms, each with private bath, have four-poster beds and other antiques of the Federal period. The front doorway was copied in *Gone With the Wind.* Rate includes early morning coffee, a full southern plantation breakfast, and a tour of the house. Limited smoking allowed. Children over 10 welcome.

Host: Jeanette S. Feltus
Rooms: 7 (PB) $90-120
Full Breakfast
Credit Cards: None
Notes: 2, 5, 9, 10, 11, 12, 14, 15

Monmouth Plantation

36 Melrose Avenue, 39120
(601) 442-5852; (800) 828-4531
FAX (601) 446-7762
e-mail: luxury@monmouthplantation.com

Monmouth Plantation is a glorious return to the antebellum South. A national historic landmark. Built in 1818, it is rated by *USA Today* and *Glamour* as one of the "top 10 most romantic places in the USA." Each room integrates modern comforts with period art and furnishings. Twenty-six acres of manicured gardens burst with magnolias and moss-draped oaks, making Monmouth Plantation's return to antebellum glory complete. Unforgettable gourmet five-course dinner by candlelight.

Rooms: 28 (PB) $125-225
Full Breakfast
Credit Cards: A, B, C, D, E
Notes: 2, 4, 5, 7, 9, 10, 12, 14

Natchez Trace Bed and Breakfast Reservation Service

P.O. Box 193, Hampshire, TN 38461
(931) 285-2777; (800) 377-2770
e-mail: natcheztrace@worldnet.att.net

Bed and Breakfast on the Bluff. Victorian home, built in 1894, with a panoramic view of the majestic Mississippi River, this home has one suite for guests, with a parlor with a gas fireplace, private porch, and private entrance. There are rollaway beds that can be used for extras and children of all ages are welcome—even a cable TV with the Disney channel and

VCR, with children's videos. Only blocks from historic downtown and Natchez Under the Hill. $110.

The Coyle House. Newly restored home in the old Spanish section of downtown Natchez, this home was a winner of Natchez's Historic Preservation Award and is in the National Register of Historic Places. Two spacious suites: one with private parlor accommodates four with a day bed; one with a veranda and large bathroom with whirlpool accommodates three with day bed; each has private entrance. Beautifully landscaped grounds. Many other historic homes are within walking distance. $110.

Elgin Plantation. Set on 25 acres, four miles south of Natchez, built in 1772; in the national register and featured in *Country Inns*. Splendid columned two-story 1840 wing is set aside for guests, with three bedrooms upstairs and living room, dining room (where a full southern breakfast is served), and kitchen downstairs. Two-bedroom suite also available. Double-tiered gallery with jib windows opening out to both levels. Magnificent grounds with huge moss-draped oaks, beautiful antiques. A tour of the main house, including antebellum costumes for photographs, is available to guests. $90-130.

Governor Holmes House. Milepost 8. Built in 1794, this is one of the oldest and most historic homes in Natchez, having been the home of the last governor of the Mississippi Territory and first governor of Mississippi. Listed in the National Register of Historic Places, it is beautifully decorated with period furnishings, porcelain, paintings, and oriental carpets. It features suites with private, modern baths. A delicious plantation breakfast is served in the formal dining room or the quaint breakfast room. Small children cannot be accommodated. $95.

Hope Farm. Milepost 8. This Natchez home, built between 1774 and 1789, is listed in the National Register of Historic Places and was owned by the first Spanish governor of the territory. It features exquisite antique furniture from the early 18th century. Each guest room is furnished with a distinctive four-poster bed with draped testers. Private baths. No small children. A large southern-style breakfast and tour of the home are included. Twenty dollars for each additional person. $90-100.

Main Street Balcony Bed and Breakfast. Milepost 11. In a building built in 1887, this luxurious two-bedroom apartment is just across from a trolley stop. The building facade has cast-iron posts and a balcony overlooking the street and is central to antique shops, restaurants, and all the Natchez attractions. Two guest rooms with private baths, a kitchen, and living room. Guests can choose either a Continental breakfast or a coupon for a buffet at the hotel across the street. Twenty-five dollars for each additional person. $140.

Ravennaside. Built around 1870 and in the national register, this home has entertained famous writers, publishers, politicians, dignitaries, and the elite of Natchez. It is convenient to the downtown historic area but boasts three acres of gardens. One of the few remaining old stables is on the grounds, and guests can have a complimentary carriage ride around town. Beautiful antiques throughout. Two rooms in an adjoining cottage available at $85 each. Rooms in the main house are $95-115.

Terrace Suite Bed and Breakfast. In downtown Natchez on "Antiques Row," this award-winning restoration/conversion houses an apartment on the second floor, with 14-foot ceilings, 10-foot windows, brick walls, and a rooftop terrace with a panoramic view of the historic district. One bedroom, full bath with whirlpool tub, kitchen, sleeper-sofa, and a half-bath in the living room. Cable TV, microwave, parking garage. Complimentary bottle of wine and hors d'oeuvres, Continental breakfast. Twenty-five dollars for each additional person. $150.

Wensel House. This 1888 Victorian townhouse completely renovated and beautifully furnished with antiques. In the heart of the historic district across from Natchez Pilgrimage headquarters, shopping, touring, and dining. Guests enjoy the parlor and dining room where complimentary fresh fruit and drinks are available. Generous plantation breakfast served in the dining room. Three large bedrooms, private bath, cable TV, telephone, iron and ironing board, and hair dryer. Fifteen dollars for additional persons. $75.

Oakland Plantation

1124 Lower Woodville Road, 39120
(601) 445-5101; (800) 824-0355

This charming retreat is about eight miles south of Natchez, with 360 acres of pastures, nature trails, fishing ponds, and a tennis court. The guest house dates back to 1785, and guests to the estate include Andrew Jackson and his wife, Rachel. Come for the peace and quiet and relax in an 18th-century atmosphere. Smoking outside only.

Hosts: Andy and Jeanie Peabody
Rooms: 3 (2 PB; 1 SB) $65-75
Full Breakfast
Credit Cards: A, B, C
Notes: 2, 5, 8, 9, 10, 11, 12, 14

NEW ALBANY

Natchez Trace Bed and Breakfast Reservation Service

P.O. Box 193, Hampshire, TN 38461
(931) 285-2777; (800) 377-2770
e-mail: natcheztrace@worldnet.att.net

Heritage House. Twenty miles from the trace and in a quiet neighborhood, this historic home was built in 1906 and has six guest rooms. There is a shaded front porch for reading the morning paper, and inside are rooms with 12-foot ceilings and antique furnishings. Suite with two bedrooms, sitting room with TV, and bathroom available. Children welcome. $65-75.

OXFORD

Barksdale-Isom House

1003 Jefferson Avenue, 38655
(601) 236-5600; (800) 236-5696
FAX (601) 236-6763

Recently renovated antebellum home. Each room has marble private baths, telephone, cable TV. House furnished with beautiful mid-19th century French antiques. Wander through lush gardens. Enjoy a full gourmet breakfast or relax in a rocking chair on the porch. One block north of town square.

Host: Susan Barksdale
Rooms: 6 (PB) $120-150
Full Breakfast
Credit Cards: A, B, C
Notes: 2, 4, 5, 7, 9, 12

PASS CHRISTIAN

Lincoln, Ltd.; Bed and Breakfast Mississippi

P.O. Box 3479, Meridian, 39303
(601) 482-5483 (information)
(800) 633-MISS (reservations)
FAX (601) 693-7447
e-mail: blincolnh@aol.com

77. Across from Pass Christian Yacht Harbor, this three-story home allows guests to enjoy a harbor view from the front porches, with French doors opening onto the porches from all rooms facing the gulf. As guests stay among the family antiques and art, they may enjoy the reception and dining parlors, play cards or billiards in the kitchen or den, or simply enjoy the peaceful harbor view. Five rooms. Children over 14 are welcome. $78-98.

PORT GIBSON

Lincoln, Ltd.; Bed and Breakfast Mississippi

P.O. Box 3479, Meridian, 39303
(601) 482-5483 (information)
(800) 633-MISS (reservations)
FAX (601) 693-7447
e-mail: blincolnh@aol.com

26. Enjoy a night in one of the South's most beautiful antebellum mansions. In the National Register of Historic Places, this home is furnished with family heirlooms. Visitors will step back in history to an era of gracious living. Includes a full southern-style breakfast and a tour of the home. Eleven guest rooms. $85-125.

66. Circa 1832. This late Federal-style home is noted for its beautiful three-story curved show-off stairway. Once owned by Judge Harry T. Ellet, who drew up the secession paper for the Confederacy. Enjoy one of five guest rooms beautifully decorated or one large suite complete with Jacuzzi. Listed in the National Register of Historic Places. Full southern breakfast. $75-115.

Natchez Trace Bed and Breakfast Reservation Service

P.O. Box 193, Hampshire, TN 38461
(931) 285-2777; (800) 377-2770
e-mail: natcheztrace@worldnet.att.net

Oak Square. This home in Port Gibson is two miles from the trace. The grounds of this 1850 mansion contain three guest houses with 12 rooms for guests, each with a massive four-poster canopied bed and other antique furnishings. A tour of the full house and grounds is conducted every evening. A full southern breakfast, complete with grits and biscuits, is served each morning. $85.

Oak Square Plantation

Oak Square Plantation

1207 Church Street, 39150
(601) 437-4350; (800) 729-0240

Oak Square, circa 1850, is Port Gibson's largest and most palatial Greek Revival antebellum mansion. Visitors experience a quiet retreat into the past. Family heirloom antiques, canopied beds, full southern breakfast, and a tour of the mansion and grounds. In the National Register of Historic Places. Port Gibson is the third oldest town in Mississippi, referred to by Gen. U. S. Grant as "the town too beautiful to burn." Area attractions include antebellum homes, churches, a military state park, Civil War battlefields, and museums. Inquire about accommodations for children. Limited social drinking permitted. Limited handicapped accessible.

Hosts: Mr. and Mrs. William D. Lum
Rooms: 12 (PB) $85-95
Full Breakfast
Credit Cards: A, B, C, D
Notes: 2, 5, 7, 10, 11, 12

SLATE SPRING

Lincoln, Ltd.; Bed and Breakfast Mississippi

P.O. Box 3479, Meridian, 39303
(601) 482-5483 (information)
(800) 633-MISS (reservations)
FAX (601) 693-7447
e-mail: blincolnh@aol.com

65. Circa 1890. This lovely old farmhouse with curved staircase has been lovingly restored to its present beauty with half-tester Victorian beds and heirloom antiques. Walk the 150-acre farm with its beautiful wildflowers, colorful birds, and trees. Enjoy a full southern breakfast and a full-course dinner included in the price. Three guest rooms with private baths. $75-105.

TUPELO

The Mockingbird Inn

The Mockingbird Inn Bed and Breakfast

305 North Gloster, 38801
(601) 841-0286

Discover the romance of a different place and time in an award-winning enchanting getaway in the heart of Tupelo. Guest rooms have international decor, private baths, telephones, modem hookup, cable TVs, and alarm clocks. One guest room has a double Jacuzzi, another a fireplace, and another a sitting area. Light evening snack and beverages are complimentary. Two Civil War battlefields are nearby; five minutes to Elvis's birthplace. Just off the Natchez Trace Parkway. Near the coliseum and popular restaurants. Rated in the top 10 best bed and breakfasts in Mississippi. Children over 10 welcome. Inquire about accommodations for pets.

Hosts: Jim and Sandy Gilmer
Rooms: 7 (PB) $65-125
Full Breakfast
Credit Cards: A, B, C, D
Note: 5, 7, 9, 10, 11, 12, 14, 15

Natchez Trace Bed and Breakfast Reservation Service

P.O. Box 193, Hampshire, TN 38461
(931) 285-2777; (800) 377-2770
e-mail: natcheztrace@worldnet.att.net

Mockingbird Inn. In downtown Tupelo—across the street from Elvis's school—and about two miles from the trace, each room in this home is of a different theme, each reflecting the style and charm of a different part of the world. Private telephones, internet connection, evening snacks, handicapped accessible. Special romance package available. Rated in the Top Ten Best Bed and Breakfasts in Mississippi. $75-125.

VICKSBURG

Annabelle

501 Speed Street, 39180
(601) 638-2000; (800) 791-2000
FAX (601) 636-5054
e-mail: annabelle@vicksburg.com
www.missbab.com/annabelle

Overnight memories are taken from this historic 1868 two-story Victorian home in Vicksburg's historic garden district. Elegantly, but comfortably, furnished in beautiful antiques, Annabelle offers king- and

Annabelle

NOTES: Credit cards accepted: A MasterCard; B Visa; C American Express; D Discover; E Diner's Club; F Other; 2 Personal checks accepted; 3 Lunch available; 4 Dinner available; 5 Open all year; 6 Pets welcome;

queen-size beds, 12-foot-high ceilings, in-room cable TV, air conditioning, a beautiful Vieux Carré courtyard, and sparkling swimming pool surrounded by crepe myrtle, pecan, and magnolia trees. A delicious southern breakfast is served in the formal dining room. AAA three-diamond rating. Mobil Travel Guide three-star rating. German spoken.

Hosts: Carolyn and George Mayer
Rooms: 5 (PB) $90-110
Suites: 2 (PB) $125-145
Full Breakfast
Credit Cards: A, B, C, D
Notes: 2, 5, 7, 9, 10, 11, 12, 14

Belle of the Bends

508 Klein Street, 39180
(800) 844-2308

The Belle of the Bends is a Victorian mansion, built in 1876 in classic Italianate architecture. It is nestled on a bluff providing a view of the Mississippi River from the verandas that wrap around three sides of this charming southern mansion. The home is elegantly decorated in period family antiques. In-residence owners, Wally and Jo Pratt, will conduct a personal tour of the home and gardens.

Host: Jo Pratt
Rooms: 5 (PB) $95-130
Full Breakfast
Credit Cards: A, B, C, D
Notes: 2, 5, 7, 8, 9, 14

Belle of the Bends

Cedar Grove Mansion Inn

Cedar Grove Mansion Inn

2300 Washington Street, 39180
(800) 862-1300; FAX (601) 634-6126

Make Cedar Grove the next romantic escape. Capture *Gone With the Wind* elegance and romance in exquisite guest rooms/suites. Each room is lavishly decorated and furnished with period antiques combined with the conveniences of private bath, cable TV, telephone, and air conditioning. Relax with a mint julep in the piano bar—the perfect prelude to a romantic gourmet candlelight dinner in the Garden Room Restaurant. Awake to a full southern breakfast followed by a historic tour.

Host: Rhonda Abraham
Rooms: 29 (PB) $85-165
Full Breakfast
Credit Cards: A, B, C, D
Notes: 4, 5, 7, 8, 9, 10, 11, 12, 14, 15

The Corners Mansion

601 Klein Street, 39180
(800) 444-7421

Step back to 1873 in this beautiful southern residence with its high ceilings, period antique furnishings, 68-foot verandas overlooking the Mississippi, and fragrant gardens filled with blossoms throughout the summer. The hosts introduce their guests to the traditional southern lifestyle by encouraging them to relax throughout the home. A full plantation breakfast is served in the

7 No smoking; 8 Children welcome; 9 Social drinking allowed; 10 Tennis nearby; 11 Swimming nearby; 12 Golf nearby; 13 Skiing nearby; 14 May be booked through a travel agent; 15 Handicapped accessible.

formal dining room and is followed by an enjoyable tour and historical narrative of the mansion and the original parterre gardens.

Hosts: Cliff and Bettye Whitney
Rooms: 15 (PB) $85-120
Full Breakfast
Credit Cards: A, B, C, D, E
Notes: 2, 5, 6, 7, 8, 9, 10, 12, 14, 15

Lincoln, Ltd.; Bed and Breakfast Mississippi

P.O. Box 3479, Meridian, 39303
(601) 482-5483 (information)
(800) 633-MISS (reservations)
FAX (601) 693-7447
e-mail: blincolnh@aol.com

35. This home, circa 1873, was built as a wedding present from father to daughter. It is an interesting mixture of Victorian and Greek Revival architectural styles. All bedrooms are furnished with antiques and have private baths. Some rooms are available with fireplaces and TVs. Enjoy a spectacular view of the Mississippi River and valley from a rocking chair on the front gallery. Full plantation breakfast is included. Listed in the National Register of Historic Places. Six guest rooms. $85-120.

36. Lavish antebellum mansion built between 1840 and 1858 as a wedding present from a wealthy businessman to his bride. *Gone With the Wind* elegance that guests won't soon forget. Exquisitely furnished with many original antiques. Enjoy the beautiful formal gardens, gazebos, and fountains. Relax in the courtyard. Pool and spa available. Listed in the National Register of Historic Places. Its 17 guest rooms have private baths. $85-160.

41. Elegant antebellum mansion, circa 1856, in Vicksburg's historic district. It is the best example of Palladian architecture found in Mississippi. Used as a hospital during the Civil War, it was shelled during the siege of Vicksburg. Listed in the National Register of Historic Places. A welcoming beverage, tour of the home, and full breakfast are included. Eight guest rooms. $95 and up.

73. This historic home, circa 1876, was named after an excursion riverboat and overlooks the Mississippi River. Sit on the porch and watch riverboats pass by, or stroll in the informal gardens. The home is an easy walk to other historic homes, restaurants, and attractions. Enjoy one of the three guest rooms filled with family antiques. $95 and up.

96. Circa 1835, frequented by notable military leaders such as General Stephen D. Lee. Complemented by its enchanting three-story elliptical spiral staircase, Balfour House is considered to be one of the first Greek Revival structures in Mississippi. Listed in the National Register of Historic Places. Arrangements for groups include candlelight tours, basket lunches, refreshments on the galleries, and southern breakfasts. Welcoming beverage and plantation breakfast included. Telephone and cable TV. Four guest rooms. $95 and up.

Natchez Trace Bed and Breakfast Reservation Service

P.O. Box 193, Hampshire, TN 38461
(931) 285-2777; (800) 377-2770
e-mail: natcheztrace@worldnet.att.net

The Corners. Milepost 60 or 67. In historic Vicksburg, 15 miles from the trace, this circa 1873 mansion, built as a wedding present to a daughter, is listed in the National

Register of Historic Places. All rooms are furnished with antiques and include TV; some have working fireplaces. There is a 68-foot gallery with a spectacular view of the Mississippi River. Full plantation breakfast is included. $85-120.

Stained Glass Manor. "One of the most lavish residential displays of leaded & stained glass," according to the National Register of Historic Places. A fine example of Mission-style architecture, built by a descendant of the founder of Vicksburg. Beautiful furnishings—working fireplaces in many rooms. One room very suitable for families, with children welcome. Smoking permitted in some areas. $60-150.

WEST

The Alexander House

210 Green Street, P.O. Box 187, 39192
(601) 967-2266; (800) 350-8034

The Alexander House

Step inside the front door of the Alexander House bed and breakfast and return to a more leisurely and gracious way of life. The Alexander House represents Victorian decor at its prettiest and country hospitality at its best. Captain Alexander, Dr. Joe, Ulrich, Annie, and Miss Bealle are the names of the rooms waiting to cast a spell over those who visit. Day trips to historic or recreational areas may be charted or chartered.

Hosts: Ruth Ray and Woody Dinstel
Rooms: 5 (3 PB; 2 SB) $65
Full Breakfast
Credit Cards: A, B, C, D
Notes: 2, 3, 4, 5, 8, 9, 14

7 No smoking; 8 Children welcome; 9 Social drinking allowed; 10 Tennis nearby; 11 Swimming nearby; 12 Golf nearby; 13 Skiing nearby; 14 May be booked through a travel agent; 15 Handicapped accessible.

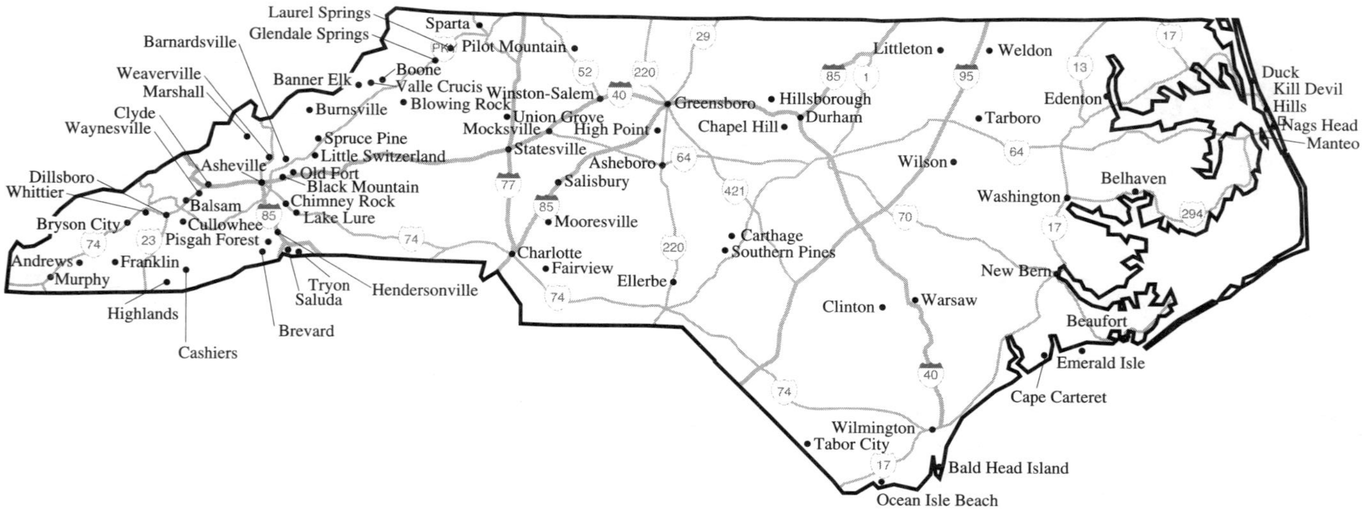

North Carolina

North Carolina

ANDREWS

Carolina Mornings, Inc.

(800) 770-9055; (888) MORNINGS (667-6467)
FAX (919) 929-5061
e-mail: carolinamornings.com
www.carolinamornings.com

26. Come, sit a spell on the comfortable front porch and watch the Great Smoky Mountains Railroad pull into town. In one of western North Carolina's most beautiful valleys, this relaxing inn is furnished with antiques collected by the innkeeper and her family. Carriage house apartment available. $75-80.

28. On 20 acres of land adjoining Nantahala National Forest, this bed and breakfast boasts a rushing stream just outside its door. Cozy guest rooms open onto a great room with a two-story stone fireplace. Take a llama trek to a hidden waterfall on the grounds. Apartment available. $60-100.

ASHEBORO

The Doctor's Inn

716 South Park Street, 27203
(336) 625-4916; (336) 625-4822

The Doctor's Inn is a home filled with antiques. It offers its guests the utmost in personal accommodations. Amenities include a gourmet breakfast served on fine china and silver, fresh flowers, terry-cloth robes and slippers, homemade goodies, and a refrigerator stocked with soft drinks, juices, and ice cream parfaits. Nearby are 60 potteries and the North Carolina Zoo.

Hosts: Marion and Beth Griffin
Rooms: 2 (1 PB; 1 SB) $95
Full Breakfast
Credit Cards: None
Notes: 2, 5, 7, 9, 10, 12

ASHEVILLE

Acorn Cottage

25 St. Dunstans Circle, 28803
(828) 253-0609; (800) 699-0609
FAX (828) 258-2129

An Art and Crafts bungalow country cottage in the heart of Asheville. The four individually decorated guest rooms feature queen-size beds, fine linens, air conditioning, TVs, and private baths. Come relax in this 1925 architecturally designed home built of North Carolina granite, maple hardwood floors, and a beautiful stone fireplace. Acorn Cottage is in a natural woodland setting only one-quarter mile from the Biltmore Estate. Inquire about accommodations for children.

Host: Sharon Tabor
Rooms: 4 (PB) $80-100
Full Breakfast
Credit Cards: A, B, C, D
Notes: 2, 5, 7, 9, 10, 11, 12, 13, 14

Acorn Cottage

NOTES: Credit cards accepted: A MasterCard; B Visa; C American Express; D Discover; E Diner's Club; F Other; 2 Personal checks accepted; 3 Lunch available; 4 Dinner available; 5 Open all year; 6 Pets welcome; 7 No smoking; 8 Children welcome; 9 Social drinking allowed; 10 Tennis nearby; 11 Swimming nearby; 12 Golf nearby; 13 Skiing nearby; 14 May be booked through a travel agent; 15 Handicapped accessible.

Advance Accommodations of Western North Carolina

P.O. Box 1008, 28802
(704) 645-6420; (800) 854-4924
e-mail: advncaccom@aol.com
www.advanceaccommodations.com

This reservation service has more than 35 properties in western North Carolina. Bed and breakfasts, inns, lodges, resorts, cabins, and cottages are available for daily, weekend, weekly, and monthly rental. Rates are from moderate to upper price range.

Contact: Denise Steier
Credit Cards: A, B, D
Notes: 2, 5, 7, 9, 12, 13

Applewood Manor Inn

62 Cumberland Circle, 28801-1718
(828) 254-2244; (800) 442-2197
FAX (828) 254-0899
www.comscape.com/apple

A fine turn-of-the-century Colonial Revival manor set on one and one-half acres of rolling lawn and woods in Asheville's historic Montford district. Within 15 minutes of the finest restaurants, antique shops, and area attractions, including the Biltmore Estate. Amenities include private baths, queen-size beds, fireplaces, balconies, full gourmet breakfasts, and complimentary beverages. Bikes, badminton, and croquet are available.

Hosts: Coby and John Verhey
Rooms: 4 (PB) $95-115
Cottage: 1

Applewood Manor Inn

Full Breakfast
Credit Cards: A, B
Notes: 2, 5, 7, 9, 10, 12, 13, 14

Beaufort House Victorian

Beaufort House Victorian Bed and Breakfast

61 North Liberty Street, 28801
(828) 254-8334: www.beauforthouse.com

Built in 1894, Beaufort House stands today as an eloquent testimony to the gentle style of living prevalent at the turn of the century. Encompassing romance, history, and elegance, Beaufort House offers guests the comforts of modern luxuries such as central air conditioning, TVs, VCRs, telephones, Jacuzzis, and fitness facility. Enjoy bicycles and mountain views. The Beaufort House is listed in the National Register of Historic Places and was previously featured in *National Geographic Traveler* magazine. AARP, corporate, and government rates. Inquire about accommodations for children.

Hosts: Robert and Jacqueline Glasgow
Rooms: 12 (PB) $85-195
Full Breakfast
Credit Cards: A, B
Notes: 2, 5, 7, 9, 10, 11, 12, 13, 14

The Black Walnut Bed and Breakfast Inn

288 Montford Avenue, 28801
(828) 254-3878; (800) 381-3878
www.blackwalnut.com

The Black Walnut is a turn-of-the-century Shingle-style home in the heart of the

Montford historic district just minutes from downtown and the Biltmore Estate. Amenities include large guest rooms with air conditioning, working fireplaces, TVs, VCRs, and private baths. Jacuzzi suites are also available. Full breakfast served by candlelight includes a special blend coffee, homemade coffee cakes, muffins, and preserves. Private cottage and loft suite available with kitchenette.

Hosts: Randy and Sandra Glasgow
Rooms: 7 (PB) $95-160
Full Breakfast
Credit Cards: A, B, C, D
Notes: 2, 5, 7, 8, 10, 11, 12, 13, 14

The Black Walnut

Cairn Brae

217 Patton Mountain Road, 28804
(828) 252-9219

Cairn Brae is in the mountains above Asheville. Very private, on three acres of woods, but only 12 minutes from downtown. Private guest entrance to living room with fireplace. Afternoon refreshments served on the terrace overlooking Beaverdam Valley. Beautiful views. Woodsy trails. Air conditioned. All rooms have private baths. Quiet and secluded. Closed December through March. Children over 10 welcome.

Hosts: Milli and Ed Adams
Rooms: 3 (PB) $95-110
Full Breakfast
Credit Cards: A, B, D
Notes: 2, 7, 9, 10, 11, 12, 14

Carolina Bed and Breakfast

177 Cumberland Avenue, 28801
(828) 254-3608; (888) 254-3608
FAX (704) 252-0640
www.bbonline.com/nc/carolina/

Comfortable turn-of-the-century home on an acre of beautiful gardens in the historic Montford district. Charming guest rooms, four with fireplaces, have antiques and collectibles, as well as private baths. Convenient to downtown shopping, galleries, restaurants, and the Biltmore Estate. A quiet, relaxing getaway in the heart of the city. Outdoor Jacuzzi and chef-prepared full gourmet breakfast. Smoking permitted in designated areas only. Children over 12 welcome.

Host: Connie Stahl
Rooms: 6 (PB) $95-140
Cottage: $150
Full Breakfast
Credit Cards: A, B, D
Notes: 2, 5, 9, 10, 11, 12, 13, 14

Carolina Mornings, Inc.

(800) 770-9055; (888) MORNINGS (667-6467)
FAX (919) 929-5061
e-mail: carolinamornings.com
www.carolinamornings.com

A reservation service for bed and breakfasts and country inns in Asheville and throughout western North Carolina. The service is able to assist travelers wishing to visit the Biltmore Estate with comfortable accommodations at in-town sites. Many of the bed and breakfasts are in historic homes elegantly furnished with antiques. The service is also able to find lodging for those who want to explore the mountains, visit the Piedmont, and enjoy the sandy beaches. Offering lakeside lodges or hilltop retreats close to the Blue Ridge Parkway. Also the service offers secluded cabins and guest houses throughout the area.

Rates: $70-385
Full Breakfast
Credit Cards: A, B, C, D
Notes: 2, 3, 4, 5, 7, 8, 9, 10, 11, 12, 13

01. This 1925 home is built of North Carolina granite, with maple floors and a beautiful stone fireplace. In the heart of Asheville, in a lovely wooded setting, Acorn Cottage is only one-fourth mile from the entrance to the Biltmore Estate. Children welcome. TV available. $85-100.

02. Welcoming refreshments await guests upon their arrival at this finely preserved Shingle-style home built in 1899. The main house and garden cottage interiors are a wonderful mix of antiques and fine traditional furniture. Elegant, candlelit full breakfast served on beautiful English china. $95-150.

03. In the National Register of Historic Places, this 1883 house is a comfortable blend of Victorian elegance and southern charm. A full breakfast is served in the dining room or opt for a Continental basket in guests' room. Tandem biking packages and weekend workshops available. $105-125.

05. Sitting in a quiet neighborhood and minutes from the Biltmore Estate, this quaint one-room cottage offers convenience and flexibility. Prepare own breakfast from the stocked refrigerator and relax in the loft in the queen-size bed. $85.

08. Fine Old World charm in the secluded gardens surrounding a heated swimming pool on the grounds of this estate. Rooms feature Jacuzzi baths, four-poster beds, and fireplaces. Delightful British innkeepers serve tea every afternoon at four. TV and telephone on request. $75-95.

18. Enjoy a gourmet breakfast at this wonderful, restored 100-year-old stone and shingle home just one mile from the Biltmore Estate entrance. Amenities include antique mahogany furniture, as well as other English antiques and wrought-iron canopied beds. TV in the rooms. $85-110.

20. A picket fence with climbing primrose surrounds the lovely gardens and pond at this 1889 English Shingle-style home. Heart-pine floors, elegant antiques, and original light fixtures are featured throughout the inn. Many rooms have fireplaces. Suites and a guest cottage. $100-150.

22. The original tin roof still graces this grand Victorian "painted lady." Two- and three-room suites, many with Jacuzzi baths, all with TV, VCR, telephone, and full kitchen make guests' stay comfortable, convenient, and memorable. Guest cottage available. Children welcome. From $115.09.

24. An elegant mansion in the National Register of Historic Places featuring lovely tea gardens and a wraparound porch. Some rooms have one- or two-person Jacuzzis and fireplaces. TV, VCR, and telephone in rooms, as well as a fitness facility and bicycles. $115-250.

40. Some of the finest interior woodwork in Asheville graces this 1905 Colonial Revival home, furnished with period antiques. Breakfast is served on heirloom china and linens. Enjoy afternoon tea and crumpets or catch a mountain breeze while rocking on one of the large porches. $110-125.

41. Be surrounded with the romance, history, and elegance of this century-old inn. Listed in the National Register of Historic Places, Richmond Hill offers mountain views, gourmet dining, croquet court, stream, and waterfall. TV and telephone in each room. $145-375.

NOTES: Credit cards accepted: A MasterCard; B Visa; C American Express; D Discover; E Diner's Club; F Other; 2 Personal checks accepted; 3 Lunch available; 4 Dinner available; 5 Open all year; 6 Pets welcome;

Cedar Crest Victorian Inn

674 Biltmore Avenue, 28803
(828) 252-1389

An 1890 Queen Anne mansion listed in the National Register of Historic Places features carved oak paneling, ornate glasswork, authentic Victorian decor with period antiques, and romantic guest rooms. Croquet court, fireplaces, and English gardens. A full breakfast is served buffet style. One-quarter mile from the entrance to the Biltmore Estate and four miles from the Blue Ridge Parkway. AAA four-diamond-rated. Children over 10 welcome.

Hosts: Jack and Barbara McEwan
Rooms: 9 (PB) $130-195
Suites: 2
Full Breakfast
Credit Cards: A, B, C, D, E
Notes: 2, 5, 7, 10, 11, 12, 14

The Colby House

230 Pearson Drive, 28801
(828) 253-5644; (800) 982-2118

This elegant and charming Dutch-Tudor house in the Montford historic district is known as a special place. There are beautiful gardens, an outdoor porch, and inviting fireplaces. The home has four guest rooms, each with individual decor, queen-size beds, and private baths. A full breakfast is varied daily. Southern hospitality abounds in the hosts' personal attention to every guest's needs.

Hosts: Everett and Ann Colby
Rooms: 4 (PB) $95-135
Full Breakfast
Credit Cards: A, B, C
Notes: 2, 7, 9, 10, 11, 12, 13

Corner Oak Manor

53 St. Dunstans Road, 28803
(828) 253-3525

Corner Oak Manor

This lovely English Tudor home is just minutes away from the famed Biltmore Estate and Gardens. Antiques, handmade wreaths, weavings, and stitchery complement the restored elegance of this home. Breakfast specialties include orange French toast, blueberry-ricotta pancakes, or four-cheese herb quiche. A living room with fireplace and baby grand piano and outdoor deck with Jacuzzi are among the gracious amenities.

Hosts: Karen and Andy Spradley
Rooms: 4 (PB) $100-160
Full Breakfast
Credit Cards: A, B, C, D
Notes: 2, 5, 7, 9, 10, 11, 12

Flint Street Inns

116 Flint Street, 28801
(828) 253-6723

Two lovely old homes on an acre lot with century-old trees. Comfortable walking distance to town. Guest rooms, furnished with antiques and collectibles, have air conditioning and queen-size beds, and some have fireplaces. The inns provide complimentary beverages and restaurant menus. Breakfast is full southern style, featuring home-baked breads and iron-skillet biscuits. Smoking in designated areas only.

Hosts: Rick, Lynne, and Marion Vogel
Rooms: 8 (PB) $100
Full Breakfast
Credit Cards: A, B, C, D
Notes: 2, 5, 9, 10, 11, 12, 14

7 No smoking; 8 Children welcome; 9 Social drinking allowed; 10 Tennis nearby; 11 Swimming nearby; 12 Golf nearby; 13 Skiing nearby; 14 May be booked through a travel agent; 15 Handicapped accessible.

The Inn on Montford

296 Montford Avenue, 28801
(800) 254-9569; www.innonmontford.com

A turn-of-the-century Arts and Craft home by Asheville's most famous architect. Filled with light, it is a perfect setting for the owners' eclectic collection of antiques, Victorian silver napkin rings, tea caddies, Staffordshire pottery, maps, Baxter prints, period cut glass, and Persian rugs. Fireplaces in all rooms, whirlpools in three rooms, a wide front porch with antique wicker furniture. The inn is in the Montford historic district, close to downtown and a 10-minute drive from the Biltmore Estate.

Hosts: Lynn and Ron Carlson
Rooms: 4 (PB) $175
Full Breakfast
Credit Cards: A, B, C, D, E
Notes: 2, 5, 7, 9, 10, 12, 13, 14

The Old Reynolds Mansion

100 Reynolds Heights, 28804
(828) 254-0496

Bed and breakfast in an antebellum mansion listed in the National Register of Historic Places. Beautifully restored with furnishings from a bygone era. Country setting with acres of trees and mountain views from all rooms. Wood-burning fireplaces, two-story verandas, and pool. Two-night minimum weekends and holidays. Open weekends only January through May.

Hosts: Fred and Helen Faber
Rooms: 10 (8 PB; 2 SB) $60-120
Cottage: $130
Continental Breakfast
Credit Cards: None
Notes: 2, 7, 9, 11, 12, 13

The Old Reynolds Mansion

Richmond Hill Inn

Richmond Hill Inn

87 Richmond Hill Drive, 28806
(800) 545-9238; FAX (704) 252-8726

Historic Victorian mansion built in 1889 overlooking the Blue Ridge Mountains and the Asheville skyline. Listed in the National Register of Historic Places. Magnificently restored mansion, cottages, and garden pavilion. This AAA four-diamond inn features 36 guest rooms, all with private baths and many with fireplaces. Fine dining in the AAA four-diamond gourmet restaurant. Close to the Blue Ridge Parkway and Biltmore Estate.

Host: Susan Michel
Rooms: 36 (PB) $145-375
Full Breakfast
Credit Cards: A, B, C
Notes: 2, 4, 5, 7, 8, 9, 10, 11, 12, 14, 15

The Secret Garden Bed and Breakfast

56 North Main Street, P.O. Box 2226,
Weaverville, 28787
(704) 658-9317; (800) 797-8211
e-mail: garden56@aol.com
www.bbonline.com/nc/secretgarden

Just seven miles north of Asheville, this beautiful, circa 1904, Low Country Charleston-style home offers elegant

NOTES: Credit cards accepted: A MasterCard; B Visa; C American Express; D Discover; E Diner's Club; F Other; 2 Personal checks accepted; 3 Lunch available; 4 Dinner available; 5 Open all year; 6 Pets welcome;

ambiance and gracious hospitality. The world-renowned Biltmore Estate is just 20 minutes away. Golfing, hiking, white-water rafting, unique shopping, and sumptuous dining are all in close proximity. Evening libations on the charming veranda are a highlight, as are the fabulous gourmet breakfasts that are offered. Children 10 and older welcome.

Hosts: Karen and Jack Hultin
Rooms: 4 (PB) $110-135
Full Breakfast
Credit Cards: A, B, D
Notes: 2, 5, 7, 9, 12, 13

The Wright Inn and Carriage House

235 Pearson Drive, 28801
(828) 251-0789; (800) 552-5724
FAX (828) 251-0929

Elegantly restored, circa 1898-1899, a fine example of Queen Anne architecture. Listed in the National Register of Historic Places, centrally air conditioned, with eight distinctive bedrooms (one with fireplace), and a luxurious suite with a fireplace; all with private baths, cable TVs, and telephones. Full scrumptious breakfast, afternoon tea, and refreshments. Children 12 and older welcome. The three-bedroom carriage house is ideal for groups/families and children of all ages.

The Wright Inn and Carriage House

Hosts: Carol and Art Wenczel
Rooms: 8 (PB) $105-150
Suite: 1 (PB) $150
Carriage House: 3 (S2B) $225
Full Breakfast
Credit Cards: A, B, D
Notes: 2, 5, 7, 9, 10, 11, 12, 13

BALD HEAD ISLAND

Theodosia's Bed and Breakfast

P.O. Box 3130, 28461
(910) 457-6563; (800) 656-1812
FAX (910) 457-6055

Theodosia's is a modern Victorian structure on the marina of Bald Head Island. The decor of the 10 carefully appointed rooms is diverse, variously incorporating floral and Virgin Island motifs. Everywhere there are balconies offering spectacular views of the harbor, river, or inland marshes. A full gourmet breakfast with special touches, afternoon wine, hors d'oeuvres are just some of the ways the host makes guests' stay more memorable. Children 10 and older welcome.

Hosts: Lydia and Steve Love
Rooms: 10 (PB)
Full Breakfast
Credit Cards: A, B, C, D
Notes: 2, 5, 7, 9, 10, 11, 12, 14, 15

BALSAM

Balsam Mountain Inn

P.O. Box 40, 28707
(704) 456-9498; (800) 224-9498

Nestled among lofty peaks in the Great Smoky Mountains and just off the Blue Ridge Parkway, this historic inn was built in 1908 to serve the highest railroad depot in the East. The inn was restored in 1991, and now offers 50 cheerful rooms, two 100-foot

7 No smoking; 8 Children welcome; 9 Social drinking allowed; 10 Tennis nearby; 11 Swimming nearby; 12 Golf nearby; 13 Skiing nearby; 14 May be booked through a travel agent; 15 Handicapped accessible.

porches with rockers and a view, a 2,000-volume library, and gracious dining. Plump pillows and soft comforters inspire pleasant dreams! Hiking, biking, relaxing, rafting, rail excursions, and shopping abound. Lunch is available Sundays and dinner every day. Box lunches all year when arranged by 6 P.M. the previous evening. Smoking permitted in designated areas only. Inquire about the age of children welcome.

Host: Merrily Teasley
Rooms: 50 (PB) $90-150
Full Breakfast
Credit Cards: A, B, D
Notes: 2, 4, 5, 9, 10, 11, 12, 13, 14, 15

BANNER ELK

Archers Mountain Inn

Route 2, Box 56 A, 28604
(704) 898-9004; www.arhersinn.com

Archers Mountain is nestled on Beech Mountain at nearly 5,000 feet above sea level, where activities abound for each season. The inn features 15 rooms, all of which have fireplaces, private baths, and porches overlooking outstanding mountainside views. Room amenities vary from suites which offer private balconies, hot tubs, Jacuzzi bathtubs, and first-class appointments to smaller more traditional bed and breakfast-style rooms to efficiency-style rooms perfect for families. All rooms include a full gourmet breakfast that is served in the mountain-view dining room. Evening meals are prepared nightly by chef Paul Janik. The dining room is handicapped accessible.

Hosts: Candi and Tony Catoe
Rooms: 14 (PB) $60-200
Full Breakfast
Credit Cards: A, B, D
Notes: 2, 4, 5, 7, 9, 10, 11, 12, 13

The Banner Elk Inn Bed and Breakfast

Highway 194 North, 407 Main Street East, 28604
(704) 898-6223

A charmingly restored cozy little inn close to fine restaurants and the major attractions of Grandfather Mountain, Valle Crucis, Sugar and Beech Mountain ski resorts, and the nearby towns of Boone and Blowing Rock. There are four guest rooms, two with private large baths and two sharing baths for a four-person suite. There is also an attic honeymoon suite with garden tub for two and cable TV. A wonderful great room, cable TV, stereo, and fireplace. Gourmet full breakfast weekends; simpler breakfast weekdays. Inquire about accommodations for pets. Children over five are welcome.

Host: Beverly Lait
Rooms: 5 (3 PB; 2 SB) $75-110
Full Breakfast
Credit Cards: A, B
Notes: 2, 5, 7, 9, 10, 12, 13, 14

The Banner Elk Inn

BARNARDSVILLE

Carolina Mornings, Inc.

(800) 770-9055; (888) MORNINGS (667-6467)
FAX (919) 929-5061
e-mail: carolinamornings.com
www.carolinamornings.com

41. A charming 1910 farmhouse and guest cottage on 24 acres surrounded by wildflower meadows, a swimming lake, wonderful mountain views, woods, and the Ivy River. Offering simple elegance and country comfort with antiques, down comforters, and fine linens. Children welcome. $75-125.

BEAUFORT

Delamar Inn

217 Turner Street, 28516
(919) 252-4300; (800) 349-5823

Enjoy the Scottish hospitality of this Civil War home in the heart of Beaufort's historic district. The inn offers three guest rooms with antique furnishings and private baths. After a delightful breakfast, enjoy a stroll to the waterfront, specialty shops, or historic sites. Borrow the hosts' bicycles or beach chairs, and upon return, guests will find soft drinks, cookies, and a smile waiting. The hosts are pleased to have been selected for Beaufort's 1992-95 historic homes tour. The Delamar Inn is rated three diamonds by AAA and three stars by Mobil.

Delamar Inn

Hosts: Mabel and Tom Steepy
Rooms: 3 (PB) $78-108
Continental Breakfast
Credit Cards: A, B
Notes: 2, 5, 7, 8, 9, 10, 11, 12, 14

Pecan Tree Inn

116 Queen Street, 28516
(919) 728-6733

A gracious 1866 Victorian home filled with antiques, one-half block from the waterfront in Beaufort's historic district. Relax on one of the three porches or stroll through the large English garden. There are seven air-conditioned rooms, all with private baths. Two bridal suites feature a Jacuzzi tub for two and a king-size canopied bed. Guests will enjoy the delicious breakfast with freshly baked homemade muffins, breakfast cakes, and breads, along with a choice of fruit, cereal, and beverages for breakfast. Only a few blocks from wonderful restaurants and quaint shops.

Hosts: Susan and Joe Johnson
Rooms: 7 (PB) $70-135
Continental Breakfast
Credit Cards: A, B, D
Notes: 2, 5, 7, 9, 10, 11, 12, 14

BELHAVEN

River Forest Manor and Marina

738 East Main Street, 27810
(919) 943-2151; (800) 346-2151

River Forest Manor is an ornately decorated Victorian mansion, with a private bath in each room. The inn is appropriately furnished with period furniture. Other amenities include a delicious Continental breakfast, tennis court, swimming pool, hot tub Jacuzzi, bar lounge, and marina. The world famous smorgasbord is served each night and includes southern-style cooking, from oyster fritters and seafood casserole

7 No smoking; 8 Children welcome; 9 Social drinking allowed; 10 Tennis nearby; 11 Swimming nearby; 12 Golf nearby; 13 Skiing nearby; 14 May be booked through a travel agent; 15 Handicapped accessible.

River Forest Manor

to homemade lemon pie. A Sunday brunch is available each Sunday.

Hosts: Melba G. Smith and sons,
Axson and Mark Smith
Rooms: 9 (PB) $50-85
Continental Breakfast
Credit Cards: A, B, C
Notes: 4, 5, 9, 10, 11, 12

BLACK MOUNTAIN

Black Mountain Inn

718 West Old Highway 70, 28711
(704) 669-6528; (800) 735-6128

Quiet romance in an unparalleled setting, tucked away on three secluded acres, one mile from town. Built as a stagecoach stop originally and restored in 1990. For more than two decades, this home served as a studio and haven for some of America's most accomplished writers, such as John Steinbeck, Ernest Hemingway, Norman Rockwell, Helen Keller, and many others. The Black Mountain Inn offers eight comfortable guest rooms with private baths, and a full home-cooked breakfast is served every morning.

Host: June Bergeron
Rooms: 8 (PB) $78-98
Full Breakfast
Credit Cards: A, B
Notes: 2, 5, 6, 7, 8, 9, 10, 11, 12, 14

Friendship Lodge Bed and Breakfast

P.O. Box 877, 28707
(828) 669-9294

A cozy 10-bedroom bed and breakfast at the edge of Black Mountain and dedicated to the task of helping guests enjoy the natural beauty and the abundant attractions the area has to offer. Start the day with a sumptuous breakfast and follow one's heart to whatever one desires. The cozy bedrooms have two double beds and private baths; each room is delightfully different.

Hosts: Bob and Sarah LaBrant
Rooms: 10 (8 PB: 2 SB) $50-55
Full Breakfast
Credit Cards: None
Notes: 2, 7, 8, 9, 10, 11, 12

The Red Rocker Country Inn

136 North Dougherty Street, 28711
(828) 669-5991; (888) 669-5991

The Red Rocker Inn is a meticulously restored 18-room inn, on a quiet tree-lined street in beautiful Black Mountain. Each of the rooms has a private bath, some have fireplaces, all have the comforts of home. The inn is famous for friendly southern hospitality. Enjoy a peaceful afternoon rocking on the covered front porch, or take a quiet stroll through the wonderful antique and furniture shops of Black Mountain. And in the evening, save time to feast on famous mountain dinners, four courses served family style in one of the three lovely dining rooms. Open year-round, offering a perfect setting for group meetings and family reunions. Special rates available during the off-season.

Hosts: Craig and Margie Lindberg
Rooms: 18 (PB) $70-135
Full Breakfast
Credit Cards: None
Notes: 2, 3, 4, 5, 7, 8, 10, 11, 12, 13

BLOWING ROCK

The Inn at Ragged Gardens

203 Sunset Drive, P.O. Box 1927, 28605
(828) 295-9703
e-mail: ragged-gardens.inn@blowingrock.com
www.ragged-gardens.com

Built at the turn of the century, nestled in the village amidst an acre of gardens. Enter the gracious inn with rich hardwood-paneled walls, antique furnishings, covered porches, fireplaces, and a unique stone staircase. Stroll the lovely lawn and gardens. Retire to one of the splendid guest rooms, each with private bath and fireplace complemented by a delicious breakfast. Discover the quiet corner in the heart of the village of Blowing Rock. Children 12 and older welcome.

Hosts: Lee and Jama Hyett
Rooms: 12 (PB) $125-200
Full Breakfast
Credit Cards: A, B
Notes: 2, 5, 7, 9, 10, 11, 12, 13, 14

The Inn at Ragged Gardens

Maple Lodge

Box 1236, Sunset Drive, 28605
(704) 295-3331

Elegant furnishings reflect the simplicity and charm of an earlier time. Guest rooms, filled with antiques, goose down comforters, lace, and handmade quilts, have private baths and king- or queen-size beds; some are canopied. A short stroll to craft shops, art galleries, professional summer theater, and fine restaurants. Grandfather Mountain, Linville Falls, the Blue Ridge Parkway, hiking, golf, and white-water rafting nearby.

Hosts: Marilyn and David Bateman
Rooms: 11 (PB) $85-140
Full Breakfast
Credit Cards: A, B, C, D, E
Notes: 2, 7, 9, 10, 11, 12, 13, 14

BOONE

Carolina Mornings, Inc.

(800) 770-9055; (888) MORNINGS (667-6467)
FAX (919) 929-5061
e-mail: carolinamornings.com
www.carolinamornings.com

62. This historic home sits on 16 acres at 3,300 feet, complete with trout streams and hiking trails. Enjoy this charming antique-furnished home from guests' own porch or by one of six fireplaces. This home is truly a step back into history and nostalgia. $95-120.

BREVARD

The Red House Inn Bed and Breakfast

412 Probart Street, 28712
(828) 884-9349

The Red House on Probart Street was built in 1851 to be a trading post. Through the years it has been a railroad station, a court house, a post office, a private school, and a college. The Red House has been loving restored and is now a bed and breakfast. It is charmingly furnished with turn-of-the-century period antiques. Convenient to many area sites of interest and recreational activities. In the evening the famous Flat Rock Playhouse is nearby and, of course, the wonderful music of Brevard's very own nationally acclaimed Music Center.

Host: Lynne Ong
Rooms: 5 (3 PB; 2 SB) $49-99
Full Breakfast
Credit Cards: A, B
Notes: 2, 7, 9, 10, 11, 12, 14, 15

Womble Inn

301 West Main, P.O. Box 1441, 28712
(704) 884-4770

Two blocks from the center of Brevard, the Womble Inn invites guests to relax in a welcoming, comfortable atmosphere. Each of the six guest rooms is specially furnished in antiques. All of the guest rooms have private baths and air conditioning. After a sound sleep, guests will be served breakfast on a silver tray, or guests may prefer to be seated in the dining room. Full breakfast is an option.

Hosts: Steve and Beth Womble
Rooms: 6 (PB) $52-62
Continental Breakfast
Credit Cards: A, B
Notes: 2, 3, 5, 7, 8, 9, 10, 11, 12

BRYSON CITY

Folkestone Inn

101 Folkestone Road, 28713
(828) 488-2730; (888) 812-3385
FAX (828) 488-0722
e-mail: innkeeper@folkestone.com
www.folkestone.com

The Folkestone Inn is a charming 1920s farmhouse nestled among Norway spruces, across a mountain brook, in a valley just a quarter-mile from the Deep Creek entrance to the Great Smoky Mountains National Park. Take a short walk to three sparkling waterfalls, or hike the park's trails. Enjoy nearby white-water rafting, fishing, horseback riding, and a scenic railway. Or just stay "home" at the inn and enjoy the view from a front porch rocker.

Folkestone Inn

Hosts: Ellen and Charles Snodgrass
Rooms: 10 (PB) $69-98
Full Breakfast
Credit Cards: A, B, C, D
Notes: 2, 5, 7, 9, 10, 12, 14

BURNSVILLE

Hamrick Inn

Hamrick Inn Bed and Breakfast

7787 Highway 80 South, 28714
(704) 675-5251

This charming three-story Colonial-style stone inn is nestled at the foot of Mount Mitchell, highest mountain east of the Mississippi. Much of the lovely furniture was built by the hosts. There is a private porch off each guest room, where the view and cool mountain breezes may be enjoyed. Golf, hiking, fishing, rock hounding, and craft shopping are local activities. Near the Blue Ridge Parkway. Open April 1 through October 31.

Hosts: Neal and June Jerome
Rooms: 4 (PB) $70-80
Full Breakfast
Credit Cards: A, B
Notes: 2, 7, 9, 10, 11, 12

CAPE CARTERET

Harborlight Guest House Bed and Breakfast

332 Live Oak Drive, 28584
(800) 624-VIEW

The Harborlight, on the central North Carolina coast, is on a peninsula with water on three sides; thus, all suites offer panoramic water views. All suites offer private

NOTES: Credit cards accepted: A MasterCard; B Visa; C American Express; D Discover; E Diner's Club; F Other; 2 Personal checks accepted; 3 Lunch available; 4 Dinner available; 5 Open all year; 6 Pets welcome;

entrances, private baths, individual climate controls. Luxury suites offer two-person Jacuzzis, fireplaces, and in-room breakfasts. The inn is minutes from secluded island excursions, Cape Lookout Lighthouse, and waterfront shopping villages. A gourmet breakfast is served outdoors overlooking the water each morning.

Hosts: Bobby and Anita Gill
Rooms: 9 (PB) $75-200
Full Breakfast
Credit Cards: A, B, C
Notes: 5, 7, 9, 10, 11, 12, 15

CARTHAGE

The Blacksmith Inn

703 McReynolds Street, P.O. Box 1480, 28327
(910) 947-1692; (800) 284-4515

Pinehurst (the golf capital of the world) is just 12 minutes away. This beautiful example of 1870 southern architecture has been lovingly restored and is the former home of the blacksmith for the Tyson and Jones Buggy Factory. Four spacious, tastefully decorated rooms are available, with a fireplace in each room. Just 20 minutes from Seagrove (the pottery center of North Carolina), and Cameron and Aberdeen's antique shops and historic districts. In the National Register of Historic Places. In a historic district. No smoking inside.

Hosts: Gary and Shawna Smith
Rooms: 4 (2 PB; 2 SB) $50
Full Breakfast
Credit Cards: A, B
Notes: 2, 5, 8, 12, 14

CASHIERS

High Hampton Inn and Country Club

Highway 107 South, P.O. Box 338, 28717
(704) 743-2411; (800) 334-2551 (reservations)
FAX (704) 743-5991

High Hampton Inn, listed in the National Register of Historic Places, is a 1,400-acre estate, at 3,600 feet in the Blue Ridge Mountains, with a history going back more than a century. High Hampton accommodations are simple and rustic. With no TVs or telephones, guests fill their days with golf, tennis, boating, fishing, and hiking. In the evening, guests gather by the four-sided stone fireplace for conversation and tea. All meals are served buffet style and are included in the room rate. High Hampton also features an excellent children's program for young guests ages 5 to 12.

Rooms: 120 (PB) $160-202
Full Breakfast
Credit Cards: A, B, C, D
Notes: 2, 3, 4, 8, 9, 10, 11, 12, 13, 14

CHAPEL HILL

Carolina Mornings, Inc.

(800) 770-9055; (888) MORNINGS (667-6467)
FAX (919) 929-5061
e-mail: carolinamornings.com
www.carolinamornings.com

A reservation service for bed and breakfasts and country inn specializing in Asheville and western North Carolina. The service is able to assist travelers wishing to visit the Biltmore Estate with comfortable accommodations at in-town sites. Biltmore Estate bed and breakfast packages are also available. Many of the bed and breakfasts are in historic homes elegantly furnished with antiques. The service is also able to find lodging for those who want to explore the mountains, visit the Piedmont, or enjoy the beaches. Offering lakeside lodges or hilltop retreats close to the Blue Ridge Parkway. Also service offers secluded log cabins and guest houses throughout the area. There is no charge for the service. All credit cards accepted. Full breakfast. $70-385.

101. A mile from UNC in a new old-fashioned neighborhood. Relax in spacious guest rooms, slumber soundly in comfortable beds, savor a bountiful breakfast, linger by the fire, mosey in the garden, and experience true southern hospitality. $110.

The Fearrington House Inn

The Fearrington House Inn

2000 Fearrington Village Center, Pittsboro, 27312
(919) 542-2121; www.fearrington.com

In a cluster of low, attractive buildings grouped around a courtyard and surrounded by gardens and rolling countryside, this elegant inn offers luxurious quarters in a country setting. A member of Relais et Châteaux. The restaurant's sophisticated regional cuisine has received national acclaim, including AAA's five-diamond award.

Hosts: The Fitch Family
Rooms: 31 (PB) $165-325
Full Breakfast
Credit Cards: A, B, C
Notes: 3, 4, 5, 7, 9, 10, 11, 12, 14, 15

The Inn at Bingham School

P.O. Box 267, 27514
(919) 563-5583; (800) 566-5583
FAX (919) 563-9826; e-mail: fdeprez@aol.com

The Inn is an award-winning restoration of a National Trust Property. A unique combination of Greek Revival and Federal styles. Listed in the historic registry. Stroll the surrounding woodlands or curl up by the fire. Welcome the day over an elaborate southern breakfast. Just 11 miles west of Chapel Hill, offering a charming combination of peace and history close to gourmet dining, shopping, and UNC. Smoking permitted outside only.

Hosts: François and Christina Deprez
Rooms: 5 (PB) $75-120
Full Breakfast
Credit Cards: A, B, C, D
Notes: 2, 5, 7, 8, 9, 10, 12

CHARLOTTE

The Carmel Bed and Breakfast

4633 Carmel Road, 28226
(704) 542-9450; (800) 229-5860

Classic elegance and charm. Four guest rooms, all with private baths. In southeast Charlotte, minutes from Southpark, Charlotte's prestigious business, retail, dining, and shopping area. Also minutes from the premier Phillips Place complex, with gourmet restaurants, elegant shops, and 10-theater movie houses. Easy access to I-485, I-85, and I-77. Nonsmoking house. Children over 12 welcome.

Hosts: Tom and Linda Moag
Rooms: 4 (PB) $79-109
Full Breakfast
Credit Cards: A, B, C
Notes: 2, 5, 7, 9, 12, 14

The Elizabeth Bed and Breakfast

2145 East Fifth Street, 28204
(704) 358-1368

This 1923 lavender "lady" is in historic Elizabeth, Charlotte's second-oldest neighborhood. European country-style rooms are beautifully appointed with antiques, ceiling fans, decorator linens, and unique collections. All rooms have central air and private baths; some have TVs and telephones. Enjoy a generous breakfast, then relax in the garden courtyard, complete with charming gazebo, or stroll beneath giant oak trees to convenient restaurants and shopping.

The Elizabeth

Host: Joan Mastny
Rooms: 4 (PB) $79-109
Full Breakfast
Credit Cards: A, B, D
Notes: 2, 5, 7, 9, 11

The Homeplace

5901 Sardis Road, 28270
(704) 365-1936

Restored 1902 country Victorian with wraparound porch and tin roof, nestled amid two and one-half wooded acres. Secluded "cottage-style" gardens with a gazebo, brick walkways, and a 1930s log barn further enhance this nostalgic oasis in southeast Charlotte. Experienced innkeepers offer two guest rooms and one suite and a full breakfast. Opened in 1984, the Homeplace is "a reflection of the true bed and breakfast experience." Children over 12 welcome.

The Homeplace

Hosts: Peggy and Frank Dearien
Rooms: 2 (2 PB) $115
Suite: 1 (PB) $135
Full Breakfast
Credit Cards: A, B, C
Notes: 2, 5, 7, 14

The Inn Uptown

129 North Poplar Street, 28202
(704) 342-2800; (800) 959-1990

Constructed in 1890 and historically listed as the Bagley-Mullen House, this chateauesque home has been restored into "an elegant alternative in uptown hospitality." Convenient for corporate and leisure travelers. Six beautifully appointed rooms feature private baths, complimentary wine, remote control cable TVs, and telephones. A complimentary full breakfast features specialties from the inn's kitchen and is served in the dining room. Three-diamond AAA rating. Corporate rates are available.

Host: Elizabeth J. Rich
Rooms: 6 (PB) $109-159
Full Breakfast
Credit Cards: A, B, C, D, E
Notes: 2, 5, 7, 9, 14

The Morehead Inn

1122 East Morehead Street, 28204
(704) 376-3357; (888) MOREHEAD
FAX (704) 335-1110

A historic property nestled in the heart of Dilworth, Charlotte's oldest neighborhood. The "Old Coddington House," as locals refer to it, has served as host to North Carolina's most prominent families and public servants. Built in 1917, the estate was the home of Charles and Marjorie Coddington, owners of all the Buick dealerships south of the Mason-Dixon linc. The inn now serves as "the single most unique experience in Charlotte." The Georgian Revival mansion boasts all period and European antiques. Continental plus breakfast served.

Hosts: Billy Maddalon and Helen Price
Rooms: 12 (PB) $110-230
Continental Breakfast
Credit Cards: A, B, C, D, E
Notes: 2, 5, 7, 8, 9, 10, 11, 12, 14

Still Waters

6221 Amos Smith Road, 28214
(704) 399-6299

A log resort home on two wooded acres overlooking the Catawba River at the upper end of Lake Wylie; within 15 minutes of downtown Charlotte. Full breakfast is served on glassed-in porch overlooking the lake. Enjoy the sport court, the garden, swimming, boating, fishing, or sitting in the lakeside gazebo. Convenient to I-85, airport, and Billy Graham Parkway.

Hosts: Janet and Rob Dyer
Rooms: 4 (PB) $55-85
Full Breakfast
Credit Cards: A, B, E
Notes: 2, 5, 7, 8, 9, 10, 11, 12, 14

CHIMNEY ROCK VILLAGE

The Dogwood Inn

P.O. Box 159, Highway 64-74, 28720
(828) 625-4403

A charming, white two-story European-style bed and breakfast. Come enjoy the five porches that grace this wonderful early 1900s inn on the banks of the peaceful Rocky Broad River. Massive Chimney Rock Mountain can be seen from any of the porches. A full

The Dogwood Inn

gourmet breakfast is served each morning. Children over 12 are welcome. Come rest a while. The river is calling.

Host: Marsha Reynolds
Rooms: 11 (7 PB; 4 SB) $79-129
Full Breakfast
Credit Cards: A, B, C, D
Notes: 2, 7, 9, 10, 11, 12, 14

CLINTON

The Shield House Inn

The Shield House Inn, Inc.

216 Sampson Street, 28328
(910) 592-3933; (910) 592-2634 (phone/FAX)
(800) 462-9817 (reservations only); (800) 463-9817 (reservations only)

These lodgings consist of two estates and three duplex guest houses. The Shield House Inn, circa 1916, is reminiscent of *Gone With the Wind* and the Courthouse Inn, circa 1818, is a recently renovated courthouse. Both are listed in the National Register of Historic Places. These inns have wraparound porches and many dramatic features. Spacious bedrooms are decorated with period antiques, many marble-topped. Lounging areas are available. Direct-dial telephones, cable TV, and refrigerators. Continental plus breakfast served. Full breakfast is served in the main house. Smoking permitted in guest house and porches only. Children welcome by prior arrangements. Courthouse Inn is handicapped accessible.

Hosts: Juanita McLamb and Anita Green
Rooms: 15 (PB) $60-125
Guests houses: 3; $50-150
Full and Continental Breakfast

NOTES: Credit cards accepted: A MasterCard; B Visa; C American Express; D Discover; E Diner's Club; F Other; 2 Personal checks accepted; 3 Lunch available; 4 Dinner available; 5 Open all year; 6 Pets welcome;

Credit Cards: A, B, C, D, E
Notes: 2, 5, 9, 10, 12, 14

CLYDE

Windsong: A Mountain Inn

459 Rockcliffe Lane, 28721
(704) 627-6111

Enjoy a secluded, romantic interlude at this contemporary log inn high in the breathtaking Smoky Mountains. Though the inn is small and intimate, the rooms are large and bright, with high-beamed ceilings, pine log walls, and Mexican tile floors. Rooms have a fireplace, tub for two, separate shower, and private deck or patio. Guest lounge with billiards. Full breakfast included. On 25 acres, with pool, outdoor hot tub, tennis, hiking, and lovable llamas. For families with children, there is the Pond Lodge, a separate two-bedroom log guest house with full kitchen. Luncheon and dinner llama treks in the forest, as well as overnight treks, are available. Open year-round. Children 12 and older welcome in the main inn. All ages welcome in the Pond Lodge.

Hosts: Russ and Barbara Mancini
Rooms: 7 (PB) $120-175
Full Breakfast
Credit Cards: A, B, D
Notes: 2, 5, 7, 9, 10, 11, 12, 13, 14

Windsong: A Mountain Inn

CULLOWHEE

Carolina Mornings, Inc.

(800) 770-9055; (888) MORNINGS (667-6467)
FAX (919) 929-5061
e-mail: carolinamornings.com
www.carolinamornings.com

45. A rustic lodge built with 100-year-old hand-hewn logs on the sparkling, trout-filled Tuckasegee River. Relax in front of the massive stone fireplace or enjoy billiards in the great room. Breakfast in the dining room or at a table on the porch overlooking a waterfall. Bedrooms with balconies. $90-130.

DILLSBORO

Olde Towne Inn Bed and Breakfast

300 Haywood Road, P.O. Box 485, 28725-0485
(704) 586-3461

Enjoy mountain views and breezes while rocking on the front porch of this 1878 home in Dillsboro, the "town of magic." Walk to all gift shops, galleries, restaurants, and the Great Smoky Mountains Railroad excursions. Go hiking, rafting, tubing, fishing, panning for various gems, or visit Cherokee Indian Reservation. Four guest rooms with air conditioning, ceiling fans, and decorated in country decor with antiques. Children over 10 welcome.

Host: Lera Chitwood
Rooms: 4 (PB) $65-80
Full Breakfast
Credit Cards: A, B
Notes: 2, 5, 6, 7, 11, 12, 13

DUCK

Advice 5¢: a bed and breakfast

111 Scarborough Lane, P.O. Box 8278, 27949
(252) 255-1050; (800) ADVICE5 (238-4235)

Advice 5¢ may very well be "one of the best kept secrets" on the northern beaches of the Outer Banks. In the heart of Duck, this refreshing seaside haven exudes an air of casual simplicity. All guest rooms have private decks, plus a suite which includes a sitting area, cable TV, and Jacuzzi-style bathtub. Enjoy refreshing outdoor showers, beach chairs, books galore, and home-baked treats during daily afternoon tea.

Hosts: Nancy Caviness and Donna Black
Rooms: 5 (PB) $80-160
Continental Breakfast
Credit Cards: A, B
Notes: 2, 5, 7, 9, 10, 11, 12

The Sanderling Inn Resort

1461 Duck Road, 27949
(919) 261-4111; (800) 701-4111

Year-round luxurious resort (1985) five miles north of Duck—all rooms with baths, color cable TV/VCRs, and private porches. Complete with kitchens, wet bars, and refrigerators. Wheelchair accessible. Historic restaurant and bar as well as meeting rooms for 10 to 100 people. Health club with weight room, sauna, pool, hot tub, message therapy, and tennis courts. Secluded beach, private conference center, and off-season packages available. Also available are suites and three-bedroom villas which are suitable for families.

Manager: Christine Berger
Rooms: 88 (PB) $123-432
Continental Breakfast
Credit Cards: A, B,C, D, E
Notes: 2, 3, 4, 5, 9, 10, 11, 12, 14, 15

DURHAM

Arrowhead Inn

106 Mason Road, 27712
(919) 477-8430; (800) 528-2207

This restored 1775 manor house on four rural acres offers homey hospitality in an atmosphere that evokes colonial Carolina. But along with 18th-century architecture, decor, and furnishings, the inn features contemporary comfort, sparkling housekeeping,

Arrowhead Inn

and bounteous home-cooked breakfasts that are different each morning of stay. Open year-round. Written up in *Food and Wine*, *USA Today*, and *Southern Living*. Celebrating 14 years in business. Smoking permitted in designated areas only.

Hosts: Jerry, Barbara, and Cathy Ryan
Rooms: 8 (PB) $90-210
Full Breakfast
Credit Cards: A, B, C, D, E
Notes: 2, 5, 8, 9, 10, 12, 14, 15

EDENTON

Granville Queen Themed Inn

108 South Granville Street, 27932
(919) 482-5296

A romantic bed and breakfast in Edenton's historic district. Each oversize room has large separate bath, TV, VCR, telephone, and museum-quality furniture from Italian villas. Decor themes include: French

Granville Queen Themed Inn

NOTES: Credit cards accepted: A MasterCard; B Visa; C American Express; D Discover; E Diner's Club; F Other; 2 Personal checks accepted; 3 Lunch available; 4 Dinner available; 5 Open all year; 6 Pets welcome;

Provincial, Roman, Victorian, nautical, English farm, and Egyptian (replete with a pair of 10-foot bronze sphinxes flanking Pharaoh's throne). Most rooms have fireplaces and private patios. Breakfast is a five-course gourmet including filet mignon and chicken tarragon. There are weekend wine and cheese tastings. Walk to downtown, restaurants, antiques, and impeccably maintained antebellum homes. Boat tours of Albermarle Sound adjacent.

Hosts: Marge and Ken Dunne
Rooms: 9 (PB) $90-105
Full Breakfast
Credit Cards: None
Notes: 2, 5, 7, 9, 10, 12, 15

The Lords Proprietors' Inn

The Lords Proprietors' Inn

300 North Broad Street, 27932
(919) 482-3641

Establishing a reputation for the finest accommodations in North Carolina, the inn offers 20 elegantly appointed rooms with private baths and spacious parlors for gathering for afternoon tea by the fire. A four-course dinner is served Tuesday through Saturday by reservation. MAP rates Tuesday through Saturday. One room is handicapped accessible.

Hosts: Arch and Jane Edwards
Rooms: 20 (PB) $185-235
Full Breakfast
Credit Cards: None
Notes: 2, 5, 8, 9, 10, 11, 12, 14, 15

Trestle House Inn

632 Soundside Road, 27932
(800) 645-8466; e-mail: thinn@coastalnet.com
www.edenton.com/trestlehouse

Inn overlooks wildlife preserve surrounded on three sides by water. Golfing, hiking, biking, swimming, tennis, sightseeing, fishing, and bird watching available. Inside, the inn has California redwood beams from trees estimated to be over 450 years old. TV/game room. Fireplace, deck overlooking lake and pond. Historic Edenton was original colonial capital of North Carolina. The town retains the elegant charm of a bygone era including many of the most beautiful older homes in the country.

Hosts: Peter L. Bogus and Wendy S. Jewett
Rooms: 5 (PB) $80-100
Full Breakfast
Credit Cards: A, B, C, F
Notes: 2, 5, 7, 8, 9, 10, 11, 12, 14

ELLERBE

Ellerbe Springs Inn

2537 North Highway 220, 28338
(910) 652-5600; (800) 248-6467
www.ellerbesprings.com

Ellerbe Springs Inn is a beautiful, historic country inn on 50 acres of rolling hills. Established in 1857, the manor has been

Ellerbe Springs Inn

completely renovated and redecorated. Fourteen charming guest rooms feature antique furniture, private bathrooms, and cable TVs. Historic cottage overlooking lake has two suites. First-floor dining room serves breakfast, lunch, and dinner daily. Easy drive from Charlotte, Greensboro, Raleigh, and Myrtle Beach. National Register of Historic Places.

Host: Beth Cadieu
Rooms: 16 (PB) $54-98
Full Breakfast
Credit Cards: A, B, C, D
Notes: 2, 3, 4, 5, 7, 8, 9, 10, 12, 14

EMERALD ISLE

Emerald Isle Inn and Bed and Breakfast By the Sea

502 Ocean Drive, 28594
(919) 354-3222
e-mail: adetwiller@coastalnet.com

Emerald Isle Inn Bed and Breakfast is the only bed and breakfast in Emerald Isle. It offers four unique accommodations, including the newly featured King Suite with ocean view. Enjoy a full gourmet breakfast and freshly ground coffee daily. The inn features porches with rockers, swings, ocean/bay views, and friendly conversation. With direct beach access, experience the warm blue Atlantic, colorful sunsets, and restful sounds of waves breaking on white sands, only steps from guests' suite. In-state checks accepted. AAA- and Mobil-rated.

Hosts: Marilyn and A. K. Detwiller
Rooms: 4 (PB) $75-165
Full Breakfast
Credit Cards: A, B
Notes: 5, 7, 10, 11, 12, 14

FAIRVIEW

Carolina Mornings, Inc.

(800) 770-9055; (888) MORNINGS (667-6467)
FAX (919) 929-5061
e-mail: carolinamornings.com
www.carolinamornings.com

32. Experience the elegance of this distinguished guest house on 80 rolling acres. Magnificent mountain views and fireplaces in each of the five beautifully appointed rooms. Indulge in the romantic and luxurious suite and spa complete with Jacuzzi. Gourmet breakfast and champagne reception each evening. $190-385.

FRANKLIN

The Franklin Terrace

159 Harrison Avenue, 28734
(704) 524-7907; (800) 633-2431
e-mail: terrace@dnet.net
www.intertekweb.com/terrace

The Franklin Terrace, built as a school in 1887, is listed in the National Register of Historic Places. Wide porches and large guest rooms filled with period antiques will carry guests to a time gone by when southern hospitality was at its best. Antiques, crafts, and gifts are for sale on the main floor. Within walking distance of Franklin's famous gem shops, clothing boutiques, and fine restaurants. Air conditioning. Cable TV. Open April 1 through November 15. Smoking permitted outside only. Children over the age of three are welcome. Social drinking permitted in rooms only.

Hosts: Ed and Helen Henson
Rooms: 9 (PB) $52-69
Full Breakfast
Credit Cards: A, B, C, D
Notes: 2, 7, 10, 11, 12, 14

The Heritage Inn

43 Heritage Hollow Drive,
(Just off Route 441 Business), 28734
(828) 524-4150; (888) 524-4150
FAX (828) 524-8167; e-mail: heritage@dnet.net

In Heritage Hollow, a quaint seven-acre country village within the town of Franklin, with restaurants, antique and mountain craft shops within walking distance. Near Cowee Valley where guests can try their hands at gem mines. Area

The Heritage Inn

also offers hiking trails, whitewater rafting, waterfalls, golfing, country auctions, antiques, and seasonal skiing. Within 45 minute's drive of Great Smoky Mountains National Park and Cherokee Indian Reservation and New Harrah's Casino. Gorgeous mountain views.

Innkeepers: Tina and Jim Bottomley
Rooms: 6 (PB) $75
Full and Continental Breakfasts
Credit Cards: A, B, C
Notes: 2, 5, 7, 10, 11, 12, 13

GLENDALE SPRINGS

Glendale Springs Inn and Restaurant

7414 NC Highway 16, P.O. Box 117, 28629
(336) 982-2103 (office); (800) 287-1206

Since 1892 the Glendale Springs Inn has been a welcome landmark for visitors to Ashe County and the Blue Ridge Parkway.

Glendale Springs Inn

Excellent water, pure mountain air, a superb dining menu, and a good night's rest continue to restore weary travelers. Enjoy the safe, unhurried mountain way of life. Canoe the exquisite New River. Explore back roads, scenic byways, and the region's many park trails. Visit the nearby university town. Return for afternoon tea or an evening cappuccino on the eastern Continental Divide's friendliest front porch. Smoking permitted outside.

Host: Amanda Smith
Rooms: 9 (PB) $95-115
Full Breakfast
Credit Cards: A, B, C, D
Notes: 2, 3, 4, 5, 7, 8, 9, 12, 13, 15

GREENSBORO

Greenwood

Greenwood

205 North Park Drive, 27401
(910) 274-6350; (800) 535-9363

"A culinary escape," where a New Orleans chef prepares abundant breakfasts to order and evening desserts in this 1900s chalet in the park. Candlelight packages include room service to five distinctive rooms with private baths. Dinner by special arrangement.

Hosts: Bob and Dolly Guertin
Rooms: 5 (PB) $95-160
Full Breakfast
Credit Cards: A, B, C, D, E
Notes: 2, 5, 7, 9, 10, 11, 12, 14

7 No smoking; 8 Children welcome; 9 Social drinking allowed; 10 Tennis nearby; 11 Swimming nearby; 12 Golf nearby; 13 Skiing nearby; 14 May be booked through a travel agent; 15 Handicapped accessible.

HENDERSONVILLE

Apple Inn

1005 White Pine Drive, 28739-3951
(704) 693-0107; (800) 615-6611

There's no place like home, unless it's the Apple Inn. Only two miles from downtown Hendersonville, the inn is on three acres featuring charmingly comfortable rooms, each with modern private bath that awaits guests' arrival. Delicious home-cooked breakfasts (served al fresco, weather permitting), fresh flowers, and antiques complement the ambiance of this turn-of-the-century home. Enjoy billiards, tennis, swimming, hiking, antiquing, bird watching, or just plain relaxing. Create tomorrow's memories amidst yesterday's charm!

Hosts: Bob and Pam Hedstrom
Rooms: 5 (PB) $75-140
Cottage: 1 (PB)
Full Breakfast
Credit Cards: A, B
Notes: 2, 5, 7, 9, 10, 11, 12, 13, 14

Carolina Mornings, Inc.

(800) 770-9055; (888) MORNINGS (667-6467)
FAX (919) 929-5061
e-mail: carolinamornings.com
www.carolinamornings.com

12. Experience a tasteful blend of European and American antiques and culture in an elegantly warm setting. Gourmet breakfast served in the formal dining room or on a covered porch with Turkish tiles. TV/VCR in all rooms. Rich video library. Walk to downtown Hendersonville. $85-175.

38. Offering a comfortable, homelike atmosphere, each charmingly decorated room bears the name of an apple. Relax on the secluded parklike grounds in hammocks and rockers or play badminton, horseshoes, or croquet. Mountain views with delicious home-cooked breakfasts. $79-125.

Claddagh Inn

Claddagh Inn

755 North Main Street, 28792
(800) 225-4700; FAX (828) 697-8664
e-mail: innkeepers@claddaghinn.com
www.claddaghinn.com

Hendersonville's first bed and breakfast can be found on Main Street. Newly renovated guest rooms have private baths, telephones, air conditioning, and TVs. Early risers enjoy coffee or tea while a full country breakfast is being prepared. Specially commissioned, Irish influenced, stained-glass windows adorn the doorways to some guest rooms. Enjoy the charm of rocking on the veranda and visiting with the innkeepers or other guests after a day of hiking, sightseeing, or shopping. There is always a special treat in the cookie jar. After strolling back home from a wonderful dinner, enjoy the porch swing before retiring to one's room. Listed in the National Register of Historic Places. Member of NCBBI, PAII. Relive an American tradition.

Hosts: Augie and Gerri Emanuele
Rooms: 16 (PB)
Full Breakfast
Credit Cards: A, B, C, D
Notes: 2, 5, 7, 8, 9, 10, 11, 12, 14

The Waverly Inn

783 North Main Street, 28792
(828) 693-9193; (800) 537-8195
FAX (828) 692-1010; e-mail: waverlyinn@ioa.com

Listed in the National Register of Historic Places, the Waverly Inn is the oldest inn in

The Waverly Inn

Hendersonville. The recently renovated inn has something for everyone, including claw-foot tubs and king- and queen-size canopied beds. Convenient to restaurants, shopping, Biltmore Estate, Carl Sandburg home, Blue Ridge Parkway, and Flat Rock Playhouse. Member of NCBBI and IIA. Picnic lunch available.

Hosts: John and Diane Sheiry
Rooms: 15 (PB) $89-149
Full Breakfast
Credit Cards: A, B, C, D
Notes: 2, 5, 7, 8, 9, 10, 11, 12, 14

HIGHLANDS

Colonial Pines Inn

541 Hickory Street, 28741
(828) 526-2060

A quiet country guest house with lovely mountain view. Comfortably furnished with

Colonial Pines Inn

antiques and many fine accessories. One-half mile from Highlands' fine dining and shopping area. Full breakfast includes egg dishes, homemade breads, fresh fruit, coffee, and juice. Two separate guest houses with kitchens and fireplaces are great for families. Children over 12 welcome.

Hosts: Chris and Donna Alley
Rooms: 6 (PB) $80-115
Suites: $105-135
Guest House: $105-250
Full Breakfast
Credit Cards: A, B
Notes: 2, 5, 7, 9, 10, 11, 12, 13

The Laurels

The Laurels: Freda's Bed and Breakfast

3309 Horse Cove Road, 28741
(704) 526-2091

The Laurels is in historic Horse Cove, two and one-half miles from Highlands, on seven acres. Serves an English tea in the afternoon. Two fireplaces warm the cool evenings. A large English country breakfast features fruit, bacon, ham, eggs, pancakes. The hosts grind their own whole wheat that makes crunchy toast. Homemade jams and lemon curd. Fish the one-half-acre pond stocked with rainbow trout. No smoking.

Hosts: Warren and Freda Lorenz
Rooms: 5 (PB) $70-80
Full Breakfast
Credit Cards: None
Notes: 2, 7, 8, 9, 15

7 No smoking; 8 Children welcome; 9 Social drinking allowed; 10 Tennis nearby; 11 Swimming nearby; 12 Golf nearby; 13 Skiing nearby; 14 May be booked through a travel agent; 15 Handicapped accessible.

Ye Olde Stone House Bed and Breakfast

1337 South 4th Street, 28741
(828) 526-5911

This house built of stone is a mile from town. Rooms are bright, cheerful, and comfortably furnished. Perfect places for relaxing include a sunroom, porch, 30-foot deck, and attached year-round gazebo, all with view. Two fireplaces provide gathering spots. After a restful night's sleep, rise to the smell of freshly brewed coffee and a full country breakfast. Separate, completely furnished chalet and log cabin with fireplaces and meadow views. Featured on the cover of 1996 edition of *The Annual Directory of American and Canadian Bed and Breakfasts.*

Hosts: Jim and Rene Ramsdell
Rooms: 4 (PB) $75-90
Chalet and cabins: $105-170
Full Breakfast
Credit Cards: A, B
Notes: 2, 5, 7, 8, 9, 10, 11, 12, 13

HIGH POINT

The Bouldin House Bed and Breakfast

4332 Archdale Road, Archdale, 27263
(336) 431-4909; (800) 739-1816

This finely crafted historic four-square sits on three acres of a former tobacco farm. Country atmosphere; relaxed and casual, yet elegant. Warmly decorated rooms combine old and new, each with spacious, modern, private bathrooms. America's largest concentration of furniture showrooms is only minutes away. Awaken to early morning coffee/tea service. Follow the aroma of a gourmet breakfast to the oak-paneled dining room.

Hosts: Larry and Ann Miller
Rooms: 4 (PB) $85-95
Full Breakfast
Credit Cards: A, B, D
Notes: 2, 5, 7, 9, 10, 12, 14

HILLSBOROUGH

The Colonial Inn

153 West King Street, 27278
(919) 732-2461

A charming old country inn in historic Hillsborough, the Colonial Inn has served guests continuously since 1759, among them Lord Cornwallis and Aaron Burr. A short distance from Chapel Hill, Durham, and Duke University. Convenient to I-85 and I-40. Famous for its southern cooking and homelike comfort. Great antique shopping nearby. Indoor swimming nearby.

Hosts: Carlton and Sara McKee
Rooms: 8 (6 PB; 2 SB) $55-65
Full Breakfast
Credit Cards: A, B
Notes: 2, 3, 4, 5, 8, 9, 11,

KILL DEVIL HILLS

Cherokee Inn

500 North Virginia Dare Trail, 27948
(919) 441-6127; (800) 554-2764

This large beach house with cypress-wood interior is 500 feet from ocean beach. Quiet and restful. Ideal for relaxing and romance. Close to fine restaurants, golf, hang-gliding, kayaking, scuba diving, wind surfing, deep-sea fishing, shopping, and other attractions. Three-night minimum stay required for holidays. Closed November through March.

Hosts: Bob and Kaye Combs
Rooms: 6 (PB) $70-110
Continental Breakfast

Cherokee Inn

NOTES: Credit cards accepted: A MasterCard; B Visa; C American Express; D Discover; E Diner's Club; F Other; 2 Personal checks accepted; 3 Lunch available; 4 Dinner available; 5 Open all year; 6 Pets welcome;

Credit Cards: A, B, C
Notes: 2, 7, 9, 10, 11, 12, 14

LAKE LURE

Carolina Mornings, Inc.

(800) 770-9055; (888) MORNINGS (667-6467)
FAX (919) 929-5061
e-mail: carolinamornings.com
www.carolinamornings.com

11. With a rare and wonderful combination of elegance and rustic charm, this inn rests on the shores of a mountain lake. Canoes, swimming, fishing, and a daily afternoon cruise with the owners make this a memorable bed and breakfast stay. $89-145.

LAUREL SPRINGS

Burgiss Farm Bed and Breakfast

294 Elk Knob Road, 28644
(800) 233-1505; e-mail: tburgiss@aol.com
www.breakfastinn.com

Honeymooners and anniversary couples love Burgiss Farm! This 1897 farmhouse high in the mountains has lots of space and privacy. Mountain biking, dancing at the barn, wading in the clear cool mountain water. Guests can select their breakfast from seven different selections and choose the time. By reservations only. Best time to call is around 10 P.M.

Hosts: Nancy and Tom Burgiss
Rooms: 2 (PB) $90
Full Breakfast
Credit Cards: A, B
Notes: 2, 7, 8, 9, 10, 12, 13

LITTLE SWITZERLAND

Alpine Inn

Highway 226 A, P.O. Box 477, 28749
(828) 765-5380

Alpine Inn is a small, quaint establishment with rustic mountain charm. An excellent view, from all rooms, of mountain ranges and valleys. One mile from the Blue Ridge Parkway. Guest rooms are cozy and comfortable with a homelike atmosphere. There is a variety of accommodations from a one bedroom to a full apartment. Breakfasts, which are optional, are hearty and healthful and range from $1 to $5. Full vegetarian breakfast available. Breakfast is served on the main balcony. Commune with nature's sunrises!

Hosts: Sharon E. Smith and William M. Cox
Rooms: 14 (PB) $38-60
Full and Continental Breakfast
Credit Cards: A, B
Notes: 2, 8, 9, 12

LITTLETON/LAKE GASTON

Littleton's Maplewood Manor Bed and Breakfast

120 College Street, P.O. Box 1165, 27850
(919) 586-4682

This bed and breakfast is in a small, quaint town at the gateway to beautiful Lake Gaston. Hosts offer king-, queen-size, or twin beds. There are a TV, VCR, videos, CDs, and games. Outdoor grill, horseshoes, croquet, sitting areas. Parklike grounds all for guests to enjoy. Guests may like to walk the tree-lined streets in town. A full breakfast is served on the screened sitting area. Wine and crackers served in the evening. The inn is halfway between I-95 and I-85 just off Route 158. Inquire about accommodations for children.

Hosts: Helen and Alan Burtchell
Rooms: 2 (SB) $60
Full Breakfast
Credit Cards: A, B
Notes: 5, 7, 12

MANTEO

Tranquil House Inn

405 Queen Elizabeth Avenue, 27954
(919) 473-1404

The Tranquil House Inn is a beautiful 19th-century-style inn with 20th-century convenience. Relax on the second-floor deck and enjoy the cool coastal breezes. Listen to the soothing sounds of the marina while enjoying the Continental plus breakfast, lemonade, and wine and cheese reception. Guests are invited to use the bikes while sightseeing, shopping, or discovering the history of Roanoke Island. Guests will be minutes from the beaches but a world apart. Dinner available in restaurant in season. Water-skiing available.

Host: Donnie Just Jr.
Rooms: 25 (PB) $79-169
Continental Breakfast
Credit Cards: A, B, C, D
Notes: 5, 7, 8, 9, 10, 11, 12, 14, 15

MARSHALL

Marshall House Bed and Breakfast Inn

100 Hill Street, P.O. Box 865, 28753
(828) 649-9205; FAX (828) 649-2999
e-mail: twaq42a@prodigy.com

Truly in the mountains, overlooking the quaint town of Marshall, and the French Broad River, this 1903 house is decorated with fancy chandeliers, mirrors, and lots of antiques. Resident cats add extra charm, and the porch is for rocking in this very relaxed atmosphere. Listed in the National Register of Historic Places, the house welcomes all in an atmosphere of bygone days. Continental plus breakfast served. Pets are welcome. Self-provided social drinking permitted. Limited handicapped accessibility.

Hosts: Ruth and Jim Boylan
Rooms: 9 (2 PB; 7 SB) $39-75
Continental Breakfast
Credit Cards: A, B, C, D, E
Notes: 5, 6, 8, 11, 12, 13, 14

MOCKSVILLE

Boxwood Lodge

Highway 601 South at 132 Becktown Road, 27028
(336) 284-2031

Boxwood Lodge, a Colonial Revival 25-room country mansion by Delano and Aldrich, is on 51 acres of beautifully wooded land. Convenient to I-85 or I-40 travelers. Enjoy a nearby game of golf, leisure walk, fishing, game of billiards, afternoon tea, reading by the fireside in the library, or just browsing around the lodge. Smoking permitted in designated areas only.

Host: Martha Hoffner
Rooms: 8 (5 PB; 3 SB) $55-95
Cabin: $85-95
Full Breakfast
Credit Cards: A, B, C
Notes: 2, 11, 12, 14

MOORESVILLE

Oake Ridge Farm

1108 Oak Ridge Farm Highway, 28115
(704) 663-7085

Enjoy gracious southern hospitality at Oak Ridge Farm bed and breakfast. This charming, traditionally furnished home, built in 1871, offers a step back in time to a quiet and peaceful country atmosphere. Breakfast at Oak Ridge Farm is a delightful experience with an abundance of home-baked goods and fresh fruit, served by candlelight with classical music in the background. Guests can stroll amid 18 wooded acres or enjoy the comfort of the rockers on the spacious wraparound porch. Children five and older welcome.

Hosts: Harold and Rustina Hansen
Rooms: 2 (1 PB; 1 SB)
Full Breakfast
Credit Cards: None
Notes: 2, 5, 7, 10, 11, 12, 14

MURPHY

Park Place

100 HIll Street, 28906
(828) 837-8842

Partake of congenial atmosphere in this circa 1900 three-story clapboard home with eclectic decor of family treasures, antique furnishings, interesting collectibles, and hand-knotted oriental rugs. For guests' comfort, there are three well-appointed guest rooms and a gourmet breakfast that will tickle one's palate. Shoot the breeze on the treetop-level porch, watch park activities, or just rock the time away. *Willkommen—Wir sprechen Deutsch*!

Hosts: Rikki and Neil Wocell
Rooms: 3 (PB) $75-90
Full Breakfast
Credit Cards: F
Notes: 2, 5, 9, 10, 11, 12

NAGS HEAD

First Colony Inn™

6720 South Virginia Dare Trail, 27959
(252) 441-2343; (800) 368-9390 reservations
FAX (252) 441-9234
e-mail: innkeeper@firstcolonyinn.com
www.firstcolonyinn.com

Enjoy southern hospitality at the Outer Banks's only historic bed and breakfast inn (national register). Private beach access, pool, wraparound verandas with rockers, elegant library, antique-filled rooms with private tiled baths, heated towel bars, Jacuzzis, wet bars with microwave ovens or kitchenettes, and remote-controlled heat pumps. Enjoy the complimentary breakfast buffet and afternoon tea in the sunny breakfast room. See *The Lost Colony* and Wright Brothers Memorial, fish, windsurf, hang glide, or stroll the beach. Honeymoons, anniversaries, weddings, and small conferences are specialties. AAA four-diamond-rated. Personal checks are accepted 30 days in advance.

First Colony Inn™

Hosts: The Lawrences
Rooms: 26 (PB) $80-250 seasonal
Full Breakfast
Credit Cards: A, B, C, D
Notes: 3, 5, 7, 8, 9, 10, 11, 12, 14, 15

NEW BERN

Harmony House Inn

215 Pollock Street, 28560
(919) 636-3810 (phone/FAX); (800) 636-3113
e-mail: harmony@cconnect.net
www.harmonyhouseinn.com

The Harmony House Inn is in the historic district of New Bern and is listed in the National Register of Historic Places. This unusually spacious house has eight guest rooms, the spacious two-room Benjamin Ellis Suite, and the newly decorated, romantic Eliza Ellis Suite with heart-shaped Jacuzzi. All rooms are furnished with ceiling fans, central air conditioning, cable TVs, telephones, and decorative fireplaces. Within walking distance to quaint shops, fine dining restaurants, and many historic sites. The Harmony House, rated three-diamonds by AAA, welcomes business travelers. Complimentary local calls and off-street parking. Many extras.

Hosts: Ed and Sooki Kirkpatrick
Rooms: 10 (PB) $99-155
Full Breakfast
Credit Cards: A, B, D
Notes: 2, 5, 7, 8, 9, 11, 12, 14

New Berne House Inn

709 Broad Street, 28560
(800) 842-7688

Listed in the National Register of Historic Places and one block from Tryon Palace, New Berne House offers the charm and ambiance of English country house decor. Guest rooms all have private baths, some with claw-foot tubs and pedestal sinks. Antique beds piled with pillows; crisp eyelet sheets; fireplaces in some rooms. The inn is noted for its fine breakfasts, including southern specialties such as pralines 'n' cream waffles and peach French

New Berne House Inn

toast. Special packages and rates, including mystery weekends, are available.

Hosts: Marcia Drum and Howard Bronson
Rooms: 7 (PB) $68-88
Full Breakfast
Credit Cards: A, B
Notes: 2, 5, 7, 9, 11, 12, 14

OCEAN ISLE BEACH

The Winds-Clarion Inn

310 East First Street, 28469
(800) 334-3581; FAX (910) 579-2884
e-mail: info@thewinds.com
www.thewinds.com

This delightful inn, surrounded by palm trees and lush subtropical landscaping, is on the oceanfront on an island beach just 20 minutes from North Myrtle Beach, South Carolina. The Winds features oceanfront rooms and one-, two-, and three-bedroom suites with kitchens and seaside balconies. Also four-bedroom beach houses. Amenities include daily housekeeping, a heated pool (enclosed in winter), whirlpool, beach volleyball, fitness room, rental bicycles, golf on more than 98 courses, and free tennis on the island. Complimentary hot breakfast buffet. Ask about free summer golf.

Hosts: Miller and Helen Pope
Rooms: 73 (PB) $59-182
Continental Breakfast
Credit Cards: A, B, C, D, E, F
Notes: 3, 5, 7, 8, 9, 10, 11, 12, 14, 15

OLD FORT

The Inn at Old Fort and Gardens

116 West Main Street, 28762
(704) 668-9384; (800) 471-0637 PIN 1709

The Inn at Old Fort is a restored two-story Victorian country home built in 1880. The Inn, decorated with antiques, is set on over three and one-half acres. The grounds are shaded by walnut and hemlock trees over 100 years old. The terraced lawn includes a variety of gardens. Along with a front porch for rocking and large, comfortable bedrooms, a parlor and a library are for guests' use.

Hosts: Chuck and Debbie Aldridge
Rooms: 4 (PB) $50-70
Continental Breakfast
Credit Cards: None
Notes: 2, 5, 7, 8, 9, 10, 11, 12, 14

PILOT MOUNTAIN

The Blue Fawn Bed and Breakfast

3052 Siloam Road, P.O. Box 986, 27041
(336) 374-2064; (800) 948-7716

The Blue Fawn Bed and Breakfast offers country charm in a restored, circa 1892, Greek Revival farmhouse overlooking the Yadkin River Valley. Featuring two guest rooms and one suite. Each room is furnished with period antiques, reminding guests of that simpler time. Explore the

The Blue Fawn

NOTES: Credit cards accepted: A MasterCard; B Visa; C American Express; D Discover; E Diner's Club; F Other; 2 Personal checks accepted; 3 Lunch available; 4 Dinner available; 5 Open all year; 6 Pets welcome;

rolling countryside or simply relax and view it from one of the porches. Area attractions include Pilot Mountain, canoeing, hiking, golfing, and quiet rest and relaxation. Restricted smoking.

Hosts: Terri and Geno Cella
Rooms: 3 (PB) $65-85
Full Breakfast
Credit Cards: A, B
Notes: 2, 3, 4, 5, 8, 9, 11, 12

PISGAH FOREST

The Pines Country Inn

719 Hart Road, 28768
(704) 877-3131

The Pines Country Inn is in the Blue Ridge Mountains overlooking a beautiful valley. Truly a country inn, where guests are treated like family at Grandma's house. Available by day, week, or month. Three cottages available by week or more. Between Brevard and Hendersonville.

Hosts: Tom and Mary McEntire
Rooms: 18 (16 PB; 2 SB) $55-65
Full Breakfast
Credit Cards: F
Notes: 2, 7, 8, 11, 12, 15

SALISBURY

Rowan Oak House

208 South Fulton Street, 28144-4845
(704) 633-2086; (800) 786-0437
www.bbonline.com/nc/rowanoak/

"Romantic" and "lavish" describe this Queen Anne Victorian mansion: wraparound porch, rocking chairs, elaborate woodwork, stained glass, and original fixtures. Bedrooms are enormous with central air conditioning, English and American antiques, fruit, and flowers. One room has a double Jacuzzi and gas log fireplace. A full gourmet breakfast will be served with silver, crystal, and china. Murder mystery weekends available. In the heart of the historic district, one mile from I-85, exit 76B.

Rowan Oak House

Thirty minutes to High Point furniture shopping. Charlotte Motor Speedway.

Hosts: Barbara and Les Coombs
Rooms: 4 (PB) $85-125
Full Breakfast
Credit Cards: A, B, C, D
Notes: 2, 5, 7, 9, 10, 11, 12, 14

SALUDA

The Oaks

339 Greenville Street, 28773
(704) 749-9613; (800) 893-6091

Charm and comfort await guests in this beautifully furnished 1894 Victorian home in the North Carolina mountain town of Saluda. Thirty-five miles from Greenville,

The Oaks

7 No smoking; 8 Children welcome; 9 Social drinking allowed; 10 Tennis nearby; 11 Swimming nearby; 12 Golf nearby; 13 Skiing nearby; 14 May be booked through a travel agent; 15 Handicapped accessible.

Asheville, and Spartanburg, the Oaks is well positioned for hiking to waterfalls or exploring antique shops. All four bedrooms are attractively furnished with period and antique furniture, four-poster beds, cable TVs, and private baths. Guests will enjoy rocking on the wraparound porch, reading in the library, and fabulous full breakfasts.

Rooms: 4 (PB) $85-125
Full Breakfast
Credit Cards: A, B, C, D
Notes: 2, 5, 7, 8, 9, 10, 12

SOUTHERN PINES

Knollwood House

1495 West Connecticut Avenue, 28387
(919) 692-9390

A luxurious English manor house appointed with 18th-century antiques and contemporary comforts. On three acres of longleaf pines, dogwoods, magnolias, holly trees, and hundreds of flowering shrubs. Less than 100 feet to the 15th fairway of a championship golf course. And there are more than 42 courses just minutes away. Tennis and swimming. Suites and guest rooms, all with private baths. Meeting rooms, wedding facilities, and catering are available. Smoking permitted in designated areas only.

Hosts: Mimi and Dick Beatty
Rooms: 6 (PB) $100-150
Full Breakfast
Credit Cards: A, B
Notes: 2, 5, 9, 10, 11, 12, 14

Knollwood House

SPARTA

Turby-villa

2072 NC Highway 18 North, 28675
(336) 372-8490

The Turby-villa is on 20 acres of beautiful mountain farmland. Breakfast is selected from a menu and served on a glassed-in porch with a beautiful view of the mountains. The bed and breakfast is 10 miles from the Blue Ridge Parkway, which is maintained by the National Park Service, on Highway 18, 2 miles from Sparta. Dinner available by prior arrangement. Smoking permitted outside only.

Host: Maybelline Turbiville
Rooms: 3 (PB) $53
Full Breakfast
Credit Cards: None
Notes: 2, 5, 7, 8, 9, 10, 12

SPRUCE PINE

Ansley/Richmond Inn

101 Pine Avenue, 28777
(828) 765-6993

This lovely half-century-old elegant country inn, specializing in pampering guests, is nestled into the hills overlooking the town of Spruce Pine and the Blue Ridge Parkway just four miles to the south. Ideal for hiking, crafts, skiing, golf, and gem mining, the inn has seven luxurious rooms, all with private baths, and serves a full breakfast each morning and a complimentary glass of wine in the evening.

Hosts: Bill Ansley and Lenore Boucher
Rooms: 7 (PB) $55-75
Full Breakfast
Credit Cards: A, B, D
Notes: 2, 5, 7, 8, 9, 10, 11, 12, 13, 14

Pinebridge Inn

101 Pinebridge Avenue, 28777
(704) 765-5543; (800) 356-5059
FAX (704) 765-5544

A unique, historic schoolhouse inn. High ceilings and broad windows lend a mountain majestic atmosphere. Each room has all the modern amenities. Three miles off the Blue Ridge Parkway in the western North Carolina mountains, Pinebridge Inn is connected to downtown Spruce Pine by a 410-foot-long footbridge spanning the town's park. The area is a mecca for world-renowned artists and crafts people. Also called the gem capital of the world; gemstone mining and other outdoor activities abound. AAA three-diamond-rated, Pinebridge Inn is off 226N.

Hosts: Mike and Teresa Thomas
Rooms: 46 (PB) $43-135
Continental Breakfast
Credit Cards: A, B, C, D
Notes: 5, 7, 8, 9, 10, 11, 12, 13, 14, 15

STATESVILLE

Cedar Hill Farm Bed and Breakfast

778 Elmwood Road, 28625
(704) 873-4332; (800) 948-4423

An 1840 farmhouse and private cottages on a 32-acre sheep farm in the rolling hills of North Carolina. Antique furnishings, air conditioning, color cable TVs, and telephones in rooms. After a full country breakfast, swim, play badminton, or relax in a porch rocker or hammock. For a busier day, visit two lovely towns with historic districts, Old Salem, or two large cities in a 45-mile radius. Convenient to restaurants, shopping, and three interstate highways. Smoking in designated areas only.

Hosts: Jim and Brenda Vernon
Rooms: 3 (PB) $70-95
Full Breakfast
Credit Cards: A, B, C
Notes: 2, 5, 8, 9, 11, 12, 14

Madelyn's in the Grove

P.O. Box 298, Union Grove, 28689
(704) 539-4151; (800) 948-4473
FAX (704) 539-4080

Fresh flowers and homemade cookies await guests' arrival at the new location in Union Grove. Madelyn's in the Grove now has five comfortable bedrooms, in-room telephones, TVs, a Jacuzzi and garden tub. A perfect location for the business traveler and tourist, just two miles from I-77 and 12 minutes from I-40. Return from dinner and sit in the gazebo or on the deck and watch the stars or listen to the birds. It's peacefulness at its best.

Hosts: Madelyn and John Hill
Rooms: 5 (PB) $75-100
Full Breakfast
Credit Cards: A, B, C
Notes: 2, 3, 5, 7, 9, 10, 12, 14

TABOR CITY

Four Rooster Inn

403 Pireway Road, Route 904, 28463
(910) 653-3878; (800) 653-5008
FAX (910) 653-3878
e-mail: 4rooster@intrstar.net
www.bbonline.com/nc/rooster

"Such a fine place, we crowed over their outstanding hospitality, beautiful antiques and excellent food"—*Southern Living* magazine. Experience the gracious hospitality of the Old South in the charm of a small-town setting. This family home has been restored to a comfortable elegance with antiques, china and crystal, beautiful fabrics, and fine linens. Afternoon tea awaits guests' arrival. Turndown service is accented with chocolates at bedtime. Awaken to a tray of coffee or tea and the morning news at guests' door. A full southern gourmet breakfast is served in the dining room. Myrtle Beach golf courses begin four miles from the inn.

Hosts: Gloria and Bob Rogers
Rooms: 4 (2 PB; 2 SB) $55-85
Full Breakfast
Credit Cards: A, B, C, D, E
Notes: 2, 5, 7, 9, 10, 12, 14

TARBORO

Little Warren Bed and Breakfast

304 East Park Avenue, 27886
(919) 823-1314 (phone/FAX); (800) 309-1314

Established in 1984, Little Warren is a large, gracious Edwardian family home,

Little Warren

renovated and modernized, in a quiet neighborhood in the historic district. Furnished with family English and American antiques and collectibles, the house has a fireplaced common room and a deeply set wraparound front porch that overlooks the town common, one of two originally chartered commons remaining in the United States. Charter member of North Carolina Bed and Breakfast Association. Children over six welcome. Spanish spoken.

Hosts: Patsy and Tom Miller
Rooms: 3 (PB) $68.90
Full and Continental Breakfasts
Credit Cards: A, B, C, D
Notes: 2, 5, 9, 10, 14

TRYON

The Foxtrot Inn Bed and Breakfast

800 Lynn Road, P.O. Box 1561, 28782
(828) 859-9706

This 1915 architect-designed home is on six wooded acres and offers guests many options and amenities to enhance their stay. Beginning each day with a gourmet breakfast, guests will enjoy walking the trails through the woods, lounging at the pool, and amiable evenings reading, playing cards, or watching TV in the living room and game room. A two-bedroom guest house with fully equipped kitchen, deck, fireplace, and cable TV are also available.

Host: Wim Woody
Rooms: 4 (PB) $75-125
Full Breakfast
Credit Cards: None
Notes: 2, 5, 7, 8, 9, 10, 11, 12, 13, 14

Pine Crest Inn

200 Pine Crest Lane, 28782
(828) 859-9135; (800) 633-3001

The four-diamond Pine Crest Inn is nestled in the foothills of the Blue Ridge Mountains. Listed in the National Register of Historic Places, the inn has 35 private rooms, suites, or cottages from which to choose. The gourmet restaurant, fireplaces, wide porches, and beautiful grounds complement each other and combine to create a casual elegance and a relaxing atmosphere. Nearby attractions include the Blue Ridge Parkway and the famous Biltmore Estate and Gardens.

Hosts: Jeremy and Jennifer Wainwright
Rooms: 35 (PB) $125-185
Continental Breakfast
Credit Cards: A, B, C, D
Notes: 2, 4, 5, 7, 8, 9, 10, 11, 12, 14

Pine Crest Inn

Stone Hedge Inn

300 Howard Gap Road, P.O. Box 366, 28782
(704) 859-9114; (800) 859-1974

A stunning 28-acre estate in the shadow of Tryon Mountain, surrounded by gardens and meadows. Two rooms in the main house; three guest house rooms, one with a fireplace; and a poolside cottage with a fireplace; each has private bath, telephone, cable TV, and air conditioning. A lavish breakfast is served in the dining room where picture windows afford mountain views. Dinner by candlelight in crystal globes is a mix of contemporary specials and traditional favorites. Limited handicapped accessibility.

Hosts: Tom and Shaula Dinsmore
Rooms: 6 (PB) $85-120
Full Breakfast
Credit Cards: A, B
Notes: 2, 4, 5, 7, 9, 10, 11, 12

The Mast Farm

UNION GROVE

Madelyn's in the Grove

P.O. Box 298, 28689
(704) 539-4151; (800) 948-4473
FAX (704) 539-4080

Fresh flowers and homemade cookies await guests' arrival at the new location in Union Grove. Madelyn's in the Grove now has five comfortable bedrooms, in-room telephones, TVs, a Jacuzzi and garden tub. A perfect location for the business traveler and tourist, just two miles from I-77 and 12 minutes from I-40. Return from dinner and sit in the gazebo or on the deck and watch the stars or listen to the birds. It's peacefulness at its best.

Hosts: Madelyn and John Hill
Rooms: 5 (PB) $75-100
Full Breakfast
Credit Cards: A, B, C
Notes: 2, 3, 5, 7, 9, 10, 12, 14

VALLE CRUCIS

The Mast Farm Inn

2543 Broadstone Road, P.O. Box 704, 28691
(828) 963-5857; (888) 963-5857
FAX (828) 963-6404

The Mast Farm Inn, in the historic rural mountain community of Valle Crucis, specializes in peaceful surroundings and simple joys, like freshly brewed coffee delivered to guests' door, quiet breakfasts, creative Southern dinners with vegetables fresh from the garden, and inviting porches with swings and rockers. In winter, enjoy a fire followed by a refreshing night's sleep nestled under handmade quilts and comforters. Come visit the Mast Farm Inn.

Hosts: Kay Philipp and Wanda Hinshaw
Rooms: 13 (PB) $100-215
Full Breakfast
Credit Cards: A, B, C, D
Notes: 4, 5, 7, 8, 9, 12, 13, 15

WARSAW

Squire's Vintage Inn

748 NC Highwy 24 and 50, 28398
(910) 296-1831; FAX (910) 296-1431

"You're inn for something special." The rural setting adds to the privacy and relaxed atmosphere for a feeling of getting away from it all. After a restful night's sleep, guests can gaze out at the beautiful garden or take a walk on brick sidewalks and rustic paths flanked by tall pines and towering oaks. Adjacent is the famous Country Squire Restaurant. Weekend package available. Take exit 364 from I-40. AAA-rated and Mobil Travel Guide. Free HBO.

Host: Iris Lennon
Rooms: 16 (PB) $52-79
Continental Breakfast
Credit Cards: A, B, C, E
Notes: 2, 3, 4, 5, 7, 8, 9, 12, 14, 15

WASHINGTON

Acadian House Bed and Breakfast

129 Van Norden Street, 27889
(919) 975-3967

Acadian House Bed and Breakfast is in colonial Washington in a 1900 home. It is decorated throughout with antiques and local crafts. Johanna and Leonard Huber, transplants from New Orleans, serve a full breakfast featuring southern Louisiana specialities such as beignets and café au lait as well as traditional breakfast foods. Acadian House is in the historic downtown district one block from the beautiful Pamlico River within walking distance of shopping and restaurants. Also available is a two-bedroom suite. Children over six welcome.

Hosts: Johanna and Leonard Huber
Rooms: 4 (PB) $55-65
Suite: $100
Full Breakfast
Credit Cards: A, B, C
Notes: 2, 7, 9, 12, 14

Pamlico House

400 East Main Street, 27889
(252) 946-7184; (800) 948-8507
FAX (252) 948-8507
www.bbonline.com/nc/pamlico

In the center of a small, historic town, this stately Colonial Revival homes has large rooms that are a perfect foil for the carefully chosen antique furnishings. Guests are drawn to the classic Victorian parlor or to the spacious wraparound porch for relaxing conversation. Take a self-guided walking tour of the historic district or a stroll along the picturesque waterfront. Be sure to visit the brand new Estuarium just two blocks away.

Pamlico House

Hosts: George and Jane Fields
Rooms: 4 (PB) $65-85
Full Breakfast
Credit Cards: A, B, C, D
Notes: 2, 5, 7, 9, 10, 12, 14

WAYNESVILLE

Carolina Mornings, Inc.

(800) 770-9055; (888) MORNINGS (667-6467)
FAX (919) 929-5061
e-mail: carolinamornings.com
www.carolinamornings.com

9. With four charming guest rooms, this wonderful turn-of-the-century home is graced with antique furnishings, oak paneling, cabinets, and mantels. Enjoy a full home-baked breakfast and rock on the veranda with its panoramic view of the mountains. Walk to Main Street's shops and restaurants. $65-90.

13. Have your moment in the mountains while lounging on the deck of this five-acre estate, listening to the rushing creek 100 feet below. Or watch the sunset over the mountains while sitting inside by the roaring fire. Champagne Continental breakfast. Complimentary cocktail hour. $85.

42. From the balconies and veranda to elegant interiors reminiscent of the French countryside, everything at the Yellow House spells romance. Bedrooms are lavishly decorated. All have fireplaces; some have Jacuzzi baths and wet bars. Be pampered with a gourmet breakfast bedside. $115-225.

Grandview Lodge

466 Lickstone Road, 28786
(828) 456-5212; (800) 255-7826
www.bbonline.com/nc/grandview/

A country inn in the western North Carolina mountains; open all year. Southern home cooking, with breakfast featuring homemade breads, jams, and jellies. Dinner includes fresh vegetables, freshly baked breads, and desserts. Meals, served family style, are included in the rates. Private bath and cable TV. Reservations required.

Hosts: Stan and Linda Arnold
Rooms: 11 (PB) $105-115
Full Breakfast
Credit Cards: None
Notes: 2, 4, 5, 7, 8, 9, 10, 11, 12, 13, 14

Haywood House

Haywood House Bed and Breakfast

409 South Haywood Street, 28786
(704) 456-9831

Built at the turn of the century, this historic home is graced with antique furnishings, beautiful oak paneling, cabinets, and mantels. Enjoy the cozy library for books and games, or great conversation in the parlor. A large veranda with rockers offers a panoramic view of the mountains. Walk to Main Street's shops and restaurants. Home-baked breakfast is served in the lovely dining room. A perfect home for small groups of family or friends.

Hosts: Lynn and Chris Sylvester
Rooms: 4 (2 PB; 2 SB) $70-95
Full Breakfast
Credit Cards: A, B, C, D
Notes: 2, 5, 7, 9, 12, 13, 14

Mountain Creek

146 Chestnut Walk, 28786
(828) 456-5509; (800) 557-9766
FAX (828) 456-6728; e-mail: guylah@aol.com
www.bbonline.com/nc/mcbb

This 1950s ex-corporate retreat lodge is nestled on six acres surrounded by the lull of two creeks. There is a 1,600-square-foot wraparound deck overlooking the mountain range, 100 feet above the creek, mill wheel, and trout pond. The lodge has original knotty pine and wormy chestnut walls, with cedar-lined closets. Each of the six rooms is uniquely decorated with its own private bath, two rooms having a whirlpool tub and two rooms having a balcony overlooking the treetops. Innkeepers are avid cyclists both on road and off.

Hosts: Hylah and Guy Smalley
Rooms: 6 (PB) $90-120
Full Breakfast
Credit Cards: A, B, D
Notes: 2, 5, 7, 9, 10, 11, 12, 13, 14

The Old Stone Inn

109 Dolan Road, 28786
(828) 456-3333; (800) 432-8499

The kind of mountain inn guests always hoped to find, this inn has the feel of a rustic

The Old Stone Inn

hunting lodge with cozy, simple rooms, lots of privacy, handmade quilts on wonderful beds, mountain and woodland views. Romantic candlelight dinners by the fire feature superb regional cuisine. Bountiful breakfasts at guests' own private table highlight every visit. Close to all mountain activities and within walking distance to the craft and antique shops of Waynesville.

Hosts: Robert and Cindy Zinser
Rooms: 20 (PB) $95-150
Suites: 2 (PB) $150
Full Breakfast
Credit Cards: A, B, D
Notes: 2, 4, 9, 10, 11, 12, 13

WEAVERVILLE

Carolina Mornings, Inc.

(800) 770-9055; (888) MORNINGS (667-6467)
FAX (919) 929-5061
e-mail: carolinamornings.com
www.carolinamornings.com

54. Built in 1849 as a parsonage, this charming home is decorated with country antiques and watercolors by the owner/artist. Many rooms have four-poster beds, and there's a grand piano in the parlor. Enjoy the surrounding mountain air from the outdoor hot tub. Ten minutes from downtown Asheville. $80-110.

WELDON

Weldon Place Inn

500 Washington Avenue, 27890
(919) 536-4582; (800) 831-4470

This home-away-from-home is only two miles or five minutes off I-95, exit 173. Sleep in a canopied bed, wake to singing sparrows, stroll through the nationally registered historic district, and savor a gourmet breakfast. At the Weldon Place Inn the guest's peace of mind begins with antiques and country elegance. Personal attention is provided to ensure the guest the ultimate in solitude and relaxation. Local attractions include state historic site, early canal system, and railroad.

Weldon Place Inn

Hosts: Angel and Andy Whitby
Rooms: 4 (PB) $65-99
Full Breakfast
Credit Cards: A, B, C
Notes: 5, 7, 8, 10, 14

WHITTIER

Carolina Mornings, Inc.

(800) 770-9055; (888) MORNINGS (667-6467)
FAX (919) 929-5061
e-mail: carolinamornings.com
www.carolinamornings.com

59. Experience the traditions, congeniality, and hearty breakfast of an alpine *Gasthaus* but with Smoky Mountain views. Relax with a book or explore at this hideaway on 22 acres of forested mountainside with babbling book and hiking trails. All rooms have private porches with views. $85-125.

WILMINGTON

Anderson Guest House

520 Orange Street, 28401
(910) 343-8128

An 1851 Italianate townhouse with separate guest quarters overlooking the private garden. Furnished with antiques, ceiling

NOTES: Credit cards accepted: A MasterCard; B Visa; C American Express; D Discover; E Diner's Club; F Other; 2 Personal checks accepted; 3 Lunch available; 4 Dinner available; 5 Open all year; 6 Pets welcome;

Anderson Guest House

fans, and working fireplaces. Drinks on arrival. A delightful gourmet breakfast is served. Smoking permitted in designated areas only. Inquire about accommodations for children.

Hosts: Landon and Connie Anderson
Rooms: 2 (PB) $65-85
Full Breakfast
Credit Cards: None
Notes: 2, 5, 6, 9, 10, 11, 12

Carolina Mornings, Inc.

(800) 770-9055; (888) MORNINGS (667-6467)
FAX (919) 929-5061
e-mail: carolinamornings.com
www.carolinamornings.com

203. A restored and elegant yet comfortable bed and breakfast with an eclectic mix of antiques, sumptuous fabrics, fine linens, and beautiful gardens. Each of the large rooms has been individually designed and decorated. $90-140.

Catherine's Inn

410 South Front Street, 28401
(910) 251-0863; (800) 476-0723

Experience the gracious atmosphere of this restored 1883 classic Italianate home featuring wrought-iron fence and gate, a Colonial Revival wraparound front porch, and two-story screened rear porch. The 300-foot private lawn, overlooking the Cape Fear River, are beautifully landscaped with a fountain and gazebo for guests to enjoy the beautiful sunsets. Catherine's Inn offers deluxe personal services; charming rooms, each with private bath; central air conditioning and ceiling fans; cozy library with cable TV and VCR; horseshoes, croquet, and bicycles at guests' disposal. Complimentary refreshments. Off-street parking. Corporate rates available. Smoking permitted in designated areas only. Children over 10 welcome.

Host: Catherine-Walter Ackiss
Rooms: 5 (PB) $75-99
Suite: $175
Full Breakfast
Credit Cards: A, B, C
Notes: 2, 5, 9, 10, 11, 12, 14

Catherine's Inn

The Curran House

312 South Third Street, 28401
(910) 763-6603; (800) 763-6603
FAX (910) 763-5116

Come and enjoy this 1837 home in historic Wilmington. The three guest rooms all offer private baths, bath robes, hair dryers, cable TV/VCRs, telephones. Complimentary refreshments are always available, and a hearty full breakfast will start the day. Walk to great restaurants, museums, galleries, even carriage and riverboat rides. Atlantic beaches are a short drive. Corporate rates, fax on-site, central air conditioning, three-diamond-rated by AAA.

The Curran House

Hosts: Vickie and Greg Stringer
Rooms: 3 (PB) $69-119
Full Breakfast
Credit Cards: A, B, C
Notes: 2, 5, 7, 10, 11, 12, 14

Graystone Inn

100 South Third Street, 28401
(910) 763-2000; FAX (910) 763-5555
e-mail: grastone@wilmington.net

Palatial mansion, built in 1906, is the most imposing structure downtown and a historic landmark. Vast ground floor includes fireplaces in each room, hand-carved oak Renaissance-style staircase, and library paneled in Honduras mahogany. Frequently used as a set for the movie industry. New owners have completely remodeled/ redecorated in period furnishings and fixtures. Fireplaces, PC data ports, TVs available, two suites, one junior suite, and five large rooms, easy access to all downtown attractions. Children over 12 welcome.

Graystone Inn

Hosts: Paul and Yolanda Bolda
Rooms: 7 (PB) $165-225
Full Breakfast
Credit Cards: A, B, C, D, E, F
Notes: 2, 5, 9, 10, 11, 12, 14

The Inn on Orange

410 Orange Street, 28401
(910) 815-0035; (800) 381-4666

The Inn on Orange is a lovely 1875 Italianate Victorian home. It offers four bedrooms, all with private baths and two with sitting rooms. A full breakfast is served each morning in the elegant dining room or around the small backyard swimming pool. The Inn is in the heart of the largest historic district in North Carolina. It is just a short walk to the Cape Fear River and Wilmington's great restaurants, shopping, and night spots.

Hosts: The Vargas Family
Rooms: 4 (PB) $75-115
Full Breakfast
Credit Cards: A, B, D
Notes: 2, 5, 7, 9, 10, 11, 12, 14

James Place Bed and Breakfast

9 South Fourth Street, 28401
(910) 251-0999 (phone/FAX); (800) 303-9444
e-mail: jamesinn@wilmington.net

This bed and breakfast is within Wilmington's historic district, minutes from some of Carolina's finest beaches. A carefully restored turn-of-the-century home with large front porch for rocking and reminiscing. The Renewal Room has a special quality of intimacy with a Jacuzzi bathroom, queen-size bed, and personal balcony. The Nesting Suite has a queen-size canopied nesting bed, sitting area, and private bath. The Shaker Room has a queen-size bed, twin bed, and private bath.

Hosts: Maureen and Tony Spataro
Rooms: 3 (PB) $75-105

Full and Continental Breakfast
Credit Cards: A, B, C
Notes: 2, 5, 7, 8, 11, 12, 14

Live Oaks

Live Oaks Bed and Breakfast

318 South Third Street, 28401
(910) 762-6733; (888) 762-6732

In the historic downtown area, this circa 1883 home has been restored by its present owners to its original grandeur and decorated in a Victorian style with antiques and reproductions. Within walking distance are wonderful shops and restaurants, antiquing, museums, and galleries. Take a horse-drawn carriage ride or the walking tour or a house tour and relive a bit of the past. Golf and beaches just 20 minutes away. Children over 12 welcome.

Hosts: Margi and Doug Erickson
Rooms: 3 (PB) $95-125
Full Breakfast
Credit Cards: A, B, D
Notes: 2, 5, 7, 9, 11, 12, 14

Rosehill Inn

114 South Third Street, 28401
(910) 815-0250; (800) 815-0250
FAX (910) 815-0350; www.rosehill.com

Rosehill Inn is an exceedingly comfortable Neoclassical Revival home in the heart of Wilmington's historic district. Just a few minutes' walk from the Cape Fear River with abundant dining and shopping destinations. Restored in 1995, the house offers a wonderful combination of antique charm and beauty with the finest in up-to-date conveniences. Breakfast is served in the formal dining room fresh each morning. Come experience the romance. AAA three-diamond-rated.

Hosts: Laurel Jones and Dennis Fietsch
Rooms: 6 (PB) $85-165
Full Breakfast
Credit Cards: A, B, C, D
Notes: 2, 5, 7, 9, 12, 14

The Verandas

202 Nun Street, 28401
(910) 251-2212; www.verandas.com

In the heart of the historic district, this elegant mansion provides luxurious accommodations two quiet blocks from the Cape Fear River and Riverwalk. This award-winning inn offers large guest rooms with lounge furniture, desks, marble bathrooms, private telephones with modem jacks, color TV, and individual climate control. Spacious public and outdoor space. Affordable elegance.

Hosts: Dennis Madsen and Charles Pennington
Rooms: 8 (PB) $95-165
Full Breakfast
Credit Cards: A, B, C, D
Notes: 2, 5, 7, 9, 10, 11, 12, 14

The Verandas

The Worth House

412 South Third Street, 28401
(910) 762-8562; (800) 340-8559

Romantic Queen Anne Victorian inn in historic district, short walk to riverfront, restaurants, and shopping. Antiques, period furniture, and art in parlor, library, and formal dining room. Seven guest rooms, all with private baths and sitting areas, some with fireplaces and enclosed porches. Full breakfast, free soft drinks, and snacks. Laundry facilities. Large-screen TV, room telephones, fax, copier, and modem link available.

Rooms: 7 (PB) $80-120
Full Breakfast
Credit Cards: A, B. C
Notes: 2, 5, 7, 9, 10, 11, 12, 14

WILSON

Miss Betty's Bed and Breakfast Inn

600 West Nash Street, 27893-3045
(919) 243-4447; (800) 258-2058 (reservations only)

Selected as one of the "Best Places to Stay in the South," Miss Betty's is comprised of four beautifully restored historic homes. In a gracious setting in the downtown historic section, where quiet Victorian elegance and charm abound in an atmosphere of all modern-day conveniences. Guests may browse for antiques at Miss Betty's or in any of the numerous antique shops that have given Wilson the title of "Antique Capital of North Carolina." A quiet town also known for its famous eastern Carolina barbecue, Wilson features four beautiful golf courses, numerous tennis courts, and an Olympic-size pool. Midway between Maine and Florida, along the main north-south route I-95.

Miss Betty's

Hosts: Betty and Fred Spitz
Rooms: 10 (PB) $60-80
Full Breakfast
Credit Cards: A, B, C, D, E, F
Notes: 2, 5, 7, 9, 10, 11, 12, 14, 15

WINSTON-SALEM

A. T. Zevely Inn

803 South Main Street, 27101
(800) 928-9299; FAX (910) 721-2211

A. T. Zevely Inn, circa 1844. National register, museum-quality restoration. Only inn in historic Old Salem. Moravian style. Rooms have king- or queen-size beds, private bath, TV, and telephone. Some have fireplaces and/or whirlpool/steam baths. Complimentary breakfast and evening wine and cheese. AAA-rated. Full breakfast served on weekends; Continental breakfast on weekdays. Featured in *Country Living*, *Tasteful*, *Washington Post Travel*, *Southern Living*, and *Home Access* America cable program.

Host: Linda Anderson
Rooms: 12 (PB) $85-205
Full and Continental Breakfast
Credit Cards: A, B, C
Notes: 2, 5, 6, 8, 9, 10, 11, 12, 14, 15

Lady Anne's Victorian Bed and Breakfast

612 Summit Street, 27101
(336) 724-1074
www.bbonline.com/nc/ladyannes

Warm southern hospitality surrounds guests in this 1890 historic Victorian. An aura of romance touches every suite and room, all of which are individually decorated with period antiques and treasures, while skillfully including modern luxuries, such as private baths with two-person Jacuzzis, balconies, porches, cable TV with HBO, stereos with music and tapes, telephones, room refrigerators, coffee makers, and microwaves. An evening dessert/tea tray and a delicious full breakfast are served on fine china and lace. Near downtown attractions, performances, restaurants, and shops. Near Old Salem historic village. Smoking is not permitted inside.

Host: Shelley Kirley
Rooms/Suites: 4 (PB) $55-160
Full Breakfast
Credit Cards: A, B, C, D
Notes: 5, 7, 9, 10, 11, 12

Mickle House Bed and Breakfast

927 West Fifth Street, 27101
(910) 722-9045

Step back in time to a quaint 1892 Victorian cottage. A gracious welcome, lovely antiques, restful canopied and poster beds, and a delicious breakfast served in the spacious dining room or on the brick patio.

Mickle House

The old-fashioned rocking chairs and swing on the porch and the boxwood gardens offer guests a respite from all cares. In the picturesque national historic district of West End, it is only five minutes from Old Salem, the Medical Center, and the downtown/convention center. Walk to fine restaurants, parks, shops, the YMCA, churches, and library. Golf, tennis, and swimming nearby.

Host: Barbara Garrison
Rooms: 2 (PB) $85-95
Full Breakfast
Credit Cards: A, B
Notes: 2, 5, 7, 9, 10, 11, 12, 14

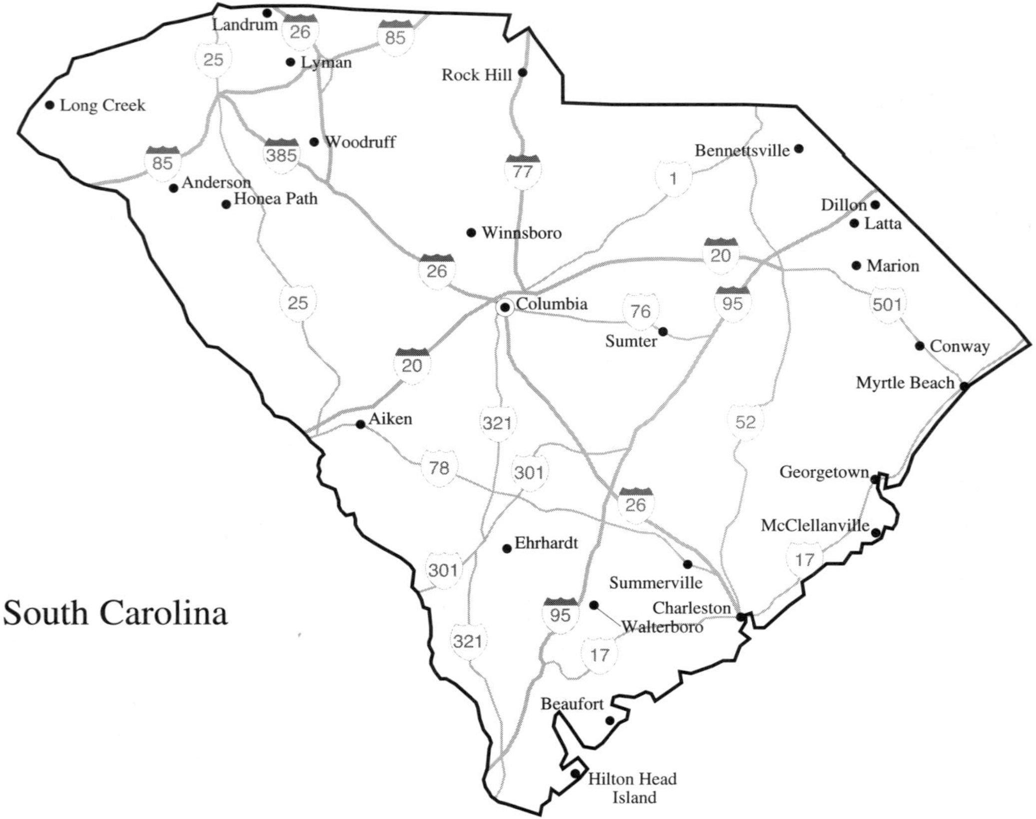

South Carolina

South Carolina

White House Inn

AIKEN

White House Inn

240 Newberry Street Southwest, 29801
(803) 649-2935

The White House Inn is a two-story Dutch Colonial home, furnished with antiques, in a parklike surrounding. Guests start their day with a full breakfast, visit the antique shops or the historical district of Old Aiken, golf, horseback ride, and finish the evening with dinner at one of the fine restaurants near the inn. Government rate honored. Weddings hosted.

Hosts: Mary Ann and Hal Mackey
Rooms: 4 (PB) $69-109
Full Breakfast
Credit Cards: A, B, C, D, E
Notes: 2, 5, 7, 9, 10, 12, 14

ANDERSON

Anderson's River Inn

612 East River Street, 29624
(864) 226-1431; FAX (864) 964-9789
e-mail: andersonin@carol.net

Constructed of heart pine, inn was completed in 1914 by Dr. Smethers, founder of one of Anderson's first hospitals. In the first established residential area in Anderson, it features 10-foot ceilings and walnut-stained woodwork. Each bedroom has a private bath and fireplace. A full breakfast is served. There is a side porch with rockers for guests and a hot tub in the backyard for relaxation. Water skiing nearby. On I-85 corridor, two hours from Atlanta, Georgia, and Charlotte, North Carolina.

Hosts: Pat Clark and Wayne Hollingsworth
Rooms: 3 (PB) $55-155
Full Breakfast
Credit Cards: A, B, C
Notes: 2, 5, 9, 10, 11, 12, 13, 14

BEAUFORT

Bay Street Inn

601 Bay Street, 29902
(843) 522-0050; (800) 256-9285
FAX (843) 521-4086
www.bbonline.com/sc/baystreet/

Circa 1852. Built as a townhouse retreat from plantation life, this grand antebellum, Beaufort-style mansion welcomes guests with warmth and spaciousness reminiscent of another time that stirs the imagination. Sweeping staircases, marble fireplaces, 14-foot-high ceilings, and double verandas will make a stay here unforgettable. A mere stroll through the historic landmark district, the Bay Street Inn sits in stately elegance on the bay and Intracoastal Waterway. All rooms have fireplaces, telephones, and cable TV. Filming site for *The Prince of Tides*. Smoking permitted in designated areas only.

NOTES: Credit cards accepted: A MasterCard; B Visa; C American Express; D Discover; E Diner's Club; F Other; 2 Personal checks accepted; 3 Lunch available; 4 Dinner available; 5 Open all year; 6 Pets welcome; 7 No smoking; 8 Children welcome; 9 Social drinking allowed; 10 Tennis nearby; 11 Swimming nearby; 12 Golf nearby; 13 Skiing nearby; 14 May be booked through a travel agent; 15 Handicapped accessible.

Bay Street Inn

Host: Peter Steciak, manager
Rooms: 9 (PB) $125-195
Full Breakfast
Credit Cards: A, B, C, D, E
Notes: 2, 5, 9, 10, 11, 12, 14, 15

The Rhett House Inn

1009 Craven Street, 29902
(843) 524-9030; FAX (843) 524-1310
e-mail: rhetthse@hargray.com

Nestled in historic Beaufort is an authentic inn that beautifully recreates the feeling of the Old South, when this was the most cultivated and enchanting town of its size in America. All of the guest rooms have been individually decorated for guests' comfort and convenience. All guest rooms have TVs, telephones, private baths, and eight rooms feature fireplaces and Jacuzzis. Enjoy afternoon tea with linzer tortes or homemade chocolate chip cookies in front of the fire or out on the veranda. In the morning, guests will wake up to the smell of freshly brewed coffee and homemade bread and muffins. Picnic lunches available. Children five and older welcome.

Hosts: Marianne and Steve Harrison
Rooms: 17 (PB) $125-225
Full Breakfast
Credit Cards: A, B, C
Notes: 2, 5, 7, 9, 10, 11, 12, 14, 15

TwoSuns Inn Bed & Breakfast

1705 Bay Street, 29902
(843) 522-1122 (phone/FAX); (800) 532-4244
e-mail: twosuns@islc.net; www.twosunsinn.com

Enjoy the charm of Beaufort's most popular bed and breakfast. The panoramic bay view is spectacular, the historic setting idyllic, and the atmosphere casually elegant with antiques, collectibles (including a mini-banana museum just for fun) and modern amenities. Set in a certified historic 1917 grand home, TwoSuns features an afternoon "tea and toddy," comfortable king- or queen-size beds, sumptuous breakfasts and gracious, resident owners. Highly rated nationally, and enjoyed by more than 11,000 since 1990.

Hosts: Carrol and Ron Kay
Rooms: 6 (PB) From $105
Full Breakfast
Credit Cards: A, B, C, D, E
Notes: 2, 5, 7, 9, 10, 11, 12, 14, 15

BENNETTSVILLE

The Breeden Inn and Carriage House

404 East Main Street, 29512
(843) 479-3665; FAX (843) 479-7998
www.bbonline.com/sc/breeden

In Bennettsville's historic district, this 1886 mansion offers the opportunity to experience true southern hospitality. Well-preserved architectural delights and beautiful antique decor highlight the interior in both houses. The inn is 20 minutes off I-95. A great halfway point between Florida and New York. Enjoy bird watching on the two-acre backyard habitat, swim or sun by the pool, browse in the inn's collectibles shop, walk Bennettsville's sidewalk-lined streets, relax on the rocker-lined veranda and portico. Cable TV and telephone in all rooms. Come...a good night's sleep and a delicious, elegant breakfast in a wonderful, warm old home await.

Hosts: Wesley and Bonnie Park
Rooms: 6 (PB) $65-95
Full Breakfast
Credit Cards: A, B
Notes: 2, 5, 7, 8, 10, 11, 12, 14

CHARLESTON

Ann Harper's Bed and Breakfast

56 Smith Street, 29401
(843) 723-3947

This circa 1870 home is in Charleston's historic district. Two rooms with connecting bath and sitting area with TV. The owner is a retired medical technologist and enjoys serving a full breakfast. Two-night minimum stay requested. Extra charge for single night. Smoking in designated areas only. Children over 10 welcome.

Host: Ann D. Harper
Rooms: 2 (PB) $70-110
Full Breakfast
Credit Cards: None
Notes: 2, 5, 9, 10, 11, 12

Ashley Inn Bed and Breakfast

201 Ashley Avenue, 29403
(843) 723-1848; (800) 581-6658

Circa 1832 historic home offers seven bedrooms, beautifully decorated with antique canopied beds. A place to be pampered and sleep in until the aroma of sizzling sausage and home-baked biscuits announces a full breakfast on the columned piazza overlooking the garden and fountain. Tour nearby historic sites on complimentary bicycles and return to more pampering with afternoon tea, sherry, and sumptuous home-baked goods. Private baths, color TV, off-street parking, and very special southern hospitality. AAA three-diamond-rated. Featured on TV's *Country Inn Cooking*. Children over 10 welcome.

Ashley Inn

Hosts: Bud and Sally Allen
Rooms: 7 (PB) $69-150
Full Breakfast
Credit Cards: A, B, C, D
Notes: 2, 5, 7, 9, 10, 11, 12, 14

Barksdale House Inn

27 George Street, 29401
(843) 577-4800; FAX (843) 853-0482

One of Charleston's most luxurious 14-room inns. A 200-year-old home featuring individually designed rooms, some with whirlpool tubs and fireplaces. Flowers daily with newspaper, tea, sherry, turndown service with chocolates. Fountain in courtyard and free parking.

Rooms: 14 (PB) $80-195
Continental Breakfast
Credit Cards: A

The Battery Carriage House Inn (1843)

20 South Battery, 29401
(800) 775-5575

Stay in the carriage house of this landmark antebellum mansion at White Point Gardens (on the waterfront), the most elegant residential district of old and historic Charleston. Eleven rooms. Ample street parking. Silver tray Continental breakfast in room or garden. Fluffy robes and towels. Turndown service. Afternoon refreshments. Quiet garden. Cable TV and HBO.

Private steam baths. Whirlpool tubs. Friendly, professional staff. Described by *Elegant Small Hotels*, 1996, as "Garden-centered, history-laden, romantic and intimate." Highly recommended.

Host: Katharine Hastie
Rooms: 11 (PB) $79-199
Continental Breakfast
Credit Cards: A, B, C, D
Notes: 2, 5, 7, 9, 10, 11, 12, 14

Bed and Breakfast at 27 State Street

27 State Street, 29401
(843) 722-4243

Guests can surround themselves with history and southern hospitality in the French Quarter of the old walled city of Charlestowne. Stroll to major points of interest, dining, shopping, and touring. Guests enter the courtyard with their own personal key. Enjoy sea breezes on the veranda. Private entrances and private baths. Antiques, reproductions, high poster queen-size beds. Newspaper, fresh flowers, fruit, cable TV, telephones, and bicycles. Continental plus breakfast.

Hosts: Paul and Joye Craven
Rooms: 5 (PB) $100-165
Continental Breakfast
Credit Cards: None
Notes: 2, 5, 7, 8, 9, 10, 11, 12

Bed and Breakfast at 27 State Street

The Belvedere

The Belvedere

40 Rutledge Avenue, 29401
(843) 722-0973

A Colonial Revival mansion built in 1900 with an exquisite Adamesque interior taken from the circa 1800 Belvedere plantation house. In the downtown historic district, on Colonial Lake, within walking distance of historical points of interest, restaurants, and shopping. Guests are welcome to use the public areas and piazzas in this romantic, beautifully restored and refurbished mansion. Closed December 1 to February 1. Children over eight welcome.

Hosts: David S. Spell and Rick Zender
Rooms: 3 (PB) $125-150
Continental Breakfast
Credit Cards: None
Notes: 2, 7, 9, 10, 11, 12, 14

Brasington House Bed and Breakfast

328 East Bay Street, 29401
(843) 722-1274

Elegant accommodations in a splendidly restored Greek Revival Charleston single house, furnished with antiques, in Charleston's beautiful historic district. Four lovely, well-appointed guest rooms with central heat and air conditioning include

NOTES: Credit cards accepted: A MasterCard; B Visa; C American Express; D Discover; E Diner's Club; F Other; 2 Personal checks accepted; 3 Lunch available; 4 Dinner available; 5 Open all year; 6 Pets welcome;

private baths, telephones, cable TVs, and tea-making services. King-, queen-, and twin-size beds available. Included is a bountiful family-style breakfast, wine and cheese served in the living room, liqueurs and chocolates available in the evening. Off-street parking.

Hosts: Dalton K. and Judy Brasington
Rooms: 4 (PB) $115-154
Full Breakfast
Credit Cards: A, B
Notes: 2, 5, 7, 9, 10, 11, 12

Cannonboro Inn Bed and Breakfast

184 Ashley Avenue, 29412
(843) 723-8572; (800) 235-8039
FAX (843) 723-8007; e-mail: cannon@cchat.com

This circa 1853 historic home skillfully combines old and new, offering six beautifully decorated bedrooms with four-poster and canopied beds. Known for its hearty full breakfast, the Cannonboro Inn is a place to be pampered. The aroma of freshly brewed coffee and home-baked French puff muffins entice guests to a delicious breakfast on the columned piazza overlooking the garden. After breakfast guests can tour nearby historic Charleston on complimentary bicycles, on foot, or by horse-drawn carriage. Return in the afternoon to relax in the parlor and enjoy high tea with fresh home-baked treats such as raspberry almond short bread and English toffee bars or guests might enjoy sherry and mint juleps. This, along with the off-street parking, private baths, cable TV, central air conditioning, and warm professional staff are what Charleston is all about. Children 10 and older welcome.

Cannonboro Inn

Hosts: Bud and Sally Allen (owners); Lynn Bartosh (manager)
Rooms: 6 (PB) $69-180
Full Breakfast
Credit Cards: A, B, C, D
Notes: 2, 5, 9, 10, 11, 12, 14

Country Victorian Bed and Breakfast

105 Tradd Street, 29401-2422
(843) 577-0682

Rooms have private entrances and contain antique iron and brass beds, old quilts, oak and wicker antique furniture, and braided rugs over the heart-of-pine floors. Homemade cookies will be waiting. The house, built in 1820, is within easy walking distance of restaurants, antique shops, churches, art galleries, museums, and all points of historical interest. Parking and bicycles are available for guests. Many extras are provided. Featured in the fall 1997 issue of *Country Quilts* magazine. Children over 10 are welcome.

Host: Diane Deardurff Weed
Rooms: 2 (PB) $75-125
Continental Breakfast
Credit Cards: None
Notes: 2, 5, 7, 9, 10, 11, 12

East Bay Bed and Breakfast

301 East Bay Street, 29401
(843) 722-4186; FAX (803) 720-8528

Elegant 200-year-old Federal single house and birthplace of Civil War heroine Phoebe Pember. Easy walk to Old City Market, King Street shops, College of Charleston, Medical University, restaurants, and day-spa. Exquisitely decorated. Silver tray service. Private

East Bay

carriage house also available. Meeting and reception space. Desks, fax, telephone, cable TV, and off-street parking. Smoking permitted on piazzas only. Inquire about accommodations for children.

Host: Carolyn Rivers
Room: (PB) $125-185
Continental Breakfast
Credit Cards: A, B
Notes: 2, 5, 11, 12, 14

1837 Bed and Breakfast and Tea Room

126 Wentworth Street, 29401
(843) 723-7166

These delightful accommodations are in a wealthy cotton planter's home and brick carriage house, now owned by two artists. In the center of the historic district, within walking distance of boat tours, Old City Market, antique shops, restaurants, and main attractions. Full gourmet breakfast is served in the formal dining room or on the outside piazzas. Visit with others while enjoying such specialties as sausage pie, eggs Benedict, ham omelets, and home-baked breads (lemon, apple spice, banana, and cinnamon swirl). Afternoon tea is served. Canopied poster rice beds, verandas, rockers, and southern hospitality. Smoking permitted in designated areas only.

Hosts: Sherri Weaver and Richard Dunn
Rooms: 8 (PB) $69-129
Full Breakfast
Credit Cards: A, B, C
Notes: 2, 5, 10, 11

Fulton Lane Inn

202 King Street, 29401
(843) 720-2600; (800) 720-2688

Set off King Street on a quiet pedestrian lane in the heart of the antique and historic district. Many rooms have cathedral ceilings or fireplaces, canopied beds, and large whirlpool baths to give a special romantic feeling of a bygone era. The gracious southern hospitality includes a silver-service breakfast, wine and sherry, turndown with chocolates, and a newspaper. AAA four diamonds. No smoking.

Host: Randall Felkel
Rooms: 27 (PB) $120-275
Continental Breakfast
Credit Cards: A, B, D, E
Notes: 2, 5, 7, 8, 9, 10, 11, 12, 14, 15

Historic Charleston Bed and Breakfast

57 Broad Street, 29401
(843) 722-6606; (800) 743-3583
FAX (843) 722-9589
www.charleston.net/com/bed&breakfast

Representing more than 50 bed and breakfast properties in and around Charleston's historic district. Accommodations include private homes and carriage houses. Call for details.

Ashley Avenue. Two lovely rooms with a full breakfast. The first room is on the second floor with a private hall bath. The second room is a suite on the third floor with a rooftop view, full bath, and separate sitting room. $130-200.

Broad Street. Third-floor suite with kitchen, sitting room, queen-size bedroom, and bath. Also available is an accommodation with private entrance, kitchen, king-size bedroom, and bath with shower only. $115-135.

Chapel Street. Private entrance, garden level. Queen-size bed, living room, kitchen, private bath, lovely antiques. Lovely garden with fountain. $135-150.

Church Street. Two rooms on third floor. Both rooms have private baths and beautiful harbor views from piazza. $110-115.

East Bay. Spacious one-bedroom apartment and a two-bedroom carriage house. $125-225.

Hasell Street. Carriage house with living room, full kitchen with breakfast area, and private patio. Two bedrooms, one full bath with washer and dryer. Off-street parking. $170-215.

Limehouse Street. Carriage house with living room, kitchen, second-floor bedroom with queen-size bed and full bath. Off-street parking. $100-125.

Water Street. Third-floor suite with bedroom, full bath, living room, small kitchen, and large porch with a lovely harbor view. $195-215.

Wentworth Street. Carriage house with two separate units to be rented individually or as an entire unit. The first unit has a large room with queen-size poster bed, full bath, refrigerator, and separate sink in one room, large patio with seating. Off-street parking. No inside smoking. The second unit has two rooms, one with queen-size bed, fireplace, bath (shower only); additional room has fireplace, sofa, wet bar, and small refrigerator. Bikes and patio seating available. Off-street parking. Nonsmoking. $90-120.

John Rutledge House Inn

116 Broad Street, 29401
(843) 723-7999; (800) 476-9741

This national landmark was built in 1763 by John Rutledge, a framer and signer of the U.S. Constitution. Large rooms and suites in the main and carriage houses offer the ambiance of historic Charleston. Rates include wine and sherry upon arrival, turndown service with brandy and chocolate, and breakfast with newspaper delivered to guests' room. Free parking. AAA-rated four diamonds and Mobil-rated four stars. Historic Hotels of America. Nonsmoking rooms available. Limited handicapped accessibility.

Rooms: 19 (PB) $165-335
Continental Breakfast
Credit Cards: A, B, C, D, E
Notes: 2, 5, 8, 9, 10, 11, 12, 14

King George IV Inn

32 George Street, 29401
(843) 723-9339; (888) 723-1667
FAX (803) 723-7749; www.virtualcities.com
www.bbonline.com/sc/kinggeorge/
www.webpost.com/hia/listings/k-george.htm

"Step into the past, feel the history of Charleston around you." Historic inn circa 1790s. Named Peter Freneau House after a prominent Charlestonian, merchant, shipowner, Jeffersonian politician in charge of President Thomas Jefferson's election. The inn is Federal style, four stories tall, three levels of old Charleston porches. All rooms have decorative fireplaces, tall ceilings, plaster moldings, hardwood floors, antiques. Parking, air conditioning, private baths, refrigerators, Continental plus breakfast. In the heart of historic district, five-minute walk to the historic market. Personal checks accepted in advance.

Hosts: Debra, Terry, and Debbie
Rooms: 10 (8 PB; 2 SB) $85-155
Continental Breakfast
Credit Cards: A, B
Notes:5, 7, 8, 9, 10, 11, 12, 13

Kings Courtyard Inn

198 King Street, 29401
(843) 723-7000; (800) 845-6119

Kings Courtyard Inn, circa 1853, is in the heart of the antique and historic district. Convenient to attractions, shops, and restaurants. Rate includes Continental breakfast, newspaper, and wine and sherry served in the lobby. Turndown service with chocolate and brandy. AAA four diamonds. Historic Hotels of America. Double, king-, and queen-size beds and suites are available. Nonsmoking rooms available.

Host: Reg Smith
Rooms: 41 (PB) $125-215
Continental Breakfast
Credit Cards: A, B, C, D, E
Notes: 2, 5, 8, 9, 10, 11, 12, 14, 15

King's Inn

136 Tradd Street, 29401
(843) 577-3683

This fully restored 1885 home in the historic district includes two bed and breakfast units with separate entrances. One has a full kitchen. The waterfront, antique shops, and house museums are minutes away. The entire historic area can be covered on foot. Enjoy blooming gardens and magnificent house tours in April, the international arts festival—Spoleto—in May, and warm beaches in June. The hostess is a registered tour guide for the city and also a Charlestonian.

King's Inn

Host: Hazel King
Rooms: 2 (PB) $100-120
Continental Breakfast
Credit Cards: None
Notes: 2, 7, 9, 10, 11, 12, 14, 15

The Kitchen House (Circa 1732)

126 Tradd Street, 29401
(843) 577-6362

Nestled in the heart of the historic district, the Kitchen House is a completely restored 18th-century dwelling. Southern hospitality and a decanter of sherry await guests' arrival. The refrigerator and pantry are stocked for breakfast. Absolute privacy, cozy fireplaces, antiques, patio, and colonial herb gardens. This pre-Revolutionary home was featured in *Colonial Homes* magazine and the *New York Times*. Complete concierge services. Honeymoon packages.

Host: Lois Evans
Rooms: 3 (1 PB; 2 SB) $145-225
Full Breakfast
Credit Cards: A, B
Notes: 2, 5, 7, 8, 9, 10, 11, 12, 14

The Lodge Alley Inn

195 East Bay Street, 29401
(843) 722-1611; (800) 845-1004
FAX (843) 722-1611; e-mail: LodgeAlley@aol.com

Nestled in the historic district within strolling distance of fine dining and attractions. Luxurious inn rooms and suites surround an enchanting courtyard with fountain. Many rooms/suites appointed with pine floors, oriental carpets, fireplaces, and period reproductions reflecting Charleston's European heritage. Meals served daily in the French Quarter Restaurant. Enjoy amenities including complimentary valet parking, morning coffee, daily newspaper, afternoon sherry, and turndown service with chocolates.

Host: Norma Armstrong
Rooms; 95 (PB) $144-360
Full Breakfast
Credit Cards: A, B, C
Notes: 2, 3, 4, 5, 8, 9, 12, 14, 15

NOTES: Credit cards accepted: A MasterCard; B Visa; C American Express; D Discover; E Diner's Club; F Other; 2 Personal checks accepted; 3 Lunch available; 4 Dinner available; 5 Open all year; 6 Pets welcome;

Maison DuPré

317 East Bay Street, 29401
(843) 723-8691; (800) 844-INNS

Three restored Charleston single houses and two carriage houses constitute Maison DuPré, originally built in 1804. The inn features period furniture and antiques and is in the historic Ansonborough district. Complimentary Continental breakfast and a Low Country tea party are served. "Maison DuPré, with its faded stucco, pink brick, and gray shutters is one of the city's best-looking small inns"—*New York Times.*

Hosts: Lucille, Bob, and Mark Mulholland
Rooms: 15 (PB) $98-200
Continental Breakfast
Credit Cards: A, B
Notes: 2, 7, 8, 9, 10, 11, 12, 14

Palmer Home Bed and Breakfast

5 East Battery, 29401
(843) 853-1574; (888) 723-1574

Fabulous rooms with a view overlooking Charleston Harbor and historic Fort Sumter. Locally known as the "Pink Palace" it is one of the 50 most famous homes in Charleston. The forerunner of the submarine, *The David*, was invented in this house. The Palmer House is in the center of the historic district. Off-street parking and bicycles are provided for guests.

Room: 3 (PB) $100-150
Continental Breakfast
Credit Cards: None
Notes: 2, 5, 7, 8, 9, 11, 12

The Planters Inn

112 North Market Street, 29401
(843) 722-2345; (800) 845-7082
www.plantersinn.com

The Planters Inn is the heart and soul of historic Charleston, steps away from landmark houses, gardens, and Waterfront Park. The newly renovated inn has 62 spacious rooms and suites featuring oversized private baths and large closets. Guests are treated to refreshments each afternoon and turndown service each night. The acclaimed Peninsula Grill serves dinner seven nights a week. AAA-rated four diamonds. Silver-service breakfast and valet parking available.

Host: Larry Spelts
Rooms: 62 (PB) $105-250
Continental Breakfast
Credit Cards: A, B, C, D, E
Notes: 2, 4, 5, 7, 8, 9, 10, 11, 12, 14, 15

Rutledge Victorian Inn and Guest House

114 Rutledge Avenue, 29401
(843) 722-7551; (888) 722-7553
FAX (843) 727-0065

Elegant old Charleston house in the downtown historic district. This century-old house with decorative Italianate architecture was originally the Brodie-Pinkussohn House. All rooms have fireplaces, 12-foot ceilings, hardwood floors, 10-foot doors and windows, and antiques. Lovely round 120-foot porch overlooks the park and Roman columns, the remains of the Confederate Soldiers Reunion Hall. Air conditioning, private baths, TVs, telephones, fax, turndown service, parking, refreshments, and Continental plus breakfast. A 5- to 20-minute walk to all historic sights. Smoking permitted on porches only. Water and lots of beaches nearby. Detached kitchen house,

Rutledge Victorian Inn

7 No smoking; 8 Children welcome; 9 Social drinking allowed; 10 Tennis nearby; 11 Swimming nearby; 12 Golf nearby; 13 Skiing nearby; 14 May be booked through a travel agent; 15 Handicapped accessible.

built in 1832, with two bedrooms, private garden is also available. Children 12 and older welcome.

Hosts: Lyn and Norm
Rooms: 10 (7 PB; 3 SB) $60-155
Continental Breakfast
Credit Cards: A, B
Notes: 2, 5, 9, 10, 11, 12, 14

Thomas Lamboll House

19 King Street, 29401
(843) 723-3212; FAX (843) 723-3216

This Charleston single house was built in 1735 by Thomas Lamboll, a notable colonial judge, and is just off the Battery in the heart of the historic district. It offers two large, handsome bedrooms with private baths and French doors leading onto the piazza. The bedrooms are centrally air conditioned and have fireplaces, cable TVs, and telephones. Each room is tastefully furnished with reproduction and antique furniture. A Continental breakfast is served in the dining room on the first floor. Off-street parking available.

Rooms: 2 (PB) $95-145
Continental Breakfast
Credit Cards: A, B
Notes: 2, 5, 7, 8, 9, 10, 11, 12

Two Meeting Street Inn

2 Meeting Street, 29401
(843) 723-7322

"The Belle of Charleston's bed and breakfasts." This Queen Anne Victorian mansion, circa 1890-92, has welcomed guests for more than 50 years. In the historic district overlooking the Battery, the inn charms its visitors with exquisite Tiffany windows, canopied beds, oriental rugs, and English antiques. The day starts with freshly baked muffins served in the oak-covered dining room or courtyard, then afternoon tea, and ends with evening sherry on the wraparound piazza. The epitome of southern hospitality and turn-of-the-century luxury. Two-night minimum stay requested for weekends and holidays.

Two Meeting Street Inn

Hosts: The Spell Family
Rooms: 9 (PB) $145-275
Continental Breakfast
Credit Cards: None
Notes: 2, 5, 7, 10, 11, 12

Vendue Inn

19 Vendue Range, 29401
(843) 577-7970; (800) 845-7900
FAX (843) 577-2913
www.charleston.net/com/vendueinn

Elegant 18th-century-style inn at the beautiful harbor and historic waterfront in the heart of the historic district. Beautiful rooms and suites, some with water views, many with Jacuzzis, marble baths, and fireplaces. Included in stay are full buffet breakfast and wine and cheese. Large suites include full breakfast, wet bar, fresh fruit baskets, and so forth. Excellent restaurant, the Library, features progressive southern cuisine. Rooftop terrace and bar overlooking harbor and city. Smoking permitted on designated floors only.

Hosts: Evelyn and Morton Needle
Rooms: 45 (PB) $120-235
Full Breakfast
Credit Cards: A, B, C, D, E
Notes: 2, 3, 4, 5, 8, 9, 10, 11, 12, 13, 14

Victoria House Inn

208 King Street, 29401
(843) 720-2944; (800) 933-5464

Built in 1889, this Romanesque-style building has 18 elegantly renovated guest rooms.

Modern amenities are provided in every room, including a stocked refrigerator. Guests receive evening turndown service, and wine and sherry are served in the lobby. Continental breakfast and newspaper delivered to the room each morning. AAA four diamonds. Nonsmoking rooms available. Limited handicapped accessibility.

Host: Mary Kay Smith
Rooms: 18 (PB) $120-245
Continental Breakfast
Credit Cards: A, B, D, E
Notes: 2, 5, 8, 9, 10, 11, 12, 14

Villa de la Fontaine Bed and Breakfast

138 Wentworth Street, 29401
(843) 577-7709

This columned Greek Revival mansion is in the heart of the historic district. It was built in 1838 and boasts a three-quarter-acre garden with fountain and terraces. Restored to impeccable condition, it is furnished with museum-quality furniture and accessories. The hosts are retired ASID interior designers and have decorated the rooms with 18th-century American antiques. Several of the rooms feature canopied beds. Breakfast is prepared by a master chef who prides himself on serving a different menu every day. Off-street parking. Minimum-stay requirements for weekends and holidays. There are four rooms and two suites.

Hosts: William Fontaine and Aubrey Hancock
Rooms: 6 (PB) $100-150
Full Breakfast
Credit Cards:None
Notes: 2, 5, 7, 9, 10, 11, 12

COLUMBIA

Claussen's Inn

2003 Greene Street, 29205
(803) 765-0440; (800) 622-3382

Restored bakery, circa 1928, listed in the National Register of Historic Places and within walking distance of shopping, restaurants, and entertainment. Luxurious rooms with private baths, outdoor Jacuzzi, and four-poster beds. Rates include a Continental breakfast delivered to the room, complimentary wine and sherry, turndown service with chocolates and brandy, and a newspaper. Nonsmoking rooms available.

Host: Ron Jones
Rooms: 29 (PB) $120-135
Continental Breakfast
Credit Cards: A, B, C, D, E
Notes: 2, 5, 8, 9, 10, 12, 14, 15

CONWAY

The Cypress Inn

16 Elm Street, P.O. Box 495, 29528
(843) 248-8199; (800) 575-5307
FAX (843) 248-0329

Coastal South Carolina is the location of this divine bed and breakfast where guests will find excellence in the little details, and it is never forgotten that this is where memories are created. On the edge of the Waccamaw River overlooking a private marina, guests enjoy Jacuzzis, TVs, and telephones with data ports for the business travelers. Morning breakfast is alive with aromas and enthusiastic voices. Days are spent in bird watching, ocean walks, exploring sculpture gardens, and much more.

Host: Jim and Carol Ruddick
Rooms: 12 (PB) $105-140
Full Breakfast
Credit Cards: A, B, C
Notes: 2, 5, 7, 9, 10, 11, 12, 14, 15

DILLON

Magnolia Inn

601 East Main Street, 29536
(843) 774-0679

Magnolia Inn is two and one-half miles from exit 190 on I-95 in South Carolina. The inn has four spacious and individually appointed guest rooms in a century-old

Greek Revival mansion. Just 60 minutes from the Grand Strand beaches at Myrtle Beach and 40 minutes from Darlington International raceway. Children 12 and older welcome.

Hosts: Alan and Eileen Kemp
Rooms: 4 (PB) $60-70
Full Breakfast
Credit Cards: A, B, C, D
Notes: 2, 5, 7, 11, 12

EHRHARDT

Ehrhardt Hall Bed and Breakfast

400 South Broadway, P.O. Box 246, 29081
(803) 267-2020

A stay at the Ehrhardt Hall is a return to the elegance of yesterday. The inn has been restored to its original grandeur. It is reminiscent of an era when graciousness and thoughtfulness were a way of life. All rooms are oversized with ceiling fans, armoires, sitting areas, private baths, color TVs, fireplaces, and central heat and air conditioning. Indoor pool, large spa. Tennis and golf nearby.

Rooms: 6 (PB) $50-90
Continental Breakfast
Credit Cards: A, B, C
Notes: 5, 7, 8, 9, 10, 12, 14

GEORGETOWN

Ashfield Manor Bed and Breakfast

3030 South Island Road, 29440
(800) 483-5002

The inn offers southern hospitality in the style of a real southern plantation. Ashfield Manor has an elegant but comfortable country setting. All room are oversized and redecorated with period furnishings, private entrance, and color cable TV. Enhanced Continental menu for breakfast served in guests' room, the parlor, or on the 57-foot screened porch overlooking a lake with wildlife—even an alligator!

Hosts: Dave and Carol Ashenfelder
Rooms: 4 (2 PB; 2 SB) $55-65
Continental Breakfast
Credit Cards: A, B, D
Notes: 2, 5, 7, 8, 10, 12, 14

King's Inn at Georgetown

230 Broad Street, 29440
(803) 527-6937; (800) 251-8805
FAX (803) 527-6937
www.bbonline.com/sc/kingsinn/

Magnificent moldings, crystal chandeliers, and gleaming original floors grace the foyer and three antique-filled parlors of this 1825 Federal manse. Exquisitely decorated guest rooms provide the ultimate in romantic relaxation, from canopied king-size bed adjoining private piazzas to dreamy postered queen-size rooms with an in-room Jacuzzi tub for two. The garden breakfast room overlooks lap pool and screened porch. Among *Country Inns* 1995 Top 12 Inns.

Hosts: Marilyn and Jerry Burkhardt
Rooms: 7 (PB) $89-139
Full Breakfast
Credit Cards: A, B, C
Notes: 2, 3, 4, 5, 7, 8, 9, 10, 11, 12, 14

1790 House

630 Highmarket Street, 29440
(803) 546-4821; (800) 890-7432
e-mail: jwiley@aol.com
www.bbonline.com/sc/1790house
www.1790house.com

Meticulously restored, this 200-year-old Colonial plantation-style inn is in the heart of historic Georgetown. Spacious, luxurious rooms with sitting areas and central heat and air. Stay in the Rice Planters Room, the beautiful romantic cottage with Jacuzzi tub, or in one of the other lovely rooms. Gourmet breakfasts. Walk to shops, restaurants, and historic sights. Just a short drive to Brookgreen Gardens, Myrtle Beach, and the Grand Strand—a golfer's paradise. One hour to Charleston. Rated

NOTES: Credit cards accepted: A MasterCard; B Visa; C American Express; D Discover; E Diner's Club; F Other; 2 Personal checks accepted; 3 Lunch available; 4 Dinner available; 5 Open all year; 6 Pets welcome;

excellent by ABBA, three diamonds by AAA and Mobil.

Hosts: John and Patricia Wiley
Rooms: 6 (PB) $85-135
Full Breakfast
Credit Cards: A, B, C, D, E
Notes: 2, 5, 7, 8, 9, 10, 12, 14

The Shaw House

The Shaw House

613 Cypress Court, 29440
(843) 546-9663

A spacious two-story Colonial home in a serene natural setting overlooking Willowbank Marsh. It is a wonderful setting for bird watching. The rooms are spacious—all private baths—have many antiques, are air-conditioned, carpeted. Queen-size rice beds, a full southern breakfast. Nighttime chocolate on pillows along with turndown service. Walk to restaurants, shops, and historic sights. A golfer's paradise. Beaches 10 minutes away. Children permitted.

Hosts: Mary and Joe Shaw
Rooms: 3 (PB) $60-70
Full Breakfast
Credit Cards: C
Notes: 2, 5, 8, 9, 10, 11, 12, 14, 15

"ShipWright's"

609 Cypress Court, 29440
(843) 527-4475

Serving tourists or boaters. Quiet, spacious with a tasteful decor of heirlooms and antiques. Experience the breathtaking view of the Avenue of Live Oaks and the Alive Marshes of the Black River while rocking on the large porch or gazing out the parlor window. Taste Grandma Eicher's pancakes, freshly ground coffee, and fresh fruit. Guests say, "I feel like I just visited my best friend." AAA-approved.

Host: Leatrice Wright
Rooms: 2 (PB) $60
Full Breakfast
Credit Cards: None
Notes: 2, 5, 7, 8, 9, 10, 11, 12

HILTON HEAD ISLAND

Ambiance

8 Wren Drive, 29928
(843) 671-4981

Marny welcomes guests to sunny Hilton Head Island. This cypress home, nestled in subtropical surroundings, is in Sea Pines Plantation. Ambiance reflects the hostess's interior decorating business by the same name. All the amenities of Hilton Head are offered in a contemporary, congenial atmosphere. The climate is favorable year-round for all sports. Ambiance is across the street from a beautiful beach and the Atlantic Ocean. Smoking outside only.

Host: Marny Kridel Daubenspeck
Rooms: 2 (PB) $80
Continental Breakfast
Credit Cards: None
Notes: 2, 5, 7, 9, 10, 11, 12, 14

HONEA PATH

Sugarfoot Castle's Bed and Breakfast

211 South Main Street, 29654
(864) 369-6565

Enormous trees umbrella this circa 1880 brick Victorian home. Fresh flowers grace the 14-inch-thick walled rooms furnished with family heirlooms. Enjoy the living room's interesting collection or the library's

Sugarfoot Castle's

comfy chairs, TV, VCR, books, fireplace, desk, and game table. Upon rising, guests will find coffee and freshly squeezed orange juice outside their doors, followed by a breakfast of fresh fruit, cereal, hot breads, and beverages served in the dining room by candlelight. Rock away the world's cares on the screened porch overlooking peaceful gardens. Children over 10 welcome. TVs in all rooms.

Hosts: Cecil and Gale Evans
Rooms: 3 (SB) $68
Continental Breakfast
Credit Cards: A, B
Notes: 2, 5, 7, 9, 10, 11, 12

LANDRUM

The Red Horse Inn

310 North Campbell Road, 29356
(864) 895-4968

The Red Horse Inn is on 190 acres in the midst of horse country. Charming Victorian cottages are exquisitely furnished and decorated. Each offers a kitchen, separate bedroom, sitting area with a fold-out bed, full bath, TV, air conditioning, and beautiful mountain views from the rocking porch. Three rooms have Jacuzzis and three have lofts. Inquire about accommodations for pets. Additional charge for extra person up to four per cottage.

Hosts: Mary and Roger Wolters
Cottages: 5 (PB) $95
Continental Breakfast
Credit Cards: A, B
Notes: 2, 5, 7, 8, 9, 10, 12, 14

LATTA

Abingdon Manor

307 Church Street, 29565
(803) 752-5090; (888) 752-5090

Six miles from I-95 and halfway between New York City and Miami, this 8,000-square-foot Greek Revival mansion is the closest four-diamond property in the Carolinas to I-95. Completed in 1905, the inn is listed in the national register. Filled with unique architectural details, and furnished with antiques, the house is comfortably elegant. Feather beds, robes, high-quality linens, turndown service, complimentary wine and sherry among the many amenities included.

Hosts: Michael and Patty Griffey
Rooms: 5 (PB) $105-140
Full Breakfast
Credit Cards: A, B, C, D
Notes: 2, 5, 7, 9, 10, 12, 14

LONG CREEK

Chauga River House

P.O. Box 309, 29658
(800) 451-9972

The Chauga River House is a private home on the shoals of the Chauga River and is open to guests of Wildwater, Ltd. Wildwater is a white-water rafting company in the beautiful mountains of upstate South Carolina. The Chauga River House serves a Continental-style breakfast and features comfortable home-style accommodations. Children eight and older welcome.

Hosts: Jim and Jeanette Greiner
Rooms: 5 (3 PB; 2 SB) $46-85
Continental Breakfast
Notes: A, B, D
Notes: 2, 9, 11

LYMAN (GREENVILLE/SPARTANBURG)

Walnut Lane Bed and Breakfast

110 Ridge Road, 29365
(864) 949-7230; FAX (864) 949-1633

Reminiscent of the grand plantations of yesterday, the Walnut Lane Bed and Breakfast stands as a beacon of the past on its lush acreage surrounded by an abundance of fruit trees. Conveniently between Spartanburg and Greenville. Surrounded by great area outlet shopping, art centers, concert facilities, many fine universities, and cultural centers. For business or leisurely travelers the Walnut Lane is where guests want to be. Chair lift available in house.

Hosts: Marie and Park Urquhart
Rooms: 4 (PB) $75-90
Full Breakfast
Credit Cards: A, B, C, D
Notes: 2, 3, 4, 5, 7, 9, 10, 11, 12, 14

MARION

Montgomery's Grove

408 Harlee Street, 29571
(803) 423-5220

Montgomery's Grove is an 1893 Victorian manor nestled among five acres of century-old trees. Listed in the national historic register, it's known for unique architecture, dramatic 14-foot interior archways, woodwork, and five beautifully appointed bedrooms. Sip tea on wraparound porches or stroll under Spanish moss-draped trees to Marion's quaint shops and restaurants. Minutes from I-95, the perfect midway stopping point north or south. Close to the fun and excitement of Myrtle Beach.

Hosts: Coreen and Rick Roberts
Rooms: 5 (3 PB; 2 SB) $80-100
Full Breakfast
Credit Cards: None
Notes: 2, 3, 4, 5, 8, 9, 10, 11, 12, 14

MCCLELLANVILLE

Laurel Hill Plantation

8913 North Highway 17, P.O. Box 190, 29458
(843) 887-3708; (888) 887-3708

Laurel Hill faces the Intracoastal Waterway and the Atlantic Ocean. Porches provide a scenic view of marshes and creeks. The house is furnished in charming country and primitive antiques that reflect the Low Country lifestyle. Thirty miles north of Charleston, and only 60 miles south of Myrtle Beach. Smoking is allowed in designated areas only. Inquire about accommodations for children.

Hosts: Jackie and Lee Morrison
Rooms: 4 (PB) $95-115
Full Breakfast
Credit Cards: A, B, C, D, E, F
Notes: 2, 5, 9, 10, 11, 12, 14

Laurel Hill Plantation

MYRTLE BEACH

Serendipity Inn

407 71st Avenue North, 29572
(803) 449-5268; (800) 762-3229

Award-winning Spanish-style inn. Unique, elegant, and secluded. Only 300 yards from 60 miles of white sand beaches. Amenities include an outdoor hot tub, heated pool, shuffle board, Ping-Pong table, and gas grill. Choice of five queen-size, two master doubles, seven minisuites, or two suites. Air conditioning, TVs, refrigerators, and private baths in all rooms. Close to all of the country theaters, more than 90 golf courses, tennis, deep-sea fishing, and great shopping.

Hosts: Terry and Sheila Johnson
Rooms: 14 (PB) $45-129
Continental Breakfast
Credit Cards: A, B
Notes: 2, 8, 9, 10, 11, 12, 14, 15

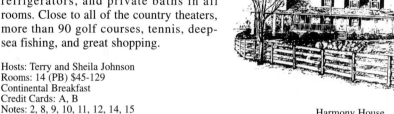

ROCK HILL

East Main Guest House

600 East Main Street, 29730
(803) 366-1161
www.bbonline.com/sc/eastmain/

In the downtown historic district, this Craftsman-style bungalow has been completely renovated and has been beautifully decorated. Guest rooms include private baths, cable TVs, telephones, fireplaces, and queen-size beds. The Honeymoon Suite has a canopied bed and a whirlpool tub. A TV/sitting/game room is provided, and breakfast is served in the beautifully appointed dining room or under the patio pergola. AAA three-diamond-rated and Mobil three-star-rated.

Hosts: Jerry and Melba Peterson
Rooms: 3 (PB) $59-79
Continental Breakfast
Credit Cards: A, B
Notes: 2, 5, 7, 9, 10, 11, 12, 14

Harmony House Bed and Breakfast

3485 Harmony Road, Catawba, 29704
(803) 329-3924; (888) 737-0016
www.bbonline.com/sc/harmony

Harmony House

Victorian-style farmhouse built in 1991. Nestled on a 36-acre countryside tract just four miles off I-77 on the outskirts of Rock Hill. Beautifully decorated with antiques and family treasures. Two common sitting areas, one with TV/VCR, Primestar satellite, movies, games, stocked refrigerator with drinks, snacks, etc. Peace and tranquility are definite assets, with city life just minutes away. Ample attractions nearby. Continental plus breakfast served. Children six and older welcome.

Hosts: Winky and Cecil Staton
Rooms: 3 (PB) $65-75
Continental Breakfast
Credit Cards: None
Notes: 2, 5, 7, 12

SUMMERVILLE

Bed and Breakfast of Summerville

304 South Hampton Street, 29483
(803) 871-5275

Sleep in the slave quarters of an 1862 house in a quiet historic district. Near restaurants, antique and speciality shops. Queen-size bed, telephone, TV, kitchenette, bath with shower, bikes, and pool. Short drive to Charleston, Middleton and Magnolia Gardens. Winter breakfast is self-prepared from the stocked refrigerator. For the rest of the year, breakfast in the greenhouse is an option. Advance reservation, please.

Hosts: Dusty and Emmagene Rhodes
Room: 1 (PB) $60
Continental Breakfast
Credit Cards: None
Notes: 2, 5, 7, 9, 10, 11, 12

Woodlands Resort and Inn

125 Parsons Road, 29483
(803) 875-2600; (803) 875-2603; (800) 774-9999

Woodlands Resort and Inn nestled in the woods on 42 acres, with 19 handsomely appointed rooms. No two are exactly alike, but all feature residential advantages such as fireplaces, sitting areas, heated towel racks, whirlpool baths, and personal amenities. Signature yellow roses and iced split of Perrier-Jouet champagne greet each guest upon arrival. Turndown service includes chocolates handmade by Woodlands' pastry chef. Dine in the five-diamond dining room. Heated swimming pool, clay tennis courts, croquet lawn, and bicycles are just a few of the many things available during a stay in South Carolina's only five-diamond, Relais et Chateaux property. Breakfast is served at the five-diamond restaurant, which opens at 7:00 A.M., or guests can order room service.

Host: Marty Wall
Rooms: 19 (PB) $225-325
Credit Cards: A, B, C, D, E
Notes: 2, 3, 4, 5, 7, 9, 10, 11, 12, 14, 15

SUMTER

Bed and Breakfast of Sumter

6 Park Avenue, 29150
(803) 773-2903; (888) 786-8372 (toll free)

This restored 1896 Prairie-style home sits in the heart of Sumter's historic district across from Memorial Park. Large front porch with swings and rocking chairs. Gracious guest rooms with antiques, fireplaces. Formal Victorian parlor and TV sitting room. Cable. Fax. Gourmet breakfast (fruit, entrée, home-baked breads). Antique shops, Swan Lake, and golf courses are all nearby. AAA-rated three diamonds.

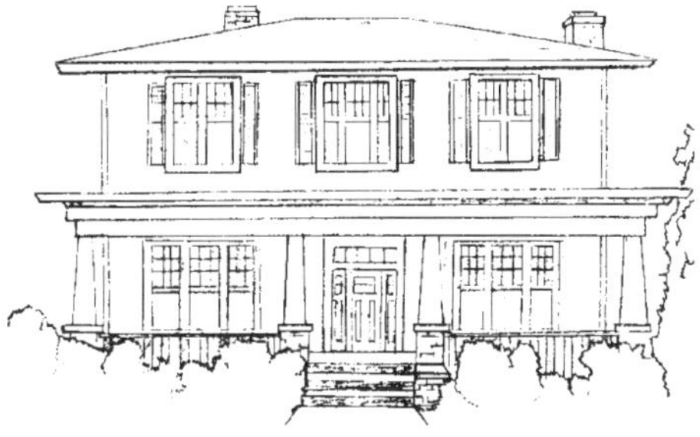
Bed and Breakfast of Sumter

Hosts: Jess and Suzanne Begley
Rooms: 5 (PB) $75
Full Breakfast
Credit Cards: A, B
Notes: 2, 5, 7, 10, 12, 14

Calhoun Street Bed and Breakfast

302 West Calhoun Street, 29150
(803) 775-7035; (800) 355-8119

Built in 1890s by a great-uncle, this Victorian home features a comfortable living room, dining room, four foyers, and reading area called the Yosemite Room. In the upstairs front foyer, guests may browse through the costume library or sit comfortably and watch TV. Furnished with family antiques and books. The front porch has a swing and joggling board, while the screened back porch overlooks the rose gardens. On pleasant evenings play croquet or sit in the gardens and watch the moon rise. In the historic district. Evening refreshments and full breakfast are served.

Rooms: 4 (PB) $65-75
Full Breakfast
Credit Cards: A, B
Notes: 2, 5, 7, 8, 9, 10, 11, 12

WALTERBORO

Old Academy Bed and Breakfast

904 Hampton Street, 29488
(843) 549-3232

Originally built in 1834 as Walterboro's first school, this grand two-story home is now a charming bed and breakfast. Just off exit 53 and exit 57 from I-95.

Centrally in historic Walterboro, it is only one hour from Charleston, Savannah, and Hilton Head. Peaceful and quiet surroundings in a small southern town. Canadian money at PAR.

Hosts: Don and Jean Sterling
Rooms: 4 (1 PB; 3 SB) $60-75
Full Breakfast
Credit Cards: None
Notes: 2, 5, 7, 8, 10, 12

WINNSBORO

Songbird Manor

116 North Zion Street, 29180
(803) 635-6963; FAX (803) 635-6963

Elegant 1912 William Morris-style home is a showcase of southern craftsmanship. Extensive oak and chestnut woodwork and doors, exquisite molded plaster ceilings and fireplaces in all rooms. Comfortably appointed bedrooms, two with sitting areas. Three baths have original claw-footed tubs. In historic district close to shops and restaurants. Wraparound veranda with swings and rockers. Gourmet breakfast and complimentary afternoon refreshments.

Host: Susan Yenner
Rooms: 5 (PB) $65-110
Full Breakfast
Credit Cards: A, B, C, D
Notes: 2, 5, 7, 9, 10, 12

WOODRUFF

The Nicholls-Crook Plantation House Bed and Breakfast

120 Plantation Drive, 29388
(864) 476-8820 (phone/FAX)

Be surrounded with the atmosphere of times gone by in this Georgian-style plantation house built in 1793 and listed in the National Register of Historic Places. Delight in historic ambiance enhanced by period antique furnishings and beautiful gardens. A bountiful breakfast adds to guests' pleasures. Guest rooms are cozy and inviting. Near Spartanburg, Greenville, Cowpens and Kings Mountain battlefields, historic Walnut Grove Plantation, BMW Zentrum, antique shopping, and more. Take exit 28 from I-26. Smoking permitted outside only. Children over six welcome.

Hosts: Suzanne and Jim Brown
Rooms: 3 (2 PB; 1 SB) $75-95
Full Breakfast
Credit Cards: C
Notes: 2, 5, 7, 9, 12, 14

The Nicholls-Crook Plantation

NOTES: Credit cards accepted: A MasterCard; B Visa; C American Express; D Discover; E Diner's Club; F Other; 2 Personal checks accepted; 3 Lunch available; 4 Dinner available; 5 Open all year; 6 Pets welcome;

Tennessee

ATHENS

Majestic Mansion Bed and Breakfast

202 East Washington Avenue, 37303
(423) 746-9041; e-mail: eden@cococo.net

Rest awhile at this beautiful 1909 home centrally located in downtown Athens. Select either the Old World charm of the Ambassador Room, the Japanese decor of the Empress Room, the country living of the King of the Mountain Room, or the whimsey of the Aslan Room. A full power breakfast or fitness fare is available every morning. Midway between Chattanooga and Knoxville off I-75.

Hosts: Richard and Elaine Newman
Rooms: 4 (3 PB; 1 SB) $65-75
Full Breakfast
Credit Cards: A, B
Notes: 2, 5, 7, 10, 12

Woodlawn

110 Keith Lane, 37303
(615) 745-8211; (615) 745-6029

Woodlawn is an elegant bed and breakfast in historic downtown Athens. The antebellum Greek Revival mansion is filled with family antiques. Built in 1858 by Alexander Keith, it was a Union hospital during the Civil War. Listed in the National Register of Historic Places. Thirteen-foot ceilings, large bedrooms with private baths. Halfway between Chattanooga and Knoxville off I-75. The *Tennessean* calls Woodlawn a classic bed and breakfast. On five acres, Woodlawn is filled with warm, friendly southern hospitality in the heart of Athens.

Hosts: Barry and Susan Willis
Rooms: 4 (PB) $60-140
Full Breakfast
Credit Cards: A, B, D
Notes: 2, 5, 7, 9, 10, 11, 12, 13, 14

BRISTOL

New Hope Bed and Breakfast

822 Georgia Avenue, 37620
(423) 989-3343; (888) 989-3343

All the charm of a late Victorian home, yet comfort and convenience were high on the agenda when decorating decisions were being made. "Come home to New Hope" is the hosts' motto. There are four guest rooms with large private baths. A full breakfast is always served. Arrange for a guided walking tour of the historic neighborhood or call ahead and inquire about the murder mystery weekends.

Hosts: Tom and Tonda Fluke
Rooms: 4 (PB) $75-105
Full Breakfast
Credit Cards: A, B, C
Notes: 2, 5, 7, 12

CHATTANOOGA

Adams Hilborne Mansion Inn

801 Vine Street, 37403
(423) 265-5000; FAX (423) 265-5555

Cornerstone to the Fort Wood historic district, this majestic Romanesque Victorian mansion is built in castlelike proportions of native mountain stone. The Adams Hilborne pampers guests with fine antiques, original artwork, and exquisite fabrics in all the oversized guest suites.

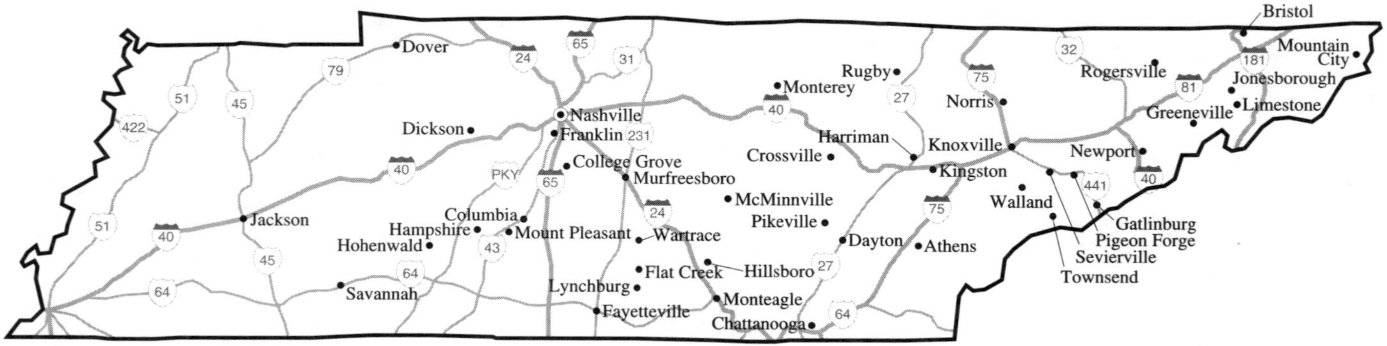
Bristol
Mountain City
Jonesborough
Limestone
Greeneville
Rogersville
Newport
Gatlinburg
Pigeon Forge
Sevierville
Townsend
Walland
Knoxville
Norris
Kingston
Athens
Harriman
Rugby
Monterey
Crossville
Dayton
McMinnville
Pikeville
Hillsboro
Monteagle
Chattanooga
Flat Creek
Wartrace
Murfreesboro
College Grove
Nashville
Franklin
Mount Pleasant
Columbia
Hampshire
Hohenwald
Lynchburg
Fayetteville
Savannah
Dickson
Dover
Jackson
PKY

Tennessee

Adams Hilborne Mansion Inn

The Designer Showhouse for the city of Chattanooga and winner of the prestigious National Trust Great American Home Awards. The reception rooms are resplendent with heavily carved moldings, coffered ceilings, 16-foot-tall arched pocket doors with silver-plated hinges. Fine candlelight dining in the restaurant. Minutes from the Tennessee Aquarium, Civil War sites, and Tennessee River.

Hosts: Wendy and Dave Adams
Rooms: 10 (PB) $100-295
Continental Breakfast
Credit Cards: A, B, C, E
Notes: 2, 3, 4, 5, 7, 8, 9, 10, 11, 12, 14, 15

Alford House Bed and Breakfast

5515 Alford Hill Drive, 37419
(423) 821-7625

Gracing the entrance to Lookout Mountain, this 18-room home offers a peaceful, quiet atmosphere. Towering trees surround the decks where one can read or relax from the day's cares. Rhoda's antique glass baskets, bears, heirlooms, and Victorian clutter can be found throughout. The Tennessee Aquarium, Rock City, and Ruby Falls, all within five miles. Hiking trails begin here. Early coffee is available and breakfast is served in the dining room or on upper deck. Inquire about accommodations for children. Mid-week and off-season discounts.

Host: Rhoda (Troyer) Alford
Rooms: 4 (2 PB; 2 SB) $65-95
Suite: 1 (PB) $145
Full and Continental Breakfast
Credit Cards: None
Notes: 2, 5, 7, 9, 10, 11, 12, 14

Bluff View Inn

411 East Second Street, 37403
(423) 265-5033; FAX (423) 757-0124

Overlooking the Tennessee River, in the Bluff View Art District, the Bluff View Inn offers refined accommodations in three turn-of-the-century restored homes. Guests enjoy Old World elegance, a spectacular view, and an exciting blend of gourmet restaurants, gardens, galleries, meeting rooms, banquet halls, private parlors, terrace cafés, working artists' studios, and the new Bluff View Scenic Overlook. Conveniently connected to downtown Chattanooga's major attractions and the popular North Shore via the Tennessee Riverwalk and Walnut Street Pedestrian Bridge. Private parking.

Host: Julie Poston, innkeeper
Rooms: 16 (PB) $115-250
Full Breakfast
Credit Cards: A, B, C, D
Notes: 2, 3, 4, 5, 7, 8, 9, 12

Bluff View Inn

NOTES: Credit cards accepted: A MasterCard; B Visa; C American Express; D Discover; E Diner's Club; F Other; 2 Personal checks accepted; 3 Lunch available; 4 Dinner available; 5 Open all year; 6 Pets welcome; 7 No smoking; 8 Children welcome; 9 Social drinking allowed; 10 Tennis nearby; 11 Swimming nearby; 12 Golf nearby; 13 Skiing nearby; 14 May be booked through a travel agent; 15 Handicapped accessible.

The Captain's Quarters Bed and Breakfast Inn

13 Barnhardt Circle
Fort Oglethorpe, GA 30742-3601
(706) 858-0624; (800) 710-6816
FAX (706) 861-4053
e-mail: innkeeper@captains-qtrs-inn.com
www.captains-qtrs-inn.com

Circa 1902, this beautifully renovated Classic Renaissance Revival home was built in 1903 by the US Army for two captains and their families. Rooms are individually decorated and some have working fireplaces. The spacious common areas are filled with family antiques. A hot tub spa is available with robes and slippers provided. In the suburbs of Chattanooga on the northern border of the Chickamauga and Chattanooga National Military Park, just 20 minutes from the Tennessee Aquarium and Lookout Mountain. Smoking permitted outside only. Children over 10 welcome. Cat in residence. No pets. Three-course breakfast served.

Hosts: Betty and Daniel McKenzie
Rooms: 7 (PB) $85-125
Full Breakfast
Credit Cards: A, B, C, D
Notes: 2, 5, 7, 9, 10, 12, 14

COLLEGE GROVE

Peacock Hill Country Inn

6994 Giles Hill Road, 37046
(615) 368-7727; (800) 327-6663
www.bbonline.com/tn/peacock/

Ten luxury accommodations on a 700-acre cattle farm, convenient to Franklin and Nashville. A historic 1850s farmhouse, two-story log cabin, a two-level granary suite and new/old McCall House. Private baths with whirlpools, power showers, king-size beds, fireplaces. Fireside suppers by reservation. Featured in *National Geographic Travel*, *Southern Living*, *Romantic Homes*, and *Country Accents*. No smoking. Inquire about accommodations for pets.

Hosts: Anita and Walter Ogilvie
Rooms: 10 (PB) $125-225
Full Breakfast
Credit Cards: A, B, C, D
Notes: 2, 3, 4, 5, 7, 8, 9, 10, 11, 12, 14, 15

COLUMBIA

Locust Hill Bed and Breakfast

1185 Mooresville Pike, 38401
(913) 388-8531; (800) 577-8264

Historic 1840 antebellum home and two-story smokehouse with fireplace, both furnished with family antiques, handmade quilts, and embroidered linens. Guests are pampered with morning coffee in their room. Delicious gourmet breakfasts feature country ham, biscuits, and homemade jams. Enjoy the fireplaces, relax in the library, on the porches, in the flower gardens to make this a perfect getaway. Fireside gourmet dinners available. AAA three-diamond-rated.

Hosts: Bill and Beverly Beard
Rooms: 4 (PB) $90-125
Full Breakfast
Credit Cards: A, B, C, D
Notes: 2, 4, 5, 7, 12

Locust Hill

Natchez Trace Bed and Breakfast Reservation Service

P.O. Box 193, Hampshire, 38461
(931) 285-2777; (800) 377-2770
e-mail: natcheztrace@worldnet.att.net

Sweetwater Inn. Milepost 409. Thirteen miles from Columbia and just five miles from Interstate 65, this 1901 farmhouse has been newly restored to elegant perfection.

Double wraparound porch provides view of the Middle Tennessee countryside. The Columbia area is the antebellum home capital of Tennessee. A gourmet breakfast is served on fine linens and china. $100-125.

Sweetwater Inn

2436 Campbells Station Road, 38401
(931) 987-3077; (800) 335-3077
FAX (931) 987-2525

This turn-of-the-century Gothic steamboat-style country home, set in the middle of Tennessee, is a perfect base to explore the surrounding area. There are two wraparound porches, and lots of rocking chairs to sit in while viewing the breathtaking vistas of soft rolling hills. Each of the four bedrooms has access to the second-floor porch, where guests can watch the sunrise or sunset with morning coffee or evening dessert. A sumptuous gourmet breakfast is served by candlelight. Near Columbia, home of President James K. Polk, antebellum home tours, Saturn car factory, Civil War history, and Mule Day Celebration. Near I-65 south, exit 32, it is 45 miles south of Nashville. Dinner available by reservation.

Host: Sandy Shotwell
Rooms: 4 (PB) $100-125
Full Breakfast
Credit Cards: A, B, D
Notes: 2, 5, 7, 8, 10, 11, 12, 14

CROSSVILLE

Betty's Bed and Breakfast and Made By Hand Gift Gallery

5241 Peavine Road, 38558-7915
(931) 484-8827

Just down the road from the nationally acclaimed Fairfield Glade resort, Betty's Bed and Breakfast provides a warm and friendly atmosphere for that special getaway. Sit on the wraparound porch and enjoy the beauty of the Cumberland Plateau. Wake up to the aroma of a delicious full breakfast, served in Aunt Hattie's dining room. Nearby are the Cumberland County Playhouse and the Cumberland State Park. Fully air conditioned and open year-round. Lunch is available with reservations.

Host: Betty Bryan
Rooms: 4 (PB) $65
Full Breakfast
Credit Cards: A, B
Notes: 2, 5, 8, 9, 10, 11, 12

DAYTON

Rose House

123 Idaho Avenue, 37321
(423) 775-3311; (423) 877-4275

Built in 1892, Rose House is the perfect place to get away. Only 30 minutes from historic Chattanooga. Guests can enjoy hiking, fishing, or just taking it easy on the front porch swing. It is furnished in period antiques with modern seating and bedding. Dayton is home to the famous Scopes Monkey Trial reenactment every July.

Host: Leana Leighton
Rooms: 3 (2 PB; 1 SB) $65-75
Full Breakfast
Credit Cards: A, B, C, D
Notes: 2, 5, 7, 10, 11, 12

DICKSON

East Hills Bed and Breakfast Inn

100 East Hill Terrace, 37055
(615) 441-9428; FAX (615) 446-2181
www.bbonline.com/tn/easthills/

This fully restored traditional home with southern charm was built in the late forties by the current owner's father. The house is near Luther Lake, Greystone Golf Course, and is only six miles from Montgomery Bell State Park; convenient to shopping, hospital, restaurants, and downtown area. Large living room, library/den with fireplace, and TV for guests to enjoy. Furnished throughout with period antiques. The long front

7 No smoking; 8 Children welcome; 9 Social drinking allowed; 10 Tennis nearby; 11 Swimming nearby; 12 Golf nearby; 13 Skiing nearby; 14 May be booked through a travel agent; 15 Handicapped accessible.

East Hills

porch has rocking chairs and a swing. Enjoy the big front yard with lots of trees.

Hosts: John and Anita Luther
Rooms: 5 (PB) $65-95
Cottage: 1
Full and Continental Breakfast
Credit Cards: A, B, C
Notes: 2, 5, 7, 10, 11, 12, 15

DOVER

Riverfront Plantation Inn

190 Crow Lane, P.O. Box 349, 37058
(931) 232-9492

Experience the southern hospitality of this splendidly restored Civil War era home. The inn features five elegant guest rooms with private baths, screened porches, and a gourmet plantation breakfast. The historic waterfront estate is adjacent to Fort Donelson National Battlefield and minutes from Land Between the Lakes.

Hosts: Lynn and Fulton Combs
Rooms: 5 (PB) $85
Full Breakfast
Credit Cards: A, B, D
Notes: 2, 3, 4, 5, 7, 9, 10, 11, 12, 14

FAYETTEVILLE

The Heritage House

315 East College Street, 37334
(931) 433-9238; (888) 629-4422

Visit this charming pre-Civil War antebellum brick Italianate-style home with high ceilings, thick walls, and pocket doors in the historic district. Relax in comfortably furnished rooms with all premium cable TV, in-room refrigerator, and antiques. Guests are welcome to enjoy the swing on the balcony or wicker chairs on the long front porch. Within walking distance of churches, movie theater, restaurants, historical district, museum, and gift and antique shops. Other points of interest include Tims Ford Lake, U.S. Space and Rocket Center, and the Jack Daniel's Distillery. Smoking permitted in designated areas only.

Hosts: Nina and Ken May
Rooms: 2 (PB) $60-100
Continental Breakfast
Credit Cards: None
Notes: 2, 5, 9, 10, 11, 12

The Heritage House

FLAT CREEK (SHELBYVILLE)

Bottle Hollow Lodge

111 Gobbler Ridge Road, P.O. Box 92,
Shelbyville, 37160
(931) 695-5253

Nestled high in the rolling hills of Middle Tennessee, Bottle Hollow Lodge occupies 68 acres of beautiful countryside and magnificent views. The ultimate in peace, quiet, and solitude, this inn is just minutes from Lynchburg's Jack Daniel's Distillery and the site of the Tennessee Walking Horse National Celebration in Shelbyville. Bottle Hollow Lodge, with its inviting rockers on the front porch and plush sofas in front of the large stone fireplace, will add to the enjoyment of activities in the area. Lunch and dinner available by reservation for groups of 12 to 23. Children over 12 welcome.

Host: Pat Whiteside
Rooms: 4 (PB) $90
Full Breakfast
Credit Cards: A, B
Notes: 2, 5, 7, 9, 12, 14, 15

FRANKLIN

Blueberry Hill Bed and Breakfast

4591 Peytonsville Road, 37064
(615) 791-9947

Blueberry Hill is eight miles from historic Franklin—rich in Civil War history. It is perched near the top of a high hill with breathtaking views of the rolling hills and valleys of Middle Tennessee from the great room, deck, porch, and gardens. The original house was built in the Federal style with fireplaces in every room. There are two guest rooms with four-poster beds and gas log fireplaces. Full breakfast with blueberry specialties.

Hosts: Art and Joan Reesman
Rooms: 2 (PB) $75-85
Full Breakfast
Credit Cards: A, B, D
Notes: 2, 5, 7, 9, 12

Natchez Trace Bed and Breakfast Reservation Service

P.O. Box 193, Hampshire, 38461
(931) 285-2777; (800) 377-2770
e-mail: natcheztrace@worldnet.att.net

Blueberry Hill Bed and Breakfast. Twelve miles from the Natchez Trace and convenient to Franklin, I-65, and Nashville, this home has a breathtaking view of the valley. A replica of a Federal-period home, there are old heart-pine flooring and a fireplace in every room. The modern addition boasts a great room with books, a piano, a pub table, and large-screen TV, with a collection of movies. Queen-size beds; full breakfast with blueberry specialties. Children over 10 welcome. $70-80.

Namaste Bed and Breakfast. Milepost 436. Set in the lovely Leipers Creek valley near the village of Leipers Fork, this country home is only two and one-half miles from the Natchez Trace. There are facilities for horses; the trail along the trace is just minutes away. Large guest rooms with private baths. Enjoy a full breakfast and look out over the peaceful setting. Swimming pool and exercise room available. $80.

The Old Marshall House Bed and Breakfast

1030 John Williams Road, 37067
(615) 591-4121; (800) 863-5808
FAX (615) 591-4174
www.bbonline.com/tn/oldmarshall

Beautiful 1869 home in serene pastoral setting with pond and old log cabin. Three minutes from I-65, 3.5 miles from historic downtown Franklin, and 18 miles from downtown Nashville. Three porches to lounge on, twin parlors with library, TV, and games, three individually decorated, charming guest rooms with fireplaces and private bathrooms. Come to relax and to enjoy the peace and quiet of southern country living. Smoking permitted outside only.

Hosts: Glenn and Ursula Houghton
Rooms: 3 (PB) $85-110
Full Breakfast
Credit Cards: A, B, C, D
Notes: 2, 5, 7, 9, 10, 11, 12

Sweeney Hollow Bed and Breakfast

3454 Sweeney Hollow Road, 37064
(615) 591-0498; e-mail: jpf0498@aol.com
www.members.tripod.com/~Claudia3848/index.html

Turn off the Natchez Trace Parkway to discover this country hideaway nestled amid the rolling hills of charming Leipers Fork.

Just 35 miles from downtown Nashville and 35 minutes to three major shopping malls, this cozy brick ranch home is also near historic Franklin with its numerous Civil War sites, antique malls, golf courses, and restaurants. Spend a peaceful evening watching the wildlife or strolling through the five-acre woods. The innkeepers blend down-home friendliness with international experience. The spacious guest quarters include a private bath en suite, a separate sitting area, and kitchen privileges. Computer services are available in the office. Smoking is permitted on the patio only.

Hosts: Claudia and John Finnegan
Rooms: 1 (PB) $125
Full Breakfast
Credit Cards: None
Notes: 7, 8, 12

GATLINBURG

Butcher House in the Mountains

1520 Garrett Lane, 37738
(423) 436-9457

Tucked away upon a mountain is an indescribable view from this Swiss chalet. The breakfasts here are gourmet and bountiful. Most people don't require lunch after this meal. Almost three miles from the village of Gatlinburg. AAA three-diamond-rated. ABBA-rated excellent. Color TV in every room, guest kitchen, and telephone. "We look forward to sharing our beautiful home with you." The hosts have been innkeepers for eight years.

Butcher House in the Mountains

Hosts: Hugh and Gloria Butcher
Rooms: 5 (PB) $89-129
Full Breakfast
Credit Cards: A, B, C
Notes: 2, 5, 7, 9, 10, 11, 12, 13, 14

The Colonel's Lady Inn

1120 Tanrac Trail, 37738
(423) 436-5432; (800) 515-5432
e-mail: colonel@colonelsladyinn.com

Magnificent panoramas, impeccable privacy, marvelously romantic—all describe the elegant charm of the Colonel's Lady. Ideal for all intimate celebrations. One cottage, two rooms, and five suites, all with king- or queen-size beds and private baths; some kitchens, fireplaces, and TVs. Children over 12 welcome. No pets.

Hosts: Anita and Bill Cate
Rooms: 8 (PB) $89-159
Full Breakfast
Credit Cards: A, B, D
Notes: 5, 7, 9, 10, 11, 12, 13, 14

Eight Gables

219 North Mountain Trail, 37738
(423) 430-3344; (800) 279-5716

Guests of this bed and breakfast are welcomed by a peaceful mountain setting. Near the trolley stop, it features a unique design and decor. Comfort is assured in the spacious guest rooms, each decorated with an individual theme and style. Each first-floor guest room has a private entrance, and all of the second-floor guest rooms are graced with cathedral ceilings and arched windows. There are gathering rooms for relaxing and viewing TV. Full sit-down breakfast. Dramatic surroundings inside and out. Everything a guest might need marks this tribute to southern hospitality. AAA four-diamond-rated. Dinner available on Saturday only.

Hosts: Don and Kim Cason
Rooms: 12 (PB) $109-179

Eight Gables

Full Breakfast
Credit Cards: A, B, C, D
Notes: 2, 3, 5, 7, 8, 9, 10, 11, 12, 13, 14

GREENEVILLE

Hilltop House Bed and Breakfast Inn

6 Sanford Circle, 37743
(423) 639-8202

Come and experience the serenity of a 1920s manor house overlooking the Nolichucky River Valley with the Appalachian Mountains in the background. All three guest rooms have private baths and spectacular mountain views, and two have their own verandas. Enjoy afternoon tea at 4:00 P.M. each day and sumptuous breakfasts. Nearby golf, mountain hiking and biking, trout fishing, white-water rafting, horseback riding, or antiquing. The house is beautifully furnished with oriental rugs, English antiques, and reproduction pieces. Children over three welcome.

Host: Denise M. Ashworth
Rooms: 3 (PB) $75-80
Full Breakfast
Credit Cards: A, B, C
Notes: 2, 5, 7, 9, 12, 14

Nolichuckey Bluffs

400 Kinser Park Lane, 37743
(423) 787-7947; (800) 842-4690
FAX (423) 787-9247; e-mail: cabins@usit.net

Luxury bed and breakfast and fully equipped large, two-bedroom cabins. Full breakfasts with home-baked goodies. Laundry and exercise area. Spectacular mountain views in a beautiful country setting. Children's playground, trails, and picnic pavilion. Asheville, North Carolina, Gatlinburg, antiques, historical spots, and Appalachian Trail nearby. Enjoy evenings around the fireplace as someone puts another roll in the player piano, or enjoy freshly baked cookies while watching the sun set behind the mountains.

Hosts: Patricia and Brooke Sadler
Rooms: 7 (PB) $70-95
Full Breakfast
Credit Cards: A, B, D
Notes: 2, 5, 7, 8, 10, 11, 12, 14

HAMPSHIRE

Natchez Trace Bed and Breakfast Reservation Service

P.O. Box 193, Hampshire, 38461
(931) 285-2777; (800) 377-2770
e-mail: natcheztrace@worldnet.att.net

Ridgetop Bed and Breakfast. Milepost 392. Contemporary cedar home furnished with antiques, set on 170 acres of wooded hills near the village of Hampshire, between Columbia and Hohenwald. Picture windows look out over the woods; have coffee on the spacious deck. Clear streams, a waterfall, birds, and wildflowers. Near Meriwether Lewis Park, Metal Ford, and Jackson Falls on the trace. The hosts are experts on local wildflowers. Full breakfast served. There is one guest room in the home, a cottage for up to four people, and an 1830 log cabin with fireplace. $65-85.

HARRIMAN

Bushrod Hall Bed and Breakfast

422 Cumberland Street, Northeast, 37748
(423) 882-8406; (888) 880-8406

This Queen Anne Victorian home was built in 1892 by S. K. Paige for $18,000. Later purchased for the American Temperance University, it became the Bushrod W. James Hall of Domestic Science for young ladies.

Bushrod Hall

In June 1996, Bob and Nancy Ward began restoring the house to its former splendor while welcoming guests to come and enjoy its charm and elegance. Special features include a massive oak staircase, imported from Sweden, wainscoting, and exquisite wood detailing, including five fireplaces with original mantels.

Hosts: Nancy and Bob Ward
Rooms: 3 (PB) $75-125
Full Breakfast
Credit Cards: A, B, C
Notes: 2, 5, 7, 9, 14

HILLSBORO

Lord's Landing Bed and Breakfast

375 Lord's Landing Lane, 37342
(931) 467-3830; FAX (931) 467-3032
e-mail: lordslanding@blomand.net

Central Tennessee's 50-acre paradise awaits guests from near and far. Drive in for a relaxing retreat, or fly in to a 2,400 x 80-foot turf airstrip for a quiet getaway. Near the base of the Cumberland Plateau, the main house boasts breathtaking views from every window. A leisurely stroll takes guests to the seven-bedroom, seven-bath country cottage, beautifully decorated with antiques and fine furnishings. Fireplaces and Jacuzzi tubs in most rooms.

Hosts: Denny and Pam Neilson
Rooms: 7 (PB) $95-150
Full Breakfast
Credit Cards: A, B, D
Notes: 2, 3, 4, 5, 8, 12, 14

HOHENWALD

Natchez Trace Bed and Breakfast Reservation Service

P.O. Box 193, Hampshire, 38461
(931) 285-2777; (800) 377-2770
e-mail: natcheztrace@worldnet.att.net

Armstrong's Bakery Bed and Breakfast. Just seven miles from the Natchez Trace in Hohenwald, this home has been freshly restored and opened as a bed and breakfast. Once the town jail, it is now beautifully decorated with antiques and has a comfortable balcony that can be used as a sitting area for two of the guest rooms. "High Forest" in German, Hohenwald is known for its small-town charm and outdoor activities, including canoeing, cycling, and hunting. Convenient to Meriwether Lewis Park on the trace. Full breakfast. $65.

Avaleen Springs Bed and Breakfast. Sixteen miles west of the trace on Highway 412, this is a truly magical 30-acre retreat, a rustic cedar home nestled against a bluff, with a mile-long series of springs and streams that runs under the house. Guests can actually observe creek life through a glass coffee table in the sitting room. Canoeing and fishing in the area, and convenient to the Tennessee River, the Buffalo River, Shiloh Battlefield, and Mousetail Landing State Park. $50-85.

JACKSON

Highland Place Bed and Breakfast

519 North Highland Avenue, 38301
(901) 427-1472

This noted historic home of Jackson, known locally as the Hamilton-Butler

Highland Place

Mansion, contains a treasure of unique and interesting woodwork and antiques. The architectural jewel of the house is a cherry-paneled library. The one guest room and three suites offer an unusual degree of flexibility in accommodations. One suite has a custom-built walnut queen-size canopied bed with easy chairs grouped in front of an operating fireplace and is available with an adjoining bedroom, making it suitable for a family of four. The four full baths include one with a restored antique claw-foot tub, and one with an oversized tub large enough for two. Dinner available by reservation.

Hosts: Glenn and Janice Wall
Rooms: 4 (PB) $75-135
Full Breakfast
Credit Cards: A, B, C
Notes: 2, 5, 7, 10, 11, 12, 14

JONESBOROUGH

Jonesborough Bed and Breakfast

100 Woodrow Avenue, P.O. Box 722, 37659
(423) 753-9223

This beautifully restored home was built in 1848 and is in Jonesborough's historic district. All restaurants and shops are within easy walking distance. To make a visit memorable, guests will find robes, high beds, antique furnishings, fireplaces, large porch with rocking chairs, secluded terrace, air conditioning, and a big breakfast. Private baths. Seasonal rates.

Host: Tobie Bledsoe
Rooms: 3 (PB) $79-99
Full Breakfast
Credit Cards: None
Notes: 2, 5, 7, 8, 9, 11, 12

KINGSTON

Whitestone Country Inn

1200 Paint Rock Road, 37763
(423) 376-0113; FAX (423) 376-4454

A luxurious, secluded 275-acre country estate on the shores of Watts Bar Lake provides a perfect escape for a getaway. Each of the 12 bedrooms has a fireplace, whirlpool tub, TV/VCR. Fishing and hiking are also available on the property. Surrounded by a wildlife and waterfowl refuge, Whitestone Inn brings guests close to all East Tennessee attractions, but far enough away to find sanctuary, relaxation, and the tranquility of God's creation.

Hosts: Paul and Jean Cowell
Rooms: 12 (PB) $85-145
Full Breakfast
Credit Cards: A, B, C, D
Notes: 2, 3, 4, 5, 7, 8, 10, 12, 14, 15

KNOXVILLE

Maplehurst Inn

800 West Hill Avenue, 37920
(423) 523-7773 (phone/FAX)

Built in 1917 as a single-family home on the Tennessee River, adjacent to the University of Tennessee. In 1981, the Maplehurst Inn was converted to a European-style bed and breakfast inn. It remains an exquisite inn for special guests in Knoxville's historic and peaceful Maplehurst Park. The Penthouse Honeymoon Suite and the

Anniversary Suite have Jacuzzis and king-size beds. Other rooms feature sunken or marble tubs, a fireplace, and a king-size or two double beds. A bodacious buffet breakfast is served each day.

Hosts: Sonny and Becky Harben
Rooms: 11 (PB) $85-125
Full Breakfast
Credit Cards: A, B
Notes: 2, 5, 7, 9, 10, 12

Mitchell's

1031 West Park Drive, 37909
(423) 690-1488

This bed and breakfast offers a comfortable room in a private home in a pleasant tree-shaded neighborhood near fine shops and restaurants. Parking at a private entrance, double bed, TV, refrigerator, and microwave; rollaway bed and crib available. It is 45 minutes to the Smoky Mountains, 25 minutes to Oak Ridge, 1.5 miles to I-75/I-40, and 8 miles to downtown Knoxville. Ground level is handicapped accessible.

Host: Mary M. Mitchell
Room: 1 (PB) $40
Continental Breakfast
Credit Cards: None
Notes: 2, 5, 6, 8, 9, 10, 11

LIMESTONE

Snapp Inn Bed and Breakfast

1990 Davy Crockett Park Road, 37681
(423) 257-2482

These hosts will welcome guests into this gracious 1815 Federal home furnished with antiques and set in farm country. Enjoy the mountain view from the full back porch or play a game of pool. Close to Davy Crockett Birthplace State Park; 15-minute drive to historic Jonesborough or Greeneville. Third person is an additional $10.

Hosts: Dan and Ruth Dorgan
Rooms: 2 (PB) $65
Full Breakfast

Snapp Inn

Credit Cards: None
Notes: 2, 5, 6, 7, 9, 11, 12, 14

LYNCHBURG

Cedar Lane Bed and Breakfast

Route 3, Box 155E, 37352
(931) 759-6891

On the outskirts of historic Lynchburg, home of Jack Daniel's Distillery, this newly built farmhouse offers guests comfort and relaxation. Whether it be a weekend or week's stay, guests can spend their time antiquing in nearby shops or reading a book in the sunroom. The rooms are beautifully decorated in rose, blue, peach, and green with queen-size and twin beds. Telephones and TV available upon request. Continental plus breakfast. Dinner available by reservation. Children over 10 welcome.

Hosts: Elaine and Chuck Quinn
Room: 4 (PB) $65-75

Cedar Lane

Continental Breakfast
Credit Cards: A, B, C
Notes: 2, 5, 7, 9, 11, 12

Mulberry House Bed and Breakfast

8 Old Lynchburg Highway, Mulberry, 37359
(615) 433-8461

This 110-year-old home in Mulberry, where Davy Crockett spent a winter, is nestled in the hills of Middle Tennessee, only seven miles from Lynchburg, the home of Jack Daniel's Tennessee whiskey. Only 45 minutes from Huntsville, Alabama. There are numerous craft and antique shops to visit. Buggy rides available.

Host: Candy Richard
Rooms: 2 (PB) $55
Continental Breakfast
Credit Cards: A, B
Notes: 2, 5, 7, 8, 9, 14

MCMINNVILLE

Historic Falcon Manor

2645 Faulkner Springs Road, 37110
(931) 668-4444; FAX (931) 815-4444
e-mail: falconmanor@falconmanor.com
www.falconmanor.com

Relive the 1890s in one of the South's finest Victorian mansions. Indulge in the luxury of museum quality antiques. Enjoy owners' tales of the 10,000-square-foot mansion's history and their adventures restoring it. Rock on gingerbread verandas shaded by giant trees in this country setting just minutes from town. Halfway between Nashville and Chattanooga with easy access to I-24 and I-40, this is the ideal base for a Tennessee vacation. The 1997 National Trust Restoration Award winner.

Historic Falcon Manor

Hosts: George and Charlien McGlothin
Rooms: 5 (PB) $105
Full Breakfast
Credit Cards: A, B
Notes: 2, 4, 5, 7, 9, 10, 11, 12, 14, 15

MEMPHIS

The Bridgewater House Bed and Breakfast

7015 Raleigh LaGrange Road, Cordova, 38018
(901) 384-0080; e-mail: kmistilis@worldnet.att.net

A Greek Revival home converted from a schoolhouse, circa 1890. A lovely, elegant dwelling filled with antiques, family heirlooms, oriental rugs, etc. There are the original floors, enormous rooms, high ceilings, deep moldings, and faux marbleizing. Two very spacious bedrooms with private baths are available for guests along with a common room with fireplace. Guests are pampered with refreshments upon arrival, coffee outside room, and a full gourmet breakfast served by a certified chef and food and beverage director. Right off I-40, but only 20 minutes from downtown Memphis. The inn is on two and one-half acres with stately oak trees.

Hosts: Katherine and Steve Mistilis
Rooms: 2 (PB) $100
Full Breakfast
Credit Cards: A, B, D
Notes: 2, 5

Lowenstein-Long House

217 North Waldran, 38105
(901) 527-7174

This beautifully restored Victorian mansion near downtown is listed in the National Register of Historic Places. Convenient to major attractions, such as the

7 No smoking; 8 Children welcome; 9 Social drinking allowed; 10 Tennis nearby; 11 Swimming nearby; 12 Golf nearby; 13 Skiing nearby; 14 May be booked through a travel agent; 15 Handicapped accessible.

Mississippi River, Graceland, Beale Street, the Memphis Zoo, Brooks Museum, and the Victorian Village. Free off-street parking.

Hosts: Col. Charles and Dr. Margaret Long
Rooms: 4 (PB) $50-80
Full Breakfast
Credit Cards: None
Notes: 2, 5, 7, 9

MONTEAGLE

Adams Edgeworth Inn

Monteagle Assembly, 37356
(931) 924-4000; FAX (931) 924-3236

A showcase for country antiques, original paintings, handmade quilts, and quaint decor; nestled in an exclusive historic village on top of Monteagle Mountain. Two hundred feet of verandas supply ample space for rocking away the day. Fine dining by candlelight available every evening. In a 115-year-old Chautauqua village; abundant hiking, views, vistas, and natural activities in the area. Also proximity to Jack Daniel's, University of the South, Sewanee, and Arnold Engineering Center with the largest wind tunnel in the world. National register property. Independent innkeepers.

Adams Edgeworth Inn

Hosts: Wendy and Dave Adams
Rooms: 12 (PB) $95-205
Full Breakfast
Credit Cards: A, B, C
Notes: 2, 4, 5, 7, 8, 9, 10, 11, 12, 14

North Gate Inn

103 Monteagle Assembly, 37356
(931) 924-2799; FAX (931) 924-3662

The bright blue awning of this historic inn welcomes guests to warm hospitality and sumptuous breakfasts. Variety of common areas to enjoy, including the spacious Gate Room and Sun Room with blue enamel wood stove, porches, and fireplaces. Original iron beds, custom mattresses, antique quilts, and ceiling fans in each charming guest room. Exceptional personal hospitality. Special breakfasts. Close to hiking trails, waterfalls, caves, mountain vistas, antiques, and crafts. Explore the grounds of the historic Chautauqua of the South, Monteagle Assembly, or rock a while on the porch. In business for more than 15 years.

Hosts: Nancy and Henry Crais
Rooms: 7 (PB) $72-88
Full Breakfast
Credit Cards: None
Notes: 2, 5, 7, 8, 9, 10, 11, 12, 14

MONTEREY

The Garden Inn

1400 Bee Rock Road, 38574
(888) 293-1444
www.bbonline.com/tn/gardeninn

The Garden Inn sits on the very edge of the Cumberland Plateau, looking 1,000 feet down into the Calfkiller Valley. Upscale accommodations and a relaxed elegance will greet the visitor in this three-year-old inn. The inn features beautiful landscaped grounds, a simulated mountain stream that runs through the building, and an atmosphere for complete relaxation. It is also ideal for small corporate groups, weddings, and retreats.

Rooms: 11 (PB) $110-155
Full Breakfast
Credit Cards: A, B, C, D
Notes: 5, 7, 9, 12, 15

MOUNT PLEASANT

Natchez Trace Bed and Breakfast Reservation Service

P.O. Box 193, Hampshire, 38461
(931) 285-2777; (800) 377-2770
e-mail: natcheztrace@worldnet.att.net

Academy Place Bed and Breakfast. The site of an 1835 "female academy" and rebuilt in 1906 by the mayor of the town of Mount Pleasant. At his death, the spacious bedrooms were used for boarders; it continues in that tradition as a newly opened bed and breakfast, 15 miles from the Natchez Trace. Each room has a queen-size bed, comfortable seating, and a writing desk. Hot spa available, as well as basketball, horseshoes, and cable TV. Nearby are historic homes and churches and the Mount Pleasant/Maury Phosphate Museum. Full breakfast. $75-90.

MOUNTAIN CITY

Butler House Bed and Breakfast

309 North Church Street, 37683
(423) 727-4119 (phone/FAX); (888) 219-7737

Nestled in the beautiful Blue Ridge mountains of eastern Tennessee, this spacious circa 1870 national registry home is sure to please. Two blocks from downtown Mountain City on 15 acres of lawns, gardens, and treed hillsides, and just minutes from tourist attractions of North Carolina and Virginia as well as Tennessee. The upstairs porch is made for rocking and relaxing, and the comfortably appointed rooms are all accessible from it.

Hosts: Bill and Joan Trathen
Rooms: 4 (PB) $60-70
Full Breakfast
Credit Cards: A, B
Notes: 2, 5, 7, 9, 10, 11, 12, 13

Prospect Hill Bed and Breakfast

801 West Main Street, Highway 67, 37683
(423) 727-0139

Unusual tranquility, superb mountain views, and proximity to nature hikes, fishing, boating, festivals, caverns, galleries, and shopping. Between the mountains where Tennessee, North Carolina, and Virginia join. Circa 1889 solid brick mansion built by a local prospector who served in the Union army. Huge rooms, modern romantic baths, comfortable beds, and fireplaces. Innkeepers are stripping the oak moldings in the formal rooms and turning 2.5 acres into a parklike setting. Decorating in the second owner's 1910 period with antique dining set and Stickley reproductions. Comfortable hospitality from experienced innkeepers who found a lovely house in the best small town in northeast Tennessee.

Hosts: Robert and Judy Hotchkiss
Rooms: 5 (PB) $89-199
Full Breakfast
Credit Cards: A, B
Notes: 2, 5, 7, 8, 9, 10, 12, 13, 14, 15

MURFREESBORO

Clardy's Guest House

435 East Main Street, 37130
(615) 893-6030; e-mail: rdeaton@bellsouth.net
www.bbonline.com/tn/clardys/

In the historic district, this 20-room Victorian Romanesque home is filled with antiques and features ornate woodwork and fireplaces. An 8-x-8-foot stained-glass window overlooks the magnificent staircase. The area has much to offer history buffs and antique shoppers. Thirty miles from Nashville, just two miles off I-24. Continental plus breakfast served.

Clardy's Guest House

Hosts: Robert and Barbara Deaton
Rooms: 3 (2 PB; 1 SB) $45-53
Continental Breakfast
Credit Cards: None
Notes: 2, 5, 7, 8, 9, 10, 11, 12, 14

NASHVILLE

Crocker Springs Bed and Breakfast

2382 Crocker Springs Road,Goodlettsville, 37072
(615) 876-8502

Come, relax, and enjoy this country haven just 14 miles from downtown Nashville. Crocker Springs is a restored Tennessee farmhouse built circa 1890, furnished with many antiques. Listen to the rippling sounds of the creek from the porch or sunroom. Hike the wooded ridge and partake of God's beautiful nature. Escape from the busy world. Full breakfast along with sweet rolls or breads. Jack and Bev extend a warm welcome of southern hospitality to each of their guests.

Hosts: Jack and Bev Spangler
Rooms: 3 (PB) $85-100
Full Breakfast
Credit Cards: C
Notes: 2, 5, 7, 10, 11, 12

Hillsboro House Bed and Breakfast

1933 20th Avenue South, 37212
(615) 292-5501; e-mail: hilsboro@nashville.net
www.bbonline.com/tn/hillsboro

Nestled on a quiet street in historic Hillsboro/Belmont neighborhood, Hillsboro House is only blocks from Vanderbilt University and Music Row and is an easy walk to some of Nashville's finest restaurants. The three bedrooms have queen-size feather beds and private baths. A full breakfast is served in the parlor. Enjoy a unique balance of history, culture, and small-town friendliness.

Host: Andrea Beaudet
Rooms: 3 (PB) $105
Full Breakfast
Credit Cards: A, B, C
Notes: 2, 5, 6, 7, 8, 14

Hillsboro House

Morning Star Bed and Breakfast

460 Jones Lane, Hendersonville, 37075
(615) 264-2614

On six acres of rolling lawns and deep woods, Morning Star affords a potpourri of pleasant surprises. Outdoors, shoot hoops, challenge the kids to volleyball or badminton, go tobogganing (weather permitting), or tune up for serious golf on own private par-three country golf course. Try one's hand at billiards, table tennis, and

NOTES: Credit cards accepted: A MasterCard; B Visa; C American Express; D Discover; E Diner's Club; F Other; 2 Personal checks accepted; 3 Lunch available; 4 Dinner available; 5 Open all year; 6 Pets welcome;

Morning Star

darts, settle in by one of four downstairs fireplaces, inspect antiques, or avail oneself of the 60-inch theater TV with tape library.

Rooms: 3 (1 PB; 2 SB) $95-120
Full Breakfast
Credit Cards: A, B, C
Notes: 2, 5, 6, 7, 8, 9, 12

Natchez Trace Bed and Breakfast Reservation Service

P.O. Box 193, Hampshire, 38461
(931) 285-2777; (800) 377-2770
e-mail: natcheztrace@worldnet.att.net

Applebrook Bed and Breakfast. Almost 3 miles from the terminus of the Natchez Trace and 14 miles from downtown Nashville, this turn-of-the-century farmhouse is nestled on five panoramic acres. There are a swimming pool, five-stall horse barn, and a brook and natural spring. Savor their specialty—apple pancakes with real maple syrup. Convenient to Nashville attractions, as well as Franklin's Civil War sites and antique shops. Large guest rooms with queen-size beds. $95.

Chigger Ridge. Less than 10 miles from the trace, near Pegram, this home is perched on a ridgetop with 67 acres of trails and vistas in all directions. The main house, with two guest bedrooms, is a western cedar log home, with vaulted ceilings, skylights, ceiling fans, and porches everywhere. A separate guest house has three more guest rooms, two baths, a complete kitchen, and wraparound deck. Convenient to I-40 and only 30 minutes from Nashville. Guest house available at $250. Bed and breakfast rooms available at $85.

Sweet Annie's Bed and Breakfast. Milepost 438. Ten miles from the trace, this contemporary country home features a swimming pool and a hot tub. Guests can rent horses and bicycles from hosts, and they are convenient to both the bridle trail along the trace and to Fairview Nature Park's riding trails. Guests can even get a personal fitness workout for an extra charge. $65.

Woodshire Bed and Breakfast

600 Woodshire Drive, Goodlettsville, 37072
(615) 859-7369; FAX: (615) 851-9173

Family antiques, homemade preserves, and southern hospitality—all just 15 to 20 minutes from Nashville's universities, museums, Parthenon, Opryland, and many country music attractions. Private entrance, use of screened porch, and Continental breakfast. Country atmosphere with urban conveniences. Also a private telephone is available for guests and cable TV is in two rooms. A mid-1800s reconstructed log cabin is also available. Five dollars for each additional person. Minimum stay required during holidays and Fan Fair.

Hosts: John and Beverly Grayson
Rooms: 2 (PB) $65
Log Cabin: $70
Continental Breakfast
Credit Cards: None
Notes: 2, 7, 8, 10, 11, 12, 14

NEWPORT

Christopher Place, An Intimate Resort

1500 Pinnacles Way, 37821
(423) 623-6555; (800) 595-9441
e-mail: thebestinn@aol.com
www.christopherplace.com

Surrounded by expansive mountain views, this premier southern estate includes over

Christopher Place

200 acres to explore, a pool, tennis court, and sauna. Relax by the marble fireplace in the library, retreat to the game room, or enjoy a hearty mountain meal in the dining room. Romantic rooms are available with a hot tub or fireplace. Off I-40 at exit 435, just 32 scenic miles from Gatlinburg and Pigeon Forge. Handicapped accessible. AAA-rated four diamonds.

Host: Drew Ogle
Rooms: 8 (PB) $150-300
Full Breakfast
Credit Cards: A, B, C, D
Notes: 2, 3, 4, 5, 7, 9, 10, 11, 12, 13, 14, 15

NORRIS

Skunk Ridge Christmas Tree Farm

1203 Mountain Road, Clinton, 37716
(423) 494-0214; FAX (423) 494-0149
e-mail:laryhamner@aol.com

Horses, pastures, and woods surround this secluded yet convenient location. I-75, Museum of Appalachia, Lenoir Museum, historic Norris all within three miles. Twenty minutes to Knoxville and Oak Ridge. The Smoky Mountains, Big South Fork, Dollywood, and six TVA lakes within 50 miles. Rustic, two-story country home. Large bedrooms furnished with Appalachian antiques. Swimming in season. Nature trails and a Christmas tree plantation. Children over 12 welcome.

Hosts: Larry and Martha Hammer
Rooms: 3 (1 PB; 2 SB) $50-65
Full Breakfast
Credit Cards: A, B
Notes: 5, 7, 9, 10, 11, 12, 13

PIGEON FORGE

Day Dreams Country Inn

2720 Colonial Drive, 37863
(423) 428-0370; (800) 377-1469
www.daydreamscountryinn.com

Delight in the true country charm of this antique-filled, secluded, two-story log home. Six uniquely decorated guest rooms. Enjoy an evening by the cozy fireplace, relax on the front porch to the soothing sound of Mill Creek, or take a stroll around the three wooded acres. Three blocks from the parkway and minutes from most attractions and the Great Smoky Mountains National Park. Perfect for family reunions or retreats.

Hosts: Bob and Joyce Guerrera
Rooms: 6 (PB) $79-119
Full Breakfast
Credit Cards: A, B, D
Notes: 2, 3, 4, 5, 7, 8, 9, 10, 11, 12, 13, 14, 15

Day Dreams Country Inn

Hilton's Bluff Bed and Breakfast Inn

2654 Valley Heights Drive, 37863
(423) 428-9765; (800) 441-4188

On a wooded hilltop, just a quick one-half mile from the Parkway, this modern country inn boasts wide decks overlooking the Smoky Mountains. Three honeymoon/ special occasion rooms feature heart-shaped whirlpool tubs. All rooms include the southern country gourmet breakfast and evening snacks. Truly, this is "home away from home."

Hosts: Bob and JoAnn Quandt
Rooms: 10 (PB) $69-129\
Full Breakfast
Credit Cards: A, B, C
Notes: 2, 5, 7, 9, 10, 11, 12, 13, 14

PIKEVILLE

Fall Creek Falls Bed and Breakfast

Route 3, Box 298B, 37367
(423) 881-5494

Enjoy the relaxing atmosphere of a country manor home on 40 acres of rolling hillside one mile from the nationally acclaimed Fall Creek Falls Resort Park. Beautiful accommodations have a common sitting area with TV. Lodging includes a full breakfast served in a cozy country kitchen, an elegant dining room, or a sunny Florida room with a magnificent view. Assistance with touring, dining, and shopping information. Off-season rates. AAA-rated.

Hosts: Doug and Rita Pruett
Rooms: 8 (PB) $65-140
Full Breakfast
Credit Cards: A, B, C, D
Notes: 2, 3, 7, 10, 11, 12

ROGERSVILLE

Hale Springs Inn

110 West Main Street, 37857
(423) 272-5171

This elegant, three-story Federal brick building, built in 1824, is the oldest continuously run inn in Tennessee. Beautifully furnished with antiques from the period. Some of the rooms feature four-poster

Hale Springs Inn

canopied beds, and all rooms have working fireplaces. Air conditioning. Guests may bring their own wine. Candlelight dining.

Host: Capt. and Mrs. Carl Netherland-Brown
Rooms: 9 (PB) $45-75
Continental Breakfast
Credit Cards: A, B, C
Notes: 3, 4, 5, 7, 8, 9, 10, 11, 12

RUGBY

Grey Gables Bed 'n' Breakfast Inn

Highway 52, P.O. Box 52, 37733
(423) 628-5252

Nestled on the outskirts of the 1880s English village of Rugby, Grey Gables offers the best of the Victorian English and Tennessee country heritage, creatively blending Victorian and country antiques. Fare includes lodging, evening meal, and country breakfast. Visit the beautiful Cumberland Plateau, historic Rugby, and Grey Gables. In the tradition of the forebears, guests will receive a hearty welcome, a restful bed, and a full table. Reservations required. Lunch available by reservation. Smoking permitted in designated areas only. Limited handicapped accessibility.

Hosts: Bill and Linda Brooks Jones
Rooms: 8 (4 PB; 4 SB) $115
Full Breakfast
Credit Cards: A, B, C
Notes: 2, 4, 5, 9, 11, 12, 14

Newbury House at Historic Rugby

P.O. Box 8, Highway 52, 37733
(423) 628-2441; (423) 628-2430

Newbury House was Rugby's first boarding house, established in 1880. Victorian era. Beautifully restored features include board-and-batten siding, mansard roof, dormer windows, a lovely front porch, and shared parlor and sunroom. Newbury House lodged both visitors and settlers to British author Thomas Hughes's utopian colony. The national register village offers historic building tours, museum stores, specialty restaurant, and hiking trails. Victorian cottages are available for families with children.

Host: Historic Rugby
Rooms: 5 (3 PB; 2 SB) $68-82
Suite: 1
Full Breakfast
Credit Cards: A, B
Notes: 2, 3, 4, 5, 7, 9, 11

SAVANNAH

Natchez Trace Bed and Breakfast Reservation Service

P.O. Box 193, Hampshire, 38461
(931) 285-2777; (800) 377-2770
e-mail: natcheztrace@worldnet.att.net

White Elephant Bed and Breakfast. In Savannah, 30 miles from the trace, and only 10 miles from Shiloh National Military Park, this turreted Victorian home has wraparound porches and 1.5 acres of grounds. There are period antique furnishings—even claw-foot tubs—and Civil War memorabilia. The host's passion is Civil War history, and guests can sign up for a personalized tour of Shiloh Battlefield. There is an "overflow room" available for additional guests in a party for $25. $65-95.

White Elephant Bed and Breakfast Inn

304 Church Street, 38372
(901) 925-6410
www.bbonline.com/tn/elephant

Stately 1901 Queen Anne-style Victorian home on one and one-half shady acres in the Savannah historic district. Within walking distance of Tennessee River, downtown shopping, restaurants, and churches. Nearby golf courses and Civil War attractions; 10 miles to Shiloh National Military Park; innkeeper offers guided battlefield tours; 12 miles to Pickwick Dam and Lake. Three individually decorated rooms feature antique furnishings, queen-size beds, private baths. Full breakfast. Two parlors, antiques, central heat and air, wraparound porches, croquet.

Hosts: Sharon and Ken Hansgen
Rooms: 3 (PB) $65-95
Full Breakfast
Credit Cards: None
Rooms: 2, 5, 7, 9, 10, 11, 12, 14

White Elephant

NOTES: Credit cards accepted: A MasterCard; B Visa; C American Express; D Discover; E Diner's Club; F Other; 2 Personal checks accepted; 3 Lunch available; 4 Dinner available; 5 Open all year; 6 Pets welcome;

SEVIERVILLE

Blue Mountain Mist Country Inn and Cottages

1811 Pullen Road, 37862
(423) 428-2335; (800) 497-2335

On 60 acres in the country, this Victorian-style farmhouse inn offers the ultimate in relaxation. Decorated with antiques, quilts, crafts, local art, and mountain history. Innkeepers' ancestors were among the first to settle the Smoky Mountains area. Surrounded by rolling hills and mountains; views from a big wraparound porch offering rockers, hammock, or swing. Five romantic cottages, Jacuzzis, evening dessert, and full southern breakfast. Easy to get to and away from traffic. Featured in and selected by *Country Inns* magazine as one of the top 10 affordable luxuries, 1996.

Hosts: Norman and Sarah Ball
Rooms: 12 (PB) $98-140
Cottages: 5
Full Breakfast
Credit Cards: A, B
Notes: 2, 5, 7, 8, 9, 10, 11, 12, 13, 14, 15

Calico Inn

757 Ranch Way, 37862
(423) 428-3833; (800) 235-1054

Voted 1998 Inn of the Year, the Calico Inn is an authentic log inn with touches of elegance. It is decorated with antiques, collectibles, and country charm. It has a spectacular mountain view and is on a hilltop with 25 acres surrounding it. Each guest room has its own private bath. Guests will be served a full delicious breakfast daily. Only minutes away from the Great Smoky Mountains National Park, Dollywood, Gatlinburg, hiking, fishing, golfing, and all the attractions, yet completely secluded. Children six and older welcome.

Calico Inn

Hosts: Lill and Jim Katzbeck
Rooms: 3 (PB) $85-95
Full Breakfast
Credit Cards: A, B
Notes: 2, 5, 7, 10, 11, 12, 13, 14

Huckleberry Inn

1754 Sandstone Way, 37876
(423) 428-2475; (800) 704-3278
e-mail: kiba1@aol.com
www.bbonline.com/tn/huckleberry

Beautiful mountain log home high atop the Great Smoky Mountains surrounded by Gatlinburg, Pigeon Forge, Sevierville, and Dollywood. All rooms feature private whirlpool baths, and two have fireplaces. Two large screen porches with spectacular mountain view. Rustic charm and southern hospitality abound. Special events catering for small groups. Gift certificates and special packages available. Arrangements may be made for children on an individual basis at an additional cost.

Host: Karan Bailey
Rooms: 3 (PB) $69-89
Full Breakfast
Credit Cards: A, B, C, D
Notes: 2, 3, 4, 5, 7, 9, 12, 13

Little Greenbrier Lodge

3685 Lyon Springs Road, 37862
(423) 429-2500; (800) 277-8100

Little Greenbrier Lodge is at the entrance to the Great Smoky Mountains National Park. One of the oldest rustic lodges, circa 1939, nestled in the trees overlooking

Little Greenbrier Lodge

Wears Valley. The inn offers guests today's modern comforts, yet recaptures yesterday's charm with antique Victorian decor. The view of the valley provides a perfect backdrop for the country breakfast, and the lodge provides peace, quiet, and privacy.

Host: Charles and Susan Lebon
Rooms: 10 (8 PB; 2 SB) $65-110
Full Breakfast
Credit Cards: A, B, D
Notes: 2, 3, 4, 5, 7, 9, 11, 12, 13, 14

Von-Bryan Inn

2402 Hatcher Mountain Road, 37862
(423) 453-9832; (800) 633-1459
FAX (423) 428-8634
e-mail: von-bryan-inn@juno.com

Welcome to the mountaintop! A magnificent log inn with breathtaking mountain views of the Great Smokies. Enjoy the romantic, spacious accommodations and hearty Tennessee breakfast. Relax by the pool, trout fish in a clean mountain stream, take a day hike in the mountains, and come back to a hot tub and iced tea and cookies. Three-bedroom cabin great for families.

Hosts: The Vaughn Family: D. J., JoAnn, David, and Patrick
Rooms: 7 (PB) $90-135
Cabin: $200
Full Breakfast
Credit Cards: None
Notes: 2, 5, 7, 8, 9, 11, 12, 13, 14

TOWNSEND

Adobe and Beyond Bed and Breakfast

275 Little Mountain Way, 37882
(423) 448-9097; (888) TN-ADOBE (862-2633)
e-mail: info@tnabode.com; www.tnadobe.com

This beautiful Smoky Mountain woodhome contains a spacious suite including a gas stove, private bath, TV/VCR, kitchenette, and separate entrance. A second room contains a private bath (across hall), TV/VCR, with same kitchenette and separate entrance. Outdoor hot tub, wraparound porch, mountain view. Continental plus breakfast served, and cowboy cookouts can be arranged by request. Listen to Jean play folk instruments. Enjoy hiking, camping, tubing, whitewater rafting, bicycling, horseback riding, fishing, golfing, skiing. Drive through Cades Cove or the scenic Foothills Parkway. Near Pigeon Forge, Dollywood, outlet shopping, and Gatlinburg.

Hosts: David "Buffalo Bill" and Jean Nelson
Rooms: 2 (PB) $80-95
Continental Breakfast
Credit Cards: None
Notes: 2, 3, 5, 7, 9, 11, 12, 13, 14

WALLAND

Blackberry—A Country House, Hotel, and Mountain Club

1471 West Millers Cove Road, 37886
(423) 984-8166; FAX (423) 681-7753
e-mail: blkberryfrm@aol.com

Blackberry is an all-inclusive, full service country house hotel 25 mintues from Knoxville, yet peaceful and secluded on 1,100 acres adjacent to the Smoky Mountains. Ideal for relaxing getaways, corporate retreats, small meetings, and holidays. Enjoy hiking, fly-fishing with Orvisendorsed instructors, swiming, tennis, croquet, mountain biking, and rocking in the chairs on the veranda overlooking the meadows and mountains. Rates are for two people and include three gourmet meals daily, all snacks, non-alcoholic beverages, and use of all recreational equipment.

Innkeeper: Brian Lee
Owners: Sandy and Kreis Beall
Roosm: 44 (PB) $295-695
Full Breakfast
Credit Cards: A, B, C, D
Notes: 2, 3, 4, 5, 7, 9, 10, 11, 12, 13, 14, 15

WARTRACE

Ledford Mill Bed and Breakfast

Route 2, Box 152 B, 37183
(931) 455-2546

Ledford Mill

A welcome change from the daily grind! Enjoy a peaceful night's rest in a historic 1884 gristmill by a waterfall. Turn-of-the-century charm with antique mill workings. Three unique accommodations, all with views of falls, creek, and gardens. Claw-foot tubs, comfy queen-size beds. A beautiful rural setting in southern Middle Tennessee. Near many historic and natural areas. Three miles from Tullahoma. Continental plus breakfast served.

Hosts: Dennis and Kathleen Depert
Rooms: 3 (PB) $85-110
Continental Breakfast
Credit Cards: A, B
Notes: 2, 5, 7, 9, 10, 11, 12, 14

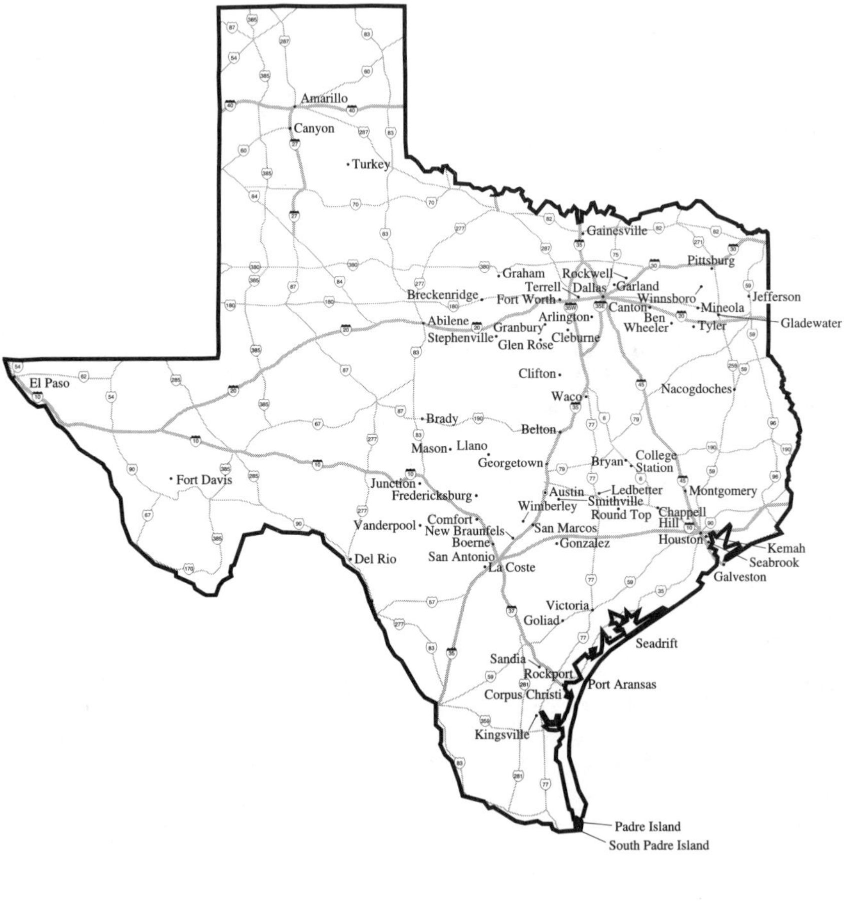
Amarillo
Canyon
Turkey
Gainesville
Pittsburg
Graham
Rockwell
Terrell
Dallas
Garland
Breckenridge
Fort Worth
Winnsboro
Jefferson
Canton
Mineola
Arlington
Ben Wheeler
Tyler
Gladewater
Abilene
Granbury
Stephenville
Glen Rose
Cleburne
El Paso
Clifton
Waco
Nacogdoches
Brady
Belton
Mason
Llano
Georgetown
Bryan
College Station
Fort Davis
Junction
Austin
Ledbetter
Montgomery
Fredericksburg
Smithville
Wimberley
Round Top
Chappell Hill
Vanderpool
Comfort
New Braunfels
San Marcos
Houston
Boerne
Gonzalez
Kemah
San Antonio
Del Rio
La Coste
Seabrook
Galveston
Victoria
Goliad
Seadrift
Sandia
Rockport
Port Aransas
Corpus Christi
Kingsville
Padre Island
South Padre Island

Texas

Texas

ABILENE

Bolin's Prairie House Bed and Breakfast

508 Mulberry, 79601
(915) 675-5855

Nestled in the heart of Abilene is a 1902 home furnished with antiques and modern luxuries combined to create a warm, home-like atmosphere. Downstairs, there are high ceilings, hardwood floors, and a wood-burning stove. Upstairs are four unique bedrooms (Love, Joy, Peace, and Patience), each beautifully decorated. Breakfast of special baked-egg dishes, fruit, and home-made bread is served in the dining room that is decorated with a collection of cobalt glass and blue-and-white china.

Hosts: Sam and Ginny Bolin
Rooms: 4 (2 PB; 2 SB) $50-65
Full Breakfast
Credit Cards: A, B, C, D
Notes: 2, 5, 7

AMARILLO

Parkview House Bed and Breakfast

1311 South Jefferson, 79101
(806) 373-9464; FAX (806) 373-3166
e-mail: parkviewbb@aol.com
www.members.aol.com/parkviewbb

This 1908 Prairie Victorian in the heart of the Texas panhandle has been lovingly restored by the present owners to capture its original charm. It is furnished with antiques and comfortably updated. Guests may relax, read, or

Parkview House

engage in friendly conversation on the wicker-filled front porch; browse through the garden; or soak leisurely in the romantic hot tub under stars. Convenient to biking, jogging, tennis, hiking, and the award-winning musical drama *Texas* in Palo Duro State Park. Old Route 66, antique shops, restaurants, various museums, and West Texas A&M University are nearby. Continental plus breakfast. Smoking outside only. Inquire about accommodations for children.

Hosts: Nabil and Carol Dia
Rooms: 5 (3 PB; 2 SB) $65-85
Cottage: $105
Continental Breakfast
Credit Cards: A, B, C
Notes: 2, 5, 7, 9, 10, 12, 14

AUSTIN

Austin-Lake Travis Bed and Breakfast

4446 Eck Lane, 78734
(512) 266-3386; (800) 484-9095 (#5348)
(reservations only)
www.laketravisbb.com

This unique waterfront retreat is a 20-minute drive from downtown Austin.

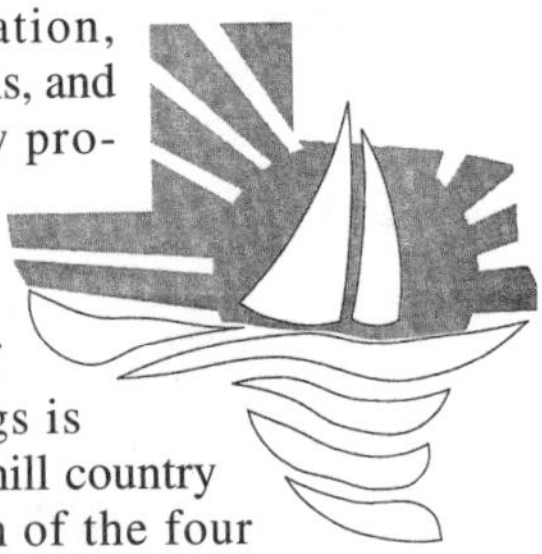

Cliffside location, crystal water, hills, and expansive view provide the setting for a luxurious getaway. The natural beauty of the surroundings is reflected in the hill country home with each of the four guest suites having a deck with view of the lake. "Intimate resort" describes the amenities available: private boat dock, pool, hot tub, fitness center, massage and spa services, and sailing/boat charters. Inside is a stone fireplace, game room, pool table, and library/theater. Nearby are a boat and Jet Ski rentals, horseback riding, bicycling, hiking, steam train, and wineries to tour. Breakfast is served in bed.

Hosts: Judy and Vic Dwyer
Rooms: 4 (PB) $145-195
Full Breakfast
Credit Cards: A, B, C
Notes: 5, 7, 9, 10, 11, 12, 14

Austin's Wildflower Inn

1200 West 221/2 Street, 78705
(512) 477-9639; FAX (512) 474-4188
e-mail: kjackson@io.com

Austin's Wildflower Inn, built in the early 1930s, is a lovely Colonial-style two-story home tucked away in a very quiet neighborhood of tree-lined streets in the center of Austin. Convenient to the University of Texas, the state capitol, and the downtown shopping and entertainment district. Every room has been carefully restored to create an atmosphere of warmth and comfort. "I invite you to come and relax here and enjoy our beautiful grounds and have one of our special breakfasts in our lovely back garden. I wish you happiness and prosperity, and may your road lead to mine."

Austin's Wildflower Inn

Host: Kay Jackson
Rooms: 4 (2 PB; 2 SB) $74-89
Full Breakfast
Credit Cards: A, B, C
Notes: 2, 5, 7, 9, 10, 11, 12

Bed and Breakfast Texas Style

4224 West Red Bird Lane, Dallas, 75237
(972) 298-8586; (800) 899-4538
FAX (972) 298-7118; e-mail: bdtxstyle1@aol.com
www.bnbtexasstyle.com

Carter Lane Bed and Breakfast. This large sprawling residence in a quiet area of bustling Austin has two guest areas, a well-stocked fish pond, pool, picnic area, and a weight and exercise room. The home is newly decorated with upscale furnishings; each guest room has a private bath. Guests are encouraged to relax in the hammock by the lake, or wor kout while watching a video in the exercise room. Weekday breakfasts are Continental. On weekends guests will be served a full breakfast with all the trimmings. The lucky guest who lands a bass from the lake may enjoy having it for breakfast. The host will also prepare vegetarian and healthy recipes. $75-85.

The Brook House Bed and Breakfast

609 West 33rd Street, 78705
(512) 459-0534

The Brook House was built in 1922 and restored to its present country charm. It is seven blocks from the University of Texas with easy access to local restaurants and live music. Enjoy one of six guest rooms, each of which has a private bath, TV, and

NOTES: Credit cards accepted: A MasterCard; B Visa; C American Express; D Discover; E Diner's Club; F Other; 2 Personal checks accepted; 3 Lunch available; 4 Dinner available; 5 Open all year; 6 Pets welcome;

The Brook House

telephone. A full breakfast is served daily in the dining room which has a fireplace or, weather permitting, outside on the veranda. No smoking in rooms. Partial handicapped accessibility.

Host: Barbara Love
Rooms: 6 (PB) $72-99
Full Breakfast
Credit Cards: A, B, C, D, E, F
Notes: 2, 5, 6, 8, 9, 10, 11, 12

Fairview—A Bed and Breakfast Establishment

1304 Newning Avenue, 78704
(512) 444-4746; (800) 310-4746
FAX (512) 444-3494; e-mail: fairview@io.com
www.fairview~bnb.com

Surrounded by huge live oak trees on an acre of landscaped grounds, this turn-of-the-century Colonial Revival historic landmark offers gracious accommodations. Carefully selected antique furnishings give each room its own unique style and romance. Fairview's six rooms range from luxury suites to elegant retreats. The gardens are a wonderful place to relax after a busy day. "Fairview is probably the grandest bed and breakfast in Austin (and one of the top two or three in the state)"—*Texas Monthly*, August 1993.

Fairview

Hosts: Duke and Nancy Waggoner
Rooms: 6 (PB) $99-149
Full Breakfast
Credit Cards: A, B, C, D, E
Notes: 2, 5, 7, 9, 10, 11, 12, 14

Gregg House and Gardens

4201 Gregg Lane, 78744
(512) 928-9777; FAX (512) 928-9776
e-mail: jim6611@aol.com

This in-town country retreat with hardwood floors and a stone fireplace is set on two acres with huge trees and a fish pond. Downtown and state capitol are 10 minutes; LBJ presidential library and shopping 15 minutes. Full kitchen, TV room, living/dining and laundry available for guests' use. Large patio and deck; bus stop. Airport 20 minutes. Hosts will help guests with their special interests and provide directions and maps. A large organic garden and nature trails are being developed. Fifteen dollars per each additional person.

Hosts: Nelda and Jim Haynes
Rooms: 2 (PB) $35-45
Full or Continental Breakfast
Credit Cards: None
Notes: 3, 4, 5, 7, 9, 10, 11, 12

Southard House

908 Blanco, 78703
(512) 474-4731

Centrally downtown off West Sixth Street are three beautifully restored homes. A two-block stroll will take guests to the wonderful West End area, full of restaurants and shopping. All of the antique-decorated rooms and suites have private baths and telephones. Some of the rooms have features such as claw-foot tubs, fireplaces, coffee makers, TVs, and small refrigerators. Continental buffet is served on weekdays; full breakfast is served on weekends. Enjoy the new swimming pool.

Hosts: Jerry and Rejina Southard
Rooms: 16 (PB) $69-169
Full and Continental Breakfast
Credit Cards: A, B, C, D, E
Notes: 2, 5, 7, 8, 11, 15

BELTON

Bed and Breakfast Texas Style

4224 West Red Bird Lane, Dallas, 75237
(972) 298-8586; (800) 899-4538
FAX (972) 298-7118; e-mail: bdtxstyle1@aol.com
www.bnbtexasstyle.com

The Belle of Belton. A beautiful antebellum home right in town with four bedrooms to charm and pamper guests. The rooms are named after the four seasons: Spring, with twin four-poster beds and claw-foot tub across the hall; Summer, with king-size bed, white wicker furniture, and shared bath; Fall, with brass bed, rocking chairs in the triple window, and private bath with shower; Winter, with a corner cupola where poinsettias are displayed, queen-size bed, and private bath. Continental breakfast includes quiche or croissants, fresh fruit, and specially blended coffees or teas. $75.

BEN WHEELER

Bed and Breakfast Texas Style

4224 West Red Bird Lane, Dallas, 75237
(972) 298-8586; (800) 899-4538
FAX (972) 298-7118; e-mail: bdtxstyle1@aol.com
www.bnbtexasstyle.com

The Arc Ridge Guest Ranch. This 600-acre ranch in East Texas near Canton and Tyler has its own lake. Three guest houses have two bedrooms, living room, complete kitchen, and shower. Fishing and paddleboats are available. No hunters allowed in this environmentally protected area. Breakfast will be left in the refrigerator for guests to prepare themselves. Family rates will be considered. Two-night minimum stay. $95.

BOERNE

Boerne Sunday House Bed and Breakfast Inn

911 South Main, 78006
(210) 249-9563; (800) 633-7339

In a quaint and appealing setting in the beautiful Texas Hill Country. Each room is unique and most are furnished with antiques. All guest rooms are delightfully decorated, cozy, and immaculate. A bountiful breakfast is served in the restored German Sunday House. Close to antique and craft shops. Twenty-five miles from San Antonio and Sea World. Fifteen miles from Fiesta Texas theme park. Smoking restricted. Inquire about accommodations for children. Minimal accessibility for handicapped.

Hostess: Faye Wilson
Owners: Lou and Mary Lou Borgman
Rooms: 13 (PB) $48-70
Full Breakfast
Credit Cards: A, B, C, D, E
Notes: 2, 5, 8, 10, 11, 12

Boerne Sunday House

NOTES: Credit cards accepted: A MasterCard; B Visa; C American Express; D Discover; E Diner's Club; F Other; 2 Personal checks accepted; 3 Lunch available; 4 Dinner available; 5 Open all year; 6 Pets welcome;

Guadalupe River Ranch

605 F.M. 474, 78006
(830) 537-4837; (800) 460-2005
FAX (830) 537-5249; e-mail: grranch@gvtc.com
www.guadalupe-river-ranch.com

The main lodge was built in 1929 (formerly owned by actress Olivia de Havilland) and restored to its original elegance. With 360 acres, the ranch provides one of the most spectacular views in the Texas Hill Country. The Guadalupe River Ranch is renowned for its gourmet cuisine, fine wines, Vintner Events, and also offers a variety of activities; river tubing, canoeing, horseback riding, and hiking trails. If one is seeking rest and relaxation, find a hammock, or the overlook swing. Enjoy the peace and serenity.

Host: Elisa McClure
Rooms: 46 (PB) $209-229
Full Breakfast
Credit Cards: A, B, C, D
Notes: 2, 3, 4, 7, 8, 9, 10, 11, 12, 14, 15

BRADY

Brady House

704 South Bridge, 76825
(915) 597-5265; (888) 272-3901
e-mail: bradyhs@centex.net

Brady is at the geographic center of Texas: the northern gateway to the Hill Country, the southern door to the Texas plains, and the portal to West Texas. Six blocks south of the square, Brady House amid its acre of landscaped grounds has three spacious guest rooms, each with private bath. The Craftsman-style home built in 1908 is furnished to reflect not only the period but also family collections.

Brady House

Hosts: Bobbie and Kelly Hancock
Rooms: 3 (PB) $85-95
Full Breakfast
Credit Cards: A, B, C, D
Notes: 3, 4, 5, 7, 10, 11, 12

BRECKENRIDGE

Bed and Breakfast Texas Style

4224 West Red Bird Lane, Dallas, 75237
(972) 298-8586; (800) 899-4538
FAX (972) 298-7118; e-mail: bdtxstyle1@aol.com
www.bnbtexasstyle.com

The Blue Rose Bed and Breakfast. This Victorian cottage is charmingly decorated with lovely antiques. The cottage has been completely remodeled and has the comforts of today, including central heat and air, washer and dryer, and a microwave oven in the kitchen. There are two bedrooms, each with one bed; one bathroom. There is also a rollaway. Breakfast fixings are left in the well-stocked kitchen and will include the Blue Rose breakfast cake. Breckenridge is a historic town south of Possum Kingdom Lake. The owners live across the street and will meet and welcome guests. Ten dollars for each additional person. $79.

The Keeping Room Bed and Breakfast. This large two-story brick inn is a place for comfort and refuge from the busy world. It was built in 1929 and has been faithfully restored to "better than original" condition. There are two large suites, Bluebonnet and Walker, that each have a sitting room, a bedroom with queen-size beds and matching day bed, and a private bath. The other two rooms, Goodwin and Rustic, also have queen-size beds and share a hall bath. All rooms have TVs.

7 No smoking; 8 Children welcome; 9 Social drinking allowed; 10 Tennis nearby; 11 Swimming nearby; 12 Golf nearby; 13 Skiing nearby; 14 May be booked through a travel agent; 15 Handicapped accessible.

Guests will be pampered with a hearty breakfast of biscuits, sausage, eggs, muffins, juice, and coffee. $65-75.

Full Breakfast
Credit Cards: A, B, C, D
Notes: 2, 3, 4, 5, 7, 9, 10, 11, 12, 14, 15

BRYAN

Bed and Breakfast Texas Style

4224 West Red Bird Lane, Dallas, 75237
(972) 298-8586; (800) 899-4538
FAX (972) 298-7118; e-mail: bdtxstyle1@aol.com
www.bnbtexasstyle.com

Wilderness Bed and Breakfast. This charming home is at the end of a cul-de-sac just three miles from Texas A&M University. There are three bedrooms, two with queen-size beds, one with two twin beds, and a private sitting room with a sleeper-sofa. The master suite downstairs has a private bath; the two rooms upstairs share a hall bath. Breakfast may be Continental with homemade breads or muffins, lots of fruit and cereals, or it may be a traditional Canadian/Texan-style breakfast. This is a nonsmoking facility. Children over 15 years welcome. $75-85.

CANTON

Heavenly Acres Bed and Breakfast

Route 3, Box 470, Mabank, 75147
(800) 283-0341; www.heavenlyacres.com

A 100-acre ranch, with two lakes and two ponds, all spring fed and fully stocked for fishing. Twelve miles southwest of Canton. Each private cabin provides unique decor, with kitchen, TV/VCR, porches with rockers to overlook water. Perfect for romantic getaways. Enjoy video library, mountain bikes, fishing, paddle boats, barnyard petting zoo, and walking paths. Conference center available for church retreats, corporate seminars, etc. No smoking indoors.

Hosts: Vickie J. and Marshall E. Ragle
Cabins: 6 (PB) $85.50-95

Texas Star Bed and Breakfast

Route 1, Box 187, Edgewood, 75117
(903) 896-4277; FAX (903) 896-7061
e-mail: ohohm@integrityonline2.com

Enjoy a peaceful day in the country nestled among large oaks, cedar trees, and green pasturelands in the gently rolling hills of East Texas. Each of the six rooms reflects a different theme of Texas history—Spanish, Native American, Old West, German, Texas country. Private baths, private entrances, and private patios are available. Full course country breakfasts. Five minutes from the world-famous First Monday Trade Days in Canton. Dinner is available by advance request.

Hosts: David and Marie Stoltzfus
Rooms: 6 (4 PB; 2 SB) $65-85
Full Breakfast
Credit Cards: A, B, C, D
Notes: 2, 5, 7, 8, 12

CANYON

Hudspeth House

1905 Fourth Avenue, 79015
(806) 655-9800; (800) 655-9809
FAX (806) 655-7457
www.Hudspethinn.com

This historic bed and breakfast is on the road to and only 20 minutes from Palo Duro Canyon, home of the famous *Texas* musical drama. The facilities offer beautiful accommodations, good ol' American breakfasts. Take a stroll to the Panhandle-Plains Historic Museum or just relax and enjoy the warm hospitality. Special candlelight dinner served in privacy of guests' room is available with reservations.

Hosts: Mark and Mary Clark
Rooms: 8 (PB) $55-110
Full Breakfast
Credit Cards: A, B, C, D, E, F
Notes: 5, 7, 8, 9, 10, 11, 12, 14

NOTES: Credit cards accepted: A MasterCard; B Visa; C American Express; D Discover; E Diner's Club; F Other; 2 Personal checks accepted; 3 Lunch available; 4 Dinner available; 5 Open all year; 6 Pets welcome;

CHAPPELL HILL

Stagecoach Inn

Main at Chestnut, P.O. Box 339, 77426
(409) 836-9515

The inn, built in 1850 by Jacob and Mary Haller, the founders of Chappell Hill, was a favorite stopping place for many notable Texans traveling from Houston to Austin or Waco over the first stagecoach line organized in Texas in 1841 by Smith and Jones. The inn, listed in the National Register of Historic Places, is a 14-room Greek Revival structure with six fireplaces, on three beautifully landscaped acres. A country breakfast is served. Two guest houses also available.

Host: Elizabeth Moore
Rooms: 5 (3 PB; 2 SB) $90
Full Breakfast
Credit Cards: None
Notes: 2, 5, 7, 9, 15

Stagecoach Inn

CLEBURNE

Bed and Breakfast Texas Style

4224 West Red Bird Lane, Dallas, 75237
(972) 298-8586; (800) 899-4538
FAX (972) 298-7118; e-mail: bdtxstyle1@aol.com
www.bnbtexasstyle.com

Cleburne Guest House. This lovely historical Queen Anne Victorian house was built near the turn of the century and is near downtown Cleburne. There are four guest rooms, two with private baths and two sharing a hall bath. All rooms have color TVs and fresh flowers. Coffee bar and refrigerator upstairs for guests' needs. A Continental breakfast will be served in the main dining room or out on the New Orleans-style patio. Area attractions include antiquing, candlewalk, Springfest, and Hot Air Balloon Festival. Walk to antique malls, tearoom, and shopping. $95-115.

CLIFTON

Bed and Breakfast Texas Style

4224 West Red Bird Lane, Dallas, 75237
(972) 298-8586; (800) 899-4538
FAX (972) 298-7118; e-mail: bdtxstyle1@aol.com
www.bnbtexasstyle.com

The Sweetheart Cottage. A historical home, once damaged in a tornado, now restored for a perfect weekend getaway. A loft room has a queen-size bed, and a pull-out sofa is available downstairs. Country breakfast fare is left in the complete kitchen for the guests to prepare. No smoking. Two-night minimum stay required. $65-75.

COLLEGE STATION

Bed and Breakfast Texas Style

4224 West Red Bird Lane, Dallas, 75237
(972) 298-8586; (800) 899-4538
FAX (972) 298-7118; e-mail: bdtxstyle1@aol.com
www.bnbtexasstyle.com

Country Gardens. A sense of peace and tranquility will descend on guests as they enter this little country hideaway on four acres. Stroll through the wooded glen, fruit orchard, grapevines, and berry patches and enjoy the birds and wildflowers. The hosts will prepare a delicious breakfast of wheat pancakes or homemade bread; coffee, tea, or milk; and fruit in season. $65-75.

COMFORT

The Comfort Common

717 High Street, P.O. Box 539, 78013
(830) 995-3030
e-mail: comfortcommon@hctc.net
www.bbhost.com/comfortcommon

Historic limestone hotel, circa 1880, listed in the National Register of Historic Places. Rooms and suites are furnished with antiques. The downstairs of the hotel features numerous shops filled with American antiques. A stay at the Comfort Common will put guests in the heart of the Texas Hill Country with Fredericksburg, Kerrville, Boerne, Bandera, and San Antonio all a brief 15-30 minutes away. Fiesta Texas theme park is only 20 minutes away. Featured in *Southern Living* and *Travel & Leisure* magazines.

Hosts: Jim Lord and Bobby Dent
Rooms: 9 (PB) $65-110
Full Breakfast
Credit Cards: A, B, C, D
Notes: 2, 5, 7, 9, 12

The Comfort Common

CORPUS CHRISTI

Bay Breeze Bed and Breakfast

201 Louisiana, 78404
(512) 882-4123
www.go-native.com/inns/0121.html

Within view of the sparkling bay waters, this fine older home features bedroom suites with private baths that radiate the charm and ambiance of days gone by. Less than a five-minute drive from the business district and city marinas, where sea vessels of every description are berthed. One can enjoy fine dining, recreation, or purchase shrimp direct from the net. Travel only a short distance to the Bayfront Convention Center, art and science museums, the Columbus ships, the preservation homes of Heritage Park, and the Harbor Playhouse Community Theater. Beach nearby.

Bay Breeze

Hosts: Frank and Perry Tompkins
Rooms: 4 (PB)
Full Breakfast
Credit Cards: A, B
Notes: 2, 5, 7, 9, 10, 11, 12

Sand Dollar Hospitality

3605 Mendenhall Drive, 78415
(512) 853-1222; (800) 528-7782
FAX (512) 814-1285
www.ccinternet.net/sand-dollar

Bay Breeze. Within view of the sparkling bay waters, this fine older home offers four accommodations, all with private baths. Guests are invited to enjoy the large sunroom, the 1930s billard table, watch TV, or just relax. A five-minute drive to the business district and city marinas, where guests can enjoy fine dining and recreation or purchase shrimp direct from the net. It is only a short strill to the city's finest bayfront park and fishing pier. Resident cat. Full breakfast. Smoking permitted outside only. $65-90.

NOTES: Credit cards accepted: A MasterCard; B Visa; C American Express; D Discover; E Diner's Club; F Other; 2 Personal checks accepted; 3 Lunch available; 4 Dinner available; 5 Open all year; 6 Pets welcome;

Camden at Villa Del Sol. A one-bedroom tastefully furnished condominium overlooking Corpus Christi Bay and the USS *Lexington* aircraft carrier/naval history musuem. The compact kitchen is stocked with basic cooking and serving ware. Sleeping accommodations include a queen-size bed, queen-size sofa bed, and two built-in bunks in the hallway. Laundry facilities are close by and elevator is down the hall. The complex includes two swimming pools, three hot tubs, and four barbecue pits. Weekly and monthly rates available. $96.

Camden House. Just five-minute's walking time from beautiful Corpus Christi Bay, this rambling white brick ranch-style home offers a spacious guest suite with a king-size bed and private bath. The adjoining sitting room is furnished with a small couch, easy chair, and has full cable TV. Step out from the suite to own private Jacuzzi or join the hosts at the pool. Have breakfast in the privacy of own suite, or in the dining room, or out by the pool. $96.

Colley House (formerly the Seagull). New England antiques collected by the hosts, a retired navy couple, add to the charm and ambiance of this lovely home. Only one block from Corpus Christi Bay, this 50-year-old home is in a quiet up-scale neighborhood just a five-minute walk from the city's largest bayside park. Guests are invited to relax in the enclosed patio/den with TV, wet bar, and cozy surroundings. Two bedrooms with private baths are available. Older children are welcome. Full breakfast. Smoking permitted outside only. $65.

Inn on the Bay. With an unencumbered view of Corpus Christi Bay and the downtown skyline, this host home offers the discriminating guest a luxurious retreat. An attractively furnished one-bedroom apartment is in the guest wing of the home with own private entrance. Within three miles of Corpus Christi Naval Air Station and Texas A&M University, this home is conveniently on Ocean Drive, a scenic expressway to downtown Corpus Christi. It is also only about 15 minutes' driving time to the gulf beaches on nearby Padre Island. $125.

La Maison du Soleil. Within a quiet gated community, reminiscent of the medieval cities of Provence, this scenic home offers a guest room with private bath, a heated pool, and access to nearby tennis courts. This charming French Provincial-style home is midway between downtown and the gulf beaches—driving time being 25 minutes in either direction. A full gourmet breakfast served. Smoking permitted outside only. $90.

Manitou Cottage. Nestled among the trees behind a charming New England-style farm house, this guest cottage is three blocks from Corpus Christi Bay and less than 10 minutes from downtown. An antique brass bed, wood floors, skylights, and ceiling fans combine to offer a relaxed and cozy atmosphere. Rockers on the porch facing the swimming pool add to the relaxed ambiance. Bicycles are available for riding through the neighborhood. Other amenities include cable TV, telephone, and fax service. A full hot breakfast is delivered to the cottage door. $96.

Smith Place. A colorfully landscaped back yard with pool and hot tub is the setting for two charming guest houses—the Garden Room and the Lodge. The sleeping accommodations for the Garden Room include a queen-size bed in the bedroom and a queen-size sofa bed in the adjoining sitting room. The Lodge has just a queen-size bed and easy chair. Other amenities include private entrances, off-street parking, refrigerator, microwave, coffee center, and cable TV. Breakfast provisions are brought in daily. Small pets permitted. $90.

DALLAS

Bed and Breakfast Texas Style

4224 West Red Bird Lane, Dallas, 75237
(972) 298-8586; (800) 899-4538
FAX (972) 298-7118; e-mail: bdtxstyle1@aol.com
www.bnbtexasstyle.com

Artist's Haven. This private home offers two upstairs guest rooms with lovely amenities and shared bath. One room has twin beds, and the other room has a king-size bed. Breakfast is Continental plus, with fruit, pastries, and beverages. Cat in residence. No smoking. Children are welcome. $75.

The Cloisters. This lovely home is one block from White Rock Lake in a secluded area of Dallas. There are two guest rooms, each with a private bath. Both rooms have double beds, one with an antique Mexican headboard that is a conversation piece. Breakfast will be lots of protein, eggs, and/or blueberry pancakes. A bicycle is available for riding around the lake. No smoking. $75.

Fan Room. The antique fan displayed in this lovely twin bedroom is the focal point and was the start of a large collection of fans. The home is near Prestonwood, Marshall Fields, and the Galleria Mall. Southfork Ranch is a 15-minute drive north. A full country breakfast includes jalapeño muffins for first-time Texas visitors. Second bedroom near the kitchen with a double bed and private bath. $70.

The Rose. This historical home was built in 1901 and has four guest bedrooms, each with a private bath. Guests are treated to special breakfasts on the weekends, Continental during the week. Children over 12 are welcome. Smoking is permitted. $60-85.

Tudor Mansion. Built in 1933 in an exclusive neighborhood in the shadow of downtown, this Tudor-style mansion offers queen-size bed and private bath. A full gourmet breakfast of cheddar on toast, Texas-style creamed eggs with jalapeño, or fresh vegetable omelet is served. The bus line is three blocks away. Spanish and French are spoken. Three miles from downtown. Close to a public golf course. $80.

DEL RIO

The 1890 House

609 Griner Street, 78840
(210) 775-8061; (800) 282-1360
FAX (210) 775-4667

Nestled in the heart of Del Rio guests will find this magnificent turn-of-the-century home. It boasts five charming guest rooms, private soaking tubs, and Jacuzzi. It possesses the relaxing Victorian elegance of years gone by. Awaken every morning to the aromas of homemade breads, muffins, and freshly ground coffee. Make this visit an international event by traveling three miles south of the border to Acuna, Mexico.

Hosts: Alberto and Laura Galvan
Rooms: 5 (PB)
Full Breakfast
Credit Cards: A, B, D
Notes: 5, 7, 8, 9, 10, 11, 12, 14

EL PASO

Cowboys and Indians Board and Bunk

P.O. Box 13752, 79913
(505) 589-2653; www.softaid.net/cowboys

Lie back and enjoy the wonderful panoramic view of Franklin Mountains and desert sunsets of southern New Mexico. Bunk down in one of the four theme rooms that are comfortable and decorated to make guests feel like they are a part of the Old West. Relax in the large gathering room. The grub is the best in southwestern- and chuckwagon-style cooking. Special packages for year-round golf, horseback riding, sightseeing, seminars, and workshops. Lunch and dinner available but catered only. Smoking permitted outside only. Children over 12 welcome. One room is handicapped accessible.

Hosts: Irene and Don Newlon
Rooms: 4 (PB) $64-87 per night
Full and Continental Breakfast
Credit Cards: A, B, C
Notes: 2, 5, 7, 9, 10, 11, 12, 14

FORT DAVIS

The Veranda Country Inn

The Veranda Country Inn

210 Court Avenue, P.O. Box 1238, 79734
(888) 383-2847; e-mail: veranda@overland.net
www.theveranda.com

The Veranda is a spacious historic inn built in 1883. This unique adobe building, with 2-foot-thick walls and 12-foot ceilings, has eight large rooms and suites furnished with antiques and collectibles. Its walled gardens and quiet courtyards provide travelers with a change of pace and lifestyle in mile-high Fort Davis. A large, separate Carriage House is next to the gardens in the shade of a large pecan tree. The Veranda is within minutes of sites renowned for astronomy, historical forts and buildings, and scenic hiking, biking, and bird watching.

Hosts: Paul and Kathie Woods
Rooms: 8 (PB) $67.50-99
Carriage House: $95-135
Full Breakfast
Credit Cards: A, B, D
Notes: 2, 5, 7, 9,

FORT WORTH

Bed and Breakfast at the Ranch

8275 Wagley Robertson Road, 76131
(817) 232-5522; (888) 593-0352
e-mail: bbranch@flash.net
www.fortworthians.com/bbranch

A true taste of Texas on 15 acres. Bed and Breakfast at the Ranch offers four spacious rooms with their own private baths. Two rooms have special tubs—a Jacuzzi and antique claw-foot tub. Three rooms have their own private patio. The spacious living room offers a stone fireplace, TV with video library, board games, upright grand piano, and library of books. Enclosed patio room is complete with hot tub, patio furniture, wet bar, guest refrigerator, and free pinball. Gourmet breakfast served by resident innkeeper—full on weekends and Continental on weekdays. Grounds offer tennis, putting green, gazebo, swing, and smokehouse. Unique!

Hosts: Scott and Cheryl Stewart
Rooms: 4 (PB) $85-159
Full or Continental Breakfast
Credit Cards: A, B, C
Notes: 2, 4, 5, 7, 9, 10, 11, 12

Bed and Breakfast at the Ranch

Bed and Breakfast Texas Style

4224 West Red Bird Lane, Dallas, 75237
(972) 298-8586; (800) 899-4538
FAX (972) 298-7118; e-mail: bdtxstyle1@aol.com
www.bnbtexasstyle.com

Bloomsbury House. Escape to this beautifully restored 1908 two-story Queen Anne home in one of Texas's largest historic neighborhoods, just south of downtown. Guests will be pampered in one of the four guest bedrooms; each room has its own private bath. Enjoy desserts upon arrival and full home-cooked breakfast in the morning. Attractions in Fort Worth include the Sundance Square, Kimbell Art Museum, and Billy Bob's (famous "kicker dance" club). $99-110.

Miss Molly's Hotel

109 1/2 West Exchange Avenue, 76106
(817) 626-1522; (800) 99-MOLLY (996-6559)
FAX (817) 625-2723
e-mail: missmollys@travelbase.com

An authentic turn-of-the-century boarding house in the Fort Worth stockyards national historic district, the heart of the North Texas cattle industry. Reminiscent of the Old West, seven rooms share three antique-appointed full baths (custom robes are provided during guests' stay), and Miss Josie's, the premier suite, boasts an elegant Victorian decor with draped-fabric ceiling and private bath. A Continental plus breakfast is served in the central parlor beneath a stained-glass skylight. Lunch and dinner are available within walking distance.

Host: Alice Hancock
Rooms: 8 (1 PB; 7 SB) $75-170
Full Breakfast
Credit Cards: A, B, C, D, E, F
Notes: 2, 5, 7, 8, 9, 14

The Texas White House

1417 Eighth Avenue, 76104
(817) 923-3597; (800) 279-6791
FAX (817) 923-0410

This historically designated, award-winning country-style home has been restored to its original 1910 grandeur of simple, yet elegant decor. Within five mintues of downtown, medical center, Fort Worth zoo, the cultural district, botanic gardens, water gardens, and Texas Christian University. Three guest rooms with sitting areas and private baths with claw-foot tubs. Breakfast served in either the dining room or sent to guests' room. Amenities include telephone, TV, early morning coffee service, afternoon snacks and beverages, secretarial services, laundry service for extended stays, and off-street parking.

Hosts: Jamie and Grover McMains
Rooms: 3 (PB) $85-105
Full Breakfast
Credit Cards: A, B, C, D
Notes: 2, 5, 7, 9, 10, 11, 12, 14

FREDERICKSBURG

Das College Haus

106 West College, 78624
(830) 997-9047; (800) 654-2802

Visit historic Fredericksburg and stay at Das College Haus, just three blocks from downtown. Spacious rooms with private baths; all have access to the porches, balcony with porch swing, and wicker rockers, where guests can relax and visit. Das College Haus is beautifully appointed with comfortable period furniture and original art for a wonderful "at home" atmosphere. Enjoy a full breakfast served in the old-fashioned dining room. Central heat and air, cable TV, VCR, and a collection of movies. Coffee makers and refrigerators in rooms.

Host: Myrna Dennis
Rooms: 4 (PB) $80-100
Full Breakfast
Credit Cards: A, B
Notes: 2, 5, 7, 9, 10, 11, 12, 15

Schildknecht-Weidenfeller House

Gästehaus Schmidt Reservation Service
231 West Main, 78624
(830) 997-5612; FAX (830) 997-8282

Guests can relive history in the Schildknecht-Weidenfeller House in the heart of Fredericksburg's historic district. Decorated with antiques and handmade quilts, this guest house accommodates up to 10 people. A German-style Continental plus breakfast is left for guests to enjoy at their leisure around the antique farm table in the kitchen. This 1870s German limestone house

Schildknecht-Weidenfeller House

has been featured on tours of historic homes and in *Country Decorating Ideas*. Member of Historic Accommodations of Texas. Children 12 and older welcome. Rates increase with number of people in party.

Owners: Ellis and Carter Schildknecht
House: $125
Continental Breakfast
Credit Cards: A, B, D
Notes: 2, 5, 7, 9, 10, 11, 12, 14

Schmidt Barn Bed and Breakfast

Gästehaus Schmidt Reservation Service
231 West Main, 78624
(210) 997-5612; FAX (210) 997-8282

The remnants of an 1860s limestone barn were lovingly saved to turn it into a guest house. Stone walls, brick floors, timber beams maintain century-old charm. Bathroom invites guests to a long soak in a sunken tub. Quilts, antique linens, samplers, and a collection of toys enliven the wooden-beamed loft bedrooms. Hosts live next door. Featured in *Country Living* and *Travel and Leisure*. German Continental plus breakfast is left for guests to enjoy at their leisure.

Hosts: Charles and Loretta Schmidt
Rooms: 1 (PB) $85
Continental Breakfast
Credit Cards: A, B
Notes: 2, 5, 6, 8, 9, 10, 11, 14

Watkins Hill

608 East Creek Street, 78624
(800) 899-1672; FAX (830) 997-6057

The hosts' goal for guests is relaxation and privacy. Two acres with seven buildings, seven antique-filled guest rooms, private entrances, private baths, telephone line, TV/VCR, breakfast brought to guests' door. Meeting, retreat, reunion, wedding facility for 50 persons with 1840 frontier log barn, including stage, ballroom, dining room, library, parlor, conservatory, and kitchen. Catering available. The hosts can accommodate or create guests' own special occasion or event.

Hosts: Betty O'Connor and Susan Martin
Rooms: 7 (PB) $110-165
Full Breakfast
Credit Cards: A, B
Notes: 5, 6, 7, 8, 9, 10, 11, 12, 14

GAINESVILLE

Alexander Bed and Breakfast Acres, Inc.

Route 7, Box 788, 76240
(903) 564-7440; (800) 887-8794
www.bbhost.com/alexanderbbacres

Three-story Queen Anne Victorian home on 65 peaceful acres of woods and meadows. Large wraparound porch for lounging; walking trails; near two large lakes, antiques, country farms, and zoo. Each bedroom decorated with different theme: western, antique, canopied, or Amish. Full breakfast included. Separate conference room and extra lodging on third floor. Two-story guest cottage offers three bedrooms sharing one and one-half baths, kitchen, laundry, living area, and large screened porch. Children and pets welcome in cottage only. Dinner available by arrangement.

Hosts: Jim and Pamela Alexander
Rooms: 8 (5 PB; 3 SB) $60-125
Full Breakfast
Credit Cards: A, B, D
Notes: 2, 5, 7, 9, 11, 12, 13, 14

GALVESTON

Madame Dyer's Bed and Breakfast

1720 Postoffice Street, 77550
(409) 765-5692

From the moment guests enter this carefully restored turn-of-the-century Victorian home built in 1889, they will be entranced by such period details as wraparound porches, high airy ceilings, wooden floors, and lace curtains. Each room is furnished with delightful antiques that bring back memories of days gone by. In the morning, on an antique buffet sideboard on the second floor, guests will find teas and freshly brewed coffee provided for the early riser. Breakfast is a special treat, served abundantly in the dining room. Smoking permitted on outside porches only. Children over 12 are welcome.

Hosts: Linda and Larry Bonnin
Rooms: 3 (PB) $100-125
Full Breakfast
Credit Cards: A, B
Notes: 2, 5, 7, 9, 10, 11, 12, 14

Madame Dryer's

The Queen Anne Bed and Breakfast

1915 Sealy Avenue, 77550-2312
(409) 763-7088; (800) 472-0930

This home is a four-story Queen Anne Victorian built in 1905. Stained-glass windows, beautiful floors, large rooms, pocket doors, and 12-foot ceilings with transom doors; beautifully redecorated in 1991. Walk to the historic shopping district, restaurants, 1886 opera house, museums, and the historic homes district. A short drive to the beach. A visit to Queen Anne is to be anticipated, relished, and long-remembered.

Hosts: John McWilliams and Earl French
Rooms: 5 (3 PB; 2 SB) $85-145
Full Breakfast
Credit Cards: A, B, C
Notes: 2, 5, 7, 9, 10, 11, 12, 13, 14

GALVESTON ISLAND

Bayview Inn with Hot Tub and Boatpier

P.O. Box 1326, 77553
(409) 741-0705

Waterfront casual luxury and elegance in a romantic setting complete with huge swaying palms, exotic waterfowl, and hot tub. Water views from all rooms with private baths; furnished with fabulous rare antiques from world travels. Boat dock. Golf course and beach two minutes away. Ms. Pat is an island character well worth meeting. Her specialty is adult getaways. Nearby are flight and car museums, historical homes, IMAX, rainforest-pyramid, trolley, fishing, beach, boating; 45 minutes to Houston.

Host: Ms. Pat Hazlewood
Rooms: 3 (PB) $65-145
Continental Breakfast
Credit Cards: F
Notes: 2, 5, 7, 9, 10, 11, 12, 13

GARLAND

Bed and Breakfast Texas Style

4224 West Red Bird Lane, Dallas, 75237
(972) 298-8586; (800) 899-4538
FAX (972) 298-7118; e-mail: bdtxstyle1@aol.com
www.bnbtexasstyle.com

Catnip Creek. Right on Spring Creek, the hot tub on the deck overlooks a wooded

NOTES: Credit cards accepted: A MasterCard; B Visa; C American Express; D Discover; E Diner's Club; F Other; 2 Personal checks accepted; 3 Lunch available; 4 Dinner available; 5 Open all year; 6 Pets welcome;

creek. The guest room has a queen-size bed, private bath, and private entrance. Breakfast has granola and cinnamon-raisin biscuits or other homemade muffins and breads. Weekend guests are treated to a healthy quiche or pancakes. Herbal teas and specially blended coffees are offered. Bicycles are provided. Just 30 minutes from downtown Dallas and very near Hypermart, the newest tourist attraction of the metroplex. Also near Southfork Ranch. $60-75.

GEORGETOWN

Claibourne House

912 Forest, 78626
(512) 930-3934; (512) 913-2272 (voice mail)

Claibourne House is three blocks west of the historic courthouse square in the heart of old Georgetown. Built in 1896, this spacious Victorian residence was restored during 1987-88 and adapted as a bed and breakfast inn. Guests are graciously accommodated in four bedrooms, each with private bath. An intimate upstairs sitting room and downstairs grand hall and parlor and wraparound porch are available for guests. The guest rooms are handsomely furnished with treasured family furniture, antiques, and distinctive fine art.

Host: Clare Easley
Rooms: 4 (PB) $85-120
Continental Breakfast
Credit Cards: A, B
Notes: 2, 5, 7, 9

Heron Hill Farm Bed and Breakfast

1350 County Road 143, 78626
(512) 863-0461; (800) 439-3828 (reservations)

New, old-fashioned Texas farmhouse built in 1997 especially for bed and breakfast. House sits high on a hill overlooking 13 acres of wildlife habitat and a large vegetable garden. Pick own veggies in season. The four guest rooms, each with private

Heron Hill Farm

bath, are on the second floor. Rooms feature country decor which mixes new and antique furniture. Three rooms have queen-size beds, one roo has two twin antique white iron beds. Full breakfast served daily. Enjoy antiquing, hiking, biking, and swimming and boating at local lake; golf also available nearby. Inner Space Caverns and Lady Bird Johnson Wildflower Center make good day trips.

Hosts: Ed and Linda Devine
Rooms: 4 (PB) $75
Full Breakfast
Credit Cards: A, B
Notes: 2, 5, 7, 8, 9, 11, 12

GLADEWATER

Honeycomb Suites

111 North Main Street, 75647
(800) 594-2253; FAX (903) 845-2448
www.pageboyz.com/honeycomb

Specializing in romantic getaways, offering seven suites, each in a different motif. Five suites are above scratch-recipe bakery in the antique district of Gladewater. Two suites (including the honeymoon suite) are in an adjacent building. Four suites have whirlpool tubs for two. Saturday evenings, candlelight dinners with horse-drawn carriage rides are available by reservation. Romance

7 No smoking; 8 Children welcome; 9 Social drinking allowed; 10 Tennis nearby; 11 Swimming nearby; 12 Golf nearby; 13 Skiing nearby; 14 May be booked through a travel agent; 15 Handicapped accessible.

packages and gift certificates are available. Gladewater is 120 miles east of Dallas or 60 miles west of Shreveport.

Hosts: Bill and Susan Morgan
Rooms: 7 (PB) $85-150
Full Breakfast
Credit Cards: A, B, C, D
Notes: 2, 3, 4, 5, 7, 9, 10, 11, 12

GLEN ROSE

Bed and Breakfast Texas Style

4224 West Red Bird Lane, Dallas, 75237
(972) 298-8586; (800) 899-4538
FAX (972) 298-7118; e-mail: bdtxstyle1@aol.com
www.bnbtexasstyle.com

Hummingbird Lodge. The motto of the owners for this extraordinary bed and breakfast is "Come find the trees and streams, the deer and the birds, the peace. Come find yourself." Just about two miles south of Glen Rose off the beaten path, surrounded by cedar trees and small hills, a weary city dweller will find complete serenity. There are large porches and decks with rocking chairs; the "hummers" are most entertaining; or just curl up with a book down by the hot tub in the swinging hammock. There are well marked walking trails, a waterfall, and a pond for the energetic fisherman. There are six guest rooms, all with private baths. A full gourmet breakfast is provided. $85-115.

Bussey's Something Special

202 Hereford Street, P.O. Box 1425, 76043
(817) 897-4843; (800) 700-4843 (#13)

Relax in a private country cottage in downtown Glen Rose historic district. Family-friendly with crib upstairs. Enjoy hand-crafted lounges, artwork, books, games, and toys. Seashell and oak bathroom with shower (no tub). Experience the Early American decor in a private cozy cottage with tropical bath, whirlpool jet tub/shower, and small kitchen. Both cottages have a king-size bed. Continental plus breakfast, private front porches, and attractive decor. Sweetheart packages for special occasions are available upon request.

Hosts: Susan and Morris Bussey
Cottage: 2 (PB) $80-100
Continental Breakfast
Credit Cards: A, B, C
Notes: 2, 5, 7, 8, 10, 11, 12, 14

GOLIAD

The Linburg House

736 North Jefferson Street (Highway 183 North), 77963
(512) 645-1997; e-mail: mheskett@viptx.net

An 1888 Victorian Craftsman-style residence that has been made comfortable with country antique furnishings, central air and heat. After a busy day, be prepared to relax in the exquisite charm and comfort of one of the three gracious bedrooms. Each suite has its own cable color TV. There is a front porch to relax on or guests can choose the enclosed screened back porch and enjoy a country view. Just a short drive to the historic fully restored Spanish fort Presidio La Bahia, Goliad State Historical Park, wildlife observation areas, and Coleto Creek Reservoir, which has year-round fishing.

Hosts: Mike and Terry Heskett
Rooms: 3 (PB) $65-85
Full Breakfast
Credit Cards: None
Notes: 2, 5, 7

GONZALES

St. James Inn

723 St. James, 78629
(830) 672-7066

A former cattle baron's mansion. This elegant bed and breakfast is a welcome respite from the busy life. Furnished with antiques, colorful collections, and warm hospitality. The rural area offers a fun opportunity for hiking, biking, antiquing, and roaming. Relax in the lovely setting of one of the grand historic homes of Gonzales, "the

Lexington of Texas"—once alive with cotton and cattle ranches. This area of Texas is rich in history and great scenic adventures. Experience historic and hospitable Gonzales Country. Member of Professional Innkeepers, Inc., and Texas Historic Accommodations Association.

Hosts: Ann and J. R. Covert
Rooms: 5 (4 PB) 85-100
Full Breakfast
Credit Cards: A, B, C
Notes: 2, 3, 4, 9, 10, 11, 12, 14

GRAHAM

Bed and Breakfast Texas Style

4224 West Red Bird Lane, Dallas, 75237
(972) 298-8586; (800) 899-4538
FAX (972) 298-7118; e-mail: bdtxstyle1@aol.com
www.bnbtexasstyle.com

Victorian Memories. Victorian ambiance adorns this 1900s Folk Victorian-style bed and breakfast guest house, built by one of Graham's pioneer families. Established in 1885, it has been lovingly preserved with unique stained glass, wood floors, and high ceilings. There are two guest rooms, each complimented by English ivy, floral wreaths, quilts, and charming antiques. There are two baths, one with a claw-foot tub. There is a fully equipped kitchen, where a Continental breakfast is left for guests' leisure. Relax in the sunroom while enjoying the pleasures of fresh flowers and plants. Visit historic Graham with America's largest downtown square only two blocks away. Inquire about rates for the entire house. $79.

GRANBURY

Pearl Street Inn Bed and Breakfast

319 West Pearl Street, 76048
(817) 579-7465; (888) PEARL ST

Pearl Street Inn

Relax and reminisce in the stately, stylish comfort of a 1912 Prairie-style home. Three blocks from Granbury's historic square, this tastefully restored historical home features antique furnishings, two porches, cast-iron tubs, pocket doors, outdoor hot tub, and scrumptious breakfasts. Enjoy live theater, state parks, drive-in movies, antique shopping, or festivals in a charming country setting, 30 miles south of the Dallas/Fort Worth metroplex. Enjoy overnight accommodations in a delightful home "where days move gently in all seasons."

Host: Danette D. Hebda
Rooms: 5 (PB) $59-109
Full Breakfast
Credit Cards: None
Notes: 2, 5, 7, 9, 10, 11, 12, 14

HOUSTON

The Lovett Inn

501 Lovett Boulevard, 77006
(713) 522-5224; (800) 779-5224
FAX (713) 528-6708; www.lovettinn.com

Once the home of Houston mayor and federal court judge Joseph C. Hutcheson, the Lovett Inn has all of the amenities of a first-class hotel. Within walking distance to some of the city's finest restaurants, clubs, and shopping. The George R. Brown Convention Center, downtown, Greenway Plaza, Texas Medical Center, Hobby Airport, and the Galleria are also nearby. Each room has been comfortably decorated to evoke the inn's historic past, while adding such modern amenities as in-room telephones, remote color TV, and private bathrooms. To accommodate the most discriminating traveler, suite accommodations, meeting rooms, fax service, and in-room whirlpool are available.

Host: Tom Fricke
Rooms: 9 (8 PB; 1 SB) $85-150
Continental Breakfast
Credit Cards: A, B, C, D
Notes: 5, 6, 7, 8, 9, 10, 11, 12, 14, 15

Robin's Nest

4104 Greeley, 77006
(713) 528-5821; (800) 622-8343
FAX (713) 521-2154; www.houstonbnb.com

Historic, circa 1897, two-story wooden Queen Anne. Feather beds atop fine mattresses, convenience of central location, and taste (buds) make the stay worthwhile. The rooms are spacious, furnished in eclectic Victorian with custom-made drapes, bed covers, etc. Robin's Nest is decoratively painted in concert with her sister "painted ladies." In the Museum and Arts district, surrounded by museums, art galleries, downtown, excellent restaurants, and the theater district. Inquire about accommodations for pets and children.

Host: Robin Smith
Rooms: 4 (PB) $85-120
Full Breakfast
Credit Cards: A, B, C, D
Notes: 2, 5, 7, 9, 10, 11, 12, 13

Sara's Bed and Breakfast Inn

941 Heights Boulevard, 77008
(713) 868-1130; (800) 593-1130

This Queen Anne Victorian is in the historic Heights district of Houston, a neighborhood of historic homes, many of which are in the National Register of Historic Places. Each bedroom is uniquely furnished, having either single, double, queen, or king-size beds. The balcony suite consists of two bedrooms, two baths, kitchen, living area, and balcony. The sights and sounds of downtown are only four miles away.

Sara's

Hosts: Donna and Tillman Arledge
Rooms: 14 (12 PB; 2 SB) $55-150
Continental Breakfast
Credit Cards: A, B, C, D, E, F
Notes: 2, 5, 7, 8, 9, 10, 11, 12, 14

JEFFERSON

Captain's Castle Bed and Breakfast

403 East Walker Street, 75657
(800) 650-2330
www.jeffersontx.com/captainscastle

The Captain's Castle was so named by Captain Thomas J. Rogers, a Confederate officer and local pioneer banker. In the early 1870s, he combined two older houses—the two-story front portion he moved across town on log rollers, with oxen, from down on the riverfront. This colorful old home, furnished with antiques, has a Texas Historical Medallion and is listed in the national register of homes.

Hosts: Buck and Barbara Hooker
Rooms: 7 (PB) $95-110
Full Breakfast
Credit Cards: A, B, C
Notes: 2, 5, 7, 9, 11, 12, 14

NOTES: Credit cards accepted: A MasterCard; B Visa; C American Express; D Discover; E Diner's Club; F Other; 2 Personal checks accepted; 3 Lunch available; 4 Dinner available; 5 Open all year; 6 Pets welcome;

Excelsior House Hotel

211 West Austin, 75657
(903) 665-2513

The historic Excelsior House was built in the 1850s by riverboat captain William Perry. Currently owned and operated by the Jessie Allen Wise Garden Club, the brick and timber structure has 15 guest rooms, each furnished in exquisite period furniture. The ballroom, once the location of gala balls, and the dining room are the perfect setting to enjoy the Excelsior's famous plantation breakfast, or to host receptions, weddings, luncheons, or dinners by reservation.

Rooms: 15 (PB) $65-100
Full Breakfast
Credit Cards: A, B
Notes: 2, 5, 7, 9, 11, 12

Hale House Bed and Breakfast

702 South Line Street, 75657
(903) 665-8877

Hale House Bed and Breakfast is spacious, comfortable, and furnished with gorgeous period antiques. Completely restored to include modern conveniences, the home glows with hardwood floors, antique mirrors, and chandeliers. Owners James and Nancy Rice offer a warm southern welcome to guests, along with a gourmet breakfast served with china and crystal in the formal dining room. Six beautifully appointed guest rooms, an enclosed sun porch, a broadside porch, and spacious gazebo make Hale House a delightful, romantic setting.

Hale House

Hosts: James and Nancy Rice
Rooms: 6 (PB) $75-100
Full Breakfast
Credit Cards: A, B, D
Notes: 2, 5, 7, 12

McKay House

McKay House Bed and Breakfast Inn

306 East Delta Street, 75657
(903) 665-7322
(800) 468-2627 (reservations 9 A.M.-5 P.M.)

Jefferson is a riverport town from the frontier days of the Republic of Texas. It has historical mule-drawn tours, 30 antique shops, boat rides on the Big Cypress Bayou, and a mysterious lake made famous by Walt Disney. The McKay House, an 1851 Greek Revival cottage, offers period furnishings, cool lemonade, porch swings, and fireplaces. Seven rooms that vary from the keeping room to the garden suite (with his and her antique footed tubs). A full gentleman's breakfast is served in the garden conservatory. Victorian nightclothes are laid out for guests. VIP guests have included Lady Bird Johnson, Alex Haley, and Fabio. Mobil Travel Guide.

Owner: Peggy Taylor
Innkeepers: Lisa and Roger Cantrell
Rooms: 4 (PB) $99
Suites: 3 (PB) $125-155
Full Breakfast
Credit Cards: A, B, C
Notes: 2, 5, 7, 8, 11, 12, 14

Urquhart House of Eleven Gables

301 East Walker Street, 75657
(903) 665-8442

The Urquhart House of Eleven Gables is an experience of luxuries and historical elegance. Turn-of-the-century quality of life comes alive with period decor and antiques. Further creating the yesteryear ambiance are equestrian carriages and wagons clip-clopping the street that fronts the wraparound porch of this expansive 1890 Queen Anne house. Antique wicker swing and furniture occupy the abundantly pleasant wraparound porch inviting guests to come and "sit a spell." Gourmet breakfast served with antique linens, crystal, and china.

Host: Joyce Jackson
Rooms: 4 (PB) $125
Full Breakfast
Credit Cards: A, B, C, D, E
Notes: 2, 5, 7, 8, 9, 12, 14

Urquhart House of Eleven Gables

JUNCTION

Shady Rest at the Junction Bed and Breakfast Inn

101 North 11th Street, 76849
(915) 446-4067 (phone/FAX); (888) 892-8292

Junctions's one-of-a-kind Victorian-style bed and breakfast offers guests a unique stay in downtown. This beautiful turn-of-the-century home has recently undergone a massive refurbishing inside and out. Relax on the beautiful wraparound front porch, or leisurely lounge at the umbrella table, as guests enjoy this picturesque setting nestled between the North and South Llano Rivers. Guests will be treated to a sumptuous breakfast by candlelight to Victorian love songs.

Shady Rest at the Junction

Hosts: Bill and Debbie Bayer
Rooms: 1 (PB) $65
Full Breakfast
Credit Cards: None
Notes: 2, 3, 4, 7, 12

KEMALT

The Ark on the Bay

705 Sixth Street, 77565 (location)
1302 First Street, Seabrook, 77586 (mailing)
(281) 474-5295; FAX (281) 474-7840

The Ark has a nautical theme with incredible views. The house has been carefully decorated and will make guests feel as if they were the captain of the ship. Rent a room or the whole house for a fun-packed memorable vacation. Bring one's watercraft, fishing poles, crab traps, swimsuits, beach towels, and lots of suntan lotion for a great time. Outside, under the house is a 10-person hot tub, stereo speakers, a patio area, and access to the water via a small pier. It is only three blocks from the marina and some of the best seafood restaurants on the Texas

Coast. There are also many speciality and gift shops within a half block to browse through. Unhosted.

Managed by: Suzanne Silver
Rooms: 3 (2 PB; 1 SB) $85-120
Continental Breakfast
Credit Cards: A, B, C, D
Notes: 2, 5, 7, 9, 12, 14

KINGSVILLE

B Bar B Ranch Inn

325 East County Road 2215, 78363
(512) 296-3331; FAX (512) 296-3337
e-mail: bbarb@rivnet.com

Quietly nestled beneath the rippling leaves of a south Texas mesquite grove, this 80-acre working ranch is host to a wide variety of native plants and wildlife. Originally part of the historic King Ranch, the B Bar B is a bird watching hot spot. The hosts also offer fishing and hunting trips. Their gourmet restaurant is sure to tempt guests' taste buds.

Hosts: Luther and Patti Young
Rooms: 16 (PB) $85-125
Full Breakfast
Credit Cards: A, B, D
Notes: 2, 4, 5, 11, 12, 14

LA COSTE

Bed and Breakfast Texas Style

4224 West Red Bird Lane, Dallas, 75237
(972) 298-8586; (800) 899-4538
FAX (972) 298-7118; e-mail: bdtxstyle1@aol.com
www.bnbtexasstyle.com

Swan and Railway Inn. At one time this inn was known as the City Hotel and it had only three guest bedrooms. It has now increased to five rooms, three with private baths. There is a new pool for guests to enjoy. Breakfast may be yogurt and granola or bran muffins, fruit, and herb teas. About 18 to 20 minutes from San Antonio and 10 minutes from Sea World. La Coste was a French settlement, and nearby Castroville has German roots. $75-85.

LEDBETTER

Ledbetter Bed and Breakfast

208 FM 1291, P.O. Box 212, 78946-0212
(409) 249-3066; (800) 240-3066
FAX (409) 249-3330; e-mail: jjervis@fais.net
www.ledbetter-tx.com

Ledbetter Bed and Breakfast, established in 1988, is a collection of multigenerational, family, 1800-1900s homes within walking distance of the remaining 1870s downtown businesses. A full country breakfast buffet can serve up to 70 guests daily. Hay rides, walks, fishing, horse and buggy rides, games, Christmas lights, chuck wagon or romantic dinners, indoor heated swimming pool, VCR, TV. A telephone can be made available on advance request. Each unit accommodates approximately four people. Only nonalcoholic beverages are allowed outside private quarters. Only outdoor smoking is permitted. Water skiing nearby. Establishment is semi-handicapped accessible.

Hosts: Chris and Jay Jervis
Rooms: 20 (18 PB; 2 SB) $70-150
Full or Continental Breakfast
Credit Cards: A, B, C
Notes: 2, 3, 4, 5, 7, 8, 10, 11, 12, 13, 14

MASON

Hasse House Ranch

1221 Ischar, P.O. Box 58, 76856
(888) 41-HASSE (414-2773)

The Hasse House, circa 1883, is where country quality lives in historical architecture laced with modern conveniences. Complete with period furniture, microwave, dishwasher, washer-dryer, central air, two bedrooms, two baths, living room, and complete kitchen. Guests may explore the 320-acre ranch with two-mile nature trail and abundant wildlife. Owner lives in town so party will be only one in the house. "Let us invite you to the complete peace of rural living."

Host: Laverne Lee
Rooms: 2 (PB) $95
Continental Breakfast
Credit Cards: A, B
Notes: 2, 5, 8, 9, 12

MINEOLA

The Lott Home Bed and Breakfast Cottages

311 East Kilpatrick Street, 75773
(888) 232-LOTT (5688); e-mail: lotthomecottages@tyler.net

The Lott Home Cottages, circa 1918, offers old-fashioned southern hospitality at its best. The charming, romantic cottages include queen-size beds, private baths, cable TV, antique furnishings, and a kitchen, with microwave, refrigerator, and coffee maker, fully stocked with refreshments and snacks. Each cottage has its own private porch with wooden rockers for guests to relax and view a beautiful East Texas sunset. Treat oneself to an unforgettable night, relive a moment in time and take home wonderful memories at the Lott Home Bed and Breakfast Cottages.

Hosts: Mark and Sharon Chamblee
Rooms: 2 (PB) $95
Full Breakfast
Credit Cards: A, B, D
Notes: 2, 5, 7, 9, 12, 14, 15

MONTGOMERY

Honeysuckle Rose Bed and Breakfast

820 Caroline Street, P.O. Box 1447, 77356
(409) 597-7707; (800) 341-9151
FAX (409) 582-4404; e-mail: rosebb@mcia.com

A Victorian-style home two blocks from antique shopping in downtown Montgomery. Three rooms with private baths, parlor, and library. A European-style Continental plus breakfast provided—no set time for breakfast. Hosts live off premises. The English Rose Room (queen-size bed) and Tea Room (double bed) have Victorian decor. The Rambling Rose Room is country style with twin beds. Front and back porches have rockers and a swing for guests to enjoy.

Hosts: Charlotte and Dix Cottingham
Rooms: 3 (PB) $75-85
Continental Breakfast
Credit Cards: A, B, D
Notes: 2, 5, 7, 12, 14, 15

NACOGDOCHES

PineCreek Lodge Bed and Breakfast Country Inn

Route 3, Box 1238, 75964
(409) 560-6282; (888) 714-1414
e-mail: pitts@lcc.net
www.pinecreeklodge.com

On a peaceful 140-acre wooded property near a flowing creek. Acres of beautiful grounds and flowers. Miles of surrounding country roads for driving and hiking enjoyment. Special features include large decks with swings and rocking chairs, hammock, pool, spa, fishing pond, and hiking trail. Each room has a private bath and deck with swing, air conditioning, ceiling fans, TV and VCR, refrigerator, telephone, monogrammed robes, and fresh flowers. Refreshments at check-in. Smoking outdoors only.

Hosts: The Pitts Family
Rooms: 11 (PB) $55-95
Full Breakfast
Credit Cards: A, B, C, D
Notes: 2, 3, 4, 5, 8, 12

PineCreek Lodge

NOTES: Credit cards accepted: A MasterCard; B Visa; C American Express; D Discover; E Diner's Club; F Other; 2 Personal checks accepted; 3 Lunch available; 4 Dinner available; 5 Open all year; 6 Pets welcome;

NEW BRAUNFELS

Historic Kuebler-Waldrip Haus

1620 Heuco Springs Loop, 78132
(830) 625-8372; (800) 299-8372
www.cruisingamerica.com/kuebler-waldrip

Come relax on a 43-acre ranch near San Antonio. Enjoy a delightful stay in either the Historic Kuebler-Waldrip Haus (circa 1847), a German Roch house, or the historic Danville School House (circa 1863), an original one-room schoolhouse. Rooms have air conditioning and central heat, private baths, some with whirlpool tubs, TVs, telephones, kitchen access, and porch. Create great memories when planning reunions, a wedding, honeymoon, anniversaries, receptions, or vacation. Meeting and party facility is now available. Free brochure. Quiet, well-behaved pets welcome. Airport nearby.

Hosts: Margaret and son, Darrell Waldrip
Rooms: 10 (PB) $95-145
Full Breakfast
Credit Cards: A, B, C, D
Notes: 2, 5, 7, 8, 9, 10, 11, 12, 13, 14, 15

Karbach Haus Bed and Breakfast

487 West San Antonio Street, 78130
(830) 625-2131; (800) 972-5941
FAX (830) 629-1126

Lovingly restored turn-of-the-century mansion on an acre estate in downtown New Braunfels. Walk to fine restaurants, museums, antique stores, local attractions. Experience *Gemütlichkeit* of a German *Gasthaus* with amenities of a small resort. Spacious guest rooms have private tile baths, queen- or king-size beds, cable TVs, VCRs, robes, ceiling fans, down quilts, and many antiques. Central heat and air, heated pool and spa, video library, butler's pantry with guest refrigerator, ice machine. World-class German-style breakfasts. Long-term rental available. Owner/hosts on premises.

Hosts: Captain Ben Jack Kinney, USN (Retired) and Kathleen Karbach Kinney, Ph.D.
Rooms: 6 (PB) $105-175
Full Breakfast
Credit Cards: A, B, D
Notes: 2, 5, 7, 9, 10, 11, 12

The Old Hunter Road Stagecoach Inn Bed and Breakfast

5441 FM 1102, 78132
(830) 620-9453 (phone/FAX)
e-mail: stagecoach@sat.net

Step back in time to a bygone era of Texas history and hospitality. The inn—with its hand-hewn log cabins and *fachwerk* house redolent of early Texas—was used as a stagecoach stop between 1850 and 1865. Each guest room is impeccably appointed with the rustic elegance of Texas antiques, laces, linens, quilts, and fresh flowers. All have private baths, entrances, and porches with rockers surrounded by gardens of fragrant herbs and antique roses. A gourmet breakfast with guests in mind is served in the candlelit dining room.

Rooms: 3 (PB) $85
Full Breakfast
Credit Cards: A, B, C
Notes: 2, 5, 7, 8, 9, 10, 11, 12

Prince Solms Inn

295 East San Antonio Street, 78130
(800) 625-9169; FAX (830) 625-9169

Historic landmark in historic Hill Country, circa 1898. Oldest continuous business in the state. City location in historic downtown. Two blocks from museums, water sports, and so forth. Ideal for family gatherings, small weddings, and corporate retreats. Mystery weekends (spring and fall), romance packages which include dinner in renowned Wolfgang's Keller Restaurant, rated one of the 10 most romantic restaurants by *Ultra* magazine. Continental plus breakfast served. Restaurant on premises. Smoking permitted in courtyard only.

Hosts: Larry Patton and
Beverly Talbot (general manager)
Rooms: 10 (PB) $90-150
Continental Breakfast
Credit Cards: A, B, C, D
Notes: 2, 3, 4, 5, 7, 8, 9, 10, 11, 12, 13, 14

PADRE ISLES

Sand Dollar Hospitality

35 Mendenhall Drive, Corpus Christi, 78415
(512) 853-1222; (800) 528-7782
FAX (512) 814-1285
www.ccinternet.net/sand-dollar

Fortuna Bay. This enchanting hideaway on Texas's North Padre Island is cradled between the Laguna Madre and the Gulf of Mexico. A unique bed and breakfast inn, Fortune Bay presently consists of three one-bedroom fully furnished condominums in a 10-unit complex. Each unit has a living room with cable TV, a bedroom with a queen-size bed, a fully equipped kitchen with microwave, and a washer and dryer. There is also an outside grill near the pool. The three-story, red-tile-roof structure is at the intersection of five canals. Provisions for a Continental plus breakfast are supplied. A complimentary boat ride through the canal system is offered. Weekly and monthly rates are available. $96.

PITTSBURG

Carson House Inn and Grille

302 Mount Pleasant Street, 75686
(903) 856-2468; (888) 302-1878
FAX (903) 856-0709
e-mail: carsonig@1starnet.com

Carson House

Built in 1878, the inn is a study in charm and elegance. Turn-of-the-century antiques fill the beautifully appointed rooms. The unique wood trim and wainscotting is from the now extinct curly pine tree. The serene, cozy atmosphere of the Carson House beckons guests for a relaxing long weekend or a romantic getaway. The Grille brings inviting atmosphere and exceptional food to the table. The staff is ready to make guests feel right at home.

Rooms: 5 (3 PB; 2 SB) $55-85
Full Breakfast
Credit Cards: A, B, C, D
Notes: 2, 3, 4, 5, 7, 8, 11, 12

PORT ARANSAS

Sand Dollar Hospitality

35 Mendenhall Drive, Corpus Christi, 78415
(512) 853-1222; (800) 528-7782
FAX (512) 814-1285
www.ccinternet.net/sand-dollar

Harbor View. Three-story Mediterranean-style home on the Port Aransas Municipal Harbor, offers three large bedrooms, one with private bath. The inn is within easy walking distance of the restaurants, shops, charter boats, and fishing operations. On-site mooring facilities are available for crafts up to 50 feet in length. Bikes are available at no additional charge. Full breakfast. Cots for children are available at $15 per child. $75-90.

ROCKPORT

Sand Dollar Hospitality

35 Mendenhall Drive, Corpus Christi, 78415
(512) 853-1222; (800) 528-7782
FAX (512) 814-1285
www.ccinternet.net/sand-dollar

Anthony's by the Sea. The innkeepers at Anthony's offer four guest bedrooms in the

NOTES: Credit cards accepted: A MasterCard; B Visa; C American Express; D Discover; E Diner's Club; F Other; 2 Personal checks accepted; 3 Lunch available; 4 Dinner available; 5 Open all year; 6 Pets welcome;

guest wing of the residence plus two guest cottages. All units throughout the inn include a refrigerator, cable TV and VCR. A spacious plant-filled patio with lounge chair and tables connects the main house and the two guest cottages. There guests will also find a barbecue grill for guests' use. Off to the side is a swimming pool and hot tub. A full breakfast is served. The renowned Aransas Wildlife Refuge is less than an hour's drive away. Group, weekly, and monthly rates available. $66-95.

Chandler House. The upper-level veranda of this 123-year-old house offers a view of the gulf and the town's shopping area with its many specialty shops and galleries. Each of the two large upstairs bedrooms has two queen-size beds and its own private bath. The downstairs bedroom has a king-size bed, a private attached bath, fireplace, and TV. The common area includes a great room with fireplace and parlor games and a spacious breakfast room. Lunch is also available and open to the public at the unique Chandler House Tea Room. Children over 12 welcome at $25 per each child. $100.

Cygnet. A cozy, secluded country cottage on 16 acres with a double bed, top of the line queen-size sleeper sofa, kitchenette, TV/VCR, and country Jacuzzi outside. This delightful country retreat is about five miles south of Rockport and was designed to provide guests with privacy and comfort. Guests will be provided with farm-fresh eggs, homemade bread, cereals, milk, and fresh fruit. Five dollars for each additional person. $67.

The Habitat. A unique haven of seven plus acres, in the heart of the Lamar Peninsula and near the Aransas Wildlife Refuge, this bed and breakfast consists of three log cabins. Each cabin has a fully stocked kitchen, screened front porch, and outdoor grill. Bird watchers will have a chance to identify and photograph a myrid of bird life in and around the two-acre lake that fronts each cabin. Self-serve Continental breakfast. No pets.

ROCKWALL

Bed and Breakfast Texas Style

4224 West Red Bird Lane, Dallas, 75237
(972) 298-8586; (800) 899-4538
FAX (972) 298-7118; e-mail: bdtxstyle1@aol.com
www.bnbtexasstyle.com

Barton on Boydstun. Individual cottage suites are on this large property right near downtown Rockwall. Other buildings are an art gallery, working studio, and the Bois d'Arc Chapel. The cottages are new and built specifically for guests. Each one has its own screened porch and small kitchen. Perfect place for a small wedding or honeymoon retreat. Breakfast is a prepared treat that is left in the cottage for guests to zap in the microwave. $110-140.

ROUND TOP

Broomfields

801 North Nassau Road, 78954
(409) 249-3706; FAX (409) 249-3852
e-mail: brmflds@fais.net

Country retreat five miles from Round Top on 40 acres of meadowland with wooded tracts, stocked pond with boats and gazebo. Historic restorations, classical music, and semiannual antique shows nearby. Spectacular displays of wildflowers in spring and foliage in fall. An 1800s Texas-vernacular modern home built with 100-year-old barn

Broomfields

7 No smoking; 8 Children welcome; 9 Social drinking allowed; 10 Tennis nearby; 11 Swimming nearby; 12 Golf nearby; 13 Skiing nearby; 14 May be booked through a travel agent; 15 Handicapped accessible.

beams and furnished with selected European and American antiques. Comfortable, well-appointed rooms and baths. Antiques and decorative arts gallery on the premises. Miniature donkeys raised.

Hosts: Julia and Bill Bishop
Rooms: 3 (PB) $90-140
Full Breakfast
Credit Cards: None
Notes: 2, 5, 9, 10, 11, 12

SAN ANTONIO

Academy House of Monte Vista

Academy House of Monte Vista

2317 North Main Avenue, 78212
(888) 731-8393; e-mail: academyh@netxpress.com
www.ahbnb.com

A gracious, unpretentious 1897 Victorian in San Antonio's century-old Monte Vista historic neighborhood, only minutes from the Riverwalk and Alamo. Each guest bedroom has its own unique character; elegantly decorated in rich shades of wine and burgundy, furnished with period antiques, private baths, cable TV, king-size beds. Full country breakfast. Private garden cottage with Jacuzzi. Excellent restaurants nearby. Member of Texas Historical Accommodations.

Hosts: Kenneth and Johnnie Walker Staggs
Rooms: 4 (PB) $85-145
Full Breakfast
Credit Cards: A, B
Notes: 2, 5, 7, 10, 12, 14, 15

Adams House Bed and Breakfast

231 Adams Street, 78210
(210) 224-4791; (800) 666-4810
FAX (210) 223-5125
www.san-antonio-texas.com

Enjoy gracious, southern hospitality at the Adams House Bed and Breakfast, in the King William Street Historic District of downtown San Antonio. The Riverwalk is a short two-block stroll, and the Alamo is a 15-minute walk. The two-story Adams House has been lovingly restored to its original 1902 splendor. Full-width verandas grace both floors, front and back. All rooms are furnished with period antiques, oriental rugs, and handmade reproductions. AAA three-diamond and Mobil Travel Guide.

Hosts: Nora Peterson and Richard Green
Rooms: 4 (PB) $89-125
Full Breakfast
Credit Cards: A, B, C, D
Notes: 2, 5, 8, 9, 10, 11, 12, 14

Beckmann Inn and Carriage House

222 East Guenther Street, 78204
(210) 229-1449; (800) 945-1449
FAX (210) 229-1061
www.beckmanninn.com

This elegant Victorian inn is in the heart of San Antonio in the King William Street

Beckmann Inn and Carriage House

Historic District. The wraparound porch welcomes guests to this beautiful home. All rooms are colorfully decorated, featuring ornately carved Victorian queen-size beds, antiques, private baths, TVs, telephones, refrigerators, desks, and robes. Ride the trolley or take the Riverwalk to the Alamo, restaurants, shops, Mexican market, and much more. Guests receive gracious and warm hospitality during their stay. Gourmet breakfast with a breakfast dessert. AAA-, Mobil-, and IIA-rated excellent.

Hosts: Betty Jo and Don Schwartz
Rooms: 5 (PB) $90-140
Full Breakfast
Credit Cards: A, B, C, D, E
Notes: 2, 5, 7, 8, 9, 11, 12, 14

Bonner Garden Bed and Breakfast

145 East Agartia, 78212
(800) 396-4222; FAX (210) 733-6129
e-mail: noels@onr.com
www.travelbase.com

An award-winning replica of an Italian Renaissance villa built in 1910 for internationally known artist Mary Bonner. The original villa was built in Italy in the early 1600s. Fireplaces, tile, fixtures, etc., were imported from Italy. A large swimming pool and a rooftop patio provide enjoyable respites for guests. Guest rooms have private baths, some with Jacuzzi tubs, TVs, VCRs, and telephones. A film library and Texarkana library are available for guests' enjoyment. A full gourmet breakfast is served.

Hosts: Jan and Noel Stenoien
Rooms: 5 (PB) $85-115
Full Breakfast
Credit Cards: A, B, C, D, E
Notes: 2, 5, 7, 9, 10, 11, 12, 14

Bonner Garden

Brackenridge House

Brackenridge House: A Bed and Breakfast Inn

230 Madison, 78204
(210) 271-3442; (800) 221-1412
FAX (210) 226-3139; e-mail: benniesueb@aol.com
www.brackenridgehouse.com

Native Texan owners and innkeepers will guide guests through their visit to this beautiful Greek Revival home in historic King William. Gourmet breakfast served in formal dining room or veranda, hot tub, private baths, and country Victorian decor add to guests' comfort and pleasure. Pets and children are welcome in the carriage house.

Owners and Innkeepers: Bennie and Sue Blansett
Rooms: 5 (PB) $89-175
Guest house: 2 (PB)
Full Breakfast
Credit Cards: A, B, C, D, E
Notes: 2, 5, 6, 7, 8, 9, 10, 11, 12, 14

7 No smoking; 8 Children welcome; 9 Social drinking allowed; 10 Tennis nearby; 11 Swimming nearby; 12 Golf nearby; 13 Skiing nearby; 14 May be booked through a travel agent; 15 Handicapped accessible.

Chabot Reed House

403 Madison, 78204
(210) 223-8697; (800) 776-2424
FAX (210) 734-2342; e-mail: sister@txdirect.net
www.ivylane.com/chabot

George Stooks Chabot built this Victorian home in 1876 in the heart of what is known today as the King William Street Historic District. The property, masterfully and authentically restored, is listed in the National Register of Historic Places and is a Texas historic landmark. This magnificent home offers beautiful, private, and romantic accommodations within walking distance to downtown San Antonio, Riverwalk, and the convention center. Smoking permitted outside only. Partially handicapped accessible.

Hosts: Sister and Peter Reed
Rooms: 5 (PB) $125-175
Full Breakfast
Credit Cards: None
Notes: 2, 5, 7, 8, 9, 10, 11, 12, 14

The Columns on Alamo

1037 South Alamo, 78210
(800) 233-3364
www.bbonline.com/tx/columns

Resident innkeepers welcome guests to their gracious 1892 Greek Revival home and guest house in the historic King William area. Blocks from Riverwalk, restaurants, shopping, convention center, and Alamo; short drive to Sea World and Fiesta Texas. Marvelous antiques and period reproductions, queen- and king-size beds, Jacuzzis, fireplace, telephones, TVs, large common areas, verandas, gardens, off-street parking. Full gourmet breakfast is served in the main house. Smoke free except for verandas, outdoors. Two-night minimum Saturday.

The Columns on Alamo

Hosts: Ellenor and Art Link
Rooms: 11 (PB) $89-148
Full Breakfast
Credit Cards: A, B, C, D, E, F
Notes: 5, 7, 9, 12, 14

Noble Inns

Noble Inns

107 Madison Street, 78204
(210) 225-4045; (800) 221-4045
FAX (210) 227-0877; e-mail: nobleinns@aol.com
www.nobleinns.com

Noble Inns operates two luxury Victorian properties in downtown San Antonio's King William historic district. Meticulously restored, the 1890-era bed and breakfasts are decorated with period antiques and offer full modern amenities. All accommodations feature private, marble bath with two-person Jacuzzi or claw-foot tub; antique mantel gas fireplace; sumptuous fabrics, wallpapers; color cable TV with HBO; telephone with data port and voicemail. Full and Continental breakfasts. Beautiful patios, outdoor pool and heated spa or indoor swim spa. Transportation in classic 1960 Rolls Royce available.

Hosts: Don and Liesl Noble
Rooms: 9 (PB) $120-175
Full and Continental Breakfast
Credit Cards: A, B, C, D
Notes: 2, 5, 7, 9, 10, 11, 12, 14

The Ogé House on the Riverwalk

209 Washington Street, 78204
(800) 242-2770; FAX (210) 226-5812
e-mail: ogeinn@swbell.net
www.ogeinn.com

Elegant historic antebellum mansion shaded by massive pecans and oaks, on one and one-half landscaped acres along the banks of the famous San Antonio Riverwalk in the King William Street Historic District. The inn, beautifully decorated with antiques, has large verandas and a grand foyer. All rooms have air conditioning, telephones, and TVs, many with fireplaces. Dining, entertainment, convention centers, trolley, and the Alamo are steps away. Featured in the *New York Times*, *Glamour*, *Victoria*, *Southern Living*, Travel channel. IIA-rated excellent, Mobil three-star-rated. Complimentary *Wall Street Journal*, *New York Times*, and *San Antonio Express News*. Smoking restricted. Gourmet breakfast.

Hosts: Patrick and Sharrie Magatagan
Rooms: 10 (PB) $145-205
Continental Breakfast
Credit Cards: A, B, C, D, E
Notes: 2, 5, 9, 10, 12, 14

Riverwalk Inn

329 Old Gailbeau Road, 78204
(210) 212-8300; (800) 254-4440
FAX (210) 229-9422

The Riverwalk Inn is comprised of five two-story log homes, circa 1840, that have been restored on the San Antonio Riverwalk and are tastefully decorated in period antiques. Amenities include fireplaces, refrigerators, private baths, telephones, balconies, 80-foot porch, and conference area. Continental plus breakfasts and desserts served. Swimming nearby. Smoking permitted outside only. No children.

Hosts: Johnny Halpenny; Jan and Tracy Hammer
Rooms: 11 (PB) $99-155
Continental Breakfast
Credit Cards: A, B, C, D
Notes: 2, 5, 7, 10, 11, 12, 14, 15

The Victorian Lady Inn

The Victorian Lady Inn

421 Howard Street, 78212
(210) 224-2524; (800) 879-7116
www.viclady.com

This 1898 historic mansion offers spacious guest rooms furnished with period antiques. High-back beds, claw-foot tubs, fireplaces, and verandas complete guests' pampered retreat. Savor a fabulous full breakfast each morning. Relax in the outdoor hot tub surrounded by tropical palms and banana trees. The Alamo, Riverwalk, convention center, and trolley are just blocks away. Package plans, corporate rates, and meeting space available.

Hosts: Joe and Kathleen Bowski
Rooms: 8 (PB) $69-135
Full Breakfast
Credit Cards: A, B, C, D
Notes: 2, 5, 7, 9, 10, 11, 12, 14

A Yellow Rose

229 Madison, 78204
(210) 229-9903; (800) 950-9903
www.bbonline.com/tx/yellowrose/

A Yellow Rose bed and breakfast is an 1878 Victorian home in the King William Street Historic District. It has five wonderful guest rooms appointed with antiques, and each has private bath, cable TV, and queen-size bed. Off-street, covered parking is also provided. Breakfast is served daily in the elegant 18th-century dining room, and afterwards or in the afternoon or evening guests will enjoy relaxing on the veranda. Two blocks from the Riverwalk, one block from the 50¢ trolley, five blocks from the Alamo and convention center, and within three blocks from three of the finest restaurants in San Antonio.

Hosts: Deb Field-Walker and Kit Walker
Rooms: 5 (PB) $95-140
Full Breakfast
Credit Cards: A, B, C, D
Notes: 2, 5, 7, 9, 12, 14

SANDIA

Knolle Farm and Ranch Bed, Barn, and Breakfast

Route 1, Box 81, Farm Road 70, 78383
(512) 547-2546; FAX (512) 547-3934

Bed, Barn, and Breakfast in renovated, historic dairy barn. Once boasting "World's Largest Jersey Herd," the Knolles are now pampering guests. Nestled in the Nueces River valley among towing oaks and rolling fields, upscale guest cottages contain antiques, full kitchens, patios, laundry facilities. Guests may bring private horses or ride bed and breakfast's horses. Fully equipped barn, arenas, acres of trail riding. Guided dove/duck/goose hunting, fishing, canoeing, game room all on premises. Superb bird watching, catered gourmet meals and picnics. Fun for entire family.

Host: Beth Knolle
Rooms: 4 (2 PB; 2 SB) $65-125
Full Breakfast
Credit Cards: A, B
Notes: 2, 3, 4, 5, 6, 8, 9, 11, 15

Sand Dollar Hospitality

35 Mendenhall Drive, Corpus Christi, 78415
(512) 853-1222; (800) 528-7782
FAX (512) 814-1285
www.ccinternet.net/sand-dollar

Knolle Farm and Ranch Bed and Breakfast. A true Texas ranch experience with sufficient "citified" amenities to make for a comfortable and enjoyable stay. There are four guest rooms. There are eight stalls as well as outside paddock and arena. Additional attractions and/or activities include canoeing, fishing, skeet shooting, and bird watching. Ten dollars for each additional person. $125.

SAN MARCOS

Crystal River Inn

326 West Hopkins, 78666
(512) 396-3739

Romantic, luxurious Victorian mansion that captures all the fun and flavor of the Texas Hill Country. Close to headwaters of crystal-clear San Marcos River. Antiques, fireplaces, and fresh flowers adorn the rooms. Wicker-strewn veranda, gardens, and fountains offer hours of peaceful rest

Crystal River Inn

NOTES: Credit cards accepted: A MasterCard; B Visa; C American Express; D Discover; E Diner's Club; F Other; 2 Personal checks accepted; 3 Lunch available; 4 Dinner available; 5 Open all year; 6 Pets welcome;

and relaxation. Enjoy sumptuous brunches including gourmet items such as stuffed French toast and bananas Foster crêpes. Mystery weekends, river trips, and romantic getaways are the hosts' specialities.

Hosts: Mike and Cathy Dillon
Rooms: 12 (10 PB; 2 SB) $75-135
Full Breakfast
Credit Cards: A, B, C, D, E, F
Notes: 2, 5, 7, 9, 10, 11, 12, 14

SEABROOK

Bed and Breakfast Texas Style

4224 West Red Bird Lane, Dallas, 75237
(972) 298-8586; (800) 899-4538
FAX (972) 298-7118; e-mail: bdtxstyle1@aol.com
www.bnbtexasstyle.com

Crew's Quarters. Right on Galveston Bay at the channel where shrimp boats and ocean liners go in and out, this Cape Cod-style cottage is available for families or romantic getaways. It will sleep seven to nine people with two bedrooms downstairs, each with a private bath. A loft room upstairs with two double beds and a twin bed has a half-bath. A large deck with chairs is perfect for sunning and watching birds and boats. Continental breakfast. $75-95.

The Pelican House Bed and Breakfast Inn

1302 First Street, 77586
(713) 474-5295; FAX (713) 474-7840

This 90-year-old home can be found on the Back Bay just down the street from Galveston Bay and is in the Old Seabrook Art and Antique Colony. The Pelican House is the closest bed and breakfast to Space Center Houston and is less than five minutes to the 19 Clear Lake area marinas. The Pelican House is decorated whimsically with pelicans and fish. Relax in rocking chairs on the front porch or on the back deck where water bird viewing is at its best. Children over 10 welcome.

The Pelican House

Host: Suzanne Silver
Rooms: 4 (PB) $65-75
Full Breakfast
Credit Cards: A, B, C, D
Notes: 2, 5, 7, 9, 12, 14

SEADRIFT

Hotel Lafitte

302 Bay Avenue, 77983
(512) 785-2319

A unique bed and breakfast on San Antonio Bay. Built in 1909 and fully restored in 1988. Furnished in antique Victorian style. In Seadrift, Texas, 30 miles south of Victoria on Highway 185.

Hosts: Frances and Weyman Harding
Rooms: 10 (4 PB; 6 SB) $60-115
Full Breakfast
Credit Cards: A, B, C
Notes: 2, 9, 10, 11, 12, 14

SMITHVILLE

Bed and Breakfast Texas Style

4224 West Red Bird Lane, Dallas, 75237
(972) 298-8586; (800) 899-4538
FAX (972) 298-7118; e-mail: bdtxstyle1@aol.com
www.bnbtexasstyle.com

The Doll House. A private guest area on the second level of this residence in the Lost Pines area near Bastrop is available for visitors. The large sitting-bedroom is furnished with lovely antiques and collectibles and has its own private bath. There is a small kitchen area with refrigerator and microwave. If guests prefer to eat in, Continental fixings will be left in the room. A hearty breakfast downstairs in the dining area will be served by the gracious hosts. Two decks are available for bird watching or sunning. A lovely patio is a few steps down the trail. The state park is a few miles away. Two public golf courses are within a 10-minute drive. $110-125.

SOUTH PADRE ISLAND

Brown Pelican Inn

207 West Aries, P.O. Box 2667, 78597
(956) 761-2722

The Brown Pelican Inn is a place to relax, make oneself at home, and enjoy personalized service. The porches are a great spot to sit and watch the sun set over the bay. The inn is comfortably furnished with European and American antiques; all guest rooms have private baths, and most rooms have spectacular bay views. Breakfast in the parlor includes freshly baked bread or muffins, fresh fruit, cereal, juice, and gourmet coffee or tea. Children over 12 welcome.

Hosts: Vicky and Ken Conway
Rooms: 8 (PB) $70-150
Continental Breakfast
Credit Cards: A, B
Notes: 2, 5, 7, 9, 10, 11, 12, 14, 15

STEPHENVILLE

The Oxford House

563 North Graham Street, 76401
(817) 965-6885

Stephenville is in the northern tip of the beautiful Texas Hill Country on Highway 377 west of Lake Granbury and east of Proctor Lake. Tarleton State University is in town. Only 30 minutes from Fossil Rim Wildlife Center and Dinosaur Valley State Park. The Oxford House was built in 1898 by Judge W. J. Oxford Sr., and the completely restored, two-story Victorian, presently owned by the grandson of the judge, has antique furnishings. Enjoy a quiet atmosphere and country breakfast. Shopping within walking distance. Smoking permitted in designated areas only. Children over 10 are welcome.

The Oxford House

Hosts: Bill and Paula Oxford
Rooms: 5 (4 PB; 1 SB) $65-85
Full Breakfast
Credit Cards: A, B, C, D
Notes: 2, 4, 5, 9, 10, 11, 12, 14

TERRELL

The Bluebonnet Inn

310 West College, 75160
(972) 524-2534

The turn of the century brought the railroad to Terrell, and with it, prosperity. This fine old home was a part of Terrell's grand old days, and despite many changes through the years, the Victorian beauty remains. Relax in the large rooms, all with private baths. Enjoy this house full of antiques with its two parlors, sunroom dining, country kitchen, and service area, where guests can help themselves to snacks and fountain sodas. A full breakfast is served each morning at nine, or choose a private Continental breakfast at one's leisure. Innkeepers and owners Bryan and Jan Jobe look forward to guests' visit and will answer any questions when they call.

Rooms: 4 (PB) $75-105
Full and Continental
Credit Cards: A, B, C, D
Notes: 4, 5, 7, 10, 11, 12

TURKEY

Hotel Turkey Bed and Breakfast

Third and Alexander Streets, 79261
(806) 423-1151; (800) 657-7110
www.llano.net/turkey/hotel

Built in 1927 for the early railroad traveler and rancher, it was converted to a bed and breakfast eight years ago, maintaining the 1927 decor. Listed in the National Register of Historic Places in 1991 and the Texas historic registry in 1985. Three blocks from the Rails-to-Trails park system for hiking, biking, and horseback riding. With a lovely outside patio and enclosed glass porch with 12 rocking chairs, the hotel can accommodate up to 35 guests. Group rates available.

Hosts: Gary and Suzie Johnson
Rooms: 15 (6 PB: 9 SB) $69
Full Breakfast
Credit Cards: A, B, C
Notes: 2, 5, 7, 10

TYLER

Bed and Breakfast Texas Style

4224 West Red Bird Lane, Dallas, 75237
(972) 298-8586; (800) 899-4538
FAX (972) 298-7118; e-mail: bdtxstyle1@aol.com
www.bnbtexasstyle.com

Vintage Farm Home. This newly renovated, circa 1836-1864, home, once an original dogtrot plantation home, sits in the piney woods of East Texas. Catch the morning sun or evening breeze on the large veranda where rocking chairs and a swing invite relaxation. Take a stroll through the trails during dogwood or fall foliage season. The guest room has a king-size bed and private bath. Breakfast is served downstairs in the cozy nook. $85.

Rosevine Inn Bed and Breakfast

415 South Vine, 75702
(903) 592-2221; e-mail: rosevine@iamerica.net

Rosevine Inn is in the historic Brick Street district. Come rest and relax at Rosevine Inn. Amenities include a lovely courtyard with fountain and fireplace. There are also an outdoor hot tub and game room complete with billiards for guests' enjoyment. There are now two suites available. A full gourmet breakfast is served. The hosts look forward to meeting guests and welcoming them to the Rose Capital of the World. A picnic lunch is available.

Hosts: Bert and Rebecca Powell
Rooms: 7 (PB) $85-150
Full Breakfast
Credit Cards: A, B, C, D, E
Notes: 2, 3, 5, 7, 8, 9, 10, 11, 12, 14

VAN

Tumble on Inn

P.O. Box 1249, 75790
(903) 963-7669; (888) 707-3992
e-mail: tumbleoninn@aol.com

Country casual comfort in the pine woods of East Texas. One hour from Dallas, one and one-half hours from Shreveport. Five minutes to Canton First Monday Trade Days. Community room with movies, books, music for all tastes. Hot tub under the stars. Balcony for stargazing. Deck for relaxing. Children 12 and older welcome. No pets. Discounts for two-night stay, AARP, Texas Passport.

Hosts: Gordon and Jean Jensen
Rooms: 5 (5 SB) $75
Full Breakfast
Credit Cards: A, B
Notes: 2, 3, 4, 5, 9, 15

VANDERPOOL

Texas Stagecoach Inn

HC02, Box 166, Highway 187, 78885
(830) 966-6272; (888) 965-6272
FAX (830) 966-6273 (call first)
e-mail: stageinn@swtexas

Year-round nature tourism awaits guests at Lost Maples State Natural Area and Texas Stagecoah Inn within this undiscovered area of the Texas Hill Country. The spacious riverside inn, on three acres, is designed to ensure a peaceful respite. Guest rooms and common rooms are generously appointed with Hill Country elegance and original landscapes. Breakfast buffet feasts greet each morning. If one's desire is to relax in the tranquility of the Sabinal Canyon, or enjoy nature and all its activites, guests will find it here. Smoking permitted outside only.

Hosts: Karen and David Camp
Rooms: 2 (PB) $85-115
Suites: 2 (PB)
Full Breakfast
Credit Cards: None
Notes: 2, 5, 7, 8, 9, 10, 11, 12, 14

VICTORIA

Friendly Oaks Bed and Breakfast

210 East Juan Linn Street, 77901
(512) 575-0000; e-mail: innkprbill@aol.com
www.bbhost.com/friendlyoaks

In the shelter of ancient live oaks, history comes alive at the Friendly Oaks bed and breakfast in a preservation area of 80 restored Victorian homes. Each of four guest rooms has a private bath, its own individual decor reflecting the preservation efforts of Victoria. A conference room provides a quiet setting for retreats, meetings, seminars, parties, showers, and small weddings. Here "Bed means Comfortable, Breakfast means Scrumptious."

Hosts: Bill and Cee Bee McLeod
Rooms: 4 (PB) $55-75
Full Breakfast
Credit Cards: A, B, C, D
Notes: 2, 5, 7, 9, 10, 11, 12, 14, 15

WACO

The Judge Baylor House

908 Speight, 76706
(888) JBAYLOR; FAX (817) 756-0711
e-mail: jbaylor@iamerica.net
www.eyeweb.com/jbaylor

Two blocks from Baylor University and its Armstrong Browning Library, five minutes from Waco Convention Center. A two-story red brick home with five spacious and beautifully appointed guest rooms. All have private baths and either king-, queen-size, or twin beds. Sitting in the swing hanging from a large ash tree in the front lawn, playing the grand piano, or enjoying a new book, guests are sure to relax and feel at home.

Hosts: Bruce and Dorothy Dyer
Rooms: 5 (PB) $69-89
Full Breakfast
Credit Cards: A, B, C
Notes: 2, 4, 5, 6, 7, 8, 9, 10, 11, 12, 14, 15

WIMBERLEY

Bed and Breakfast Texas Style

4224 West Red Bird Lane, Dallas, 75237
(972) 298-8586; (800) 899-4538
FAX (972) 298-7118; e-mail: bdtxstyle1@aol.com
www.bnbtexasstyle.com

Casa de Angelitas. In the heart of the Hill Country, close to what makes Wimberley so special, and yet it has a peaceful, being in the country feeling. This lovely cottage has a fireplace, three bedrooms with adjoining bath for each room, and is available for private getaways, families, or retreats. A Continental breakfast is left in the fully equipped kitchen. A special gourmet breakfast may be served upon request. A massage therapist lives nearby and private appointments can be arranged for additional fee. Lots of quaint shops and artists' galleries are nearby. $75-95.

Southwind Bed and Breakfast

2701 FM 3237, 78676
(512) 847-5277; (800) 508-5277

Southwind is five minutes from the quaint village of Wimberley and one hour from Austin or San Antonio. Rocking chairs on the porches are good places to view hills and valleys, wildlife, and sunsets, and the hot tub is grand for star gazing. Fireplaces, queen- and king-size beds, and antique and reproduction furniture. In addition to the inn, two cabins, each with king-size bed, fireplace, and whirlpool tub, are nestled in the woods and hills. No smoking. Children welcome in cabins. Inquire about accommodations for pets. Cabins are handicapped accessible.

Host: Carrie Watson
Rooms: 3 (PB) $80-90
Full Breakfast
Credit Cards: A, B, C, D
Notes: 2, 5, 7, 9, 10, 11, 12, 14

WINNSBORO

Thee Hubbell House

307 West Elm, 75494
(800) 227-0639; FAX (903) 342-6627
e-mail: hubhouse@bluebonnet.netcom
www.bluebonnet.net/hubhouse

Ninety miles east of Dallas in beautiful northeast Texas. Two-acre landscaped plantation estate with four designated Texas historical houses. Twelve bedrooms and suites. Romantic candlelight dining, hot tub house, massage. One hundred antique shops, ten lakes, and seven golf courses. Pets welcome at the pet motel. Children welcome in the family cottage.

Hosts: Dan and Laurel Hubbell
Rooms: 12 (PB) $75-175
Full or Continental Breakfast
Credit Cards: A, B, C, D, E, F
Notes: 2, 4, 5, 7, 9, 10, 11, 12, 14, 15

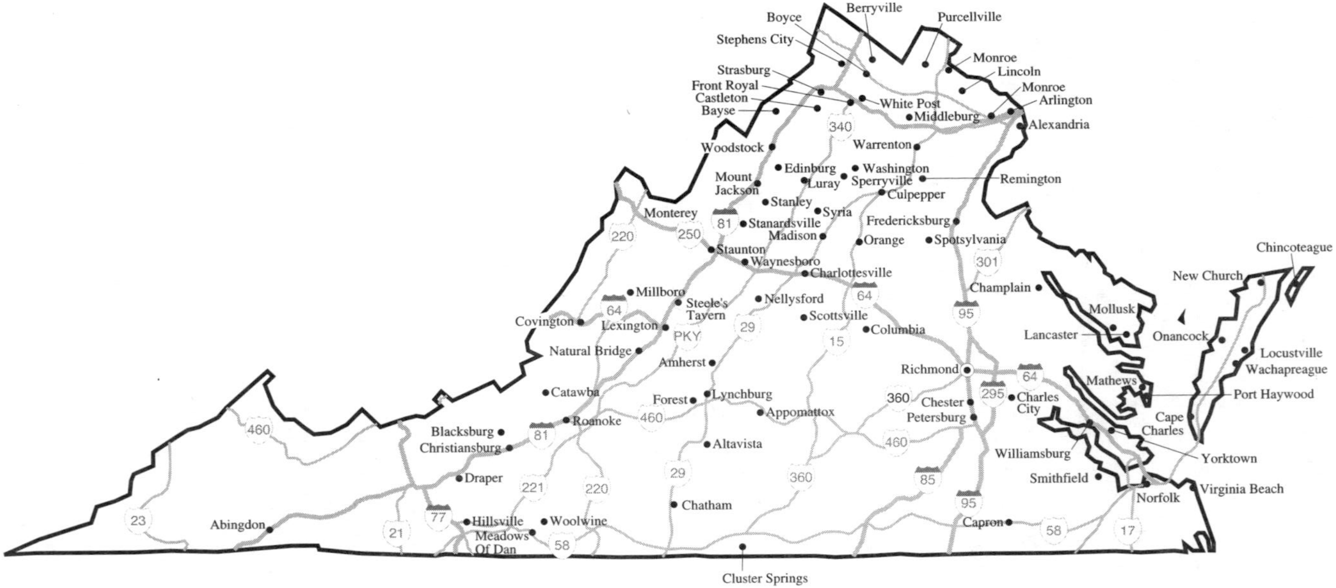
Berryville
Boyce
Purcellville
Stephens City
Monroe
Lincoln
Strasburg
Monroe
Front Royal
Arlington
Castleton
White Post
Bayse
Middleburg
Alexandria
Woodstock
Warrenton
Edinburg
Washington
Mount Jackson
Luray
Sperryville
Remington
Culpepper
Stanley
Syria
Monterey
Stanardsville
Fredericksburg
Madison
Orange
Spotsylvania
Staunton
Waynesboro
Charlottesville
Chincoteague
New Church
Champlain
Millboro
Steele's Tavern
Nellysford
Mollusk
Covington
Lexington
Scottsville
Lancaster
Onancock
Columbia
Locustville
Natural Bridge
Wachapreague
Amherst
Richmond
Mathews
Port Haywood
Catawba
Forest
Lynchburg
Chester
Charles City
Cape Charles
Appomattox
Petersburg
Blacksburg
Roanoke
Christiansburg
Altavista
Williamsburg
Yorktown
Draper
Smithfield
Virginia Beach
Norfolk
Chatham
Abingdon
Hillsville
Woolwine
Capron
Meadows Of Dan
Cluster Springs
460
340
81
250
220
301
64
95
29
PKY
15
360
295
460
81
221
220
29
360
85
95
23
77
21
58
58
17

Virginia

Virginia

Inn on Town Creek

ABINGDON

Inn on Town Creek

P.O. Box 1745, 445 East Valley Street, 24212-1745
(540) 628-4560; FAX (540) 628-9611
www.naxs.com/abingdon/innontowncreek/index.htm

A historic creek is the theme of this bed and breakfast on four acres of beautifully landscaped property. Multilevel brick patios and rock gardens provide tranquil privacy; air-conditioned, antique-filled rooms and the cordiality of the innkeepers offer a peaceful getaway to the discerning guest. Near fine dining, entertainment. Ample parking. Smoking outside. Children 10 and older welcome.

Hosts: Dr. Roger and Linda Neal
Rooms: 5 (4 PB; 1 SB) $100-250
Full Breakfast
Credit Cards: A, B
Notes: 2, 5, 7, 9, 10, 11, 12, 14

River Garden Bed and Breakfast

19080 North Fork River Road, 24210-4560
(540) 676-0335; (800) 952-4296

River Garden is nestled in the foothills of the Clinch Mountains, on the bank of the north fork of the Holston River outside historic Abingdon. Furnished with traditional, antique, and period furniture, each room has its own riverside deck overlooking the gentle rapids. Private exterior entrance, queen- or king-size bed, full bath, and central heat and air. Guests are also granted kitchen privileges. Common areas include living room, den, dining room, and recreation room.

Hosts: Carol and Bill Crump
Rooms: 4 (PB) $60-65
Full Breakfast
Credit Cards: None
Notes: 2, 5, 7, 9, 11, 12, 14

Summerfield Inn

101 West Valley Street, 24210
(540) 628-5905; (800) 668-5905

Summerfield Inn is in the Abingdon historic district, just two blocks from the world-famous Barter Theatre. Near the Appalachian Trail, Mount Rogers National Recreation Area, South Holston Lake, the Blue Ridge Parkway, Virginia Creeper Trail, excellent restaurants, and marvelous shops. Just off I-81 at exit 17. New cottage addition with Jacuzzi and in-room TV and telephone. Bikes available. Smoking restricted. Children over six welcome.

Hosts: Champe and Don Hyatt
Rooms: $70-125

Summerfield Inn

Full Breakfast
Credit Cards: A, B, C, D
Notes: 2, 9, 10, 12, 14, 15

ALEXANDRIA

Amanda's Bed and Breakfast Reservation Service

1428 Park Avenue, Baltimore, MD 21217-4230
(410) 225-0001; (800) 899-7533
FAX (410) 728-8957; e-mail:amandasrs@aol.com
www.amandas-bbrs.com

150. In historic Alexandria, a town with an interesting past and current features such as the renovated Torpedo Factory with artist shops and restaurants. The historic buildings and other shops are within easy access. Guests can walk to the Metro with access to Washington, D.C. If driving, there are several areas in the region to tour: Mount Vernon, Arlington Cemetery, and the horse country around Leesburg. Two rooms for bed and breakfast. Two-night minimum. $85-95.

ALTAVISTA

Castle to Country House

1010 Main Street, 24517
(888) 626-1825; FAX (804) 369-4911

This 1936 birch cottage-style home is decorated in Victorian and country styles. In addition to four beautifully furnished bedrooms, guests have access to a large living room with fireplace, formal dining room, and sun porches. All rooms are equipped with color cable TV, VCRs, telephones, queen-size beds, and private baths. Limousine service is offered and there is a gift shop on the premises. "Whether you are traveling on business or vacationing, we welcome you."

Hosts: Jim and Christine Critchley
Rooms: 4 (PB) $40-65
Full Breakfast
Credit Cards: A, B, C, D
Notes: 2, 3, 4, 5, 7, 10, 11, 12, 14

Castle to Country House

AMHERST

Dulwich Manor Bed and Breakfast Inn

550 Richmond Highway, 24521-3962
(804) 946-7207; (800) 571-9011

Gracious country lodging in an elegant English-style manor house with views of the Blue Ridge Mountains. Six beautifully appointed bed chambers with fireplaces; window seats or whirlpool tub; canopied, brass, and antique beds. Enjoy the hot tub in the Victorian gazebo. Surrounded by 85 acres of natural beauty at the end of a country lane. This perfect romantic getaway is convenient to Richmond, Charlottesville, Lynchburg, and Washington, D.C. A sumptuous country breakfast is served. Smoking permitted in designated areas only. Swimming 40 minutes away. Skiing 30 minutes away. Mobil three-star-rated.

Hosts: Bob and Judy Reilly
Rooms: 6 (4 PB; 2 SB) $70-98
Full Breakfast
Credit Cards: None
Notes: 2, 5, 8, 9, 10, 12, 14

Fair View Bed and Breakfast

2416 Lowesville Road, 24521
(804) 277-8500

Rusticate and relax at this peaceful country getaway with fabulous mountain views. Italianate Victorian farmhouse offers three spacious guest rooms with comfortable antique furnishings and private baths. Guests rave about the wholesome breakfasts, the stars, the panoramic view, and the teddy bears on the stairs. Families are welcome as are well-behaved pets (with prior permission). Fishing, canoeing, and hiking nearby. Thirty minutes to Blue Ridge Parkway. Centrally between Charlottesville, Lynchburg, and Lexington. Member of BBAV. Smoking permitted in designated areas only.

Hosts: Judy and Jim Noon
Rooms: 3 (PB) $70
Full Breakfast
Credit Cards: A, B, D
Notes: 2, 5, 8, 9, 12, 13, 14

APPOMATTOX

The Babcock House Bed and Breakfast Inn

Route 6, Box 1421, 106 Oakleigh Avenue, 24522
(804) 352-7532; (800) 689-6208
FAX (804) 352-5754
e-mail: richguild@earthlink.net
www.innformation.com/va/babcock

A restored turn-of-the-century inn in downtown Appomattox, less than three miles from the famous surrender site which ended the Civil War. The inn has five rooms and one suite. All rooms have private baths, ceiling fans, cable TV, and air conditioning.

Hosts: Debbie Powell, Luella Coleman, Lynah Guild
Rooms: 6 (PB) $85-110
Full Breakfast
Credit Cards: A, B, C, D
Notes: 2, 5, 7, 8, 9, 10, 12, 14, 15

ARLINGTON

Alexandria and Arlington Bed and Breakfast Network

P.O. Box 25319, 22202-9319
(703) 549-3415; (888) 549-3419
FAX (703) 549-3411; e-mail: aabbn@juno.com

Offering more than 50 private homes, bed and breakfasts, and inns, this network offers something for everyone coming to Washington, D.C., Virginia, and Maryland. Stay in a 1750s Old Town Alexandria townhouse or a glamorous highrise apartment. Hosts range from retired politicians and admirals to New Age entrepreneurs. All hosts are dedicated to guests' comfort, safety, and enjoyment of a visit in or near Washington, D.C.

Contact: Leslie Garrison
Rooms: 100+ (PB and SB) $60-325
Full and/or Continental Breakfast
Credit Cards: A, B, C
Notes: 2, 5, 6, 8, 9, 10, 11, 12, 14

The Bed and Breakfast League, Ltd./Sweet Dreams and Toast, Inc.

P.O. Box 9490, Washington, D.C. 20016-9490
(202) 363-7767; FAX (202) 363-8396
e-mail: bedandbreakfast-washingtondc@erols.com

198. A custom-built Colonial-style home within walking distance of the Ballston Metro stop offers the spacious master bedroom with a king-size and a twin bed, sitting area, and bath en suite with double Jacuzzi, shower, and three sinks. The bedroom is decorated with European linens, wallpaper, and silk curtains, and has a refrigerator, microwave, cable TV, VCR, and telephone. Internet access and a fax are also available. The gracious hostess serves a luxurious breakfast by candlelight and afternoon tea. Off-street parking available

Rates: $100-125
Credit Cards: A, B, C, E
Notes: 2, 5, 6, 7, 8, 9, 10, 11

298. A short ride to the Pentagon and Crystal City, this bed and breakfast is in a quiet, secluded area, but has easy access to Washington. Two pretty, antique-filled guest rooms have a double bed or two twin beds, each with a private bath. The hosts offer the use of a computer and fax in their office and, better still, their lovely garden with a pond. She is a costume historian, he a retired military officer; both are widely traveled, very interesting people. Parking is on-street and easy.

Rates: $70-80
Credit Cards: A, B, C, E
Notes: 2, 5, 7, 9

BASYE

Sky Chalet Mountain Lodge

P.O. Box 300, 22810
(540) 856-2147; FAX (540) 856-2436
e-mail: skychalet@skychalet.com
www.skychalet.com

Romantic, mountaintop hideaway with spectacular, breathtaking, panoramic mountain and valley views. Accommodations are rustic and comfortable. Rooms have private baths. Treetop Lodge has private baths, living rooms, fireplaces, decks. Continental breakfast delivered to guests. Welcome individuals, honeymooners, couples, families, children, groups, retreats, pets. Unique Old World Lodge with fireplaces, verandas, views, ambiance for receptions, seminars, special events. Hiking, attractions, activities, restaurants, airport nearby. "The Mountain Lovers' Paradise" since 1937, where the views remain unchallenged.

Hosts: Ken and Mona Seay
Rooms: 10 (PB) $34-79
Continental Breakfast

Sky Chalet Mountain Lodge

Credit Cards: A, B, D, E
Notes: 2, 5, 6, 8, 9, 10,11, 12, 13, 14

BERRYVILLE

Berryville Bed and Breakfast

100 Taylor Street, 22611
(540) 955-2200; (800) 826-7520
e-mail: bvillebb@shentel.net

Enjoy the in-town comfort and elegance of the Berryville Bed and Breakfast while exploring the small town of Berryville and Clarke County, in the heart of the Shenandoah Valley. Known for its apple orchards and horse farms, it is a perfect area for unwinding after a hectic week or for celebrating a special occasion. The house, built

Berryville

in 1915, is in the English country style and offers an acre of grounds for guests' enjoyment. The master suite features a fireplace. An abundant breakfast is served to each guest, and Berryville and the surrounding area offer restaurants for other meals to suit every taste and price range. "Come join us and name your pleasure."

Hosts: Don and Jan Riviere
Rooms: 4 (2 PB; 2 SB) $85-145
Full Breakfast
Credit Cards: A, B, C, D
Notes: 2, 5, 7, 9, 12

BLACKSBURG

Clay Corner Inn

401 Clay Street Southwest, 24060
(540) 953-2604; e-mail: claycorner@aol.com

A unique cluster of five houses in downtown Blacksburg one block to Virginia Tech and the Huckleberry Trail. The main house, built in 1929, reflects traditional and southwestern styles. Two guest houses have complete kitchens and living areas and are connected by wooden decks to the main house; covered patio and heated swimming pool. The Huckleberry House, circa 1911, has four very nice guest rooms. All guest rooms have cable TVs, telephones, and king- or queen-size beds.

Hosts: John and Joanne Anderson
Rooms: 12 (PB) $75-105
Full Breakfast
Credit Cards: A, B, C
Notes: 2, 5, 9, 10, 11, 12, 14

Clay Corner Inn

L'Arche

L'Arche Bed and Breakfast

301 Wall Street, 24060
(703) 951-1808

An oasis of tranquility just one block from the Virginia Tech campus, L'Arche Bed and Breakfast is an elegant turn-of-the-century Federal Revival home among terraced gardens in downtown Blacksburg. Spacious rooms have traditional antiques, family heirlooms, handmade quilts, and private baths. Delicious full breakfasts feature homemade breads, cakes, jams, and jellies.

Host: Vera G. Good
Rooms: 5 (PB) $85
Full Breakfast
Credit Cards: A, B
Notes: 2, 5, 10, 12, 13, 15

BOYCE

Amanda's Bed and Breakfast Reservation Service

1428 Park Avenue, Baltimore, MD 21217-4230
(410) 225-0001; (800) 899-7533
FAX (410) 728-8957; e-mail:amandasrs@aol.com
www.amandas-bbrs.com

333. Near Winchester and Front Royal at the northern end of Skyline Drive and the Shenandoah Valley. A rural getaway on the river, built in 1780 and 1820. Fireplaces and private baths, lots of books, full breakfast, and scenery. $80-125.

7 No smoking; 8 Children welcome; 9 Social drinking allowed; 10 Tennis nearby; 11 Swimming nearby; 12 Golf nearby; 13 Skiing nearby; 14 May be booked through a travel agent; 15 Handicapped accessible.

CAPE CHARLES

Amanda's Bed and Breakfast Reservation Service

1428 Park Avenue, Baltimore, MD 21217-4230
(410) 225-0001; (800) 899-7533
FAX (410) 728-8957; e-mail:amandasrs@aol.com
www.amandas-bbrs.com

122. Lovely, quiet, rural setting along the Chesapeake Bay featuring unspoiled land, abundant wildlife, game birds, miles of private beach, and nature's most fabulous sunsets. This two-story brick home has a great view of the bay and is decorated with antiques, reproductions, and collectibles. Four rooms with private baths. Full breakfast. $85.

138. Restored 1910 Colonial Revival. Just steps from a public beach on the bay. Relax on one of the porches, sample the cool breezes off the bay, or bike through the historic town. Guests set their own pace to explore. Four guest rooms share two baths. Full breakfast. $75-85.

183. Cape Charles is the only public beach in area. This majestic home with a wraparound porch is just a few blocks from the beach. Walk and watch the beautiful sunsets over the bay. The Eastern Shore has a unique natural splendor for guests' enjoyment. In the house, the Corinthian columns form the grand staircase leading to some of the bedrooms. A gourmet breakfast is served in the spacious sun-filled dining room. $80-110.

291. Cape Charles is on the east side of the Eastern Shore of Virginia. A small town with historic significance directly on the beautiful Chesapeake Bay. Enjoy spectacular sunsets from the breezy porch or common areas of this Victorian home. Newly refurbished large rooms, air conditioning, TV, and bicycles. Walk the beach; visit quaint shops; watch the birds, wildlife; fishing, crabbing, swimming, or sunning. Full breakfast. Indoor hot tub. Open year-round. Seasonal rates. $85.

Bay Avenue's Sunset Bed and Breakfast

108 Bay Avenue, 23310
(757) 331-2424; FAX (757) 331-4877
e-mail: info@baysunsetbb.com
www.baysunsetbb.com

Waterfront on Chesapeake Bay, 1915 cozy Victorian. Convenient in-town location. Enjoy spectacular sunsets from rockers on the porch. Unwind and relax, away from the hustle-bustle. Romantic getaways. Walk the uncrowded beach. Biking, bird watching, golf, charter boats. Full family-style breakfast, central air conditioning, four large bright rooms with private baths, cable TV/VCRs, bikes. Two rooms have fireplace stoves for cozy nights. Guests' home away from home. Wildlife refuge, state park nearby. AAA three-diamond-rating. Smoking restricted to porch.

Hosts: Al Longo and Joyce Tribble
Rooms: 4 (PB) $75-105
Full Breakfast
Credit Cards: A, B, C, D
Notes: 5, 9, 10, 11, 12, 14

Bay Avenue's Sunset

Chesapeake Charm

Chesapeake Charm Bed and Breakfast

202 Madison Avenue, 23310
(757) 331-2676; (800) 546-9215
e-mail: chesapeakecharminfo@prodigy.net

Discover the charm of historic Cape Charles on Virginia's Eastern Shore. Private baths in antique-filled rooms with individual air conditioning and heating. Plentiful breakfasts and afternoon treats. Convenient to bay beach, golf, fishing, art and antique stores. Gift certificates available.

Hosts: Phyllis and Barry Tyndall
Rooms: 3 (PB) $65-85
Full Breakfast
Credit Cards: A, B
Notes: 2, 8, 9, 10, 11, 12, 14

Sea Gate Bed and Breakfast

9 Tazewell Avenue, 23310
(757) 331-2206

In the sleepy town of Cape Charles, just steps from Chesapeake Bay on Virginia's undiscovered Eastern Shore. The day begins with a country breakfast followed by leisure, hiking, bird watching, bathing, or exploring the historic area. Tea prepares guests for the glorious sunsets over the bay. Sea Gate is the perfect place to rest, relax, and recharge—away from the crush of modern America. Winter special available. Two guest rooms have toilet and sink in room and share a bath across the hall. Smoking restricted. Children seven and older welcome.

Host: Chris Bannon
Rooms: 4 (2 PB; 2 SB) $75-85
Full Breakfast
Credit Cards: F
Notes: 2, 5, 10, 11, 12, 14

Wilson-Lee House Bed and Breakfast

403 Tazewell Avenue, 23310
(757) 331-1WLH (331-1957)
e-mail: WLHBnb@aol.com
www.wilsonleehouse.com

At the geographic center of historic Cape Charles, Wilson-Lee House is an example of the finest architecture of its time. Built in 1906, this Colonial Revival home is the work of Norfold architect James W. Lee. A modified four-square house with four rooms per floor, it has been restored to its original elegance and has been configured to accommodate the needs of a late-20th-century bed and breakfast. Six and one-half baths were added for guest comfort for each of the six luxurious bedrooms, and the butler's pantry was redesigned with the guest in mind. The grand foyer with its Ionic colonnade is bright and especially welcoming. The Eastern Shore pace is deliciously slow and sunsets on the Chesapeake Bay are breathtaking. Come rock on the porch, ride a bicycle built for two, and let the hosts arrange a romantic sunset sail, followed by a relaxing cookout on the deck.

Wilson-Lee House

Hosts: David Phillips and Leon Parham
Rooms: 6 (PB) $85-120
Full or Continental Breakfast
Credit Cards: A, B, C
Notes: 2, 5, 7, 9, 10, 11, 12, 14

CAPRON

Sandy Hill Farm Bed and Breakfast

11307 Rivers Mill Road, 23829
(804) 658-4381

Enjoy gracious southern hospitality and experience the pleasures of an unspoiled rural setting at this ranch-style farmhouse. Eleven miles from I-95 at exit 20, this working peanut and cotton farm also offers animals to visit and places to stroll in addition to a lighted tennis court on the grounds. Day trips to Williamsburg, Richmond, and Norfolk are within two hours. Fresh fruits and homemade breads are served at breakfast. Open March 25 through December 10. Reservations necessary.

Host: Anne Kitchen
Rooms: 2 (PB) $50
Full Breakfast
Credit Cards: None
Notes: 3, 4, 6, 8, 9, 10

CASTLETON

Blue Knoll Farm

110 Gore Road, 22716
(540) 937-5234

This lovingly restored 19th-century farmhouse is in the foothills of the Blue Ridge Mountains. The original house was built before the Civil War. Four guest rooms with private baths are open to guests. Blue Knoll provides a charming rural retreat minutes from a renowned five-star restaurant, the Inn at Little Washington, and other fine dining. Near Shenandoah National Park and Skyline Drive. Smoking restricted.

Hosts: Gil and Mary Carlson
Rooms: 4 (PB) $95-125

Blue Knoll Farm

Full Breakfast
Credit Cards: A, B, D
Notes: 2, 9

CATAWBA

CrossTrails Bed and Breakfast

5880 Blacksburg Road, 24070
(540) 384-8078
e-mail: xtrails@worldnet.att.net

A mountain-valley getaway in scenic Catawba Valley where the Appalachian Trail and TransAmerica Bicycle Trail cross between Roanoke and Blacksburg. World-class hiking and biking just outside the door. The 15 acres adjoined on three sides by national park property. Porches and decks designed to take advantage of commanding views. Rooms have queen-size beds and private baths. Remote carriage house, hot tub, library, cross-country skiing, fly-fishing, shuttles, full breakfast, Homeplace Restaurant nearby.

Rooms: Bill and Katherine Cochran
Rooms; 3 (PB) $70-75
Full Breakfast

Credit Cards: None
Notes: 2, 7, 9, 12

CHAMPLAIN

Linden House Bed and Breakfast and Plantation

Route 17 South, P.O. Box 23, 22438
(804) 443-1170; (800) 622-1202

Stay in one of the top-rated inns in Virginia. Rated A-plus by the ABBA and three diamonds by AAA. The 250-year-old mansion with carriage house is decorated in 18th-century reproductions and antiques. The beautifully landscaped yard and garden with gazebo and arbor provide room to relax and enjoy the quiet and serene setting. Only 45 minutes south of Fredericksburg and 75 minutes north of Williamsburg.

Hosts: Ken and Sandra Pounsberry
Rooms: 6 (PB) $85-135
Full Breakfast
Credit Cards: A, B, C, D, F
Notes: 2, 4, 5, 7, 8, 9, 11, 12, 14, 15

CHARLES CITY

Orange Hill Bed and Breakfast

18401 Glebe Lane, 23030
(804) 829-5936; (888) 889-7781

In the middle of 50 acres of working farmland, this newly renovated turn-of-the-century farmhouse offers the charm and quiet of the country. In the heart of historical plantations and only 20 minutes to Colonial Williamsburg, Jamestown, outlet shopping, and golf courses. Furnished with many antiques original to the house. A full breakfast, made from old family recipes, is served in the dining room; refreshments are served in the afternoon. Dinner available by request. Children over 12 welcome.

Hosts: Skip and Dorothy Bergoine
Rooms: 3 (2 PB; 1 SB) $80-105
Full Breakfast
Credit Cards: A, B
Notes: 2, 5, 7, 9, 12, 14

CHARLOTTESVILLE

Chester

243 James River Road, Scottsville, 24590
(804) 286-3960; www.chesterbed.com

A Greek Revival home built in 1847, Chester's seven acres include an arboretum, a century-old lily pond, spacious porches, and elegant common rooms. The gracious atmosphere combines the amenities of the finest hotel with the warmth and personal attention of a small inn. The beautifully appointed guest rooms have private baths and wood-burning fireplaces. Nearby historic sites include Monticello, Ash Lawn, the University of Virginia, and numerous Virginia wineries. Minutes away from canoeing and tubing on the James River. Dinner available for groups only.

Hosts: Jean and Craig Stratton
Room: 5 (PB) $120-140
Full Breakfast
Credit Cards: A, B
Notes: 2, 5, 7, 9, 10, 12, 13, 14

Guesthouses Bed and Breakfast

P.O. Box 5737, 22905
(804) 979-7264 (12:00-5:00 P.M. weekdays)
FAX (804) 293-7791
e-mail: guesthouses_bnb_reservations@compuserve.com
www.va-guesthouses.com

Afton House. A mountain retreat with panoramic views east to valleys and hills, this spacious home is on the old road up the mountain pass. There are four bedrooms, mostly furnished with antiques. One has a private adjoining bath, and three share two hall baths. Full breakfast is served. Antique shop on the premises and others in the village. $75-80.

Alderman House. This large, formal Georgian home is authentic in style and elegant in decor. It was built by the widow of the first president of the University of Virginia in the early 1900s and is about

Guesthouses Bed and Breakfast (continued)

one mile from the university. Breakfast is served with true southern hospitality. Two guest rooms, each with adjoining private bath. Air conditioning. No smoking in the house. $100.

Auburn Hill. An antebellum cottage on a scenic farm that was part of the original Jefferson plantation. The main house was built by Jefferson for one of his overseers. It is convenient to Monticello and Ash Lawn, just six miles east of the city. The cottage has a sitting room with fireplace, bedroom with four-poster bed, and connecting bath and shower. Guests may use the pool in summer. Scenic trails, walks, and views. Air conditioning. No smoking. Supplies provided for guests to prepare breakfast. Weekly rates available. $100-125.

Buck's Elbow Mountain Cottage. Mountaintop retreat with 360-degree views. Buck's Elbow Mountain is the highest point in Albemarle County and looks down on the Skyline Drive and Appalachian Trail, which run adjacent to the farm. Wake up and see the Valley of Virginia without getting out of bed. The cottage is contemporary with lots of glass, a cathedral ceiling in the living room, full kitchen, two bedrooms, and one and one-half baths, one with a Jacuzzi with views. Two-night minimum stay. Air-conditioned. $200.

Cross Creek. A spectacular wood, stone, and glass "cottage" on a hilltop nine miles west of Charlottesville, Cross Creek is a perennial favorite. The living room, dining room, half-bath, and kitchen are built around a massive central stone fireplace. A deck provides a wonderful wooded view. Two bedrooms are on the lower level with a full bath across the hall. Air conditioning. Supplies provided for guests to prepare breakfast. $150-200.

Duke House. Built in 1884 by Judge Duke, this Queen Anne Victorian home on historic Park Street is within walking distance to Court Square and the downtown pedestrian mall. The current owners are in the process of restoring the home to its original elegance. A large sunny guest room with private adjoining bath is available. Continental breakfast. Ceiling fan and window air conditioner. No smoking, please. $80-100.

Foxbrook. This lovely home just blocks north of the bypass is convenient to either downtown or the university area. Guest quarters consist of a sitting room overlooking a lovely garden, a bedroom, and a large bath with separate shower and sunken tub. Full breakfast. Air conditioned. No smoking. $100.

Fox Lane Farm. Lovely new home in the Victorian style built in beautiful Keswick hunt country. The guest quarters offer complete privacy in a large room with cathedral ceiling and many Victorian pieces. An old quilt hangs behind the brass bed. There is a private entrance from a lovely deck overlooking the woods and garden. There is an adjoining full bath and a pullman kitchen where breakfast supplies will be left for guests. No smoking. Air conditioning. $100.

Indian Springs. This new cottage with a rustic feel is in a lovely wooded setting on a private lake. The lake is stocked and has a small dock for fishing, basking in the sun, or swimming at guests' own risk. There is a large main room, a sitting area with a sofa bed, dining area, kitchen, and bath. This cottage has complete privacy. TV and air conditioning. Supplies are provided for guests to prepare breakfast. $125-200.

Ingleside. A farm that has been in the same family for several generations, Ingleside lies on 1,250 acres of rolling pasture backed by steep, wooded mountains. The house was built around 1840 of bricks made from the farm's red clay. Accommodations consist of a large antique-furnished room, fireplace, and adjacent bath. A tennis court is available for guest use. Air conditioning. $80.

Ingwood. In a lovely villa on six wooded acres in one of Charlottesville's most prestigious neighborhoods, Ingwood is an elegant, separate-level suite with its own drive and private entrance. The bedroom is appointed with antiques and has adjoining bath. The sitting room includes a fireplace, pullman kitchen, and sofa for an extra person. A second bedroom with twin beds and private bath is also available. Sliding glass doors open to a secluded terrace with a view of the woods. Air conditioning. Breakfast supplies are left in the suite for guests to prepare. $125-200.

Ivy Rose Cottage. An original cypress cottage, handmade by the host, is surrounded by gardens and offers mountain views. The ground floor has a double drawing room, separated by a screen, with a sitting area and a hand-wrought-iron bed. There is a rainforest sunroom with adjoining kitchen and bath with shower. Upstairs is creatively furnished with stained glass and lace curtains. It has heart-pine floors, an antique bed, and a half-bath. The host is a potter and the cottage showcases her work and that of her father, photographer Stan Jorstad. Full breakfast. Gas log stove. Air conditioned. Smoking outside only. $150-200.

Meadow Run. Enjoy relaxed rural living in this new Contemporary/Classical home six miles west of Charlottesville. Guest rooms share a bath. Guests are welcome to browse in the boat lover's library, play the grand piano, or lounge in the living room. Many windows offer bucolic vistas of the southwest range. Fireplaces in the kitchen and living room add to the homey, friendly feel. Air conditioning. $80.

Millstream. A lovely, large house about 20 minutes north of Charlottesville up a long driveway lined with old box bushes. The house, with a brick English basement, was built before the Civil War and enlarged in 1866. There are two guest rooms, each with private bath. Guests may enjoy the fireplace in the library or the mountain views from the living room. Full breakfast. No smoking. Air conditioning. $100.

Nicola Log Cabin. This is a romantic 200-year-old log cabin on a 150-acre farm in historic Ivy eight miles west of Charlottesville, with spectacular views of the Blue Ridge Mountains. The one-room cabin has a bedroom, sleeper-sofa, a new bath with shower, microwave oven, refrigerator, and wood-burning stove. Children's playset and tennis court available. Supplies provided for guests to prepare breakfast. $100-150.

Northfields. This gracious home is on the northern edge of Charlottesville. The guest room has a TV, private bath, and air conditioning. There is another bedroom available with a double four-poster bed and private hall bath. A full gourmet breakfast is served. No smoking. $68-72.

Northwood. This 1920s city house is convenient to the historic downtown area of Charlottesville, only a few blocks from Thomas Jefferson's courthouse and the attractive pedestrian mall with many shops and restaurants. The guest quarters have a private adjoining bath. Many of the furnishings are antique, and next to the bedroom there is a small, comfortable sitting room with TV. Window air conditioning. $68.

Pocahontas. A large white clapboard house built in the 1920s as a summer retreat in the countryside near Ivy, west of Charlottesville. The large porch and beautiful gardens provide a wonderful place to stop and enjoy life passing by. A large guest room, furnished in Victorian pieces, greets guests with a bright and sunny warmth and offers a private adjoining bath with shower. Other rooms are available for larger groups or families on special weekends. No air conditioning but the house stays cool through the use of attic fans and large, high-ceilinged rooms. $80.

Polaris Farm. In the middle of rolling farmland dotted with horses and cattle, this architect-designed brick home offers guests an atmosphere of casual elegance. The accommodations consist of a ground-floor room with an adjoining bath, and two upstairs rooms that share a bath. There are gardens and terraces where one can view the Blue Ridge Mountains; a spring-fed pond for swimming, boating, and fishing; miles of trails for walking or horseback riding (mounts available at nearby stables). Air conditioning. $72-100.

Recoletta. An older Mediterranean-style house built with flair and imagination. The red tile roof, walled gardens with fountain, and artistic design create the impression of a secluded Italian villa within walking distance of the University of Virginia, shopping, and restaurants. Many of the beautiful antique furnishings are from Central America and Europe. The charming guest room has a beautiful brass bed and a private hall bath with shower. Air conditioning. $80.

The Rectory. This charming home in a small village five miles west of Charlottesville was a church rectory. It is furnished with lovely antiques and has an English garden in the back. The guest room overlooking the formal rose garden has its own entrance and adjoining full bath. Air conditioning. No smoking allowed. $80.

Rolling Acres Farm. A lovely brick Colonial home in a wooded setting on a small farm, this guest house has two bedrooms with a hall bath upstairs. The house is furnished with many Victorian pieces. No smoking. Air conditioning. $68-72.

The Rutledge Place. These hosts are only the third family to own this elegant Virginia farmhouse built around 1840 with magnificent mountain views. The original brick structure has been left intact, adding only a bathroom wing. The guest accommodations are light and airy in the English basement and offer a large bedroom, a sitting room, and a full bath. The home is furnished with antiques from the hosts' family homes in the Valley of Virginia. The suite opens to a brick terrace and gardens facing the mountains. Full breakfast. Air conditioned. No smoking allowed. $125.

Upstairs Slave Quarters. A fascinating place to stay if guests want interesting decor with the privacy of their own entrance. There is a harmonious mixture of antiques and art objects. The guest suite consists of a sitting room with a fireplace and two bedrooms with bath (tub only). A sleeper-sofa in the sitting room for extra guests. Adjacent to the University of Virginia and fraternity row, it is especially convenient for university guests. Air conditioning. $120-130.

Westbury. Built around 1820, this antebellum plantation home is a beautiful reminder of what country living and southern hospitality are all about. Once a carriage stop between the James River and the Shenandoah Valley, Westbury now returns to the

NOTES: Credit cards accepted: A MasterCard; B Visa; C American Express; D Discover; E Diner's Club; F Other; 2 Personal checks accepted; 3 Lunch available; 4 Dinner available; 5 Open all year; 6 Pets welcome;

old tradition of welcoming travelers. In Batesville, a tiny community southwest of Charlottesville with a genuine country store, Westbury is only 20 minutes from Skyline Drive and the Appalachian Trail. A comfortable four-poster bed awaits in the guest room. Private hall bath. No air conditioning. $68-72.

Windrows Farm. This 200-year-old restored chestnut log cabin surrounded by large oak trees overlooks extensive vegetable and flower gardens, a pond, and lovely fields to stroll through. The cottage consists of one large room with a bed, a comfortable sitting area in front of the fireplace, a kitchen including a refrigerator, and a four-burner stove with an oven and a broiler, and a bathroom. There is a porch for rocking and picnicking. Breakfast supplies are left for guests. Window air conditioning. No smoking. No pets. $125-150.

High Meadows—Virginia's Vineyard Inn

Highmeadows Lane, Scottsville, 24590
(804) 286-2218; (800) 232-1832
e-mail: peterhmi@aol.com
www.highmeadows.com

Enchanting 19th-century European-style auberge with tastefully appointed spacious guest rooms, private baths, and period antiques. Two-room suites available. Several common rooms, fireplaces, and tranquility. Pastoral setting on 50 acres. Privacy, relaxing walks, and gourmet picnics. Virginia wine tasting and romantic candlelit dining nightly. Virginia Architectural Landmark. National Register of Historic Places. Two-night minimum stay on weekends and holidays. Closed December 24-25. One room is handicapped accessible.

High Meadows

Hosts: Peter Sushka, and Mary Jae Abbitt
Rooms: 14 (PB) $90.52-192.42
Full Breakfast
Credit Cards: A, B, C, D, F
Notes: 2, 4, 6, 7, 8, 9, 10, 11, 12, 13, 14

Inn at the Crossroads

The Inn at the Crossroads

P.O. Box 6519, 22906
(804) 979-6452

Listed in the National Register of Historic Places, the inn has been welcoming travelers since 1820. Today it continues this tradition, offering hospitality and comfort reminiscent of a bygone era. On four acres in the foothills of the Blue Ridge Mountains and convenient to Charlottesville, Monticello, and the Skyline Drive. Enjoy magnificent panoramic mountain views and a delicious country breakfast served in the keeping room.

Hosts: John and Maureen Deis
Rooms: 5 (PB) $85-115
Cottage: $125
Full Breakfast
Credit Cards: A, B
Notes: 2, 5, 7, 9, 10, 11, 12, 13, 14

The Inn at Monticello

Route 20 South, 118 Scottsville Road, 22902
(804) 979-3593; FAX (804) 296-1344
e-mail: innatmonticello@mindspring.com

Just two miles from Jefferson's Monticello, Michie Tavern, and Ash Lawn-Highland, the Inn at Monticello is the perfect place to rest and relax after visiting the historic sites in the area. The 1850 country manor house has five bedrooms, all with private baths, each decorated with antiques and fine reproductions. Each room has a special feature, such as a fireplace, porch, or romantic canopied beds. The comfortable elegance of the inn is enhanced by the gourmet breakfast served each morning, and the Virginia wine tasting offered each afternoon. Limited handicapped accessibility.

Hosts: Norm and Becky Lindway
Rooms: 5 (PB) $125-145
Full Breakfast
Credit Cards: A, B, C
Notes: 2, 5, 7, 9, 10, 12, 13, 14

The Inn at Monticello

The Mark Addy

56 Rodes Farm Drive, Nellysford, 22958
(804) 361-1101; (800) 278-2154
www.symweb.com/rockfish/mark.html

Dr. Everett's "most commanding estate in Nelson County" has been beautifully restored and lovingly appointed. The charming rooms and luxurious suites enjoy magnificent views of the beautiful Blue Ridge. The Mark Addy is between Charlottesville and Wintergreen Resort, to encourage either relaxation or adventure. Be surrounded by 12.5 acres of serenity and the romance of a bygone era. The elegant and imaginative "cuisine de grand-mère" will delight all tastes.

The Mark Addy

Hosts: John Storck Maddox; Saverio Anselmo
Rooms: 9 (PB) $90-135
Full Breakfast
Credit Cards: A, B
Notes: 2, 3, 4, 5, 7, 9, 10, 11, 12, 13, 14, 15

Mountain Meadows Bed and Breakfast

P.O. Box 4, Ivy, 22945
(804) 977-6855; (800) 395-5074

Charming bedroom suite with full bath. View of lovely secluded water garden on one side and the spectacular Blue Ridge Mountains on the other. Peaceful country setting, a short drive to Charlottesville, the University of Virginia, Monticello, Ash Lawn, vineyards, and Wintergreen ski resort. Private fishing and nature walks available on the property.

Host: Sarah Churchill
Room: 1 (PB) $70
Full and Continental Breakfast
Credit Cards: A, B
Notes: 2, 5, 7, 10, 12, 13, 15

Palmer Country Manor

Route 2, Box 1390, 22963
(800) 253-4306; FAX (804) 589-1300

A gracious 1830 estate on 180 secluded acres, Palmer Country Manor is only min-

NOTES: Credit cards accepted: A MasterCard; B Visa; C American Express; D Discover; E Diner's Club; F Other; 2 Personal checks accepted; 3 Lunch available; 4 Dinner available; 5 Open all year; 6 Pets welcome;

utes from historic Charlottesville; Monticello, Thomas Jefferson's beloved home; Ash Lawn, home of James Monroe; Michie Tavern, one of Virginia's oldest homesteads; and some of Virginia's finest wineries. Come and enjoy one of 10 private cottages. Each features a living area with fireplace, color TV, private bath, and a deck. On the grounds, enjoy the swimming pool, five miles of trails, and the fishing pond; use one of the bikes; or take a hot-air balloon ride. Golf is available nearby.

Hosts: Gregory and Kathleen Palmer
Rooms: 12 (10 PB: 2 SB) $85-300
Full Breakfast
Credit Cards: A, B, C, D, E
Notes: 2, 3, 4, 5, 8, 9, 11, 12, 14

Silver Thatch Inn

3001 Hollymead Drive, 22911
(804) 978-4686

The inn is a rambling white clapboard home dating from 1780. Its three dining rooms and seven guest rooms offer a relaxing retreat on the outskirts of Charlottesville. Modern American cuisine is served using the freshest of ingredients. The menu features grilled meats, poultry, game in season, and there is always a vegetarian selection. The inn provides a wonderful respite for the sophisticated traveler who enjoys fine food and a quiet, caring atmosphere.

Silver Thatch Inn

Hosts: Vince and Rita Scoffone
Rooms: 7 (PB) $115-150
Continental Breakfast
Credit Cards: A, B, C, E
Notes: 2, 4, 5, 7, 8, 9, 10, 11, 12, 14

200 South Street Inn

200 South Street, 22902
(804) 979-0200; (800) 964-7008
FAX (804) 979-4403

Lovely restored inn, garden terrace, sweeping veranda, in historic downtown Charlottesville, with English and Belgian antiques, six Jacuzzis, 11 fireplaces, and canopied and four-poster beds. Continental breakfast and afternoon tea (with wine) and canapés. Just four miles to Monticello and one mile to the University of Virginia.

Hosts: Brendan and Jenny Clancy
Rooms: 20 (PB) $100-200
Continental Breakfast
Credit Cards: A, B, C, E
Notes: 2, 5, 7, 8, 9, 10, 12, 13, 14, 15

CHATHAM

Eldon—The Inn at Chatham

1037 Chalk Level Road, State Road 685, 24531
(804) 432-0935

Classically restored 1835 historic plantation manor home. One-half mile from Chatham, "Virginia's prettiest town." Four guest rooms, private baths, and full gourmet country breakfast. Formal garden, wooded country setting with original dependencies (smokehouse, ice house, and servants' cottage). In-ground swimming pool, pergola. Intimate gourmet restaurant with a Culinary Institute of America graduate as chef and CHIC graduate as pastry chef. Former home of Virginia's governor and U.S. secretary of the navy, Claude A. Swanson. Member BBAV. Smoking restricted.

Hosts: Joy and Bob Lemm
Rooms: 4 (3 PB; 1 SB) $65-130
Full Breakfast
Credit Cards: A, B
Notes: 2, 4, 5, 7, 9, 10, 11, 12, 14

CHESTER

"Second Wind" Bed and Breakfast

289 Grafton Street, P.O. Box 348, 05143
(802) 875-3438

Quiet, Victorian farmhouse—comfortably applied. Two suites with queen-size beds, private sitting rooms, cable TV, and air conditioning; one common living room. A sumptuous breakfeast and warm hospitality. A short walk to Chester's main street green, and lovely restaurants. Southern exposure, wraparound deck bedecked with flowers and plants. Three inn dogs. "We're not fancy but a great place to hang your hat. Welcome!" Children 12 and older welcome.

Hosts: Stephen and Sieglinde "Siggy" Wrobel
Rooms: 3 (2 PB; 1 SB) $70
Full Breakfast
Credit Cards: None
Notes: 2, 5, 7, 9, 10, 11, 12, 13

CHINCOTEAGUE

Amanda's Bed and Breakfast Reservation Service

1428 Park Avenue, Baltimore, MD 21217-4230
(410) 225-0001; (800) 899-7533
FAX (410) 728-8957; e-mail:amandasrs@aol.com
www.amandas-bbrs.com

362. Island visitors can enjoy this seaside restored Victorian while sitting on the porch with a cool breeze. The ponies on the island are a must-see along with the many birds and animals at the national wildlife refuge. Rooms are air conditioned should the weather not cooperate. Each room is decorated with antiques, most with private baths. A full breakfast is served as well as afternoon tea. Seasonal rates. $95-135.

363. Peaceful elegance with beautifully furnished guest rooms, each with a private bath and air conditioning. Some rooms have a view of the water. Chincoteague means "Beautiful land across the water." Walk, cycle, sun, swim, gather seashells, fish, or go boating. Afternoon tea. Chincoteague is a national park and guests must drive out to the park areas and beach. $85-135.

369. In town but just a short drive or bike ride to the beach and wildlife area. Walk to shops and restaurants. Charming and romantic ambiance. A brick courtyard, fountains, and a rose garden enhance this large shore home. Rooms are furnished with antiques and art from the 18th and 19th centuries. Once two houses now joined to create one rambling bed and breakfast. $90-150.

Cedar Gables Seaside Inn

6095 Hopkins Lane, P.O. Box 1006, 23336
(757) 336-1096; (888) 491-2944
FAX (757) 336-1291
e-mail: cdrgbl@shore.intercom.net
www.intercom.net/user/cdrgbl

Cedar Gables Seaside Inn is a romantic waterfront bed and breakfast overlooking picturesque Assateague Island. The inn has upscale amenities such as a heated swimming pool, hot tub, dock, secluded shade garden, etc. The rooms all have Jacuzzi tubs, fireplaces, telephones, central heat and air conditioning, TVs, VCRs, exterior and interior entrances, and decks overlooking the water. A must for the discriminating traveler.

Hosts: Fred and Claudia Greenway
Rooms: 4 (PB) $125-195
Full Breakfast
Credit Cards: A, B, C, D
Notes: 2, 7, 9, 10, 11, 12, 14

The Channel Bass Inn

The Channel Bass Inn

6228 Church Street, 23336
(757) 336-6148; (800) 249-0818
FAX (757) 336-0600

This imposing house was built in 1892 and became the Channel Bass Inn during the 1920s. Today this elegant Chincoteague landmark has six guest rooms, beautifully furnished, spacious, and quiet. Some rooms have view of Chincoteague Bay; all have comfortable sitting areas for reading and relaxing. Afternoon tea, with "world-famous" scones, and a full breakfast included. Close to wildlife refuge and unspoiled beaches of Assateague Island. Bicycles and beach equipment available for guests' use. Mobil two-star rating. Tea room open to public. Nonsmoking. Children eight and older welcome.

Hosts: David and Barbara Wiedenheft
Rooms: 6 (PB) $89-175
Full Breakfast
Credit Cards: A, B, D
Notes: 2, 7, 9, 10, 11, 12, 14

The Garden and the Sea Inn

Virginia Eastern Shore, Route 710
P. O. Box 275, New Church, 23415
(757) 824-0672

Casual elegance and warm hospitality in a charming Victorian inn near Chincoteague and beautiful Assateague wildlife refuges and the beach. Large, luxurious rooms, romantically designed with custom beds, designer fabrics, stained glass, oriental rugs, bay windows, private baths, and skylights. Suites with whirlpools, walk-in showers, and TVs. Hearty Continental breakfast. Romantic, candlelit gourmet dinners created by chef and innkeeper Tom Baker. Patio, gardens, porches. Boating, tennis, and golf nearby. Handicapped suite available. Mobil three-star-rated. Smoking permitted in designated areas only. Inquire about accommodations for children.

Hosts: Tom and Sara Baker
Rooms: 6 (PB) $60-165
Continental Breakfast
Credit Cards: A, B, C, D
Notes: 2, 4, 6, 9, 10, 11, 12, 14, 15

The Garden and the Sea Inn

Inn At Poplar Corner

4248 Main Street, 23336
(757) 336-6115; (800) 336-6787
FAX (757) 336-5776

The Inn At Poplar Corner is a romantically decorated Victorian home, with marbletop tables and dressers, high-back walnut beds, and lace curtains. All guest rooms feature whirlpool tubs and are air conditioned for guests' comfort. After enjoying the free use of bicycles to tour Chincoteague National Wildlife Refuge and beach, guests can enjoy afternoon tea on the wraparound

7 No smoking; 8 Children welcome; 9 Social drinking allowed; 10 Tennis nearby; 11 Swimming nearby; 12 Golf nearby; 13 Skiing nearby; 14 May be booked through a travel agent; 15 Handicapped accessible.

Inn at Poplar Corner

veranda featuring wicker rockers, tables, and chairs. Full breakfast.

Room: 4 (PB) $99-149
Full Breakfast
Credit Cards: A, B
Notes: 2, 7, 9, 10, 11, 12

Miss Molly's Inn

4141 Main Street, 23336
(757) 336-6686; (800) 221-5620
FAX (757) 336-0600
e-mail: msmolly@shore.intercom.net

Built in 1886, Miss Molly's Inn is a charming Victorian on the bay, two miles from Chincoteague National Wildlife Refuge and five miles from Assateague National Seashore. All rooms are air conditioned and furnished with period antiques. Room rate includes a traditional English afternoon tea (with Barbara's superlative scones) and a full breakfast. Marguerite Henry stayed in this grand old home while writing *Misty of Chincoteague*. Complimentary bicycles and beach equipment. Mobil two-star rating. Nonsmoking. Children eight and older welcome.

Miss Molly's Inn

Hosts: David and Barbara Wiedenheft
Rooms: 7 (5 PB: 2 SB) $69-155
Full Breakfast
Credit Cards: A, B, D
Notes: 2, 7, 9, 10, 11, 12, 14

The Watson House

The Watson House

4240 North Main Street, 23336
(757) 336-1564; (800) 336-6787 (reservations)
FAX (757) 336-5776

The Watson House has been tastefully restored with Victorian charm. Nestled in the heart of Chincoteague, the home is within walking distance of shops and restaurants. Each room has been comfortably decorated, including air conditioning, private baths, and antiques. A full, hearty breakfast and afternoon tea are served in the dining room or on the veranda. Enjoy free use of bicycles to tour the island. Chincoteague National Wildlife Refuge and its beach are two minutes away, offering nature trails, surf, and Chincoteague's famous wild ponies. AAA-rated three diamonds. Smoking restricted. Inquire about accommodations for children.

Hosts: David and Jo Anne Snead and
Tom and Jacque Derrickson
Rooms: 6 (PB) $69-109
Full Breakfast
Credit Cards: A, B
Notes: 2, 7, 9, 10, 11, 12, 14

CHRISTIANSBURG

The Oaks Victorian Inn

311 East Main Street, 24073
(540) 381-1500; (800) 336-6257 (reservations)
FAX (540) 381-3036; www.bbhost.com/theoaksinn
www.innbook.com/oaks.html

Award-winning Queen Anne inn, listed in the National Register of Historic Places. Warm hospitality, comfortable, relaxed elegance, and memorable breakfasts are the hallmark of the Oaks. Antique-filled rooms with fireplaces, Jacuzzis, and canopied king- or queen-size beds. Surrounded by lawns, perennial gardens, and 300-year-old oak trees, the inn faces Main Street, once part of the Wilderness Trail blazed by Daniel Boone and Davy Crockett. Near Roanoke and the Blue Ridge Parkway. Mountain winery tours nearby, hiking, bike trails, golf, tennis, fishing, antiquing, and historic sites in the area. AAA four-diamond award for three consecutive years. Member of Independent Innkeepers Associations.

Hosts: Margaret and Tom Ray
Rooms: 7 (PB) $115-160
Full Breakfast
Credit Cards: A, B, C, D
Notes: 2, 5, 7, 9, 10, 12, 14

CLUSTER SPRINGS

Oak Grove Plantation

1245 Cluster Springs Road, P.O. Box 45, 24535
(804) 575-7137

Operated from May to September by descendants of the family who built the house in 1820. Full country breakfast in the Victorian dining room. Hiking, biking, bird watching, and wildflower walks on 400 acres of grounds. Near Buggs Island for swimming, boating, and fishing; Danville to tour the last capital of the Confederacy; and Appomattox. One hour north of Raleigh-Durham. One handicapped accessible room.

Host: Pickett Craddock
Rooms: 4 (1 PB; 3 SB) $55-120

Oak Grove Plantation

Full Breakfast
Credit Cards: None
Notes: 2, 4, 8, 9, 10, 11, 12, 14

COLUMBIA

Upper Byrd Farm Bed and Breakfast

6452 River Road West, 23038
(804) 842-2240

A turn-of-the-century farmhouse nestled in the Virginia countryside on 26 acres overlooking the James River. Enjoy fishing or tubing. Canoe rentals available. Visit Ash Lawn and Monticello plantations. See the state's capitol, or simply relax by the fire surrounded by antiques and original art from around the world. Breakfast is special. Children 12 and older welcome. Open on weekends only in winter. Winter Green skiing area is one hour away.

Hosts: Ivona Kaz-Jespen and Maya Laurinaitis
Rooms: 4 (SB) $70
Full Breakfast
Credit Cards: None
Notes: 2, 7, 9, 11, 12, 14

COVINGTON

Milton Hall Bed and Breakfast Inn

207 Thorny Lane, 24426
(540) 965-0196

Milton Hall Bed and Breakfast Inn is a Virginia Historic Landmark, listed in the

Milton Hall

National Register of Historic Places. This country manor house, built by English nobility in 1874, is on 44 acres adjoining the George Washington National Forest and one mile from I-64, exit 10. Spacious rooms are decorated in the style of the period. Rooms feature queen-size beds, private baths, and sitting areas. All guest rooms, as well as common rooms, have fireplaces.

Hosts: John and Vera Eckert
Rooms: 6 (PB) $75-140
Full Breakfast
Credit Cards: A, B, D
Notes: 2, 3, 5, 6, 8, 9, 10, 11, 12, 13, 14

CULPEPER

Fountain Hall Bed and Breakfast

609 South East Street, 22701-3222
(540) 825-8200; (800) 29-VISIT
e-mail: fhbnb@aol.com

A warm welcome awaits guests. This grand bed and breakfast is highlighted with beautiful antiques, spacious rooms, and formal gardens. Relax on own private porch, stroll the grounds, or curl up with a good book. Enjoy a filling breakfast featuring freshly baked croissants, fresh fruits, yogurt and berries, brewed coffee, and more. On the historic walking tour. Attractions: wineries, hiking, biking, canoeing, museum, battlefields, antique/craft shops, Skyline Drive, Montpelier. Golf and dinner packages. Mobil three-star- and AAA three-diamond-rated. BBAV approved.

Hosts: Steve and Kathi Walker
Rooms: 6 (PB) $95-150
Continental Breakfast
Credit Cards: A, B, C, D, E, F
Notes: 2, 5, 7, 12, 13, 14, 15

DRAPER

Claytor Lake Homestead Inn

Route 651, Brown Road, Route 1, Box 184 E5, 24324
(540) 980-6777; (800) 676-LAKE

The inn originated as a two-room log cabin over a century ago. The old Doc Brown house was renovated in 1990. The inn has six guest rooms, four overlooking the lake. The inn offers boating, fishing, and summer swimming on its own beach. Rooms are decorated with antiques, reproductions, and period furnishings from the old Hotel Roanoke. A full country breakfast is served in the dining room overlooking the lake. The inn is only a mile from the New River hiking, biking, and horse trail. The Draper golf course is five miles away. There are 550 feet of waterfront with private sand beach, fishing, and boating. Antique shops are nearby in Pulaski.

Rooms: 5 (1 PB: 4 SB) $70-85
Full Breakfast
Credit Cards: A, B, C, D
Notes: 2, 4, 5, 7, 8, 9, 11, 12, 13, 14, 15

EDINBURG

Edinburg Inn Bed and Breakfast, Ltd.

218 South Main Street, 22824
(540) 984-8286

This circa 1850 Victorian home is in the heart of the Shenandoah Valley on the edge of town next to Stoney Creek and the Edinburg Mill Restaurant. The inn is reminiscent of Grandma's country home, with a full country breakfast which includes homemade

Edinburg Inn

breads and muffins, local country eggs, bacon and sausage. Enjoy outdoor games on spacious grounds and wraparound porch with swing, rockers, and wicker. Walk to nearby restaurant and antique and craft shops. Short drive to caverns, battlefields, fishing, hiking, canoeing, horseback riding, and vineyards. Reservations appreciated.

Hosts: Judy and Clyde Beachy
Rooms: 3 (PB) $75
Full Breakfast
Credit Cards: None
Notes: 2, 5, 7, 8, 9, 10, 11, 12, 13

FAIRFAX

The Bailiwick Inn

4023 Chain Bridge Road, 22030
(703) 691-2266; (800) 366-7666
www.bailiwickinn.com

In the heart of the historic city of Fairfax, 15 miles west of the nation's capital. George Mason University is just down the street,

The Bailiwick Inn

and Mount Vernon and Civil War battlefields are nearby. In the National Register of Historic Places. Fourteen rooms with queen-size feather beds and private baths, fireplaces, Jacuzzis, and bridal suite. Afternoon tea. Candlelight dinner served by reservation. Small meetings and weddings.

Hosts: Annette and Bob Bradley
Rooms: 14 (PB) $130-299
Full Breakfast
Credit Cards: A, B, C
Notes: 2, 4, 5, 7, 8, 10, 11, 12, 14

FOREST

The Summer Kitchen at West Manor

3594 Elkton Farm Road, 24551
(804) 525-0923

Come enjoy a romantic English country cottage on a beautiful working dairy farm. This private, restored summer kitchen, circa 1840, sleeps four with fireplace, loft, sunroom, and Jacuzzi. Enjoy a full country breakfast while overlooking 600 acres of rolling cropland, pastures, cattle, and mountains. Afternoon tea and strolls through the gardens complete each day. Come escape to this country haven. Area interests include Thomas Jefferson's Poplar Forest, antique shops, and Blue Ridge Mountains.

Hosts: Sharon and Greg Lester
Cottage: 1 (PB) $115-150
Full Breakfast
Credit Cards: None
Notes: 2, 5, 7, 9, 14

FREDERICKSBURG

Amanda's Bed and Breakfast Reservation Service

1428 Park Avenue, Baltimore, MD 21217-4230
(410) 225-0001; (800) 899-7533
FAX (410) 728-8957; e-mail:amandasrs@aol.com
www.amandas-bbrs.com

310. Combine a visit to the Civil War sites between Antietam-Gettysburg and

Fredericksburg. A Classical Revival-style home with high ceilings, wide heart-of-pine floors, acorn and oak leaf moldings, and a two-story front portico. On 10 acres of grounds filled with a fine balance of mature trees and a pond. Two rooms, each with a private bath. Full breakfast served. $95.

La Vista Plantation

4420 Guinea Station Road, 22408
(540) 898-8444; (800) 529-2823
FAX (540) 898-9414; e-mail: lavistabb@aol.com
www.bbonline.com/va/lavista/

This lovely 1838 Classical Revival home is just outside historic Fredericksburg. On 10 quiet acres, the grounds present a fine balance of mature trees, flowers, shrubs, and farm fields. The pond is stocked with bass. Choose from a spacious two-bedroom apartment that sleeps six with a kitchen and a fireplace, or a formal room with a king-size mahogany rice-carved four-poster bed, fireplace, and Empire furniture. Homemade jams and farm-fresh eggs for breakfast.

Hosts: Michele and Edward Schiesser
Rooms: 1 (PB) $105
Apartment: 1
Full Breakfast
Credit Cards: A, B
Notes: 2, 5, 7, 8, 9, 10, 12, 14

FRONT ROYAL

Chester House

43 Chester Street, 22630
(540) 635-3937; (800) 621-0441
FAX (540) 636-8695
www.chesterhouse.com

A stately Georgian mansion with extensive formal gardens on two acres in Front Royal's historic district. Quiet, relaxed atmosphere in elegant surroundings, often described as an oasis in the heart of town. Easy walking distance to antique and gift shops and historic attractions; a short drive to Skyline Caverns, Skyline Drive, Shenandoah River, golf, tennis, hiking, skiing, horseback riding, fine wineries, and excellent restaurants.

Hosts: Bill and Ann Wilson
Rooms: 7 (5 PB; 2 SB) $65-190
Continental Breakfast
Credit Cards: A, B, C
Notes: 2, 5, 9, 10, 11, 12, 13, 14

Killahevlin

1401 North Royal Avenue, 22630
(540) 636-7335; (800) 847-6132
FAX (540) 636-8694; e-mail: kllhvln@shentel.net
www.vairish.com

Historic Edwardian mansion with spectacular views. Spacious bedrooms, professionally designed and restored with working fireplaces, private baths, and whirlpool tubs. Private Irish pub for guests. Complimentary beer and wine. Close to Skyline Drive, Shenandoah National Park, hiking, golf, tennis, canoeing, horseback riding, antiquing, fine dining, wineries, and live theater. Property was built in 1905 for William E. Carson, father of Skyline Drive. National Register of Historic Places and Virginia landmarks register.

Hosts: Susan and John Lang
Rooms: 6 (PB) $115-195

Killahevlin

NOTES: Credit cards accepted: A MasterCard; B Visa; C American Express; D Discover; E Diner's Club; F Other; 2 Personal checks accepted; 3 Lunch available; 4 Dinner available; 5 Open all year; 6 Pets welcome;

Full Breakfast
Credit Cards: A, B, C, D, E, F
Notes: 2, 5, 7, 9, 10, 11, 12, 14

GOODVIEW

Stone Manor Bed and Breakfast

1135 Stone Manor Place, 24095
(540) 297-1414

On beautiful Smith Mountain Lake—690 feet of waterfront, lighted boardwalk, dockage for boats, fishing, in-ground swimming pool, all-season sunroom boasting a panoramic view of the lake. Golf close by. Resort-like atmosphere. Guest rooms highlight themes of the lake activities. Magnificent lake views and sunset. Near Roanoke and Blue Ridge Parkway. Children over 12 welcome.

Rooms: 3 (PB) $85-105
Credit Cards: A, B, D
Notes: 2, 5, 7, 9, 11, 12, 14

LANCASTER

The Inn at Levelfields

10155 Mary Ball Road (State Route 3), P.O. Box 216, 22503-0216
(804) 435-6887; (800) 238-5578
FAX (804) 435-7440

A gracious antebellum manor house in the historic northern neck of Virginia. Notable features of the inn are its graceful and lofty proportions, spaciousness of its guest rooms, with king- or queen-size beds, each with a private bath and fireplace. There is a large swimming pool for guests. Championship golf, antiquing, and Tangier and Smith Island cruises in the Chesapeake Bay a short drive

The Inn at Levelfields

away. A gourmet breakfast is included and served in the formal dining room. Levelfields is the perfect place for a romantic getaway.

Rooms: 4 (PB) $95
Full Breakfast
Credit Cards: A, B, C
Notes: 2, 5, 7, 9, 11, 12

LEESBURG

The Norris House Inn

The Norris House Inn and Stonehouse Tea Room

108 Loudoun Street, SW, 20175-2909
(703) 777-1806; (800) 644-1806
FAX (703) 771-8051; e-mail: inn@norrishouse.com
www.norrishouse.com

Elegant accommodations in the heart of historic Leesburg. The six charming guest rooms are all furnished with antiques, and three of the rooms have working fireplaces. Full country breakfasts served and evening libations served. Convenient in-town location with several restaurants nearby. Only one hour's drive to Washington, D.C. In the heart of the Virginia hunt country, rich in colonial and Civil War history. Lots of antiquing and wineries. The perfect place for special romantic getaways, small meetings, and weddings. The inn is open daily by reservation. Children over 12 are welcome.

Hosts: Pam and Don McMurray
Rooms: 6 (SB) $95-140

Full Breakfast
Credit Cards: A, B, C, D, E, F
Notes: 2, 5, 7, 9, 10, 11, 12, 14

LEXINGTON

Applewood Inn

Buffalo Bend Road, P.O. Box 1348, 24450
(540) 463-1962

Spectacular passive solar country retreat on 35 hilltop acres between the Shenandoah Valley's historic Lexington and Natural Bridge with views of the Blue Ridge Mountains. Romantics and nature lovers alike enjoy the huge porches, quilt-covered queen-size beds, private baths, hot tub, hiking trails, picnic llama treks, poolside barbecues, and hearty whole-grain country breakfasts. Nearby are museums, Washington and Lee University, Virginia Military Institute, the Virginia Horse Center, summer theater, and wonderful scenic back roads.

Hosts: Linda and Chris Best
Rooms: 4 (PB) $80-125
Full Breakfast
Credit Cards: A, B, C
Notes: 2, 3, 5, 6, 7, 8, 9, 11, 12, 15

A Bed and Breakfast at Llewellyn Lodge

603 South Main Street, 24450
(540) 463-3235; (800) 882-1145
e-mail: LLL@rockbridge.net; www.llodge.com

The great in-town location of this charming Colonial, combined with the warm and friendly atmosphere, makes it the perfect home base for exploring this historic town. Ellen and John are "personalized guidebooks" in helping guests get the most out of their visit. Refreshments are served upon arrival and guests receive lots of advice on hiking, cycling, fly-fishing, and other outdoor activities. A full breakfast is served including Belgian waffles, Ellen's special omelets, meats, and homemade muffins. The decor combines traditional with antique furnishings. Walking distance to Lee Chapel, Stonewall Jackson House, Washington and Lee University, and Virginia Military Institute.

Hosts: Ellen and John Roberts
Rooms: 6 (PB) $65-98
Full Breakfast
Credit Cards: A, B, C, D
Notes: 2, 5, 7, 9, 10, 11, 12, 14

Brierly Hill Country Inn

985 Borden Road, 24450
(800) 422-4925; FAX (540) 464-8925
e-mail: cspeton@cfw.com; www.brierleyhill.com

Charming romantic country inn on eight acres of country quiet five minutes from historic Lexington. Magnificent views of Blue Ridge Mountains and Shenandoah Valley. Recently voted One of the Top 25 Inns in USA by *American Favorite Inns.* Chosen for the high standards of hospitality, cleanliness, comfort, food, and decor. Packages, corporate rates, and midweek discounts available.

Hosts: Barry and Carole Speton
Rooms: 5 (PB) $90-140
Full Breakfast
Credit Cards: A, B
Notes: 2, 4, 5, 7, 9, 11, 12, 14

Historic Country Inns

11 North Main Street, 24450
(540) 463-2044; FAX (540) 463-7262

Three historic homes restored and furnished with antiques, paintings, and amenities. In center of historic district are Alexander-Withrow, circa 1789, and McCampbell Inn, circa 1809. Museums, shops, Virginia Military Institute, and Washington and Lee University within walking distance. Maple Hall, circa 1850, six miles north of Lexington at the intersection of I-81 and Route 11, offers tennis, swimming, fishing, trails, and working fireplaces. Nightly dining for inn guests and public. Smoking permitted in designated areas only. Limited handicapped accessible.

Hosts: Don Fredenburg (innkeeper); Meredith Family (owners)
Rooms: 44 (PB)
Continental Breakfast

Credit Cards: A, B
Notes: 2, 4, 5, 8, 9, 10, 11, 14

The Hummingbird Inn

The Hummingbird Inn

30 Wood Lane, P.O.Box 147, Goshen, 24439
(540) 997-9065; (800) 397-3214
e-mail: hmgbird@cfw.com
www.hummingbirdinn.com

On a tranquil acre of landscaped grounds, the Hummingbird Inn, a unique carpenter Gothic villa, offers accommodations in an early Victorian setting. Comfortable rooms are furnished with antiques and combine an old-fashioned ambiance with modern convenience. Some have whirlpool tubs and fireplaces. Architectural features include wraparound verandas on the first and second floors, original pine floors of varying widths, a charming rustic den dating from the early 1800s, and a solarium. A wide trout stream defines one of the property lines, and the old red barn was once the town livery. Full breakfasts include unique area recipes.

Hosts: Diana and Jerry Robinson
Rooms: 5 (PB) $75-125
Full Breakfast
Credit Cards: A, B, C, D
Notes: 2, 4, 5, 6, 7, 9, 13, 14

Stoneridge Bed and Breakfast

Stoneridge Lane, P.O. Box 38, 24450
(540) 463-4090; (800) 491-2930
FAX (540) 463-6078
www.webfeat-inc.com/stoneridge

Get reacquainted at this romantic 1829 antebellum home on 26 secluded acres. Five guest rooms with private baths, ceiling fans, and queen-size beds, some featuring private balconies, double Jacuzzis, and fireplaces. Relax on the large front porch and enjoy the sunset over Short Hills mountains. Virginia wines are available and a full country breakfast is served in the candlelit dining room or on the back patio. Central air conditioning. Just five minutes south of historic Lexington.

Hosts: Norm and Barbara Rollenhagen
Rooms: 5 (PB) $115-160
Full Breakfast
Credit Cards: A, B, C, D
Notes: 2, 5, 7, 8, 9, 14

LINCOLN

Springdale Country Inn

22078
(540) 338-1832; (800) 388-1832
FAX (540) 338-1839

Restored historic landmark 45 miles west of Washington, D.C., on six acres of secluded terrain with babbling brooks, foot bridges, and terraced gardens. Meal service for groups; breakfast included in room price. Fully air conditioned. New heating system and seven fireplaces.

Host: Nancy and Roger Fones
Rooms: 9 (6 PB; 3 SB) $95-200
Full Breakfast
Credit Cards: A, B, D
Notes: 2, 5, 7, 8, 9, 11, 12, 15

LOCUSTVILLE

Amanda's Bed and Breakfast Reservation Service

1428 Park Avenue, Baltimore, MD 21217-4230
(410) 225-0001; (800) 899-7533
FAX (410) 728-8957; e-mail:amandasrs@aol.com
www.amandas-bbrs.com

143. This 18th-century Colonial is near Wachapreague and just one mile from the ocean. Quiet and comfortable. Water sports nearby. One room with double bed and private bath. Continental breakfast. $85.

LURAY

Locust Grove Inn

1456 North Egypt Bend Road, 22835
(540) 743-1804; e-mail: locustg@shentel.net
www.bbonline.com/va/locustgrove/

A time away, a place away—here mountains end, a valley starts, a river runs by. Unforgettable scenery and centuries of history make this restored colonial log house on a large farm a piece of paradise for history and nature lovers. Five spacious bedrooms, all with private bathrooms, central air conditioning, and beautiful views. Three miles west of Luray on the Shenandoah River. One mile of Shenandoah riverfront.

Hosts: Rod and Isabel Graves
Rooms: 5 (PB) $110-125
Full Breakfast
Credit Cards: A, B, D
Notes: 2, 5, 7, 8, 9, 10, 11, 12, 13, 14

The Woodruff House Bed and Breakfast

330 Mechanic Street, 22835
(540) 743-1494

This 1882 fairy-tale Victorian is beautifully appointed with period antiques, hallmarked silver, and fine china. Each room includes working fireplace and private bathroom. Some rooms have Jacuzzi tubs for two. Escape from reality, come into this fairytale where the ambiance never ends! Awaken to a choice of freshly brewed coffees (22 blends) delivered to guests' door; a gourmet candlelit breakfast follows. Sumptuous candlelit high tea buffet dinner included. Relax in the fireside candlelit garden spa. Complimentary canoes and bicycles. Inquire about accommodations for children.

The Woodruff House

Hosts: Lucas and Deborah Woodruff
Rooms: 6 (PB) $98-195
Full Breakfast
Credit Cards: A, B, D
Notes: 2, 4, 5, 7, 9, 10, 11, 12, 13, 14

LYNCHBURG

1880's Madison House Bed and Breakfast

413 Madison Street, 24504
(804) 528-1503; (800) 828-6422
e-mail: madison@lynchburg.net
www.bbhost.com/1880s-madison

Lynchburg's finest Victorian bed and breakfast, circa 1880, boasts a magnificent, authentic interior decor. Civil War library. Spacious, elegantly appointed guest rooms graced with antiques, private baths, plush robes, and linens. Some rooms have working fireplaces. Full breakfast served on antique Limoges and Wedgwood china; afternoon tea included. Central air, in-room cable TVs, in-room private-line telephones, and off-street parking. Near RMWC, Liberty University, and Lynchburg College. Mobil three-star rating.

Hosts: Irene and Dale Smith
Rooms: 3 (PB) $89-119
Suite: 1 (PB)
Full Breakfast
Credit Cards: A, B, C
Notes: 2, 5, 7, 9, 10, 11, 12, 13, 14

Federal Crest Inn Bed and Breakfast

1101 Federal Street, 24504
(804) 845-6155; (800) 818-6155
FAX (804) 845-1445
www.inmind.com/federalcrest

Relax and unwind in this elegant 1909 Georgian Revival brick home in a historical district. Enjoy unique woodwork, bedroom fireplaces, central air, down comforters, whirlpool tub, canopied queen beds, '50s café, gift shop, antiques, country breakfasts, friendly hosts, and much more! Perhaps there might even be a special invitation to visit the third-floor theater where the original owner built a stage for his children to give plays. Convenient to Jefferson's Poplar Forest and Appomattox.

Hosts: Ann and Phil Ripley
Rooms: 5 (4 PB; 1 SB) $85-125
Full Breakfast
Credit Cards: A, B, C, D
Notes: 2, 5, 7, 9, 12, 13, 14

Federal Crest Inn

Lynchburg Mansion Inn Bed and Breakfast

405 Madison Street, 24504
(804) 528-5400; (800) 352-1199

Enjoy luxurious accommodations in a 9,000-square-foot Spanish Georgian mansion on a street still paved in turn-of-the-century brick in a national register historic district. Highly rated inn, known for attention to detail. Remarkable interior cherry woodwork. King- and queen-size beds, lavish linens, private bathrooms, fireplaces, TV, telephones, turn-down with chocolates. Full silver service breakfast. Hot tub. Suites. Well-supervised children welcome.

Lynchburg Mansion Inn

Near Appomattox, Jefferson's Poplar Forest, summer baseball, Blue Ridge, antiquing, colleges.

Hosts: Bob and Mauranna Sherman
Rooms: 5 (PB) $109-144
Full Breakfast
Credit Cards: A, B, C, E
Notes: 2, 5, 7, 8, 9, 10, 11, 12, 14

MADISON

Guesthouses Bed and Breakfast

P.O. Box 5737, Charlottesville, 22905
(804) 979-7264 (12:00-5:00 P.M. weekdays)
FAX (804) 293-7791
e-mail: guesthouses_bnb_reservations@compuserve.com
www.va-guesthouses.com

Laurel Run. A recently built cottage in the woods of Madison County, 30 miles north of Charlottesville. This private cabin offers a great room, kitchen, dining area, and two bedrooms on the first floor. The loft has a double bed and cot. The broad, screened porch offers views of a stream, fields, and woods. Hiking, fishing, and riding are available in nearby Shenandoah National Park. Breakfast supplies are included for the first morning of guests' stay. $100-200.

7 No smoking; 8 Children welcome; 9 Social drinking allowed; 10 Tennis nearby; 11 Swimming nearby; 12 Golf nearby; 13 Skiing nearby; 14 May be booked through a travel agent; 15 Handicapped accessible.

MATHEWS

Ravenswood Inn

P.O. Box 1430, 23109
(804) 725-7272

A restored 1913 manor home on four acres features more than 1,000 feet of waterfront with beautiful panoramic views of Chesapeake's East River and Mobjack Bay. The area is ideal for biking with miles of serene countryside. Within an hour's drive to the historic and popular attractions of Williamsburg, Jamestown, and Yorktown.

Hosts: Ms. Ricky Durham and Ms. Sally Preston
Rooms: 5 (PB) $70-125
Full Breakfast
Credit Cards: None
Notes: 2, 5, 7, 9, 10, 11, 14

MEADOWS OF DAN

Meadowood Bed and Breakfast

Buffalo Mountain Road, Route 1, Box 28-H, 24120
(540) 593-2600; fax (540) 593-2700

Meadowood is just a short 1,000 feet off the Blue Ridge Parkway (near milepost 174) on 20 beautiful acres of fields and woods with views of the surrounding mountains. Peaceful and quiet, yet only two and one-half miles from the Chateau Morrisette Winery and two miles from famous Mabry Mill. Old split rail fences, spring-fed streams, park benches, and walking trails abound. A large den provides a fieldstone fireplace, library, and DDS satellite system/big screen TV. Reservations are suggested. "Just what a bed and breakfast should be"—*Blue Ridge Country.* "Delightful bed and breakfast just off the Blue Ridge Parkway"—*LA Times.* Children over 12 welcome.

Hosts: Frank and Leona Warren
Rooms: 4-5 (4 PB; 1-2 SB) $75-95
Full Breakfast
Credit Cards: None
Notes: 2, 5, 7, 9, 10, 12

Spangler's Bed and Breakfast

Route 2, Box 108, 24120
(703) 952-2454

On Country Road 602 within view of the Blue Ridge Parkway at milepost 180, four miles from Mabry Mill, this 1904 farmhouse has a kitchen with fireplace, piano, and four porches. There is also an 1826 private log cabin perfect for one couple. An additional 1987 log cabin has two bedrooms, complete kitchen, and wraparound porch. Fishing in the lake, swimming, three boats, bikes, and volleyball. No smoking inside. No pets.

Meadowood

NOTES: Credit cards accepted: A MasterCard; B Visa; C American Express; D Discover; E Diner's Club; F Other; 2 Personal checks accepted; 3 Lunch available; 4 Dinner available; 5 Open all year; 6 Pets welcome;

Hosts: Martha and Harold Spangler
Rooms: 7 (2 PB; 5 SB) $50-60
Continental Breakfast
Credit Cards: None
Notes: 2, 7, 8, 9, 10, 11, 12

MIDDLEBURG

The Longbarn

37129 Adams Green Lane, P.O. Box 208, 20118-0208
(540) 687-4137; FAX (504) 687-4044;
e-mail:thlongbarn@aol.com;
web: members.aol.com/thlongbarn/

Historic 100-year-old renovated barn in Middleburg surrounded by beautiful woods; European-style garden; swimming, horseback and bicycle riding nearby; golf course available. Air conditioning, fireplaces, and large library for guests' pleasure and comfort. Elegant ambiance in Italian country style; spacious bedrooms with private bath. Delicious breakfast with warm breads and other specialties from Europe. For guests' safety, no indoor smoking.

Host: Chiara Langeley
Rooms: 3 (PB) $100-125
Full Breakfast
Credit Cards: A, B, F
Notes: 2, 5, 7, 9, 10, 11, 12, 14

Middleburg Inn and Guest Suites

105 West Washington Street, P.O. Box 131, 20118
(540) 687-3115; (800) 432-6125

In the heart of hunt country, elegantly furnished living quarters for short- or long-term stays. Each centrally air-conditioned suite has a canopied bed, private bath, telephone, and color TV. Fresh cut flowers, cotton bathrobes, and a complimentary Continental breakfast at the Red Fox are a few of the extra touches that make a visit memorable.

Host: Marylin Bigelow
Room: 5 (PB) $130-195
Continental Breakfast
Credit Cards: A, B
Notes: 2, 5, 8, 9, 14

Welbourne

20117
(540) 687-3201

A seven-generation, antebellum plantation home in the middle of Virginia's fox-hunting country. On a 600-acre working farm. Full southern breakfasts, working fireplaces, and cottages. "Faded elegance." In the National Register of Historic Places.

Hosts: Nat and Sherry Morison
Rooms: 8 (PB) $64-96
Full Breakfast
Credit Cards: None
Notes: 2, 5, 6, 8, 9

MILLBORO

Fort Lewis Lodge

HCR 3, Box 21A, 24460
(540) 925-2314

At the heart of a 3,200-acre mountain plantation is a truly unique country inn. The main lodge features wildlife art and locally handcrafted Shaker-style furnishings. A silo with three bedrooms "in the round" and two historic hand-hewn log cabins with stone fireplaces are ideal for a romantic getaway. A vibrant mix of fresh tastes and interesting menus is served nightly in the historic Lewis Mill dining room.

Hosts: John and Caryl Cowden
Rooms: 13 (PB) $140-195 MAP
Cabins 2 (PB)
Full Breakfast
Credit Cards: A, B
Notes: 2, 3, 4, 7, 8, 9, 11, 12, 15

Fort Lewis Lodge

7 No smoking; 8 Children welcome; 9 Social drinking allowed; 10 Tennis nearby; 11 Swimming nearby; 12 Golf nearby; 13 Skiing nearby; 14 May be booked through a travel agent; 15 Handicapped accessible.

MOLLUSK

Guesthouses on the Water at Greenvale

Route 354, Box 70, 22517
(804) 462-5995

Two separate and private guest houses on 13 acres on the Rappahannock River and Greenvale Creek. Pool, dock, private beach, and bicycles. Each house is furnished with antiques and reproductions and has two bedrooms, two baths, living room, kitchen, and deck. Air conditioned. Enjoy sweeping water views, breathtaking sunsets, and relaxing and peaceful tranquility. Weekly rates available.

Hosts: Pam and Walt Smith
Guest Houses: 2 (PB) $85-125
Continental Breakfast
Credit Cards: A, B
Notes: 2, 5, 9, 11, 12

MONTEREY

Highland Inn

Main Street, P.O. Box 40, 24465
(703) 468-2143; (888) INN-INVA (466-4682)

Classic Victorian inn listed in the National Register of Historic Places. Tranquil location in the picturesque village of Monterey, nestled in the foothills of the Allegheny Mountains. There are 17 individually decorated rooms furnished with antiques and

Highland Inn

collectibles, each with private bath. Full-service dining room and tavern offer dinner Monday through Saturday and Sunday brunch. Antiquing, hiking, fishing, golf, and mineral baths are nearby.

Host: Michael Strand and Cynthia Peel
Rooms: 17 (PB) $55-85
Continental Breakfast
Credit Cards: A, B, C, D
Notes: 2, 4, 5, 8, 9, 11, 12, 13, 14

MOUNT JACKSON

Amanda's Bed and Breakfast Reservation Service

1428 Park Avenue, Baltimore, MD 21217-4230
(410) 225-0001; (800) 899-7533
FAX (410) 728-8957; e-mail:amandasrs@aol.com
www.amandas-bbrs.com

181. An 1830 Colonial homestead on seven acres overlooking the George Washington Mountains. Some bedrooms have wood-burning fireplaces, and the antique furniture is for sale. Pool on premises. Area activities include craft fairs, hiking, fishing, tennis, and horseback riding. Five rooms with private baths. Two guest cottages. Full breakfast. $65-85.

The Widow Kip's Country Inn

355 Orchard Drive, 22842-9753
(540) 477-2400; (800) 478-8714
e-mail: widowkips@shentel.net
www.widowkips.com

A stately 1830 Colonial on seven rural acres in the Shenandoah Valley overlooking the Blue Ridge Mountains. Romantic getaway, five rooms with fireplaces/antiques and two cottages. Locally crafted quilts adorn the four-poster, canopied, and sleigh beds. Civil War battlefields and museums, caverns, canoeing, hiking, horseback riding, golf, fishing, skiing, and pool. A comment by a recent guests: "You have set a standard of professional excellence, we will be back." Children welcome in cottages only.

Rooms: 7 (PB) $65-85
Full Breakfast
Credit Cards: A, B
Notes: 2, 5, 6, 7, 10, 11, 12, 13, 14

NATURAL BRIDGE

Burgers Country Inn

305 Rices Hill Road, 24578
(540) 291-2464

This historic inn is furnished in antiques and country collectibles. The rambling farmhouse with wraparound porch and large columns is on 10 wooded acres. Four guest rooms and three baths are available. Enjoy croquet in the summer and relax by the fire in the winter. Special Continental plus breakfast is included. Visit the Natural Bridge and historic Lexington. Beautiful Blue Ridge Parkway nearby. Call or write for brochure/reservations.

Hosts: John Burger and Mary
Rooms: 4 (2 PB; 2 SB) $60-65
Continental Breakfast
Credit Cards: None
Notes: 2, 5, 6, 8, 9, 11, 12

NELLYSFORD

Distinguished Accommodations in the Potomac Region

1428 Park Avenue, Baltimore, MD 21217-4230
(410) 728-DAPR (3277); (800) 360-DAPR (3277)
FAX (410) 728-8957; e-mail: amandasrs@aol.com
www.amandas-bbrs.com

516. Richness and romance of a bygone era, beautifully restored and lovingly appointed. Sitting atop a verdant knoll, this historic home is surrounded by the magnificence of the Blue Ridge Mountains. Charming rooms or luxurious suites offer elegant comfort, romantic privacy, and incredible views. Enjoy serenity and inspiring surroundings from any of the five porches, the hammock, or a peaceful spot on the 13 acres. Some rooms feature a double whirlpool bath or double sauna. Historic sites within a short drive or stay around the property for quiet contemplation. A delicious and satisfying gourmet breakfast is included. A prix fixe lunch or dinner is available by reservations. From $135.

Guesthouses Bed and Breakfast

P.O. Box 5737, Charlottesville 22905
(804) 979-7264 (12:00-5:00 P.M. weekdays)
FAX (804) 293-7791
e-mail: guesthouses_bnb_reservations@compuserve.com
www.va-guesthouses.com

The Mark Addy. Near Nellysford in the Rockfish Valley near the foot of Wintergreen, this inn has magnificent mountain views. Relax on one of the porches or in the library or parlor, or stroll around the beautiful grounds. This inn offers eight guest rooms or suites furnished with lovely antiques and collectibles, each with a private bath. Two rooms have Jacuzzis. A bountiful breakfast is served. Smoking outdoors on the porches only. Not suitable for children under 12. Air conditioned. $95-135.

Meander Inn. A 75-year-old Victorian farmhouse on 50 acres of pasture and woods skirted by hiking trails and traversed by the Rockfish River. The inn offers five twin or queen-size bedrooms, some with private baths. A delicious full country breakfast is served each morning. Guests may enjoy the hot tub, wood-burning stove, player piano, deck, or front porch. Wintergreen Resort and Stoney Creek golf and tennis facilities are available to guests. Smoking is permitted outdoors only. Air conditioning. $80-100.

Trillium House

P.O. Box 280, 22958
(804) 325-9126; (800) 325-9126
FAX (804) 325-1099

Trillium House was built in 1983 as a small 12-room country hotel. Relax in the great room, garden room, TV room, or

7 No smoking; 8 Children welcome; 9 Social drinking allowed; 10 Tennis nearby; 11 Swimming nearby; 12 Golf nearby; 13 Skiing nearby; 14 May be booked through a travel agent; 15 Handicapped accessible.

the outstanding library. Available to guests at preferred rates: two golf courses, swimming pool, 30 tennis courts, 25 miles of mapped hiking trails. The entry gate to the Wintergreen Mountain Village is one mile from the Blue Ridge Parkway; motorcycle restrictions. Dinner available Friday and Saturday.

Rooms: 12 (PB) $100-160
Full Breakfast
Credit Cards: A, B
Notes: 2, 5, 7, 8, 9, 10, 11, 12, 13, 14, 15

NEW CHURCH

Amanda's Bed and Breakfast Reservation Service

1428 Park Avenue, Baltimore, MD 21217-4230
(410) 225-0001; (800) 899-7533
FAX (410) 728-8957; e-mail:amandasrs@aol.com
www.amandas-bbrs.com

210. Twenty minutes from the most beautiful beaches on the East Coast and a star-rated restaurant. Elegant lodging with gourmet candlelit dining. Five rooms, some complete with Jacuzzi and canopied beds. Breakfast served in pleasant dining room. $125-155.

NORFOLK

Old Dominion Inn

4111 Hampton Boulevard, 23508
(757) 440-5100; (800) 653-9030

The Old Dominion Inn is a 60-room inn that takes its name from the Commonwealth of Virginia, "The Old Dominion." In the heart of Norfolk's west side, just one block south from the Old Dominion University campus, and only a short drive from downtown Norfolk.

Hosts: The James W. Sherrill Family
Rooms: 60 (PB) $66
Continental Breakfast
Credit Cards: A, B, C, D, E
Notes: 5, 7, 8, 12, 15

Page House Inn

Page House Inn

323 Fairfax Avenue, 23507
(757) 623-5033; (800) 599-7659
www.pagehouseinn.com

This three-story Georgian Revival in-town mansion underwent an award-winning rehabilitation, completed in 1991. New deluxe suite features incredible private bath with a sunken hot tub, steam shower for two, and a bidet. Rated four diamonds by AAA and highly rated by Mobil and Frommer's. Walk to all of the best cultural and tourist attractions and to the area's finest restaurants. Refreshments served 4:00-6:00 P.M. Complimentary beverages and snacks (self-serve). Also ask about bed and breakfast aboard the world-class yacht *Bianca*. Children over 12 welcome.

Hosts: Stephanie and Ezio DiBelardino
Rooms: 4 (PB) $120-150
Suites: 3 (PB) $140-200
Full Breakfast
Credit Cards: A, B, C
Notes: 2, 5, 7, 9, 10, 11, 12, 14

ONANCOCK

The Spinning Wheel Bed and Breakfast

31 North Street, 23417
(757) 787-7311

An 1890s folk Victorian home with antiques and spinning wheels throughout. Waterfront

The Spinning Wheel

town listed in the National Register of Historic Places. Calm Eastern Shore getaway from D.C., Virginia, Maryland, Delaware, and New Jersey. Full breakfast. All rooms with private baths, queen-size beds, and air conditioning. Walk to restaurants, shops, and deep-water harbor. Golf and tennis available at private club. Near beach, bay, and ocean. Bicycles, antiques, museums, kayaking, festivals, fishing, wildlife refuge, and Tangier Island cruise. Open May through October. AAA-approved.

Hosts: Karen and David Tweedie
Rooms: 5 (PB) $75-95
Full Breakfast
Credit Cards: A, B, D
Notes: 2, 3, 4, 7, 9, 10, 11, 12, 14

ORANGE

Hidden Inn

249 Caroline Street, 22960
(540) 672-3625; (800) 841-1253
e-mail: hiddeninn@ns.gemlink.com

A romantic Victorian featuring 10 guest rooms, each with private bath. Jacuzzis, working fireplaces, and private verandas are available. Wicker and rocking chairs on the wraparound verandas; handmade quilts and canopied beds enhance the Victorian flavor. Full country breakfast, afternoon tea, and candlelight picnics. Minutes from Monticello, Montpelier, and Virginia wineries.

Hosts: Ray and Barbara Lonick
Rooms: 10 (PB) $99-169
Full Breakfast
Credit Cards: A, B, C
Notes: 2, 5, 7, 8, 10, 11, 12, 14

PETERSBURG

Amanda's Bed and Breakfast Reservation Service

1428 Park Avenue, Baltimore, MD 21217-4230
(410) 225-0001; (800) 899-7533
FAX (410) 728-8957; e-mail:amandasrs@aol.com
www.amandas-bbrs.com

167. Traveling north or south, plan time for a stopover in Petersburg. A beautiful Queen Anne Victorian with a turret, built in the 1890s. The past and present meet in Old Towne, a revitalized commercial district of antique stores, boutiques. Craft shops and restaurants. Petersburg is convenient to the plantation country along the James River. Once guests are there, a unique adventure begins. Five spacious rooms with either a private or shared bath. A full breakfast is served. $75-85.

Mayfield Inn

3348 West Washington Street, 23804
(804) 733-0866; (804) 861-6775

Mayfield Inn is a 1750 manor house listed in the National Register of Historic Places. It was authentically restored and won the Virginia APVA Award in 1987. Guest accommodations are luxuriously appointed with oriental carpets, pine floors, antiques, period reproductions, and private baths. Situated on four acres of grounds, with a 40-foot outdoor swimming pool. Large herb

Mayfield Inn

garden and gazebo. Smoking permitted in designated areas only.

Hosts: Jamie and Dot Caudle; Cherry Turner
Rooms: 4 (PB) $69-95
Full Breakfast
Credit Cards: A, B, C
Notes: 2, 5, 8, 9, 11, 12, 14

The Owl and The Pussycat Bed and Breakfast

405 High Street, 23803
(804) 733-0505; e-mail: owlcat@ctg.net
www.ctg.net/owlcat/

An elegant turn-of-the-century Queen Anne mansion (circa 1899) a few blocks' walk to the Old Towne historic district, restaurants, antiques, and Civil War museums. Spacious guest rooms, most with private baths, air conditioning units, and beautiful wood floors. Full breakfast on weekends; Continental breakfast; discounted rates on weekdays. Easy day trips to Richmond, James River plantations, and Civil War sites. The "purr-fect" base for guests' southern Virginia discovery. Inquire about accommodations for pets. Children over eight welcome.

Hosts: Juliette and John Swenson
Rooms: 6 (4 PB: 2 SB) $75-105
Full and Continental Breakfast
Credit Cards: A, B, C, D
Notes: 2, 5, 7, 9, 10, 12, 14

PORT HAYWOOD

Tabb's Creek Inn

Route 14, Mathews County, P.O. Box 219, 23138
(804) 725-5136

Private water-view porches make this an especially attractive getaway for those seeking a dose of seclusion. On the banks of Tabb's Creek in Chesapeake Bay, this post-colonial farm features a detached guest cottage separated by pool and rose garden. Innkeeper is a well-known producing artist. The rooms are decorated with stippling, stenciling, antiques, and beds that sooth. Canoe and paddle boat provided so guests can scoot by sea. Lunch and dinner available upon request. Smoking permitted in designated areas only.

Hosts: Catherine and Cabell Venable
Rooms: 4 (PB) $75-125
Full Breakfast
Credit Cards: None
Notes: 2, 5, 6, 8, 11, 12, 14

Tabb's Creek Inn

PURCELLVILLE

Amanda's Bed and Breakfast Reservation Service

1428 Park Avenue, Baltimore, MD 21217-4230
(410) 225-0001; (800) 899-7533
FAX (410) 728-8957; e-mail:amandasrs@aol.com
www.amandas-bbrs.com

114. A spacious new log home in a meadow setting at the foothills of the Blue Ridge

NOTES: Credit cards accepted: A MasterCard; B Visa; C American Express; D Discover; E Diner's Club; F Other; 2 Personal checks accepted; 3 Lunch available; 4 Dinner available; 5 Open all year; 6 Pets welcome;

Mountains. Enjoy the sun rise with early morning coffee relaxing in a rocking chair on the front veranda. Convenient to Harpers Ferry and Shepherdstown. Two rooms, each with private bath. One with whirlpool. Continental breakfast. $85-90.

239. Be refreshed by a country setting while staying in an 18th-century home. Guest rooms are welcoming and spacious. The four private-bath bedrooms are pleasingly decorated with comfortable beds and easy chairs. One room has a Jacuzzi and one has a fireplace. A full breakfast is served. $100-125.

REEDVILLE

The Morris House

826 Main Street, P.O. Box 163, 22539
(804) 453-7016; FAX (804) 453-9032
e-mail: morrishs@crosslink.net

Guests are invited to visit the Morris House, a magnificent Queen Anne Victorian home built in 1895 on the western shore of the Chesapeake Bay. Grand architectural detail, wraparound porches, water views from every room, Jacuzzis, fireplaces, and period decor throughout are for guests to enjoy. Five comfortable guest accommodations and numerous common areas are filled with fine antiques, yet the atmosphere is relaxed and inviting. Discover the history and unspoiled beauty of Virginia's northern neck.

Hosts: Erin and Heath Dill
Rooms: 5 (PB) $70-155
Full Breakfast
Credit Cards: A, B
Notes: 2, 9, 12

REMINGTON (WARRENTON)

Highland Farm and Inn, L.L.C.

10981 Lee's Mill Road, 22734
(540) 439-0088

At the farm, south of Warrenton at Lakota, thoroughbred horses and cattle are raised on 36 secluded acres. Often fox and deer share their pastures. The accommodations, with private baths and queen-size beds, are tastefully furnished with family antiques. Guests may enjoy the spacious solarium or comfortable living room for conversation, cozy fires, and spectacular sunsets. Swim in the in-ground pool, walk along the Rappahannock River, or relax by the waterfall and ponds. Antiquing, Civil War battlefields, horse events, wineries, and fine dining are a short drive away. Enjoy afternoon refreshments and a delightful breakfast. One room is handicapped accessible.

Hosts: Ralph and Linda Robinson
Rooms: 3 (2 PB; 1 S1/2B) $60-110
Full Breakfast
Credit Cards: None
Notes: 2, 5, 7, 9, 11, 12, 14

RICHMOND

The Emmanuel Hutzler House

2036 Monument Avenue, 23220
(804) 355-4885; (804) 353-6900
e-mail: be.our.guest@bensonhouse.com
www.bensonhouse.com

This large Italian Renaissance-style inn has been totally renovated and offers leaded-glass windows, coffered ceilings, and natural mahogany raised paneling throughout the downstairs, and a large living room with marble fireplace for guests' enjoyment. Four guest rooms on the second floor, each have sitting area and private bath. One suite has a four-poster bed, love seat, and wing chair. The largest suite has a marble fireplace, four-poster mahogany bed, antique sofa, dresser, and a private bath with shower and Jacuzzi. Resident cat. Nonsmoking environment. Children over 12 welcome.

Hosts: Lyn M. Benson and John E. Richardson
Rooms: 4 (PB) $95-155
Continental and Full Breakfasts
Credit Cards: A, B, C, D, E
Notes: 2, 5, 7, 9, 10, 11, 12, 14

The William Catlin House

The William Catlin House

2304 East Broad Street, 23223
(804) 780-3746

Antiques and working fireplaces await at the William Catlin House, built in 1845, Richmond's first and oldest in the historic district. The luxury of goose down pillows and evening sherry promises a restful night. Each morning a delicious full breakfast and endless pots of steaming hot coffee or tea await guests in the elegant dining room. Numerous nearby historic sites. As seen in *Colonial Homes*, *Southern Living*, and *Mid-Atlantic* magazines.

Hosts: Robert and Josephine Martin
Rooms: 5 (3 PB; 2 SB) $75-125
Full Breakfast
Credit Cards: A, B, D
Notes: 2, 5, 7, 8, 9, 10, 14

ROANOKE

The Manor at Taylor's Store

8812 Washington Highway, P.O. Box 510,
Smith Mountain Lake, 24184
(540) 721-3951; (800) 248-6267
FAX (540) 721-5243; e-mail: taylors@symweb.com
www.symweb.com/taylors

Explore this secluded, historic 120-acre estate convenient to Smith Mountain Lake, Roanoke, and the Blue Ridge Parkway. The manor has six guest suites with extraordinary antiques and oriental rugs. Three luxury suites are also available in the West Lodge, a hand-hewn log home on a private part of the estate. Guests enjoy all luxury amenities, including central air conditioning, hot tub, fireplaces, private porches, billiard room, exercise room, guest kitchen, movies, and six private spring-fed ponds for swimming, fishing, and canoeing. A full heart-healthy gourmet breakfast served.

Hosts: Lee and Mary Lynn Tucker
Rooms: 9 (7 PB; 2 SB) $85-185
Cottage: 1 (PB) $90-190
Full Breakfast
Credit Cards: A, B, C
Notes: 2, 3, 4, 5, 7, 8, 9, 10, 11, 12, 14

SCOTTSVILLE

Guesthouses Bed and Breakfast

P.O. Box 5737, Charlottesville, 22905
(804) 979-7264; (12:00-5:00 P.M. weekdays)
FAX (804) 293-7791
e-mail: guesthouses_bnb_reservations@compuserve.com
www.va-guesthouses.com

The Prodigal. On the site of an old summer kitchen, this cottage sits behind a farmhouse built around 1830. It features a large fireplace, sleeper-sofa, pullman kitchen, full bath downstairs, and a room with a double bed upstairs. Fish in the pond, swim nearby in the Hardware River swimming hole, or rent a tube or canoe on the James River. Guests can even bring their horses. There are extra stalls and wooded trails. Air conditioning. Supplies provided for guests to prepare breakfast. $100-150.

SMITHFIELD

Isle of Wight Inn

1607 South Church Street, 23430
(757) 357-3176

This luxurious Colonial bed and breakfast inn is found in a delightful historic river-

NOTES: Credit cards accepted: A MasterCard; B Visa; C American Express; D Discover; E Diner's Club; F Other; 2 Personal checks accepted; 3 Lunch available; 4 Dinner available; 5 Open all year; 6 Pets welcome;

port town. Several suites with fireplaces and Jacuzzis. Antique shop featuring tall-case clocks and period furniture. More than 60 old homes in town dating from 1750. Just 30 minutes and a ferry ride from Williamsburg and Jamestown; less than an hour from James River plantations, Norfolk, Hampton, and Virginia Beach. No smoking allowed in common areas and some rooms.

Hosts: The Harts and the Earls
Rooms: 10 (PB) $59-119
Full Breakfast
Credit Cards: A, B, C, D
Notes: 2, 5, 8, 9, 10, 11, 12, 14

SPERRYVILLE

Sharp Rock Farm Bed and Breakfast

5 Sharp Rock Road, 22740
(540) 987-8020; www.bnb-n-va./com/sharp.htm

Sharp Rock Farm is on 23 acres in an unspoiled valley at the foot of the Blue Ridge Mountains with the Hughes River meandering through the property. It embodies the peace and pleasures of country life at its best with trout fishing, swimming, and six-acre vineyard. Hike nearby Old Rag Mountain. There are spectacular views at every turn. Hosts offer a two-bedroom cottage and a carriage house with privacy plus gourmet breakfasts. Smoking permitted outside only.

Sharp Rock Farm

Hosts: Marilyn and David Armor
Rooms: 3 (2 PB; 1 SB) $125-200
Full Breakfast
Credit Cards: A, B
Notes: 2, 5, 7, 8, 9, 11, 14, 15

SPOTSYLVANIA

Roxbury Mill Bed and Breakfast

6908 Roxbury Mill Road, 22553
(540) 582-6611; e-mail: roxburynil@aol.com

A plantation grist mill dating from 1723. Grounds and surrounding area abounds with pre-Revolution and Civil War history. Lovely ground with mill pond and waterfalls. Decks offer view of river. While one dines on the porch, scenes of nature offer a peaceful and serene atmosphere. Fifty miles from Washington, D.C. Convenient to many historical sites including Charlottesville, Fredericksburg, Williamsburg, and Richmond. Lunch and dinner available upon request. Smoking permitted on decks only. One room is handicapped accessible.

Host: Joyce Ackerman
Rooms: 3 (2 PB; 1 SB) $85-150
Full Breakfast
Credit Cards: A, B, C, D
Notes: 2, 5, 8, 9, 12, 14

STANARDSVILLE

Edgewood Farm Bed and Breakfast

1186 Middle River Road, 22973
(800) 985-3782; FAX (804) 985-6275
e-mail: edgewd1st@aol.com

Beautifully restored circa 1790 farmhouse on 130 acres in the Blue Ridge foothills. Off the beaten path yet near Skyline Drive, wineries, fine restaurants. antique and craft shops as well as Montpelier, Monticello, Ash Lawn, and University of Virginia. Accommodations include spacious, period-decorated bedrooms with private and shared baths and wood-burning fireplaces in each room. A sumptuous breakfast is served each morning on fine china; coffee, tea, or juice is brought to guests' door each morning before breakfast with the newspaper. Sparkling apple cider, cheese and crackers, and fruit served upon arrival. Lovely views, excellent bird watching, quiet and relaxing atmosphere. Skiing is one hour away.

Hosts: Eleanor and Norman Schwartz
Rooms: 3 (2 PB; 2 SB) $80-100
Full Breakfast
Credit Cards: A, B
Notes: 2, 5, 7, 8, 9, 11, 12, 14

STANLEY

Jordan Hollow Farm Inn

326 Hawksbill Park Road, 22851
(540) 778-2285; (888) 418-7000
FAX (540) 778-1759
e-mail: jhf@jordanhollow.com

Circa 1700s inn nestled at the base of the Blue Ridge Mountains. Beautiful views, 150 acres to roam, horses to ride. Relax on the spacious porches, walk the trails, and enjoy the llamas and other farm animals. Fabulous meals in the restaurant—a restored Shenandoah Valley farmhouse. New Luray Caverns, Shenandoah River, snow skiing. "We welcome you with true southern hospitality!"

Hosts: Betsy Anderson and Gail Kyle
Rooms: 20 (PB) $110-175
Full Breakfast
Credit Cards: A, B, D, E
Notes: 2, 3, 4, 5, 7, 8, 9, 10, 11, 12, 13, 14

Jordan Hollow Farm Inn

STAUNTON

Ashton Country House

Ashton Country House

1205 Middlebrook Avenue, 24401
(540) 885-7819; (800) 296-7819
FAX (540) 885-6029; www.bbhost.com/ashtonbnb

Ashton Country House, circa 1860, is a Greek Revival brick home on 25 peaceful acres on the outskirts of Staunton in the Shenandoah Valley, yet only a five-minute drive into town. Each of the five spacious guest rooms features a private bath and a queen-size bed and air conditioning. Four rooms with romantic working fireplaces. Mornings begin with a hearty breakfast. Convenient to historic attractions, fine restaurants, and area colleges. Smoking permitted outside only. Children welcome with prior notice.

Hosts: Dorie and Vince Distefano
Rooms: 5 (PB) $70-125
Full Breakfast
Credit Cards: A, B
Notes: 2, 7, 9, 10, 11, 12, 13, 14, 15

Belle Grae Inn

515 West Frederick Street, 24401-3333
(540) 886-5151; (888) 541-5151
FAX (540) 886-6641; www.valleyva.com/bellegrae/

Tucked away in the Newtown historic district of Staunton, the Belle Grae Inn is a landmark collection of beautifully restored Victorian homes dating from 1870 to the

Belle Grae Inn

early 1900s. Diners are not only invited to partake in an elegant, fine dining experience, but to indulge their senses as they explore the Old Inn, circa 1873. Here, one can enjoy a full American breakfast in the Garden Room or Azalea Courtyard, weather permitting. The parlor offers a charming space in which guests can retire in front of the fireplace or in the Music Room.

Hosts: Michael Organ, Ronn Short, and Gail Smith
Rooms: 14 (PB) $155-235 MAP
Full Breakfast
Credit Cards: A, B, C
Notes: 2, 4, 5, 7, 9, 10, 11, 12, 13, 14, 15

Frederick House

28 North New Street, 24401
(540) 885-4220; (800) 334-5575
FAX (540) 885-5180
e-mail: ejharman@frederickhouse.com
www.frederickhouse.com

A small hotel and tearoom, in the European tradition. Large, comfortable rooms or suites. Amenities include private baths, air conditioning, TV, telephones, robes, private entrances, and antique furnishings. Some balconies or fireplaces. Gourmet breakfast. Award-winning restoration and gardens. Listed in the National Register of Historic Places. Across from Mary Baldwin College. Near shops, restaurants, and the Woodrow Wilson Birthplace. In central Shenandoah Valley near Skyline Drive and Blue Ridge Parkway.

Frederick House

Hosts: Joe and Evy Harman
Rooms: 14 (PB) $75-170
Full Breakfast
Credit Cards: A, B, C, D, E
Notes: 2, 3, 4, 5, 7, 8, 9, 10, 11, 12, 13, 14

Montclair

320 North New Street, 24401
(540) 885-8832; e-mail: msbang@juno.com

Come experience the warm, intimate atmosphere of this bed and breakfast furnished with antiques and family heirlooms. In the Stuart Addition, included in the National Register of Historic Places, Montclair is a carefully restored circa 1880 Italianate townhouse in historic downtown Staunton. Guests will enjoy the relaxed ambiance of the fox hunt decor. For guests' comfort, each room is air conditioned.

Hosts: Mark and Sheri Bang
Rooms: 4 (PB) $70-85
Full Breakfast
Credit Cards: A, B
Notes: 2, 5, 7, 9, 10, 12, 13

The Sampson Eagon Inn

238 East Beverley Street, 24401
(540) 886-8200; (800) 597-9722
FAX (540) 886-8200

In the Virginia historic landmark district of Gospel Hill, this gracious, circa 1840, town residence has been thoughtfully restored and transformed into a unique inn offering affordable luxury and personal service in an intimate, inviting atmosphere. Each elegant, spacious, air-conditioned room features private bath, sitting area, canopied bed,

The Sampson Eagon Inn

TV/VCR, telephone, and antique furnishings. Adjacent to the Woodrow Wilson Birthplace and Mary Baldwin College, the inn is within two blocks of downtown dining and attractions.

Hosts: Laura and Frank Mattingly
Rooms: 5 (PB) $94-115
Full Breakfast
Credit Cards: A, B, C
Notes: 2, 5, 7, 9, 10, 11, 12, 13

Thornrose House at Gypsy Hill

531 Thornrose Avenue, 24401
(540) 885-7026

A wraparound veranda and Greek colonnades distinguish this turn-of-the-century Georgian residence. Family antiques, a grand piano, and fireplaces create an elegant, restful atmosphere. Breakfast specialties served in a formal dining room energize guests for sightseeing in the beautiful Shenandoah Valley. Beside a 300-acre park with golf, tennis, swimming, and trails. Other attractions include the Woodrow Wilson Birthplace, the Museum of American Frontier Culture, and the nearby Skyline Drive and Blue Ridge Parkway. Children six and older welcome.

Hosts: Suzanne and Otis Huston
Rooms: 5 (PB) $60-90
Full Breakfast
Credit Cards: A, B, C
Notes: 2, 5, 7, 9, 10, 11, 12, 13, 14

STEELES TAVERN

Osceola Mill Country Inn

Route 56, 24476
(540) 377-6455

This 1800s grist mill was built by Cyrus McCormick, the inventor of the reaper. The mill itself hosts four guest rooms, the Victorian Manor house has seven, and the Old Mill Store has been converted into a honeymoon cottage with Jacuzzi and fireplace. Also in the Mill, there is a restaurant for dining amongst chestnut timbers and candlelight. The inn is halfway between the towns of Staunton and Lexington and are at the foot of the Blue Ridge Mountains, close to the Appalachian Trail.

Hosts: Mercer Balliro and Brian Domino
Rooms: 12 (PB) $89-169
Full Breakfast
Credit Cards: A, B
Notes: 2, 4, 5, 7, 8, 9, 11, 12, 15

Osceola Mill Country Inn

Sugar Tree Inn

Highway 56, 24476
(540) 377-2197 (information/FAX)
(800) 377-2197 (reservations)

Sugar Tree, Virginia's mountain inn, is nestled into a mountainside less than a mile from the Blue Ridge Parkway. Guests find romantic seclusion here in rustically elegant surroundings. Each spacious room or suite offers a private wood-burning fireplace and beautiful, comfortable furnishings. There are 40-mile views from the front porch rockers. Hike Sugar Tree trails, explore historic Virginia, shop, or simply relax. Open April 1 through December 1. Great hiking, antiquing, scenery, and historic attractions nearby. One smoking room available, smoking is not permitted in public rooms.

Rooms: 11 (PB) $95-140
Full Breakfast
Credit Cards: A, B, C, D
Notes: 2, 3, 4, 9, 14, 15

STEPHENS CITY

The Inn at Vaucluse Spring

140 Vaucluse Spring Lane, 22655
(540) 869-0200; (800) 869-0525
FAX (540) 869-9546
e-mail: mail@vauclusespring.com
www.vauclusespring.com

Country Home magazine calls it "Paradise Found." "With homey three-course breakfasts, cozy rooms, and acres of Virginia landscape, it's a historic place where guests, too, find their own bit of heaven." Choose from rooms in the 1785 brick manor house, an 1850s walnut log home, the elm-paneled art gallery, or an artist's studio/mill, all in a villagelike setting surrounding a large limestone spring. Enjoy fireplaces, Jacuzzi tubs, swimming pool. Saturday-night dinner available.

Hosts: Neil and Barry Myers;
Karen and Mike Caplanis
Rooms: 12 (PB) $135-215
Full Breakfast
Credit Cards: A, B
Notes: 2, 4, 5, 7, 9, 12, 14

STRASBURG

Hotel Strasburg

213 Holliday Street, 22657
(540) 465-9191; (800) 348-8327
FAX (540) 465-4788; e-mail: thehotel@shentel.net

Like stepping back in time to the 1890s, Hotel Strasburg combines Victorian history and charm to make a special place for lodging and dining. Tastefully decorated with many antique period pieces and an impressive collection of art. Guests are invited to wander through the inn's dining rooms and quaintly renovated sleeping rooms (Jacuzzi suites). Nestled at the foot of Massanutten Mountain near the entrance to the breathtaking Skyline Drive. Inquire about accommodations for pets.

Hosts: Gary and Carol Rutherford
Rooms: 29 (PB) $74-165
Continental Breakfast
Credit Cards: A, B, C, D, E
Notes: 2, 3, 4, 5, 8, 9, 10, 11, 12, 14

SYRIA

Graves' Mountain Lodge

Route 670, 22743
(540) 923-4231; FAX (540) 923-4312

This peaceful lodge is on a large cattle and fruit farm in the shadow of the Blue Ridge Mountains next to the Shenandoah National Park. Guests enjoy three meals a day on the American plan while getting rest and relaxation during their visit. Rooms, cabins, and cottages to choose from. Trout stream and farm ponds are

7 No smoking; 8 Children welcome; 9 Social drinking allowed; 10 Tennis nearby; 11 Swimming nearby; 12 Golf nearby; 13 Skiing nearby; 14 May be booked through a travel agent; 15 Handicapped accessible.

available for fishing. Hiking trails and horseback riding are also available for guests' enjoyment. Open mid-March through November. Seasonal rates available. Inquire about accommodations for pets. Both smoking and nonsmoking rooms available.

Hosts: Rachel and Jim Graves
Rooms: 44 (38 PB; 6 SB) $60-100
Cottages: 11 (PB) $55-100
Full Breakfast
Credit Cards: A, B, D
Notes: 2, 3, 4, 8, 9, 10, 11, 12, 15

VIRGINIA BEACH

Angie's Guest Cottage

302 24th Street, 23451
(757) 428-4690

Angie's Guest Cottage is in the heart of the resort area, just one block from the ocean. Early-20th-century beach house that former guests describe as "cute, cozy, quiet, and extra clean with fresh flowers everywhere!" All rooms are air conditioned; some have small refrigerators and private entrances. A Continental plus breakfast is served on the front porch, and there are also a sun deck, barbecue pit, and picnic tables. International atmosphere. Closed mid-October through mid-March. Two-night minimum stay in season. Inquire about accommodations for pets.

Angie's Guest Cottage

Host: Barbara Yates
Rooms: 6 (1 PB; 5 SB) $52-78
Continental Breakfast
Credit Cards: None
Notes: 7, 8, 9, 10, 11, 12

Barclay Cottage

Barclay Cottage

400 16th Street, 23451
(757) 422-1956
www.inngetaways.com/va/barclay.html

Enjoy casual sophistication in a warm, historic, innlike atmosphere. Two blocks from the beach and in the heart of the Virginia Beach recreational area, the Barclay Cottage has been decorated in turn-of-the-century style with antique furniture. The hosts welcome guests to the Barclay Cottage where their theme is "We go where our dreams take us." Open April through October. AAA-approved three diamonds.

Hosts: Peter and Claire
Rooms: 5 (3 PB; 2 SB) $75-125
Full Breakfast
Credit Cards: A, B, C
Notes: 7, 9, 10, 11, 12, 14

The Picket Fence

209 43rd Street, 23451
(804) 428-8861

The furnishings in this comfortable Colonial home glow with the patina of loving care. The beach is just one block away, and beach chairs and umbrellas are provided for comfort. Near the new Virginia Marine Science Museum. One room and a suite are available year-round. A guest cottage is open May through October.

Host: Kathleen J. Hall
Room: 1 (PB) $60-90
Suite: 1 (PB)
Cottage: 1 (PB)
Full Breakfast
Credit Cards: None
Notes: 2, 3, 5, 7, 9, 10, 11, 12

WACHAPREAGUE

Amanda's Bed and Breakfast Reservation Service

1428 Park Avenue, Baltimore, MD 21217-4230
(410) 225-0001; (800) 899-7533
FAX (410) 728-8957; e-mail:amandasrs@aol.com
www.amandas-bbrs.com

267. Lovely Victorian, circa 1875, in a quaint fishing village. Four bedrooms, two full baths, contemporary kitchen, living room, dining room, fireplace, central heat and air, cable TV, and stereo. Self-catered breakfast. Whole house rental. Weekly rate is $600-700.

WARRENTON

The Black Horse Inn

8393 Meetze Road, 20187
(540) 349-4020; www.blackhorseinn.com

The Black Horse Inn is an elegant Virginia hunt country estate, only 45 minutes from Washington, D.C. Circa 1850, the original portion of this home served as a hospital during the Civil War. Fireplaces, whirlpool baths, four-poster canopied beds complement the serene setting to provide a relaxing respite for guests. The inn provides an elegant setting for family reunions, weddings, and corporate events. Equine guests are welcome. Activities include fox-hunting, horseback riding, wine-tasting, hiking, shopping at antique and specialty shops in Old Town Warrenton, bicycling, and boating.

The Black Horse Inn

Host: Lynn A. Pirozzoli
Rooms: 9 (PB) $125-295
Credit Cards: A, B C
Notes: 2, 5, 7, 9, 10, 11, 12, 14

WASHINGTON

Caledonia Farm—1812

47 Dearing Road, Flint Hill, 22627
(540) 675-3693; (800) BNB-1812

Beautifully restored 1812 stone home and romantic guest house on a farm adjacent to Shenandoah National Park. Listed in the National Register of Historic Places, offers splendor for all seasons in Virginia's Blue Ridge Mountains. Skyline Drive, wineries, caves, historic sites, and superb dining. Fireplaces, air conditioning, hay rides, hot tub, and bicycles. Only 68 miles to Washington, D.C. Children over 12 welcome.

Caledonia Farm—1812

Host: Phil Irwin
Rooms: 2 (SB) $80
Suites: 2 (PB)$140
Full Breakfast
Credit Cards: A, B, C, D
Notes: 2, 5, 7, 9, 10, 11, 12, 13, 14

The Foster-Harris House

189 Main Street, Box 333, 22747
(800) 666-0153; www.shenvalley.com/fosterharris

A turn-of-the-century home in a historic village nestled in the foothills of the Blue Ridge Mountains, with country antiques, fresh flowers, and outstanding mountain views. Near Shenandoah National Park. Five-star restaurant in town. All rooms feature private baths and central air conditioning.

Host: John and Libby Byam
Rooms: 4 (PB) $95-145
Full Breakfast
Credit Cards: A, B, C, D
Notes: 2, 5, 7, 9, 10, 11, 12, 14

WAYNESBORO

The Iris Inn

191 Chinquapin Drive, 22980
(540) 943-1991; FAX (540) 942-2093

The Iris Inn, architecturally designed and built in 1991, is on 21 wooded acres on a western slope of the Blue Ridge. It overlooks the historic Shenandoah Valley. Rooms are spacious and comfortable with king- or queen-size beds, all private baths, some whirlpools and fireplaces, porches, rockers, hot tub, full breakfast. Only five minutes to Blue Ridge Parkway and Shenandoah National Park. Near wineries, Monticello, P. Buckley Moss Museum.

Hosts: Wayne and Iris Karl
Rooms: 9 (PB) $80-140
Full Breakfast
Credit Cards: A, B
Notes: 2, 5, 7, 9, 11, 12, 13, 15

WHITE POST

L'Auberge Provençale

P.O. Box 119, 22663
(703) 837-1375; FAX (703) 837-2004

Elegant overnight accommodations, with romantic dining and the breakfast of one's dreams. L'Auberge Provençale offers the perfect getaway for pleasure or business. Superb French cuisine moderne is created by master chef Alain. Chosen by the James Beard Foundation Great Country Inn Series; four-diamond rating. L'Auberge Provençale has re-created an inn of the south of France. Country charm, city sophistication—"Where great expectations are quietly met."

Hosts: Alain and Celeste Borel
Rooms: 10 (PB) $145-250
Full Breakfast
Credit Cards: A, B, C, D, E
Notes: 2, 4, 5, 7, 9, 11, 12, 13, 14

WILLIAMSBURG

Aldrich House Bed and Breakfast

505 Capitol Ct., 23185
(757) 229-5422; e-mail: spatton@widomaker
www.aldrichhouse.com

A short stroll from the Aldrich House will transport guests to the 18th century and the heart of Colonial Williamsburg. This Colonial saltbox home offers spacious accommodations and formal living and dining areas in an unpretentious atmosphere. Innkeepers Tom and Sue Patton will help guests make their visit to the colonial past an enjoyable experience.

Rooms: 2 (PB) $80-110
Full Breakfast
Credit Cards: None
Notes: 2, 5, 7, 8, 10, 11, 12

Amanda's Bed and Breakfast Reservation Service

1428 Park Avenue, Baltimore, MD 21217-4230
(410) 225-0001; (800) 899-7533
FAX (410) 728-8957; e-mail:amandasrs@aol.com
www.amandas-bbrs.com

253. This Flemish-bond brick home was one of the first homes built on Richmond Road after the restoration of Colonial Williamsburg began in the late 1920s. The house features 18th-century decor, and the owner's apple collection is evident throughout. Four rooms with private baths. Continental plus breakfast. $95-150.

262. Three blocks from historic area and across from the College of William and Mary's Alumni House and Zable Stadium. Recent renovations have restored the house to its original charm when built in 1926. Antique furnishings throughout. Five guest rooms, each with private bath. $95-115.

361. Williamsburg is well known for its restored historic district and the depth of its history. To take advantage of this, stay a few days in one of Williamsburg's oldest and largest guest houses with 10 guest rooms. Guests are treated to southern hospitality and a full breakfast. Two of the rooms share a bath but this makes a nice family suite. Walk to the historic area and the College of William and Mary. Decorated with 18th-century reproductions and traditional antiques, with canopied or four-poster beds and quilts. $95-160.

Anne Marie's Bed and Breakfast

610 Capitol Landing Road, 23185
(757) 564-0225

Gracious hosts at Anne Marie's have a genuine interest in making a visit to Colonial Williamsburg unforgettable. A three-block stroll and guests are in the quiet restored area where history and shops abound. Evenings at Anne Marie's bring relaxation and comfort. Rooms and suite are tastefully furnished with family heirlooms and antiques. Feather beds are covered with fine linens and await guests' slumber. Guests rave about the exceptional full breakfast and the finest of hospitality.

Hosts: Marie and Ann Supplee
Rooms: 2 (PB) $85-110
Full Breakfast
Credit Cards: A, B
Notes: 2, 5, 7, 8, 9, 10, 11, 12, 14

Candlewick Bed and Breakfast

800 Jamestown Road, 23185
(800) 418-4949

In the heart of Williamsburg, Candlewick invites guests to enjoy the comforts and gracious charm of an earlier era. With 18th-century antiques and reproductions, each of the three guest bedrooms boasts a curtained canopied bed with a plush mattress decked in antique quilt and absolutely everything necessary for guests' comfort. Following a marvelous night's rest, guests will enjoy a wonderful breakfast in the keeping room. Just a whisper away from the historic area and across the street from College of William and Mary. Children over 12 welcome.

Hosts: Bernie and Mary Peters
Rooms: 3 (PB) $95-125
Full Breakfast
Credit Cards: A, B, F
Notes: 2, 7, 9, 10, 11, 12, 14

The Cedars

616 Jamestown Road, 23185
(757) 229-3591; (800) 296-3591

An eight-minute walk to historic Williamsburg and across from the College of William and Mary, this elegant three-story brick

Georgian inn offers tradition, gracious hospitality, and comfort. Scrumptious, bountiful breakfasts are served by candlelight on the tavern porch. The porch also serves as a meeting place for cards, chess, or other diversions. Each guest chamber reflects the romance and charm of the colonial era. Cottage with fireplace can accommodate five people. Off-street parking. Williamsburg's oldest, largest bed and breakfast.

Hosts: Carol, Jim, and Brona Malecha
Rooms: 8 (PB) $95-180
Cottage: 1 (PB) $150-275
Full Breakfast
Credit Cards: A, B
Notes: 2, 5, 7, 8, 9, 10, 12, 14

Colonial Capital Bed and Breakfast

501 Richmond Road, 23185
(757) 229-0233; (800) 776-0570
FAX (757) 253-7667
e-mail: ccbb@widomaker.com; www.ccbb.com

Only three blocks from the historic area, this charming Colonial Revival home, circa 1926, and its gracious hosts welcome guests. Enjoy spring gardens, summer festivities, autumn colors, and colonial Christmastide. Antique furnishings blend charm and elegance from the large parlor with wood-burning fireplace to the airy guest rooms. Full breakfast with a gourmet touch and afternoon tea and wine. Licensed for adult beverages. Bikes, and free off-street parking. Fax can receive 24 hours a day. Special rates available January through mid-March. Smoking permitted outside. Children over eight welcome. Gift certificates, package plans, and discounted attraction tickets available.

Colonial Capital

Hosts: Barbara and Phil Craig
Rooms: 5 (PB) $95-115
Suite: $140
Full Breakfast
Credit Cards: A, B, C, D
Notes: 2, 5, 9, 10, 12, 14

Colonial Gardens Bed and Breakfast

1109 Jamestown Road, 23185
(757) 220-8087; (800) 886-9715
e-mail: colgdns@widomaker.com
www.ontheline.com/cgbb

Colonial Gardens offers the perfect escape in a quiet, woodland setting. The charming interior is beautifully furnished with heirloom antiques and original art. Enjoy breakfast in the sunroom overlooking the beautifully landscaped yard. In the evening relax with other guests in the large living room around the game table and comfortable sitting areas. Ideal for Colonial Williamsburg and all area attractions. Outstanding suites and guest rooms with luxury amenities. TV/VCR, telephones. AAA three-diamond-rated.

Hosts: Scottie and Wilmot Phillips
Rooms: 4 (PB) $105-130
Full Breakfast
Credit Cards: A, B, C
Notes: 2, 5, 7, 9, 10, 11, 12, 14

For-Cant-Hill Guest Home

4 Canterbury Lane, 23185-3140
(757) 229-6623; FAX (757) 229-1863

This home is in a lovely wooded area, only five to six blocks from the colonial historic area, overlooking a lake, part of the campus of the College of William and Mary, in the heart of town. The rooms are beautifully decorated in antiques and collectibles for guests' complete comfort. The home is central heated and air conditioned with TVs in each room, and a hearty breakfast is served. The hosts make dinner reservations for guests and provide helpful information on the many attractions offered in the area.

NOTES: Credit cards accepted: A MasterCard; B Visa; C American Express; D Discover; E Diner's Club; F Other; 2 Personal checks accepted; 3 Lunch available; 4 Dinner available; 5 Open all year; 6 Pets welcome;

Telephone and fax are available in the home. Children over 10 welcome.

Hosts: Martha and Hugh Easler
Rooms: 2 (PB) $85
Full Breakfast
Credit Cards: None
Notes: 2, 5, 7, 9, 10, 11, 12, 14

Fox and Grape Bed and Breakfast

701 Monumental Avenue, 23185
(757) 229-6914; (800) 292-3699

Genteel accommodations five blocks north of Virginia's restored colonial capital. This lovely two-story Colonial with spacious wraparound porch is a perfect place to enjoy one's morning coffee, plan the day's activities, or relax with a favorite book. Furnishings include antiques, counted cross-stitch, duck decoys, and folk art Noah's arks made by the host.

Hosts: Pat and Bob Orendorff
Rooms: 4 (PB) $85-90
Full Breakfast
Credit Cards: A, B, D
Notes: 5, 7, 8, 9, 12, 14

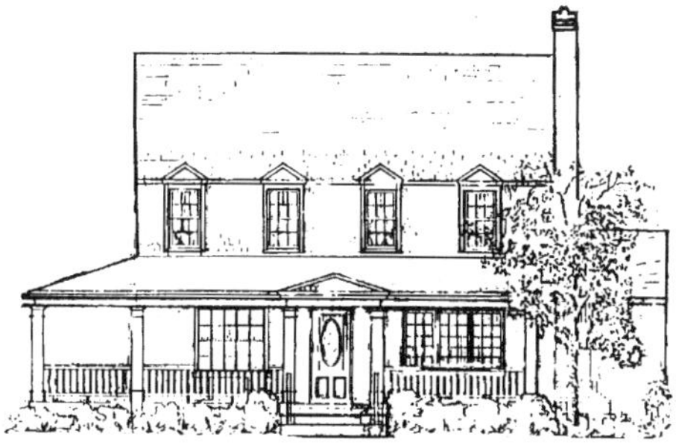

Fox and Grape

Governor's Trace

303 Capitol Landing Road, 23185
(757) 229-7552; (800) 303-7552
FAX (757) 220-2767
e-mail: govtrace@widomaker.com
www.ontheline.com/trace

Closest inn to the historic district. "Vies for the most romantic [in Williamsburg]"—*Washington Post.* Sue and Dick hold Williamsburg's record for longevity and are pioneers of the industry in town. Enjoy the special ambiance created by these long-time innkeepers: candlelit breakfasts served in the privacy of guest room, king- and queen-size beds, and spacious antique-filled rooms; one has a real wood-burning fireplace, another a private screened-in porch.

Hosts: Sue and Dick Lake
Room: 3 (PB) $105-125
Full Breakfast
Credit Cards: A, B
Notes: 2, 5, 7, 9, 10, 11, 12, 14

Hite's Bed and Breakfast

704 Monumental Avenue, 23185
(757) 229-4814

Charming Cape Cod—seven minutes' walk to Colonial Williamsburg. Large rooms cleverly furnished with antiques and collectibles. Each room has a TV, telephone, coffee maker, robes, and beautiful private bathroom with claw-foot tub. In the parlor for guest enjoyment are an antique pump organ and hand-crank Victrola. Guests can swing in the back yard and enjoy the birds, flowers, and goldfish pond.

Host: Faye Hite
Rooms: 2 (PB) $80-90
Full Breakfast
Credit Cards: None
Notes: 2, 5, 7, 8, 10, 12

The Homestay Bed and Breakfast

517 Richmond Road, 23185
(757) 229-7468 (information)
(800) 836-7468 (reservations)

Cozy and convenient. Enjoy the comfort of a lovely Colonial Revival home, furnished

The Homestay

with turn-of-the-century family antiques and country charm. It is only four blocks to Colonial Williamsburg and just minutes away from Jamestown, Yorktown, and other local attractions. Adjacent to the College of William and Mary. A full breakfast featuring homemade breads and a delicious hot dish is served in the formal dining room. Children 10 and older welcome.

Hosts: Barbara and Jim Thomassen
Rooms: 3 (PB) $80-100
Full Breakfast
Credit Cards: A, B
Notes: 2, 5, 7, 9, 12, 14

Hughes Guest Home

106 Newport Avenue, 23185-4212
(757) 229-3493

Directly opposite the Williamsburg Lodge on Newport Avenue, the Hughes Guest Home has been in operation since 1947. A lovely two-minute stroll to Colonial Williamsburg's restored district, golfing facilities, and numerous dining facilities including the colonial taverns. The College of William and Mary, Merchant's Square, and several Colonial Williamsburg museums are also within easy walking distance. The house is decorated lavishly with family antiques. Eating facilities are across the street at Williamsburg Lodge and Williamsburg Inn. Lodging only.

Rooms: 3 (1 PB; 2 SB) $50
Credit Cards: None
Notes: 2, 8, 12

Indian Springs Bed and Breakfast

330 Indian Springs Road, 23185
(800) 262-9165; e-mail: indianspgs@tri.net

Indian Springs is in downtown Williamsburg, nestled in a private wooded glade. Beautiful gardens adorn the view from each guest room. King suites open onto a shady greenery-filled veranda. The Colonial-style cottage features a king-size feather bed loft, fireplace, and wet-bar. A small library has holdings for business and leisure activities. A sunny deck is a bird watcher's haven. In-room amenities include cable, VCR, refrigerator, private bath, and private entrance.

Hosts: Kelly and Paul Supplee
Rooms: 4 (PB) $75-130
Full Breakfast
Credit Cards: A, B
Notes: 2, 5, 7, 8, 9, 10, 11, 12, 14

The Inn at 802

802 Jamestown Road, 23185
(757) 564-0845; (800) 672-4086
FAX (757) 564-7018; e-mail: 105313.42@csi.com
www.bbhost.com/innat802

A four-room bed and breakfast close to Colonial Williamsburg and adjacent to the College of William and Mary. Period decor with down comforters and dust ruffles. Four-poster beds. Large, comfortable, and private rooms, all with private bath/showers. Delicious full breakfast served daily. Two fireplaces, library, sun porch.

Hosts: Don and Jan McGarva
Rooms: 4 (PB) $115-145
Full Breakfast
Credit Cards: A, B, C, D
Notes: 2, 5, 6, 7, 8, 9, 10, 11, 12

Liberty Rose Bed and Breakfast

1022 Jamestown Road, 23185
(757) 253-1260; (800) 545-1825
www.libertyrose.com

Williamsburg's only four-diamond-awarded property. Beautifully restored 1920s clapboard-and-brick hilltop home.

Wooded setting. Only one mile from colonial district. Bedrooms have exquisite poster and French-canopied beds. Lush mattresses covered with silks and goose down. All rooms have wonderful private baths. TVs, VCRs, movies, and private-line telephones. Breakfast is delicious, hospitality is charming. Fireplaces. Grand piano. Gardens, porches, courtyards.

Hosts: Brad and Sandra Hirz
Rooms: 4 (PB) $135-205
Full Breakfast
Credit Cards: A, B, C
Notes: 2, 5, 7, 10, 12

Newport House

Newport House

710 South Henry Street, 23185-4113
(757) 229-1775

Newport House was designed in 1756 by Peter Harrison. It is furnished totally in the period, including four-poster canopy beds. Each room has a private bathroom. The full breakfast includes authentic colonial-period recipes. Only five minutes from the historic area (as close as one can get). The host is a former museum director and author of many books on colonial history. Enjoy colonial dancing in the ballroom every Tuesday evening.

Hosts: John and Cathy Millar
Rooms: 2 (PB) $120-150
Full Breakfast
Credit Cards: None
Notes: 2, 5, 7, 8, 9, 10, 11, 12, 14

Piney Grove at Southall's Plantation

P.O. Box 1359, 23187-1359
(804) 829-2480; FAX (804) 829-6888

Piney Grove is just 20 miles west of Williamsburg in the James River plantation country, among working farms, country stores, and historic churches. The elegant accommodations at this National Register of Historic Places property are in two restored antebellum homes (1790 and 1857). Also on the property is Ashland (1835), Dower Quarter (1835), and Duck Church (1900). Guests are welcome to enjoy the parlor-library, gardens, pool, nature trail, farm animals, or a game of croquet or badminton. Upon arrival, guests are served mint juleps and Virginia wine. Restaurants nearby.

Hosts: Brian, Cindy, Joan, and Joseph Gordineer
Rooms: 6 (PB) $125-160
Full Breakfast
Credit Cards: C, D
Notes: 2, 5, 7, 8, 9, 11, 12, 14

Primrose Cottage

706 Richmond Road, 23185
(757) 229-6421

A short walk from Colonial Williamsburg, Primrose Cottage is abloom with pansies, primroses, and thousands of tulips. A French double harpsichord, hand-painted antiques, German doll house, and the comforts of home including private baths, (two bathrooms have Jacuzzis) and king- or queen-size feather beds await guests. The aroma of Inge's home-cooked breakfast usually rouses even the sleepiest traveler.

Host: Inge Curtis
Rooms: 4 (PB) $95-125
Full Breakfast
Credit Cards: A, B
Notes: 2, 5, 7, 10, 11, 12, 14

War Hill Inn

4560 Long Hill Road, 23188
(757) 565-0248; (800) 743-0248

This replica of an 18th-century home sits on a 32-acre farm three miles off Route 60. Close to the College of William and Mary, Colonial Williamsburg, Busch Gardens, and shopping outlets. Seven antique-furnished guest rooms with private baths. Cable TV. Country breakfast.

Hosts: Shirley, Bill, Cherie, and Will Lee
Rooms: 7 (PB) $75-95
Suites: 2 (PB) $100-160
Cottage: 1 (PB) $120-180
Full Breakfast
Credit Cards: A, B
Notes: 2, 5, 7, 8, 9, 10, 12, 14

Williamsburg Manor

Williamsburg Manor Bed and Breakfast

600 Richmond Road, 23185
(757) 220-8011; (800) 422-8011

This 1927 Georgian home was built during the reconstruction of historic Colonial Williamsburg. Recently restored to its original elegance and furnished with exquisite pieces, including antiques and collectibles. Five well-appointed guest rooms with private baths, TVs, and central air conditioning. Guests are treated to a lavish fireside breakfast. Home is available for weddings, private parties, dinners, and meetings. Ideal location within walking distance of the historic area. On-site parking. Off-season rates available.

Host: Laura Reeves
Rooms: 5 (PB) $95-150
Full Breakfast
Credit Cards: A, B
Notes: 2, 3, 4, 5, 7, 8, 9, 10, 11, 12, 14

Williamsburg Sampler Bed and Breakfast

922 Jamestown Road, 23185
(757) 253-0398; (800) 722-1169
FAX (757) 253-2669
e-mail: wbgsampler@aol.com

An elegant 18th-century plantation-style six-bedroom Colonial proclaimed by Virginia's governor "Inn of the Year." The *Washington Post* wrote, "decorated with an eclectic assortment of antiques collected by the innkeepers." Lovely rooms and suites with four-poster beds, plus fireplace, wet bar, refrigerator, TV/VCR, and private bath. "Skip lunch" breakfast. Internationally known as a favorite for honeymoons, anniversaries, or romantic getaways. On-site parking. Walk to historic area. AAA three-diamond and Mobil three-star. Appeared on *CBS This Morning*.

Hosts: Helen and Ike Sisane
Rooms: 2 (PB) $100

Williamsburg Sampler

Suites: 2 (PB) $150
Full Breakfast
Credit Cards: A, B
Notes: 2, 5, 7, 9, 10, 11, 12, 14

WOODSTOCK

Azalea House

551 South Main Street, 22664
(540) 459-3500
www.shenwebworks.com/azaleahouse

The Azalea House dates back 100 years when it was built in the Victorian tradition and used as a church manse. The guest rooms are pleasing and comfortable, with antique furnishings and mountain views. Situated in the rolling hills of the Shenandoah Valley near fine restaurants, vineyards, shops, caverns, Civil War sites, hiking, and fishing. A great place to relax! Children over six are welcome.

Hosts: Margaret and Price McDonald
Rooms: 4 (PB) $55-75
Full Breakfast
Credit Cards: A, B, C
Notes: 2, 5, 7, 9, 10, 11, 12, 13

Azalea House

The Inn at Narrow Passage

US 11 South, P.O. Box 608, 22664
(540) 459-8000; (800) 459-8002
www.innatnarrowpassage.com

The Inn at Narrow Passage

Historic log inn with five acres on the Shenandoah River. Colonial-style rooms, most with private baths and working fireplaces. Once the site of Indian attacks and Stonewall Jackson's headquarters, it is now a cozy spot in winter with large fireplaces in the common living and dining rooms. In spring and summer, fishing and rafting are at the back door. Fall brings the foliage festivals and hiking in the national forest a few miles away. Nearby are vineyards, caverns, historic sites, and fine restaurants. Washington, D.C., is 90 miles away. Mobil, AAA, IIA.

Hosts: Ellen and Ed Markel
Rooms: 12 (PB) $90-145
Full Breakfast
Credit Cards: A, B, D
Notes: 2, 5, 8, 9, 10, 11, 12, 13, 14

WOOLWINE

Mountain Rose Bed and Breakfast

Route 1, Box 280, 24185
(540) 930-1057

"Historical country elegance in the Blue Ridge Mountains." Once a part of the Mountain Rose Distillery, this Victorian inn, circa 1901, has five spacious rooms with private baths, working antique-mantled fireplaces, and six porches. Elegant oil-lamp-lit three-course breakfast. Swimming pool,

Mountain Rose

trout-stocked creek, and 100 acres of hiking and privacy. Convenient to the Blue Ridge Parkway and Chateau Morrisette Winery. AAA three-diamond-rated. Member of BBAV and PAII. Open year-round.

Hosts: Melodie Pogue and Reeves Simms
Rooms: 5 (PB) $75-95
Full Breakfast
Credit Cards: A, B, D
Notes: 2, 5, 7, 8, 9, 10, 11, 12, 14

YORKTOWN

Marl Inn Bed and Breakfast

220 Chruch Street, P.O. Box 572, 23690
(757) 898-3859; (800) 799-6207
FAX (757) 898-3587
e-mail: EugeneM918@aol.com

Only two minutes from Williamsburg. Four rooms with private baths. Two are full suites with a bedroom, living room, kitchen. All rooms are on the second floor and have outside private entrances. Bicycles available for guests to tour battlefields and campgrounds of the Revolutionary armies. The beautiful 13-mile Colonial Parkway linking Yorktown with Williamsburg is a particularly attractive route for bicyclists and touring families. Four restaurants, upscale gift and antique shops are within walking distance, swimming and boating in the York River just two blocks from the house.

Rooms: 4 (PB) $95-120
Continental Breakfast
Credit Cards: A, B, C
Notes: 2, 7, 8, 9, 11, 12, 14

West Virginia

BRAMWELL

Three Oaks and a Quilt

P.O. Box 84, 24715
(304) 248-8316

The oaks, to keep guests cool; the quilts, to keep guests warm. Grandfather bought the home in 1904 and it has remained in the family ever since. It was restored in 1985 and 1986, using and reusing everything possible. Most people come to Bramwell to see the coal operators' mansions, which give the feeling of a town having stood still since the early 1900s. One is quickly renewed in the restful, relaxing atmosphere. A Whig Rose appliquéd quilt hangs on the front porch wall, one of three dozen at the inn. Children over 12 welcome.

Host: B. J. Kahle
Rooms: 3 (1 PB; 2 SB) $58.30
Full Breakfast
Credit Cards: None
Notes: 2, 5, 7, 9, 10, 11, 12, 13

CHARLESTON

Brass Pineapple Bed and Breakfast

1611 Virginia Street East, 25311
(304) 344-0748; (800) CALL WVA

This cozy but elegant 1910 brick home is in Charleston's historic district. The house has been carefully restored to its original grandeur, with antiques throughout, lots of stained glass, and original oak woodwork. Guest rooms are furnished in elegant style with private baths, terry robes, hair dryers, telephones, cable TVs, and VCRs. Catering to business travelers, this bed and breakfast has two business-plan rooms offering telephones with voice mail and data jacks to accommodate laptop PCs, desks, and unlimited coffee, tea, and sodas. A small copier and fax are on the first floor. Mints on pillows and turndown service add that special touch. Tea is available from 5:00 to 7:00 P.M. Candlelit breakfast is accented with crystal and silver and may be had alfresco in the petite rose garden in season. Smoking outside only. Open year-round except for holidays. Children eight and older welcome. Limited social drinking permitted.

Brass Pineapple

Host: Sue Pepper
Rooms: 6 (PB) $79-109
Continental and Full Breakfasts
Credit Cards: A, B, C, E, F
Notes: 2, 7, 10, 11, 12, 14

West Virginia

CHARLES TOWN

Cottonwood Inn

Route 2, Box 61-S
Kabletown Road and Mill Lane, 25414
(304) 725-3371; (800) 868-1188
www.mydestination.com/cottonwood

An early 1800s farmhouse, the Cottonwood is in a quiet countryside setting in the northern Shenandoah Valley, surrounded by rolling farmlands. The secluded six acres lie near Harpers Ferry and Charles Town, 65 miles west of Washington, D.C. Rich historic area; Antietam National Battlefield, 23 miles away. Antiques and period reproductions. Stream. Fireplaces in the dining room and library. Large breakfast. An inn for 11 years and home of Destination Images, producers of travel videoguides of European destinations.

Hosts: Joe and Barbara Sobol
Rooms: 7 (PB) $75-105
Full Breakfast
Credit Cards: A, B, C
Notes: 2, 5, 7, 12, 14

Cottonwood Inn

Gilbert House of Middleway Historic District: A Bed and Breakfast

P.O. Box 1104, 25414
(304) 725-0637

Near Harpers Ferry and Antietam National Battlefield. Magnificent stone house, circa 1760, listed in the National Register of Historic Places and the Historic American Building Survey (1938). Spacious, romantic rooms with wood-burning fireplaces and air conditioning. Bridal Suite has curtains around the bed and a claw-foot tub. Many European treasures, some from royal families. In the Middleway historic district. The village is one of the first European settlements in the Shenandoah Valley and is on the original settlers' trail. Colonial-era mill sites, theater at the Old Opera House, horse and auto races, rafting, outlet shopping.

Gilbert House

Host: Bernie Heiler
Rooms: 3 (PB) $80-140
Full Breakfast
Credit Cards: A, B, C
Notes: 2, 5, 7, 9, 12, 14

ELKINS

The Post House

306 Robert E. Lee Avenue, 26241
(304) 636-1792

In the heart of Elkins this bed and breakfast has five guest rooms, one of which has an adjoining children's room. Sit on the front porch or lounge in the parklike back yard with a children's playhouse. Close to Davis and Elkins College and other cultural and scenic attractions. Easy access to main roads. Certified massage is available. Handmade quilts for sale.

Host: Jo Ann Post Barlow (owner)
Rooms: 5 (2 PB; 3 SB) $60-65
Continental Breakfast
Credit Cards: None
Notes: 2, 7, 8, 10, 11, 12, 13

The Retreat

The Retreat

214 Harpertown Road, 26241
(304) 636-2960; (888) 636-2960
e-mail: retreat@nevmedia.net

The Retreat is a stately turn-of-the-century home just off the campus of Davis and Elkins College, .6 miles from downtown Elkins, gateway to the 840,000-acre Monongahela National Forest. Elkins was recently selected as one of the top 50 American small towns. Wide porches wrap around the house and five acres of old-growth trees, evergreens, rhododendron, flower and vegetable gardens make the Retreat a secluded spot to get away. Heritage music and art, as well as virtually every type of outdoor recreation, are specialties of the innkeeper.

Host: Leslie Henderson
Rooms: 6 (6 SB) $65
Full Breakfast
Credit Cards: A, B
Notes: 2, 5, 7, 8, 9, 10, 11, 12, 13

Tunnel Mountain Bed and Breakfast

Route 1, Box 59-1, 26241
(304) 636-1684; (888) 211-9123

This charming three-story fieldstone home is nestled on the side of Cheat Mountain on five private wooded acres, surrounded by scenic mountains, lush forests, and sparkling rivers. The interior is finished in pine and rare wormy chestnut woodwork. Tastefully decorated throughout with antiques, collectibles, and crafts, it extends a warm and friendly atmosphere to guests.

Hosts: Anne and Paul Beardslee
Rooms: 3 (PB) $65-75
Full Breakfast
Credit Cards: None
Notes: 2, 5, 9, 10, 11, 12, 13

Tunnel Mountain

The Warfield House

318 Buffalo Street, 26241
(888) 636-4555

The Warfield House, a grand shingle-and-brick house built in 1901, is nestled on a quiet corner in a scenic small town. Facing the forested city park, it is within walking

The Warfield House

NOTES: Credit cards accepted: A MasterCard; B Visa; C American Express; D Discover; E Diner's Club; F Other; 2 Personal checks accepted; 3 Lunch available; 4 Dinner available; 5 Open all year; 6 Pets welcome;

distance of restaurants, shops, and theaters. It contains spectacular woodwork and stained glass and has been faithfully restored with turn-of-the-century reproduction carpets and wallpapers designed to transport guests back in time. Five antique-appointed guest rooms provide comfort and privacy.

Hosts: Connie and Paul Garnett
Rooms: 5 (PB) $75-95
Full Breakfast
Credit Cards: None
Notes: 2, 5, 7, 9, 10, 11, 12, 13

HARPERS FERRY

Fillmore Street Bed and Breakfast

Fillmore Street, 25425
(304) 535-2619

With a clear mountain view, this antique-furnished Victorian home is known for its hospitality, service, and gourmet breakfast. Private accommodations and baths, TVs, air conditioning, complimentary sherry and tea, and a blazing fire on cool mornings. Closed Thanksgiving, Christmas, and New Year's Day. Smoking is permitted outside on the porch only. Children over 12 are welcome.

Hosts: Alden and James Addy
Rooms: 2 (PB) $75-80
Full Breakfast
Credit Cards: None
Notes: 2, 5, 7, 9

HEDGESVILLE

The Farmhouse on Tomahawk Run

1 Tomahawk Run Place, 25427
(304) 754-7350 (phone/FAX)
e-mail: tomahawk@intrepid.net

This beautiful, restored Civil War-era farmhouse, on 280 acres of hills and meadows, is rich in history and charm. Enjoy bountiful three-course breakfasts, spacious guest rooms with balcony or suite and king- or queen-size beds, and antiques. During the day relax on a rocking chair on the large wraparound porch, stroll the walking paths on the grounds, or visit the shops and historical sites within a short drive. In the evening luxuriate in the Jacuzzi on the back porch within earshot of the rippling brook nearby.

Hosts: Judy and Hugh Erskine
Rooms: 5 (PB) $75-110
Full Breakfast
Credit Cards: A, B, C, D, E
Notes: 2, 5, 7, 8, 12, 14

HILLSBORO

The Current Bed and Breakfast

HC 64, Box 135, 24946
(304) 653-4722; e-mail: current@inetone.net
www.carrweb.com/thecurrent

Tucked into a high mountain valley near the Greenbrier River, the Current offers a relaxing getaway. Nearby state parks and national forest provide opportunities for hiking, mountain biking, fishing, and canoeing, while the outdoor hot tub and deck beckon the star gazer and bird watcher. The 1904 farmhouse is furnished with antiques, collectibles, and quilts. Morgan horses graze in surrounding fields and serenity abounds.

Host: Leslee McCarty
Rooms: 6 (1 PB: 5 SB) $60-80
Full Breakfast
Credit Cards: A, B
Notes: 2, 5, 7, 8, 9, 11, 12, 13

The Current

7 No smoking; 8 Children welcome; 9 Social drinking allowed; 10 Tennis nearby; 11 Swimming nearby; 12 Golf nearby; 13 Skiing nearby; 14 May be booked through a travel agent; 15 Handicapped accessible.

HUTTONSVILLE

Hutton House

General Delivery, P.O. Box 88, 26273
(304) 335-6701

Enjoy the relaxed atmosphere of this historically registered and antique-filled Queen Anne Victorian. Guest rooms are individually styled, and each guest has his/her own personal favorite. Breakfast varies from gourmet to hearty. Sometimes it is served at a specific time, while at other times it is served at guests' leisure. Children can play games on the lawn. Guests can lose themselves in the beauty of the Laurel Mountains as they lounge on the wraparound porch.

Hosts: Dean Ahren and Loretta Murray
Rooms: 6 (PB) $75-80
Full Breakfast
Credit Cards: A, B
Notes: 2, 5, 7, 8, 9, 12, 13, 14

LEWISBURG

General Lewis Inn

301 East Washington Street, 24901
(304) 645-2600; (800) 628-4454

The General Lewis Inn is one of 54 historic buildings in the National Historic District of Lewisburg. It was created in 1929 by adding to an 1834 home. All rooms are furnished with antiques. The dining room serves a delicious selection of meals. A pond and garden, a living room with books, puzzles, and fireplace, and a wide veranda for rocking encourage relaxing. Two blocks away are shops for antiques, gifts, and clothing. Full breakfast is available at an extra cost.

Hosts: The Morgan Family
Rooms: 25 (PB) $70-100
Full Breakfast
Credit Cards: A, B, C, D
Notes: 2, 3, 4, 5, 6, 7, 8, 9, 12, 14, 15

MARTINSBURG

Boydville, The Inn at Martinsburg

601 South Queen Street, 25401
(304) 263-1448

This 1812 stone plantation mansion is on a 10-acre park with 100-year-old trees and boxwood. Originally part of a Lord Fairfax grant. The land, once part of a large plantation, was purchased by General Elisha Boyd in the 1790s and was a retreat for Stonewall Jackson and Henry Clay. Enjoy beautiful craftmanship from a past era, including woodwork, window glass, French chandeliers, and foyer wallpaper handpainted in England in 1812. Great porch with rockers. Continental plus breakfast. In the National Register of Historic Places. Just off of I-81, one and one-half hours from Washington, D.C., in the heart of Civil War country. Closed during the month of August.

Hosts: LaRue Frye, Bob Boege, Carolyn Snyder, and Pete Bailey
Rooms: 6 (4 PB; 2 SB) $100-125
Continental Breakfast
Credit Cards: A, B
Notes: 2, 7, 9, 12, 14

Pulpit & Palette Inn

516 West John Street, 25401
(304) 263-7012

Oriental ambiance in a Victorian home. Two bedrooms share a bath. Morning coffee/tea with shortbread and newspaper served in bed. Full breakfast, afternoon tea, evening drinks and hors d'oeuvres. Fifty-store outlet one block away. Other attractions and golf nearby. Children over 12 welcome. No smoking allowed.

Hosts: Bill and Janet Starr
Rooms: 2 (SB) $80
Full Breakfast
Credit Cards: A, B
Notes: 2, 7, 9, 12

MILTON

The Cedar House

92 Trenol Heights, 25541
(304) 743-5516; (800) CALL WVA
e-mail: vickersc@marshall.edu

The Cedar House is a hilltop, air-conditioned, tri-level ranch-style house that gives a panoramic view of surrounding hills. The five and one-half acres provide quiet and privacy within .8 of a mile of I-64, exit 28. Relax in front of the family room fire or play pool, games, or piano in the game room and use the treadmill or roller traction table. Watch skilled glass blowers at Blenko Glass, visit the covered flea market, explore the small-town shops, or attend Saturday performances at the Mountaineer Opry House.

Host: Carole Vickers
Rooms: 3 (PB) $65-75
Full Breakfast
Credit Cards: A, B, C, D
Notes: 2, 5, 7

MORGANTOWN

Appelwood Bed and Breakfast

Route 5, Box 137, 26505
(304) 296-2607

Appelwood Bed and Breakfast is a unique post-and-beam house among 35 wooded acres. Only four miles from Morgantown city limits, Appelwood provides a peaceful setting with easy access to West Virginia University, Coopers Rock State Forest, water skiing, horseback riding, and hiking areas. Awake to a full breakfast, relax by a flickering fire, or just soak away worries in the hot tub. Inquire about accommodations for pets. Smoking permitted in designated areas only.

Host: Jim Humbertson
Rooms: 3 (PB) $65-75
Full Breakfast
Credit Cards: A, B
Notes: 2, 5, 9, 10, 11, 12

Fieldcrest Manor Bed and Breakfast

1440 Stewartstown Road, 26505-3619
(304) 599-2686; (800) 765-0569
FAX (304) 599-2853
e-mail: fldcrest@access.mountain.net
www.pinnaclemall.com/fieldcrestmanor/

Stately maples and evergreens line the entrance to the affordable elegance of this premier bed and breakfast. On five beautiful acres, Fieldcrest Manor offers the finest in overnight accommodations, with private baths, telephones, and TVs in each room. The house and grounds are exceptional and the host takes great pride in the cleanliness and hospitality that are a hallmark of Fieldcrest Manor.

Host: Susan Linkous
Rooms: 5 (PB) $80-90
Full Breakfast
Credit Cards: A, B, C
Notes: 2, 5, 7, 9, 12, 13

PENCE SPRINGS

The Pence Springs Hotel

P.O. Box 90 (Route 3), 24962
(304) 445-2606; FAX (304) 445-2204

Known as the Grand Hotel, this national register inn was one of the historic mineral spas of the Virginias. A Roaring Twenties resort with casino and secret liquor rooms, it was the most popular and expensive resort in

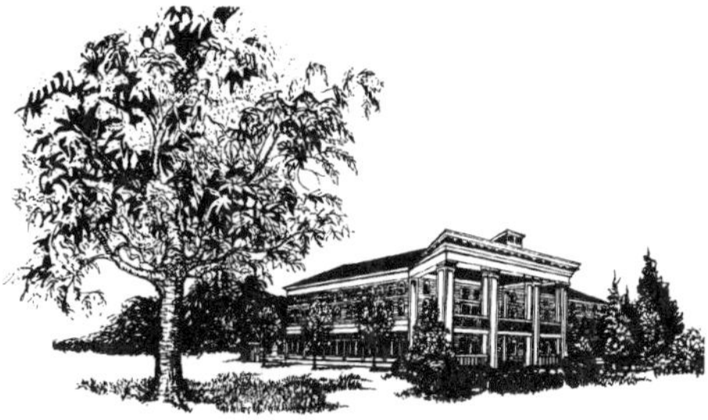

The Pence Springs Hotel

West Virginia, then a finishing school established by Eleanor Roosevelt, later the State Prison for Women, and now a fine country inn. Its gardens provide fresh herbs and vegetables for its gourmet Riverside Room restaurant. Ranked "Top Ten" for more than 20 years. Croquet, hiking, bicycles, fishing. *Southern Living*, *Gourmet*, *Mid-Atlantic*, *Blue Ridge*, and *West Virginia* magazines.

Hosts: O. Ashby Berkley and Rosa Lee Berkley Miller
Rooms: 15 (PB) $69-99
Full Breakfast
Credit Cards: A, B, C, D, E
Notes: 2, 4, 8, 9, 12, 14, 15

ROMNEY

Hampshire House 1884

165 North Grafton Street, 26757
(304) 822-7171

Completely renovated 1884 brick home. Period furniture, fireplaces, and air conditioning; quiet. Private baths and garden. The charm of the 1880s with the comforts of today in a sleepy small town on the beautiful south branch of the Potomac River. Therapeutic massage available. Golf is 20 minutes away and skiing is one hour and 15 minutes away.

Hosts: Jane and Scott Simmons
Rooms: 5 (PB) $70-95
Full Breakfast
Credit Cards: A, B, C, D, E
Notes: 2, 5, 7, 9, 10, 11, 14

SHEPHERDSTOWN

Thomas Shepherd Inn

Box 1162, 25443
(304) 876-3715; (888) 889-8952
FAX (304) 876-3313
e-mail: mrg@intrepid.net
www.intrepid.net/thomas_shepherd/

Thomas Shepherd Inn

Small, charming inn in a quaint, historic Civil War town that offers that special hospitality of the past. Guests find fresh flowers at their bedsides, fluffy towels and special soaps in their baths, complimentary beverages by the fireside, memorable breakfasts. Picnics available. Children over eight welcome. Smoking permitted in designated areas only.

Host: Margaret Perry
Rooms: 7 (PB) $65-125
Full Breakfast
Credit Cards: A, B, C, D
Notes: 2, 3, 5, 9, 12, 13

VALLEY CHAPEL/WESTON

Ingeberg Acres Bed and Breakfast

Millstone Road, P.O. Box 199, 26446
(304) 269-2834
www.tiac.net/users/mann

Guests can have a unique experience at this scenic 450-acre horse and cattle farm seven miles from Weston. The three air-conditioned guest rooms have shared bath. Private, secluded cottage with bath and kitchenette, king-size or two single beds, plus one single bed and two single sleeper loveseats, covered porch, central air and heat. Enjoy patio, deck, and pool. Casual atmosphere, private pond for fishing, seasonal hunting, hiking, and bird watching. Full breakfast. No smoking.

Hosts: Inge and John Mann
Rooms: 3 (SB) $59
Cabin: $80
Full Breakfast
Credit Cards: None
Notes: 2, 5, 7, 8, 9, 11, 12

Puerto Rico
Virgin Islands

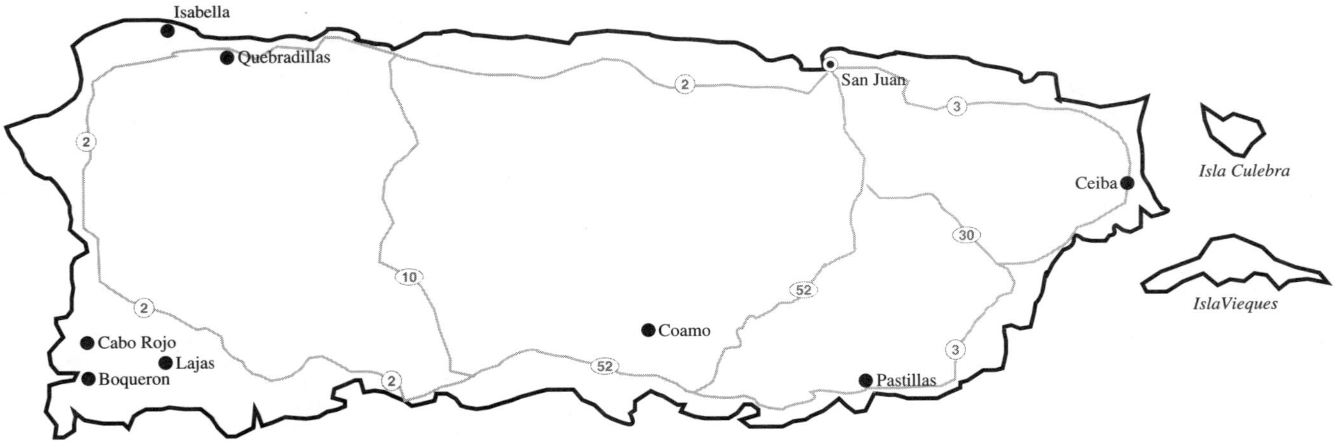
Isabella
Quebradillas
San Juan
Ceiba
Isla Culebra
IslaVieques
Cabo Rojo
Lajas
Boqueron
Coamo
Pastillas
2
3
10
30
52

Puerto Rico

Puerto Rico

BOQUERON

Parador Boquemar

P.O. Box 133, 00622
(809) 851-2158; FAX (809) 851-7600

Parador Boquemar is in walking distance to Boquerón Beach and village, one of the most visited places for local and non-local tourists year-round for its beautiful beach and warm climate. All rooms feature air conditioning, mini-refrigerators, color TVs, and private balconies (second and third floor). Also swimming pool and an excellent seafood restaurant, La Cascada Restaurant and Cocktail Lounge. Enjoy kayaking, snorkeling, swimming, fishing, scuba diving, and sailing or just relax and feel the Caribbean wind while swinging in a hammock under palm trees in this piece of paradise.

Hosts: The Rodríguez Family
Rooms: 75 (PB) $65-80
Continental Breakfast
Credit Cards: A, B, C, E
Notes: 3, 4, 5, 8, 9, 11, 12, 15

CABO ROJO

Parador Bahia Salinas

Road 301, KM 11.5, El Faro, 00623
(787) 254-1212; FAX (787) 254-1215

Beautiful gardens, ocean views, gazebos. Spacious rooms with air conditioning, balconies on most rooms. Two swimming pools, Jacuzzi, and gym. Snack bar and restaurant with typical menu and seafood. Boardwalks, live music on weekends, and lots of sunshine. Full breakfast is available at an extra charge. Smoking permitted at designated areas only.

Hosts: Miguel Rosado and Alexis Romero
Rooms: 24 (PB) $100-125
Continental Breakfast
Credit Cards: A, B, C
Notes: 3, 4, 5, 8, 9, 11, 14, 15

Parador Perichi's

Road 102, KM 14.3, Playa Joyuda, 00623
(787) 851-3131 (0590, 0560, 0620)
FAX (787) 851-0590

Parador Perichi's hotel, restaurant, and cocktail lounge in Joyuda, the site of Puerto Rico's famous resorts on the west side. Excellence has distinguished Perichi's in its 20 years of hospitality and service. The 49 air-conditioned rooms have wall-to-wall carpeting, private baths, balconies, color TVs, and telephones. Perichi's award-winning restaurant features the finest cuisine. After sunset, meet friends in the well-stocked and cozy lounge. The spacious and comfortable banquet room can accommodate up to 300 people—for those who like to combine business with pleasure.

Rooms: 49 (PB) $69.55-90.95
Full Breakfast
Credit Cards: A, B, C, D, E
Notes: 3, 4, 5, 7, 8, 9, 10, 11, 12, 13, 14

CEIBA

Ceiba Country Inn

Road 977, KM 1.2, P.O. Box 1067, 00735
(787) 885-0471; FAX (787) 885-0471

In the hills on the east coast, in a pastoral setting with a view of the sea. Quiet, serene

NOTES: Credit cards accepted: A MasterCard; B Visa; C American Express; D Discover; E Diner's Club; F Other; 2 Personal checks accepted; 3 Lunch available; 4 Dinner available; 5 Open all year; 6 Pets welcome; 7 No smoking; 8 Children welcome; 9 Social drinking allowed; 10 Tennis nearby; 11 Swimming nearby; 12 Golf nearby; 13 Skiing nearby; 14 May be booked through a travel agent; 15 Handicapped accessible.

Ceiba Country Inn

atmosphere with a cozy cocktail lounge. Convenient for trips to El Yunque, Luquillo, San Juan, Vieques, Culebra, and St. Thomas. Recommended by Frommer's, 1996. Continental plus breakfast.

Rooms: 9 (PB) $70
Continental Breakfast
Credit Cards: A, B, C, D
Notes: 5, 8, 9, 14, 15

COAMO

Parador Baños de Coamo

Bo. San Ildefonso Carr 540 Final, P.O. Box 540, 00769
(809) 825-2239; (809) 825-2186
(800) 443-0266 (US); (800) 981-7575 (PR)
FAX (809) 825-4739

The Parador Baños de Coamo is blessed for its lush, flowering vegetation, panorama, therapeutic baths, and so forth. Ponce de León missed it in his search for the Fountain of Youth. Known since 1847 (earlier by the Taino Indians). Restored to its 19th-century splendor by the Puerto Rico Tourism Company, using old aromatic wooden structures. Its 48 rooms are fully equipped to enjoy spa-style living. Individual wooden terraces; sweetwater pool for adults and children; therapeutic baths containing natural healing ingredients. Creole or international foods served. Country site. Beach nearby.

Host: Antonio Umpierre
Rooms: 48 (PB) $76
Continental Breakfast
Credit Cards: A
Notes: 3, 4, 5, 8, 9, 11

ISABELA

Costa Dorada Beach Resort

Emilio Gonzalez #900, 00662
(787) 872-7255; (888) 391-0606
FAX (787) 872-7595

Hotel in a tropical setting covered by palm trees on a mile-long stretch of white-sand beach in the lovely town of Isabela, next to a fishing village. All ocean-view rooms with air conditioning, color cable TV, direct-dial telephones. Two pools, tennis and basketball courts. Restaurant and bar. Live music on Saturdays.

Host: Mr. Carlos R. Fernandez
Rooms: 52 (PB) $107-135
Continental Breakfast

Credit Cards: A, B, C
Notes: 3, 4, 5, 8, 9, 10, 11, 12, 15

LAJAS

Parador Posada Porlamar

P.O. Box 3113, 00667
(787) 899-4015

Parador Posada Porlamar is beside the Caribbean Sea. The facilities include air-conditioned rooms with private baths, color TVs, telephones. Some rooms face the waterfront. Swimming pool facilities. Phosphorescent Bay trips available. Nightlife is exciting on weekends. Diving excursions available from the parador. Snorkeling, boating, water skiing, fishing, swimming, among other water activities available from the hotel.

Hosts: Rafy Pancorbo and Ana Pancorbo
Rooms: 38 (PB) $81.45
Full Breakfast
Credit Cards: A, B, C
Notes: 4, 5, 7, 8, 9, 11, 14, 15

LAJAS

Parador Villa Parguera

P.O. Box 273, 00667
(787) 899-7777; (787) 899-3975
FAX (787) 899-6040

A tropical paradise in Puerto Rico! It's a 70-room resort hotel in La Parguera, Lajas. Home of the world-famous Phosphorescent Bay. Most of the rooms face the Caribbean Sea. Fine cuisine, local and international. Convention hall, seminar rooms, souvenir shop, night club, dock, and swimming pool. Surrounded by beautiful patios with flowers and palm trees. Delightful tropical weather year-round. Fishing, diving, and snorkeling excursions nearby.

Rooms: 69 (PB) $95-104
Full Breakfast
Credit Cards: A, B, C, D, E
Notes: 3, 4, 5, 8, 9, 11, 14, 15

PATILLAS

Caribe Playa Beach Resort

HC 764, Box 8490, 00723
(787) 839-6339; (800) 221-4483
FAX (787) 839-1817; e-mail: geobeach@coqui.net

Thirty-two spacious beachfront studios equipped with kitchenettes, private bathrooms, ceiling fans, and patios or balconies. Deluxe studios include cable TV and air conditioning. The resort features a guest library, TV/music lounge, and the seaview terrace is open for breakfast, lunch, and dinner serving local and Continental-style meals. Hammocks and outdoor barbecues are available for guests' enjoyment and relaxation. The new free-form pool has a sun deck, whirlpool, kiddies' pool, and bar, and is surrounded by lush tropical greenery. Beach horseback riding, watersports, and scuba diving complement the services for a truly relaxing and unforgettable getaway. Small pets are welcome.

Hosts: Jenny, Ivette, Angie, or George
Rooms: 32 (PB) $65-99
Continental Breakfast
Credit Cards: A, B, C
Notes: 2, 3, 4, 5, 8, 9, 10, 11, 12, 14, 15

QUEBRADILLAS

Parador Vistamar

Road 113 N #6205, 00678
(787) 895-2065; (888) 391-0606
fax (787) 895-2294

On a hilltop with a breathtaking view of Puerto Rico's northwest Gold Coast. Rooms have ocean views, air conditioning, color cable TV, private bath; most with balconies. Two pools, tennis, basketball courts. Restaurant and bar. Live music on Saturdays.

Host: Mrs. Iris Myrna Cancel
Rooms: 55 (PB) $69-90

Continental Breakfast
Credit Cards: A, B, C
Notes: 3, 4, 5, 8, 9, 10, 11

SAN JUAN

El Canario Inn

1317 Ashford Avenue, Condado, 00907
(787) 722-3861; (800) 533-2649

San Juan's most historic and unique bed and breakfast. All 25 guest rooms are air conditioned, with private baths, telephones, and cable TVs. Beautiful tropical patio areas for relaxation. Only one block to beautiful Condado Beach, casinos, boutiques, and many fine restaurants. El Canario is perhaps the best deal for the vacation dollar in the Caribbean.

Hosts: Jude and Keith Olson
Rooms: 25 (PB) $75-100
Continental Breakfast
Credit Cards: A, B, C, D, E
Notes: 5, 8, 9, 10, 11, 14

El Canario Inn

El Consulado Hotel

Ave Ashford #1110, 00907
(888) 300-8002; FAX (787) 723-8665

An elegant European-style bed and breakfast, El Consulado preserves all the fine qualities of the Spanish mansion it has been built upon. It offers 29 ample rooms with air conditioning, cable TV, and telephone. In the most centralized and accessible point in the Condado, it is only steps from first-class restaurants, casinos, night clubs, shops, and beautiful Condado Beach.

Rooms: 29 (PB) $95-115
Continental Breakfast
Credit Cards: A, B, C, D, E
Notes: 5, 8, 11, 14, 15

Hotel La Playa

Calle Amapola #6 Isla Verde, 00979
(787) 791-1115; (787) 791-7298
FAX (787) 791-4650; e-mail: playita@icepr.com

Hotel La Playa, affectionately known for years as La Playita, has been a family-owned business for over 35 years. It is now being operated by the second generation of the Godinez family, Manuel Jr. This former private residence is on the beach just four minutes from El San Juan and Sands Hotels. The open-air restaurant and cocktail lounge with deck enjoy a cooling northeasterly breeze. Each room has a private bath, cable TV, and air conditioning. This small family-oriented hotel welcomes the opportunity to provide a relaxing atmosphere.

Hosts: Barbara and David Yourch;
Manuel Godinez
Rooms: 15 (PB) $75-105
Continental Breakfast
Credit Cards: A, B, C
Notes: 3, 4, 5, 8, 9, 11, 14, 15

Ocean Walk Guest House

Atlantic Place #1, 00911
(787) 728-0855; (800) 468-0615
FAX (787) 728-6434

The largest hostelry of its kind in Puerto Rico, with primarily an alternate lifestyle clientele. Directly on San Juan's finest beach with modest but comfortable rooms and studio apartments from single to quadruple occupancy. Majority have private baths, ceiling fans, and cable TVs (daily maid service, of course). The bar and grill patio, between the beach and pool, will keep guests in their chairs longer than they intended. Continental breakfast included in rates with breakfast and lunch menu available. Pets welcome with prior approval.

Rooms: PB, SB & Apartment; $40-140
Continental Breakfast
Credit Cards: A, B, C, D
Notes: 3, 5, 9, 11, 14

Tres Palmas Inn

2212 Park Boulevard, 00913
(787) 727-4617; FAX (787) 727-5434

Centrally positioned on one of the most beautiful sandy beaches in the San Juan area. Just 10 minutes from the airport or Old San Juan and five minutes from entertainment centers, casinos, and restaurants. All rooms include air conditioning, private baths, color cable TV, touch-tone telephones, and electronic safes. Suites with kitchenettes are available. A brand new swimming pool is available as well as oceanfront sun deck and Jacuzzi. Handicapped facilities are available. Smoking permitted in designated areas only.

Hosts: Eileen and Manuel Peredo
Rooms: 15 (PB) $55-120
Continental Breakfast
Credit Cards: A, B, C
Notes: 5, 8, 9, 10, 11, 12, 13, 14, 15

VIEQUES ISLAND

Hacienda Tamarindo

P.O. Box 1569, 00765
(787) 741-8525; FAX (787) 741-3215
www.enchanted-isle.com/tamarindo

Hosts offer a very special environment, with each room lovingly and creatively designed and decorated by owner Linda Vail. The rooms and common area are unique, imaginatively spiced with a life time's accumulation of art, antiques, and collectibles. A three-story tamarind tree rises through the center atrium. The hacienda is perched on a hilltop with a spectacular 180-degree view of the Caribbean (sunrise to sunset). The most beautiful pool on the island.

Hosts: Burr and Linda Vail
Rooms: 15 (PB) $115-140
Full Breakfast
Credit Cards: A, B, C
Notes: 2, 3, 5, 9, 10, 11, 14, 15

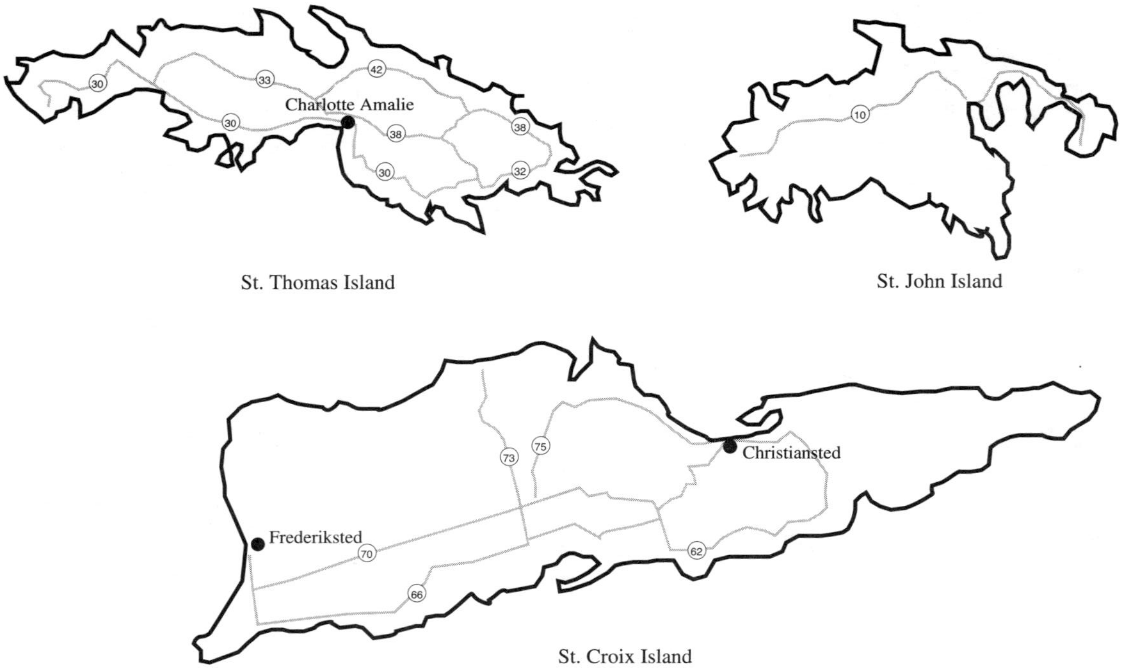

Virgin Islands

Virgin Islands

ST. CROIX—CHRISTIANSTED

The Breakfast Club

18 Queen Cross Street, Christiansted, 00820
(809) 773-7383; FAX (809) 773-8642

The Breakfast Club is a comfortable and convenient bed and breakfast just six blocks from the heart of Christiansted and minutes away from beaches, diving, water sports, dining, golf, tennis, sailing, tours, or even shopping. Upon a ridge at the top of Queen Cross Street in an old West Indian neighborhood, the Breakfast Club is the perfect setting to relish the full, complimentary breakfast in the restored 19th-century commandant's house or to "lime" on the deck and savor the cooling trade winds by the hot tub. Children over six welcome. Groups inquire about the villa.

Hosts: Toby and Barb Chapin
Rooms: 9 (PB) $55
Full Breakfast
Credit Cards: B, C
Notes: 5, 9, 10, 11, 12

Pink Fancy Hotel

27 Prince Street, 00820
(800) 524-2045; FAX (809) 773-6448
http: //www.pinkfancy.com

The Pink Fancy Hotel is a small historic inn just steps away from the shopping/restaurant area of downtown. Designated as a National Historic Trust, the hotel offers history in a tropical setting. Each room has a kitchenette, cable TV, and air conditioning. Rates include a Continental breakfast and complimentary happy hour, both served daily beside the freshwater pool. A variety

Pink Fancy Hotel

of sleeping accommodations are available to serve both the business traveler and the vacationing family.

Hosts: George and Cindy Tyler
Rooms: 13 (PB) $75-120
Continental Breakfast
Credit Cards: A, B, C, D, E
Notes: 5, 8, 9, 11, 12, 14

ST. CROIX—FREDERIKSTED

Sprat Hall Plantation

Route 63N, P.O. Box 695, 00841
(809) 772-0305; (800) 843-3584

Sprat Hall Plantation is a fine country estate by the sea dating from 1650. The furnishings of the great house are all mahogany antiques dating from all eras of occupation. Accommodations are in the great house, modern hotel rooms in the sea-view unit,

NOTES: Credit cards accepted: A MasterCard; B Visa; C American Express; D Discover; E Diner's Club; F Other; 2 Personal checks accepted; 3 Lunch available; 4 Dinner available; 5 Open all year; 6 Pets welcome; 7 No smoking; 8 Children welcome; 9 Social drinking allowed; 10 Tennis nearby; 11 Swimming nearby; 12 Golf nearby; 13 Skiing nearby; 14 May be booked through a travel agent; 15 Handicapped accessible.

efficiencies in duplex cottages, and complete one- and two-bedroom cottages. Full service on meals with lunch served at the beach. Riding stables. Excellent scuba diving. Light-tackle fishing.

Hosts: Joyce and Jim Hurd
Rooms: 12 (PB) $120-160
Continental Breakfast
Credit Cards: None
Notes: 2, 3, 4, 5, 8, 9, 10, 11, 12, 14

ST. THOMAS

Pavilions and Pools Hotel

6400 Estate Smith Bay, 00802
(340) 775-6110; (800) 524-2001

A small villa hotel on the quiet east end of St. Thomas, 400 yards away from beautiful Sapphire Beach. Each villa has its own private swimming pool within its own garden. Featured are king-size beds, garden showers, fully equipped galley-style kitchen, air conditioning, and cable TV. Personal checks accepted for deposit only.

Hosts: Tammy Waters, general manager
Becca Nelsen, sales/reservations
Rooms; 25 (PB) $180-259
Continental Breakfast
Credit Cards: A, B, C
Notes: 4, 5, 6, 8, 9, 10, 11, 12, 14

ST. THOMAS—CHARLOTTE AMALIE

Miller Manor Guest House

P.O. Box 1570, 00803
(809) 774-1535; (888) 229-0762
FAX (809) 774-5988
e-mail: millermanor-aida-leo@worldnet.att.net

The best little guest house in the Caribbean. Family-oriented, overlooking town and harbor. Five-minute walk to town. Microwave, refrigerator, air conditioning, and private bath in each room. Seasonal complimentary breakfast of breads, fruits, danishes, coffee, tea, and juices.

Hosts: Aida and Les
Rooms: 24 (PB) $54-70
Continental Breakfast
Credit Cards: A, B, C, D
Notes: 5, 8, 9, 10, 11, 12, 13, 14